MISSION FRANCE

THE TRUE HISTORY OF THE WOMEN OF SOE

KATE VIGURS

YALE UNIVERSITY PRESS
NEW HAVEN AND LONDON

For information about this and other Yale University Press publications, please contact:
U.S. Office: sales.press@yale.edu   yalebooks.com
Europe Office: sales@yaleup.co.uk   yalebooks.co.uk

Set in Minion Pro by IDSUK (DataConnection) Ltd
Printed in Great Britain by TJ Books, Padstow, Cornwall

Library of Congress Control Number: 2020949525

ISBN 978-0-300-20857-3

A catalogue record for this book is available from the British Library.

10 9 8 7 6 5 4 3 2 1

To all those who 'set Europe ablaze', but especially to Pearl Cornioley, Yvonne Burney, Bob and Mary Large and Bob Maloubier, who told me their stories and set my curiosity ablaze to tell theirs

... when the full history is written – sober history with ample documents – the poor romancer will give up business and fall to reading Miss Austen in a hermitage.

John Buchan, *Greenmantle*

CONTENTS

List of Illustrations   *ix*

List of Abbreviations   *xi*

The Women Agents of F Section   *xii*

Map of Infiltrations/Landings   *xxii*

Prologue   1

PART I: FOUNDATIONS

1   Setting Europe Ablaze   15
2   Trailblazers   42

PART II: WAR

3   The Fall of PROSPER   77
4   The Army of Shadows   107
5   D-Day   139
6   Incarceration   161

PART III: DEATH AND DELIVERANCE

7   Night and Fog   191
8   Ravensbrück   208
9   Aftermath   228

Epilogue   256

CONTENTS

Appendix: George Cross Citations *261*

Notes *265*

Bibliography *284*

Acknowledgements *292*

Index *294*

ILLUSTRATIONS

Plates

1. Tania Szabó receives her mother's medals. Courtesy of Tania Szabó.

2. Special Training School 5, Wanborough Manor, Surrey.

3. Violette Szabó, 1944. Courtesy of the National Army Museum, London.

4. Krystyna Skarbek/Christine Granville. Reproduced with kind permission from the estate of I.W. Stanley Moss.

5. Pearl Witherington's rail pass. Courtesy of Hervé Larroque.

6. Third Pattern Fairbairn–Sykes fighting knife with FS etched panel, made by Wilkinson Sword. The Ivan Gamsby Collection.

7. Julienne Aisner.

8. Yvonne Cormeau's false ID card. Printed by kind permission of the copyright owner, Yvette Cormeau Pitt.

9. Agents from Jedburgh team AUBREY prepare to be taken into occupied France post D-Day. Courtesy of RAF Harrington Museum.

10. A female agent believed to be Sonia d'Artois.

11. A young member of the Maquis of the Chartreuse mountains and Grésivaudan valley. AFP/Getty Images.

12. Pearl Witherington and Henri Cornioley with French resisters. Courtesy of Hervé Larroque.

13. Canisters dropped for the resistance and Maquis, Beuil-les-Launes, 12 August 1944. Courtesy of MRA collection, Boulay collection.

14. A resistance fighter places explosives on a French railway line. The National Archives HS7 135.

15. 84, avenue Foch, Paris. Author's photo.
16. Sturmbannführer Hans Josef Kieffer, head of the Sicherheitsdienst in Paris. From the private collection of Sarah Helm.
17. Noor Inayat Khan, 1934. Courtesy of the Nekbakht Foundation.
18. Prisoners at Ravensbrück concentration camp. BArch, Bild 183-1985-0417-015/unknown/CC-BYSA 3.0.
19. A line drawing of roll call by Violette Lecoq. The National Archives RW 2/2.
20. A prisoner at Ravensbrück shows her wounded leg. Courtesy of the United States Holocaust Memorial Museum, photographer unknown.
21. Actress Virginia McKenna with Maurice Buckmaster and Odette Hallowes (née Sansom).
22. The front cover of Jerrard Tickell's *Odette*, 1955. Courtesy of Pan Macmillan.

ABBREVIATIONS

ATS	Auxiliary Territorial Service
BCRA	Bureau Central de Renseignement et d'Action (Free France's Intelligence Service)
BEF	British Expeditionary Force
D/F	Direction Finding (van)
DZ	drop zone
FANY	First Aid Nursing Yeomanry
FS	Fairbairn–Sykes (knife)
GC	George Cross
GPO	General Post Office
JAG	Judge Advocate General's Office
MBE	Member of the Order of the British Empire
OBE	Order of the British Empire
OSS	Office of Strategic Services
PT	physical training
RAF	Royal Air Force
RSHA	Reichsicherheitshauptamt (Reich Main Security Office)
SOE	Special Operations Executive
STO	Service du travail obligatoire (compulsory work service)
STS	Special Training School
W/T	wireless telegraphist
WAAF	Women's Auxiliary Air Force

THE WOMEN AGENTS OF F SECTION

Agents arriving by boat have a single date of infiltration, whereas those arriving by aircraft have two, as the aircraft's journey started before midnight and went into the following day.

AGAZARIAN, FRANCINE
Field name: 'Marguerite'
Operational name: 'Lamplighter'
DOB: 8 May 1913
Date and method of entry: 17/18 March 1943, Lysander aircraft
Circuit: PHYSICIAN/PROSPER
Role: Courier

AISNER, JULIENNE
Field name: 'Claire'
Operational name: 'Compositor'
DOB: 30 December 1899
Date and method of entry: 14/15 May 1943, Lysander aircraft
Circuit: FARRIER
Role: Courier

BASEDEN, YVONNE
Field name: 'Odette'
Operational name: 'Burser'
DOB: 20 January 1922

Date and method of entry: 18/19 March 1944, parachute
Circuit: SCHOLAR
Role: Wireless operator

BEEKMAN, YOLANDE
Field name: 'Yvonne' and 'Mariette'
Operational name: 'Palmist'
DOB: 28 October 1911
Date and method of entry: 18/19 September 1943, Lysander aircraft
Circuit: MUSICIAN
Role: Wireless operator

BLOCH, DENISE
Field name: 'Ambroise'
Operational name: 'Secretary'
DOB: 21 January 1916
Date and method of entry: 2/3 March 1944, Lysander aircraft
Circuit: CLERGYMAN
Role: Wireless operator

BORREL, ANDRÉE
Field name: 'Denise'
Operational name: 'Whitebeam'
DOB: 18 November 1919
Date and method of entry: 24/25 September 1942, parachute
Circuit: PHYSICIAN/PROSPER
Role: Courier

BUTT, SONIA
Field name: 'Blanche'
Operational name: 'Biographer'
DOB: 14 May 1924
Date and method of entry: 28/29 May 1944, parachute

Circuit: HEADMASTER
Role: Courier

BYCK, MURIEL
Field name: 'Violette'
Operational name: 'Benefactress'
DOB: 4 June 1916
Date and method of entry: 8/9 April 1944, parachute
Circuit: VENTRILOQUIST
Role: Wireless operator

CHARLET, BLANCHE
Field name: 'Christianne'
Operational name: 'Berberis'
DOB: 23 May 1898
Date and method of entry: 1 September 1942, felucca
Circuit: VENTRILOQUIST
Role: Courier

CORMEAU, YVONNE
Field name: 'Annette'
Operational name: 'Fairy'
DOB: 18 December 1909
Date and method of entry: 22/23 August 1943, parachute
Circuit: WHEELWRIGHT
Role: Wireless operator

DAMERMENT, MADELEINE
Field name: 'Solange'
Operational name: 'Dancer'
DOB: 11 November 1917
Date and method of entry: 28/29 February 1944, parachute
Circuit: BRICKLAYER
Role: Courier

DE BAISSAC, LISE
Field name: 'Odile' and 'Marguerite'
Operational name: 'Artist'
DOB: 11 May 1905
Date and method of entry: (1) 24/25 September 1942, parachute (2) 9/10
April 1944, Lysander aircraft
Circuit: SCIENTIST
Role: Liaison officer

DEVERAUX ROCHESTER, ELIZABETH
Field name: 'Elizabeth'
Operational name: 'Typist'
DOB: 20 December 1917
Date and method of entry: 18/19 October 1943, parachute
Circuit: MARKSMAN
Role: Courier

FONTAINE, YVONNE
Field name: 'Mimi'
Operational name: 'Florist'
DOB: 8 August 1913
Date and method of entry: 25 March 1944, motor gunboat
Circuit: MINISTER
Role: Courier

GRANVILLE, CHRISTINE/KRYSTYNA SKARBEK
Field name: 'Pauline' and 'Madame Marchand'
Operational name: none in personnel file relating to F Section missions
DOB: 1 May 1908
Date and method of entry: 6/7 July 1944, parachute
Circuit: JOCKEY
Role: Courier

HALL, VIRGINIA
Field name: 'Marie'/(OSS) 'Diane'
Operational name: 'HECKLER'
DOB: 6 April 1906
Date and method of entry: (1) 23 August 1941, train from Lisbon (2) 21 March 1944, motor gunboat
Circuit: (1) HECKLER (2) (OSS) SAINT
Role: (1) Liaison officer (2) (OSS) Wireless operator

HERBERT, MARY
Field name: 'Claudine'
Operational name: 'Jeweller'
DOB: 1 October 1903
Date and method of entry: 2 November 1942, felucca
Circuit: SCIENTIST
Role: Courier

INAYAT KHAN, NOOR
Field name: 'Madeleine'
Operational name: 'Nurse'
DOB: 1 January 1914
Date and method of entry: 16/17 June 1943, Lysander aircraft
Circuit: PHONO
Role: Wireless operator

JULLIAN, GINETTE
Field name: 'Adèle'
Operational name: 'Janitress'
DOB: 8 December 1917
Date and method of entry: 6/7 June 1944, parachute
Circuit: PERMIT
Role: Wireless operator

KNIGHT, MARGUERITE
Field name: 'Nicole'
Operational name: 'Kennelmaid'
DOB: 19 April 1920
Date and method of entry: 6/7 May 1944, parachute
Circuit: DONKEYMAN
Role: Courier

LATOUR, PHYLLIS
Field name: 'Geneviève'
Operational name: 'Lampooner'
DOB: 8 April 1921
Date and method of entry: 1/2 May 1944, parachute
Circuit: SCIENTIST
Role: Wireless operator

LAVIGNE, MADELEINE
Field name: 'Isabella'
Operational name: 'Leveller'
DOB: 6 February 1912
Date and method of entry: 23/24 May 1944, parachute
Circuit: SILVERSMITH
Role: Courier

LE CHÊNE, MARIE-THÉRÈSE
Field name: 'Adèle'
Operational name: 'Wisteria'
DOB: 23 August 1891
Date and method of entry: 2 November 1942, felucca
Circuit: PLANE
Role: Courier

LEFORT, CICELY
Field name: 'Alice'
Operational name: 'Teacher'
DOB: 30 April 1900
Date and method of entry: 16/17 June 1943, Lysander aircraft
Circuit: JOCKEY
Role: Courier

LEIGH, VERA
Field name: 'Simone'
Operational name: 'Almoner'
DOB: 17 March 1903
Date and method of entry: 14/15 May 1943, Lysander aircraft
Circuit: INVENTOR
Role: Courier

NEARNE, EILEEN
Field name: 'Rose'
Operational name: 'Pioneer'
DOB: 16 January 1923
Date and method of entry: 2/3 March 1944, Lysander aircraft
Circuit: WIZARD
Role: Wireless operator

NEARNE, JACQUELINE
Field name: 'Jacqueline'
Operational name: 'Designer'
DOB: 27 May 1916
Date and method of entry: 25/26 January 1943, parachute
Circuit: STATIONER
Role: Courier

O'SULLIVAN, PATRICIA
Field name: 'Simonet'
Operational name: 'Stenographer'
DOB: 3 January 1918
Date and method of entry: 22/23 March 1944, parachute
Circuit: FIREMAN
Role: Wireless operator

OLSCHANESKY, SONIA
Field name: n/a
Operational name: n/a
DOB: 25 December 1923
Date and method of entry: n/a, locally recruited
Circuit: JUGGLER
Role: Courier

PLEWMAN, ELIANE
Field name: 'Gaby'
Operational name: 'Dean'
DOB: 6 December 1917
Date and method of entry: 13/14 August 1943, parachute
Circuit: MONK
Role: Courier

ROLFE, LILIAN
Field name: 'Nadine'
Operational name: 'Recluse'
DOB: 26 April 1914
Date and method of entry: 5/6 April 1944, Lysander aircraft
Circuit: HISTORIAN
Role: Wireless operator

ROWDEN, DIANA
Field name: 'Paulette'
Operational name: 'Chaplain'
DOB: 31 January 1915
Date and method of entry: 16/17 June 1943, Lysander aircraft
Circuit: ACROBAT/STOCKBROKER
Role: Courier

RUDELLAT, YVONNE
Field name: 'Jacqueline'
Operational name: 'Soaptree'
DOB: 11 January 1897
Date and method of entry: 17 July 1942, felucca
Circuit: PHYSICIAN/PROSPER
Role: Courier

SANSOM, ODETTE
Field name: 'Lise'
Operational name: 'Clothier'
DOB: 28 April 1912
Date and method of entry: 2 November 1942, felucca
Circuit: SPINDLE
Role: Courier

SZABÓ, VIOLETTE
Field name: 'Louise', 'Vicky', 'Corine'
Operational name: 'Seamstress'
DOB: 26 June 1921
Date and method of entry: (1) 5/6 April 1944, Lysander aircraft (2) 6/7 June 1944, parachute
Circuit: SALESMAN
Role: Courier

WAKE, NANCY
Field name: 'Hélène'
Operational name: 'Witch'
DOB: 30 August 1912
Date and method of entry: 29/30 April 1944, parachute
Circuit: FREELANCE
Role: Courier

WALTERS, ANNE-MARIE
Field name: 'Colette'
Operational name: 'Milkmaid'
DOB: 16 March 1923
Date and method of entry: 3/4 January 1944, parachute
Circuit: WHEELWRIGHT
Role: Courier

WILEN, ODETTE
Field name: 'Sophie'
Operational name: 'Waitress'
DOB: 25 April 1919
Date and method of entry: 11/12 April 1944, parachute
Circuit: LABOURER
Role: Wireless operator

WITHERINGTON, PEARL
Field name: 'Marie/Pauline'
Operational name: 'Wrestler'
DOB: 24 June 1916
Date and method of entry: 22/23 September 1943, parachute
Circuit: STATIONER/WRESTLER
Role: Courier

Map of Infiltrations/Landings

PROLOGUE

In the dead of night, autumn 1942, a Whitley bomber aircraft approached the Loire River that lay glistening below. The pilot navigated its twists and turns, its bridges and landmarks, which he had memorised in order to help him locate the drop zone. A few hours earlier, at RAF Tempsford in Bedfordshire, he had taken on board an unusual cargo – not the typical supplies for the resistance, or male parachutists about to undertake their missions of sabotage and subversion, but a very different payload.

On this night of 24 September, it was, for the first time, two women who sat closely huddled on the fuselage floor, their legs drawn up under their chins, their parachutes weighing heavily on their backs and their static lines dangling, waiting for the green light – the signal to jump. Mentally rehearsing their mission – the jump, the landing, who would meet them, the journey to the safe house – their nervous silence was masked by the roar of the engines. They had drawn straws and it was Andrée, the younger of the two, who would be the first to exit the aircraft. The dispatcher opened a circular hinged door cut into the floor and the women edged towards it, getting into position, and looking down past their feet to the roads, trees, church spires and farms of Nazi-occupied France. With the green light illuminated, 'Now!' shouted the dispatcher, and without a backward glance Andrée dropped into the cold night. Seconds later, Lise followed her. The canopies of their parachutes opened and they drifted down in the moonlight. The aircraft, silhouetted against the full moon, banked to make its return to England, taking with it the women's last links to the lives they had hitherto known and leaving them floating down to their fate.

Andrée Borrel and Lise de Baissac were the first women to parachute into occupied French territory as secret agents. Just hours earlier, they had eaten a farewell meal in a large country house, then been driven to RAF Tempsford and onto the airfield where, in a farmhouse, they were searched for cigarettes, receipts, bus tickets – anything that might give them away as having come from England. They were then zipped into their 'striptease' suits, under which they wore studiedly authentic French civilian clothing complete with French seams, zips and labels. The final accessory offered to them was an L-pill – a suicide pill, the 'L' standing for 'lethal' – before they made their way to the aircraft.

Now, they were at the Bois-Renard drop zone, not far from the village of Saint-Laurent-Nouan, roughly halfway between Blois and Orléans and close to the south bank of the Loire River. Having landed safely, the women buried their parachutes and jumpsuits, and for two days remained close together. Lise, who used to live in the free zone in the south, had not been back to France since fleeing Paris after the Nazi invasion. Andrée, on the other hand, had stayed in occupied France until 1942, working first as a nurse and then on an escape line. She was more familiar with the uniforms, the regulations and rationing, and would help Lise to adapt quickly. But after two days – a long enough time for any two agents to spend together – they went their separate ways.

Andrée and Lise were working for the British government's Special Operations Executive (SOE) French (F) Section. In 1940, a couple of years before their momentous parachute landing, the British government had recognised the urgent need for a new body, independent of the War Office, that would carry out clandestine operations behind enemy lines in order to assist the French who wished to continue fighting the Nazi threat. Duties would include sabotage, spreading of rumours and support for local resistance movements.

This new organisation would absorb the Foreign Office's existing EH Department (formed in 1938 at Electra House, after which it was named, with a primary objective to develop methods of influencing German opinion) and Section D (which although technically part of the Foreign Office was part of the Secret Intelligence Service (SIS), set up in 1938 with a view to targeting Germany's infrastructure and defending Britain against sabotage), as well as MI R (a research section of the General Staff at the War Office, established in 1939 to handle irregular warfare, including the development of weapons).

The idea for this new organisation had been mooted in several memoranda throughout the spring and early summer of 1940. Eventually, a meeting chaired by Foreign Secretary Lord Halifax was held at the Foreign Office on 1 July, in which various matters were discussed and points raised: Minister of Economic Warfare Hugh Dalton 'held that there was a clear distinction between "war from without" and "war from within", and that the latter was more likely to be better conducted by civilians, than soldiers', while Lord Hankey 'was inclined to defend the existing machinery and to attribute the failure of major sabotage schemes to the "reluctance of the Foreign Office to authorise them, or at any rate authorise them until it was too late".'[1] It was agreed that there should be a coordinator, who, 'provided he was the right man, would be able to look at the problem as a whole and, subject only to the approval of the prime minister, would be able to override if necessary any departmental objections'. The following day Dalton wrote to Halifax suggesting the new organisation should 'co-ordinate all action by way of subversion and sabotage against the enemy overseas'.[2] The letter was passed on to Neville Chamberlain, then a prominent member of the War Cabinet as Lord President of the Council, and Prime Minister Winston Churchill. After much discussion and correspondence about who should head the new organisation, on 16 July Churchill formally wrote to Dalton asking him to accept the task of forming the Special Operations Executive. On 19 July the formal charter of SOE, written by Chamberlain, was circulated, and on 22 July it was formally approved by the War Cabinet. The prime minister promptly gave the new head of SOE the much-quoted directive to 'set Europe ablaze'.[3]

SOE set up a number of different sections, which worked in various European countries, including France, Holland, Belgium, Norway, Yugoslavia,

Greece, Italy and Albania; it also operated in the Far East in a branch known as Force 136. The branch focusing on France would come to have six sections: EU/P, focusing on Polish settlements in Europe; DF, working on escape lines; AMF or 'Massingham', operating from Algiers into southern areas of France after Operation Torch in November 1942; 'Jedburgh', which was operational after D-Day; RF; and F. F was the 'independent French section', which tried to work across the whole of France and ignore the tensions that were developing between the occupied and unoccupied zones and between Pétain and de Gaulle, the self-professed leader of the Free French in exile and from whom F Section was kept secret. Indeed, RF was a separate unit set up by an 'exceedingly angry' de Gaulle when he found out about F Section, and run from London by the Free French government. There were tensions between F and RF sections all the way through the war, each believing that it was better than the other, that 'their men and methods were sound, whilst their rival's were not; each thought the other was unfairly favoured, either by the rest of the SOE war machine or by politicians outside it'.[4] In spite of these tensions, recruitment for F Section began.

F Section, or 'The Organisation' as it was known among staff, was based in Baker Street in London, but the men and women who were destined to become agents never knew the location of the section's headquarters; meetings and briefings were instead conducted at the nearby Orchard Court, an imposing block of flats on Portman Square, just off Baker Street. Originally F Section was headed by Leslie Humphreys, who started in the summer of 1940 after his own dramatic escape from France by warship, where he had been SIS Section D's representative in Paris. At the end of the year he moved over to work on escape lines and was succeeded by a civilian, H.R. Marriott, who resigned after a year over differences of opinion with various staff. He was replaced in September 1941 by 39-year-old Major Maurice Buckmaster, who remained in charge until F Section was wound up in 1946.

A senior manager for the Ford Motor Company in France before the war, Buckmaster had a sound knowledge of the country and its transportation networks, and had many useful contacts all over France. Moreover, he had a genuine love of France and plenty of enthusiasm that boded well for the difficult and contentious task ahead. He has subsequently been criticised for his many failings and mistakes: he was easily manipulated, naïve about the immediate and present danger that some of his agents were in, and reluctant to countenance the possibility that there could be double dealings, or double agents, within F Section. But, for all his faults, he had endless imagination, an undeniable commitment to the cause and boundless energy, which often saw him working day and night in the office.

Working alongside Buckmaster as his assistant was Vera Atkins. Born in Bucharest, Romania, in 1908, Vera's family moved to England in 1933, and she studied modern languages at the Sorbonne, returning to England in May 1940, where she worked as an air raid precaution officer in Chelsea. Vera joined F Section in February 1941, at the same time as Maurice Buckmaster, but in contrast to him was 'self-contained and formidably astute. She was a shrewd judge of character and had an incisive, occasionally combative manner.'[5] Vera's role meant that she often came to know agents personally; she ensured they received the right documents and cover stories, discussed agents' training reports and their suitability for work in the field, and decided which agents would work well together and their suitability for certain missions. She was there to help agents prepare their wills and ensure their wishes were met regarding contact with their families while they were away, and what should happen if they went missing. She was there for agents to confide in, and to listen to their worries and troubles. She was often present to the last minute – seeing agents dressed in their new clothes, checking their pockets for incriminating items and watching them board the aircraft to take them to France. She was respected and admired by all who came into contact with her.

Also within the F Section office were the deputy chief Nicholas Bodington (formerly of Reuters in Paris), the French briefing officer Jacques de Guélis and the signals officer Gerrard Morel. De Guélis and Morel had both been operative agents in France; Morel had survived imprisonment and serious illness, and worked in the F Section office until 1944, when he returned to France to collect a suspected double agent. Ex-accountant Robert Bourne-Paterson worked as F Section's planning officer, Selwyn Jepson as recruiting officer and Leo Marks devised codes for agents to use in the field. Between 1940 and 1944 the F Section office grew to number twenty-four men and women, many of whom had links with France or had worked in the field themselves. The first agent to be sent to France was Georges Bégué, who landed on 6 May 1941, and three days later made contact with F Section HQ.

In April 1942, two years after its creation, and in accordance with its central tenet to 'go straight for the objective, across any social or military conventions that may get in the way',[6] SOE made the groundbreaking decision to employ women in the field as secret agents. This was an unprecedented move. Up to this point, women had contributed to the war effort in a wide variety of ways, from working in munitions factories and as drivers to clerical work and nursing. They usually worked on the home front, occasionally abroad, and only a very few had recently engaged in combat behind enemy lines; indeed, the value and usefulness of women agents had just been proved to the organisation through the exploits of Virginia Hall and Krystyna Skarbek (see Chapters 1 and 2).[7] Sir Colin Gubbins, director of operations and training at SOE and the organisation's driving force, observed that, as they had already tested the value of using women in the field with Virginia and Krystyna – agents recruited and run in a fairly ad hoc manner – he knew and understood the advantages of the further use of women, and believed there was an important and niche role which only they could fulfil. Thus, SOE F Section sanctioned the systematic recruitment and training of women in larger numbers to work as agents in the field.

The initiative shocked and angered some. Vera Atkins recalled the 'heated discussion that took place when the idea was first put forward', and Dame Irene Ward, MP for Tynemouth, subsequently opined that 'the War Cabinet was [not] fully aware of what their decision involved. If they had been, permission would almost certainly have been refused.'[8] One concern was that, as with anyone undertaking clandestine operations, giving women the right to bear arms meant that they would not be protected by the Geneva Convention, and therefore could not expect to be treated as prisoners of war (POWs) if they were caught by the enemy. They would also not be in uniform and would therefore not be officially affiliated to the British armed forces. The threat to women was felt to be unconscionable. But, as F Section's recruiting officer Selwyn Jepson explained, the decision was greeted with more enthusiasm in other quarters:

> I was responsible for recruiting women for the work, in the face of a good deal of opposition from the powers that be, who said that women, under the Geneva Convention, were not allowed to take combatant duties which they regarded resistance work in France as being. ... It took me some time to find a proper answer to that and then I found it, I discovered that the anti-aircraft units always had ATS Officers on their strength and that when it came to firing an anti-aircraft gun the person who pulled the lanyard that released the trigger was a woman.... There was a good deal of opposition from various quarters until it went up to Churchill whom I had met before the war. He growled at me, 'What are you doing?' I told him and he said, 'I see you are using women to do this,' and I said, 'Yes, don't you think it is a very sensible thing to do?' and he said, 'Yes, good luck to you.' That was my authority![9]

Using women was 'sensible', Jepson felt, because in his view, 'women were very much better than men for the work. Women, as you must know, have a far greater capacity for cool and lonely courage than men. ... Men don't work alone, their lives tend to be always in company with other men.'[10] On a practical level, moreover, once in France women were less likely to attract attention because they could continue their day-to-day activities, including cycling – important for courier work – using covers such as working as district nurses or medical or cosmetic representatives, whereas from the summer of 1942, men of working age had been forced by the Nazis to undertake compulsory labour in the Service du travail obligatoire (STO). The right women, therefore, were in a more advantageous position to carry out clandestine activities undercover. Other factors may also have played a part in the British government's use of women agents in France; for instance, the

British were keen to encourage resistance in France that was not linked to de Gaulle's Free French, as the movement was untried, politically complex and of uncertain operational effectiveness. Due to one or a combination of these factors, women began to be interviewed to establish their suitability to be trained and sent behind enemy lines. This was kept top secret, known only to the recruited male agents and trainers, and the women they recruited were sworn to secrecy.

In total, F Section deployed 480 agents, 39 of whom were women. It is these 39 women who are the focus of this story. But who exactly were they? Why should they be remembered as pioneers, heroes and martyrs? And why should all these women be the focus of this book?

The night they jumped was the first time Andrée's and Lise's paths had crossed, and, as with other agents, it was not long before they parted ways. They had been recruited as agents in different ways and for different reasons. Coming from a working-class background, 23-year-old Andrée's socialist sympathies meant that she was receptive when approached in France by a hospital co-worker and friend, Maurice Dufour, to undertake secretive work on an escape line. Lise, on the other hand, originally came from an affluent British family in Mauritius, and had later settled in France. After the German occupation of Paris, she made her way to the free zone in the Dordogne, and not long after to England, where she joined SOE and was made an officer of the First Aid Nursing Yeomanry (FANY).

Andrée and Lise are not among the ranks of those women agents who became famous after the war as a result of receiving notable decorations. The thirty-nine female agents are not equally well recognised. Some agents, such as Yvonne Baseden and Lilian Rolfe, remain very much overlooked in today's history books. Yet Yvonne, an agent whom I had the pleasure of interviewing, was a skilled wireless operator and helped in receiving one of the biggest daylight drops of supplies during the war. The next day, she was betrayed to the Gestapo. Lilian Rolfe sent sixty-seven faultless wireless messages over three months before she was arrested. Other agents were less successful, but still made contributions to the war effort.

Violette Szabó's image and story have been used so often in connection with the female agents of F Section that she has come to represent all the other women too. This is amply demonstrated by a memorial on the Albert Embankment in London featuring a bust of Violette, erected in 2009 'in honour', the plinth states, 'of all the courageous S.O.E. Agents: those who did survive and those who did not survive their perilous missions'. The artist intended the face of the sculpture to express as many emotions as possible, including the ability to withstand.[11] In this way Violette's image stands for all those agents whose stories are not written.

Far from seeking to undermine the images of high-profile agents, I aim to redress the clear imbalance of recognition. So the primary purpose of this book is to bring to light, however briefly, the journeys of all thirty-nine women, showing how they came to be recruited as SOE agents; how some met and worked with each other in the field while others were more isolated; how some would stay in occupied France for the duration of war and others would return within days of being infiltrated; how some would fall in love and others would lose their loved ones; how some would survive and others would not. Another purpose of this book is to show the deeper connections between all agents, even if they served in SOE only for a short time. We will consider how successful agents were in their training and sabotage work, and in doing so reveal the reality of all the women's experiences, thereby enabling an enhanced understanding of the more over-shadowed agents.

In the opening sentence of his book *The Women Who Lived for Danger*, Marcus Binney claims: 'The girls who served as secret agents in Churchill's Special Operations Executive were young, beautiful and brave.'[12] It arguably encapsulates public perception of the female agents. Yet such a claim is at best reductive, at worst a misleading distortion. Some of the thirty-nine women were indeed young, some were beautiful (although why this should be a criterion at all is unclear – perhaps merely for the alliterative flourish), and some did have certain characteristics which made them more suited to the job than others. However, all deserve attention. By bringing forward the stories of all the women, including those less in the limelight, this book will show the women's characters and attitudes in their full diversity and explore how they shared a common mission.

Telling the stories of the female agents is facilitated, and sometimes limited, by how much it is possible to know of them. This book has been greatly enhanced by the first-hand interviews I was able to carry out with those who had served in or had links with SOE – the agents Yvonne Baseden and Pearl Witherington; Professor M.R.D. Foot, a Special Air Service intelligence officer who was the first to undertake an official history of SOE in France; Flight Lieutenant Bob Large, who brought Violette Szabó back from the field; Bob Maloubier, who worked alongside Violette – all of whom have since passed away. In addition, interviews with their descendants have all proved helpful: Tania Szabó, Violette's daughter; Tim Buckmaster, Maurice Buckmaster's son; Yvette Pitt, the daughter of Yvonne Cormeau; and Julie Clamp, the granddaughter of Yvonne Rudellat. Drawing on the insights shared by this group of people, this book will provide a window onto the world of SOE's female agents – the daily grind, their hardships, noteworthy successes and failures as they occurred – and not as some films and TV programmes would have us believe.[13]

The other main sources I draw on are the SOE files at the UK National Archives. In the 1990s, formerly secret SOE files began to be released and now there is an almost full complement of personnel files (not all of which are complete) carrying information on agents' training, development and service. Many of the files also contain a record of the 'interrogation' or debrief that the agent received upon their return: this was an opportunity for agents to relate what had happened to them and their colleagues while working behind enemy lines, and provides the clearest way of understanding their thoughts immediately after their return from the field or from a concentration camp. The National Archives also contains operational and circuit reports, as well as a collection of files on the concentration camps and war trials. Several interviews, affidavits and letters with concentration camp staff are contained within the files and have been drawn on in some detail in this book.

However, while there is an immense collection of SOE files at the National Archives, it is incomplete. Some files remain closed and public access is not permitted, such as those relating to agents or their family members who are still alive (at the time of writing, the files of Phyllis Latour remain unreleased), while others, such as Lilian Rolfe's personnel file, have simply disappeared. In 1946, a fire at SOE HQ in Baker Street destroyed many SOE FANY files.[14] In addition to this, files considered to be of no further importance were destroyed in a 'weeding' process undertaken by office staff.[15] Whether any of what was lost was significant is impossible to know. It is estimated by an SOE archivist that '87 per cent of the files were destroyed between 1945 and 1950', leaving only a small proportion of the original records to work with, which makes it very difficult to reconstruct a complete picture of an agent or of F Section using these archives alone.[16] Maurice Buckmaster, head of F Section, maintained that, in any case, full records were not kept during the war as he did not want information to fall into the wrong hands.[17] Nonetheless, we can gain a more accurate picture of the women of SOE through drawing on the personal interviews conducted, as well as the rich holdings of audio archives at Imperial War Museum, which have been thoroughly consulted and are crucial to the accuracy and perspective of this book.

I will refer to the files discussed above as 'personnel files' as opposed to 'personal files' as this is how they are listed in the catalogue of the National Archives. I have chosen to refer to the female agents by their first names, and men by their last names, predominantly to avoid confusion as there are so many who feature in this book, many with similar first names.

Over the course of the following pages some agents will appear more in the foreground than others. But far from being based on which agent has in subsequent decades become a national heroine or more widely recognised, the focus on some agents over others is in part due to the incomplete records – which in certain cases severely limits what we can know about them – and in part in order to facilitate the narrative. For instance, Sonia Olschanesky has been included in this narrative, despite being recruited locally in the field and not attending training in Britain, and therefore not being an accredited 'agent' in the full sense of the term. This is because she served in an important role in an F Section circuit and, after capture, she was treated as an agent by her captors. The number of women agents therefore stands at thirty-nine, and not thirty-eight as Buckmaster stated in his prologue to the 1950 film *Odette*.[18] All thirty-nine women are included in a way that seeks to bring due recognition to their endeavours, and which offers criticism as well as plaudits to those who undertook SOE work behind enemy lines.

PART I
FOUNDATIONS

1

SETTING EUROPE ABLAZE

Some readers may be appalled at the suggestion that it should be necessary for human beings of the twentieth century to revert to the grim
brutality of the stone-age in order to live. But it must be realised that,
when dealing with an utterly ruthless enemy who has clearly expressed
his intention of wiping this nation out of existence, there is no room for
any scruple or compunction about the methods to be employed in
preventing him.

Introduction to W.E. Fairbairn's All-in Fighting, 1942[1]

In the early hours of Friday, 10 May 1940, seven of the Wehrmacht's panzer
divisions crossed the German–Belgian border, making their way westwards
through the heavily forested Ardennes region. Surprise and speed were
essential for the Germans traversing its few, narrow roads, snaking through
valleys and forests. Because of its difficult roads, the area was poorly defended
by the Belgians and unguarded further west by the French Army's Maginot
Line – a string of defensive concrete fortifications, some 450 km long, which
ran along the Franco-German border line further south. This had been built
after the First World War to protect against another German attack. The
French and Belgians had considered the Ardennes forest to be impenetrable
to fast-moving armoured formations, but the Wehrmacht proved otherwise.

Within two days the leading panzers had reached the Franco-Belgian frontier near the River Meuse. By crossing the Meuse at Sedan and elsewhere, the
northern end of the Maginot Line was outflanked, rendering it redundant.
Instead of heading towards Paris they turned north, towards the English

Channel, which the first units reached on 20 May. This split the larger forces of the French and their British allies in two. Those in the north were pushed back to the coast, eventually to the coastal town of Dunkirk, where the German advance was then then halted on 26 May by order of the local commander, Von Rundstedt, in a decision endorsed by Hitler. This was almost certainly a response to Hermann Göring's concern that the panzers would take all the glory for the Franco-British defeat. He lobbied for his Luftwaffe to bomb their foes into submission. They failed, and thus enabled the evacuation of a large proportion of the British Expeditionary Force (BEF), along with many French troops, some of whom would return as *résistants* and SOE agents.

In just six weeks the Nazis overran France and the French government was forced to sign a humiliating armistice on 22 June 1940 in the same railway carriage in which the 1918 Armistice had been signed. The fall of France was a catastrophe, and it was in the wake of this that Prime Minister Winston Churchill, appointed on the same day the Germans had begun their western offensive, gave the go-ahead for the creation of a body to coordinate and assist local clandestine activity against the Axis powers and their occupying forces in territories across Europe and beyond so that, when the time came, they would pave the way for the returning Allied armies. SOE was born.

Polish-born Krystyna Skarbek was in Ethiopia with her husband, Jerzy Gizycki, when war broke out. The daughter of a Polish aristocrat and a Jewish banking heiress, her ancestors had saved Poland from medieval invaders, and served royalty, so Krystyna was brought up with a heritage of pride and patriotism. She was said to have had a tomboyish nature, enjoying the outdoors, maintaining her fitness and riding horses on the family estate. She was persuasive, selfless and loyal, and it was these traits that led to her becoming involved with clandestine work and eventually SOE. Aged 18, she had married businessman Karol Getlich, but they soon divorced. In 1938 she remarried and moved to Kenya.

On her arrival in London from Africa in late 1939 Krystyna was asked to join Section D, part of the SIS (otherwise known as MI6), a world dominated by men recruited through the 'old boys' network. Being neither British nor male, this was not an obvious job for Krystyna, but she was recommended to Section D, which needed agents to open lines of communication between Hungary and Poland, as German propaganda controlled all of the news and Poland was effectively cut off from the outside world. Krystyna made an 'excellent' first impression, and her 'flaming' patriotism and 'smart' looks were noted.[2] She spoke Polish, French and English and had excellent contacts in Warsaw and across Poland – exactly what Section D needed from an agent – and she was recruited.

Krystyna undertook four hazardous missions for Section D. Skiing from neutral Hungary to Nazi-occupied Poland she carried intelligence, money and propaganda to the resistance circuits that were developing there. She undertook intelligence-gathering missions, and smuggled information, radio codes, coding books and sometimes microfilm – which she hid inside her gloves. One such film contained the first evidence of German preparations for Operation 'Barbarossa', the invasion of the Soviet Union.

Alongside Krystyna was fellow Pole Andrzej Kowerski. He had lost a leg in a shooting accident before the war, but did not let it hinder his resistance work, which included smuggling dozens of Polish soldiers and Allied POWs over the Hungarian border. The pair became lovers, and made a formidable team.[3] Together Krystyna and Kowerski gathered intelligence on river and rail transport between Germany and Romania, as well as tracking the movements of border guards between Yugoslavia and Slovakia. The work was constant and eventually it took its toll. Kowerski was travelling thousands of miles to help smuggle Polish airmen out of the country so they could join the Allied war effort and was exhausted, and Krystyna became seriously ill.

The pair were also known to the Hungarian police and the Gestapo who were keen to find them. On 24 January 1941 they were arrested and interrogated. They gave nothing away but the Gestapo employed more brutal means of interrogation to extract what they wanted from them. In an act of sheer bravery and determination Krystyna bit her tongue so hard that it bled, she then coughed up the blood and said she thought she had TB. A chest X-ray confirmed scars on her lungs (caused by previous lung damage from exhaust fumes) and, concluding that she was ill with a highly contagious disease, the doctor ordered their immediate release. With a price on her head, Krystyna was smuggled out of Hungary in the trunk of a Chrysler car belonging to the British ambassador, Sir Owen O'Malley. They crossed into Yugoslavia with Kowerski following behind in an Opel, then the two made their way hundreds of miles overland until they reached SOE headquarters in Cairo, Egypt.

On arrival in Cairo they were regarded with great suspicion by both the Poles and the British in the city, but Krystyna and Kowerski did not know why. It became clear that Anglo-Polish relations were very strained and that Krystyna, with a foot in each camp, was open to suspicion by each side. The pair were also suspected of being having been turned by the enemy – since they had passed through Syria, which was controlled by the Vichy government, it was assumed they could not have made the trip successfully unless they were double agents. After a considerable period of investigation in London, Krystyna was vindicated, partly because of the fact that she had smuggled microfilm across Europe, which had alerted the Allies to the German preparations for a Soviet invasion across borders, which occurred on 22 June 1941.

SOE (which had absorbed parts of Section D in 1940) considered sending her back to Hungary or Poland, but this was deemed too dangerous. She stayed in Egypt, Palestine and North Africa, where she undertook intelligence work as well as training in coding, Morse code, wireless transmission, parachuting, weapons and explosives, and Silent Killing against the day she might return to occupied Europe.

Virginia Hall, a US national, was in Paris when the Battle of France took place and volunteered with the ambulance services, working under enemy bombardment with the friend with whom she had volunteered at the outbreak of war, transporting the wounded to safety. French soldiers were deserting and France was on the verge of collapse as the Germans advanced. When the capital was occupied, she left France via Spain, where she met

British secret agent George Bellows in August 1940. Impressed by her 'courage, powers of observation, and most of all her unqualified desire to help the French fight back', he gave her a number to call when she reached London.[4] It was the phone number of F Section's Nicholas Bodington. They arranged to meet at his house in Mayfair, near where she was staying, on 14 January 1941. It was a meeting that would change her life.

Thirty-four-year-old Virginia was already determined to serve the Allied effort. Born into a wealthy family in Baltimore, Maryland, she had attended schools in France, Germany and Austria. She had a natural talent for languages, and a desire to travel, and so wanted to join the Foreign Service. In 1931, she was appointed as a Consular Service clerk at the US embassy in Warsaw. Her next assignment was in Izmir, Turkey, where she spent her spare time at shooting parties with her friends and colleagues. On one such occasion Virginia stumbled as she climbed over a wire fence in the wetlands, her 12-bore shotgun slipped from her grasp and, as she reached out to retrieve it, she caught the trigger and shot her own leg at point-blank range. Gangrene set in before she could reach a hospital, leaving her delirious and in agony. Her life hung in the balance and only the amputation of her lower left leg could save her. When she eventually recovered she was fitted with a prosthetic limb, which she nick-named 'Cuthbert'. The loss of her leg put a premature end to Virginia's dream of becoming a diplomat and she resigned from the State Department in 1939. But she had not lost the determination which had spurred her to join the Foreign Service in the first place. She wanted more than ever to help to halt the advance of the German war machine in France.

On her arrival in London, Virginia went to the US embassy where she was debriefed about all that she had witnessed in France. She was subsequently hired by the US military attaché's office. During those months the Battle of Britain raged and she experienced countless attacks by the Luftwaffe during the Blitz, which reinforced her determination to join the war effort. She left the embassy in February 1941 and, following the phone call with Bodington, joined SOE.

Virginia's determined and independent-spirited route to SOE chimed with the experiences of some of the thirty-eight other women who were already in the United Kingdom at the outbreak of the war. Unaware that an organisation like SOE existed, some had enlisted in the armed forces, but found the work frustrating and yearned for adventure.

The paths the women took to SOE were as diverse as they themselves were. In its formative months, SOE was something of an old-boy network: word-of-mouth recruitment was encouraged, and male friends and colleagues from schools, universities, regiments and businesses sought each other out to work together. Of course, there was no women's equivalent, and neither was there any prescribed method for recruiting female agents, partly as a result of which SOE recruited an extraordinary range of women, from the ranks of the aristocracy to those of working-class backgrounds, and of all ages (the youngest, Sonia Butt, was 19, while the oldest, Marie-Thérèse le Chêne, was 51).

Although no particular experience of war service was required, perhaps the most apposite recruits for SOE were women who had fled France, either at the outset or in the early years of the war, and so had some experience of living in occupied France, perhaps even working with the resistance. Four of the female agents recruited into F Section – Andrée Borrel, Vera Leigh, Madeleine Damerment and Nancy Wake – had previously worked on escape lines, a form of resistance which helped downed British airmen, escaped POWs or stranded servicemen to find their way out of occupied territory and back to safety. This usually meant a journey across the mountains into Spain, then travelling to Gibraltar or Portugal before finally making it to Britain. These women who possessed knowledge of France, an understanding of life under the occupation and excellent language skills were a very strong asset to SOE.

Several of the women were mothers or housewives who found themselves called to interview through various ruses, such as, in the case of Violette Szabó, to discuss her war widow's pension. Marguerite 'Peggy' Knight was overheard speaking French at a party and was called for an interview, while Yvonne Rudellat was approached through contacts at the Ebury Court Club in London where she worked. A few of the women, including Lise de Baissac, Eliane Plewman and Francine Agazarian, already had spouses or siblings in SOE who put them forward as viable candidates to be considered by the organisation.

The Women's Auxiliary Air Force (WAAF) was instructed to look out for exceptional women who might be useful to SOE, and indeed it identified a number of women who became SOE agents: Yolande Beekman, Sonia Butt, Yvonne Baseden, Yvonne Cormeau, Diana Rowden, Noor Inayat Khan, Anne-Marie Walters, Cicely Lefort, Mary Herbert, Paddy O'Sullivan, Muriel Byck, Lilian Rolfe, Marguerite Knight and Phyllis Latour. Re-formed in June 1939 having been disbanded at the end of the Great War, the WAAF was part of the Royal Air Force (RAF) and individual members reported to various RAF commands. Roles within the WAAF included basic duties such as clerical work, working in kitchens and driving, as well as telephony, telegraphy and signals intelligence, including at the Government Code and Cypher School at Bletchley Park. For some of these jobs good wireless skills were paramount and knowledge of a language could be a distinct advantage. SOE used the WAAF like a recruitment agency, whereby women who were identified as having relevant skills were put forward for interview, potentially (usually unbeknown to them) to become SOE recruits. One such woman was 21-year-old Yvonne Baseden, who had joined the WAAF, after seeking her father's permission, at the outbreak of the war. Having been born in France in 1922 to a French mother and an English father, in 1939 she moved to Southampton, where she worked as a bilingual shorthand typist at an engineering firm. She had an excellent grasp of French, which did not go unnoticed by the WAAF. In early 1943, she was invited for an interview in London. As soon as the interview started, Yvonne realised it was something to do with languages, though she was not given the full details at first. An opportunity to use her language skills in a way that might serve her country and allow her to see action was just what she wanted, and she was delighted to think she could do something for the war effort other than be a WAAF officer. Her F Section training began in the summer of 1943.[5]

Some of the women who were recruited through the WAAF came from overseas and undertook war work once they had arrived safely in

Britain. For Lilian Rolfe, it wasn't just a case of travelling a short distance to the local recruiting office – she boarded a ship in Brazil. Lilian was born in 1914 and originally raised in Paris, her education continuing in Brazil after her family relocated there. She was working for the British embassy in Rio de Janeiro when war broke out; her duties included the monitoring of German shipping movements in the harbour. After five Brazilian ships were attacked off the coast of Bahia in August 1942, Brazil declared war on Germany on 22 August. Several expatriates were keen to join the war effort and within months a contingent of men and women had left for Britain, their expenses (and their return journey at war's end) paid by a British community fund. In 1943 Lilian decided that she too wanted to go to Britain, and made the difficult decision to leave her parents and her twin sister, Helen. The ship sailed via New York, where Lilian stayed for several days. It was badly damaged as it crossed the Atlantic, probably by a mine, and one passenger was drowned. When Lilian finally reached London and joined the WAAF, her fluent French brought her to the attention of SOE, and like the others she was interviewed and sent for training.[6]

Mary Herbert joined the WAAF in September 1941. She trained at Innsworth in the intelligence section and remained there until March 1942, when she came to the attention of F Section. Born in Ireland in 1903, her life before the war had been varied and stimulating, and a love of learning took her to London University, the University of Cairo and the Slade School of Fine Art. She also had various jobs, each offering exciting and different challenges: she had been employed at the British embassy in Poland, had accompanied orphaned children emmigrating to Australia and worked at the Air Ministry in London as a civilian translator. Mary was fluent in Italian, Spanish, German and, of course, French. Her worldly knowledge and language skills made her an ideal candidate for SOE training, and, although her instructors initially thought her 'too fragile for resistance work', she showed promise and went on to complete the training.[7]

The FANY was also vital to the success of SOE, both as a cover and as a useful source of personnel. The FANY had originally been set up in 1907 by a rather eccentric cavalryman, Captain Edward Baker. He had a vision of scarlet-clad women galloping side-saddle onto battlefields where they would tend to the wounded before bringing them back to the casualty clearing stations. At the outbreak of the Great War the British Army declined their offer of help so they worked for the Belgian Army, with whom they served for two years. Eventually, the British Army took them on. Surgeon-General Woodhouse said of the FANY that 'they're neither fish nor fowl, but damned fine red herring'.[8]

During the Second World War the FANY was divided into two. One part became the Women's Transport Service (WTS FANY), which provided drivers to the RAF and the army. The other part was an autonomous FANY HQ which continued to run in London and it was this organisation that worked alongside SOE. SOE recruiting officer Jepson saw to it that he dressed the 'women recruits in FANY uniforms, which were very pretty and very nice and gave them complete cover, because they could always be drivers or whatever it might be; most of the army drivers of the higher echelons of the army were FANY'.[9] Not only did FANY provide cover for agents, it also paired agents with wireless operators who would get to know their 'fist' – the uniquely recognisable way that they tapped the Morse key while sending – and so would be able to work out if something were wrong or if agents were transmitting under duress. Some SOE conducting staff for women trainees were also recruited through FANY; they would accompany an agent through training, providing pastoral care at difficult times in the programme, and would report back on a recruit's strengths and weaknesses. They would be there when an agent was about to depart for occupied territory, perhaps handing them a make-up compact for luck, or a cyanide pill, or both in the form of a deadly lipstick.[10] FANY accounted for a significant proportion of SOE's workforce and, according to SOE historian Professor William Mackenzie, when SOE 'reached its maximum expansion in the late summer and early Autumn of 1944 . . . its total British strength was probably just under 13,000 . . . [including] about 450 ATS [Auxiliary Territorial Service], 60 WAAF and 1,500 FANY as well as nearly 1,200 civilian women: [totalling] about 3,200 women'.[11]

SOE was able to gain access to the information provided on the many forms that civilians had to fill out for various reasons. These could be applications for identity cards, to join services or even to get permission to fly abroad, and they could provide a wealth of details that would show whether a person had the right qualities to warrant an SOE interview. British Customs also agreed to inform SOE should anyone suitable pass through their offices, in addition to which suitable candidates who were spotted at the London Reception Centre in Wandsworth, south-west London, where MI5 interrogated all foreign nationals who had reached Britain from enemy-occupied territory, might also have their details passed on to SOE.

Although, as we have seen, age and social background were not determining factors in SOE's recruitment process, the candidate's experience, motives and personality were considered extremely important. 'The first qualification' for an F Section candidate 'was that they had to be able to pass as a native of the place they were in, so they had to be French or speak native French and they had, obviously, to look French and as if they would be able to have all the other necessary qualities for it'.[12] They ideally needed to have knowledge of France and the French way of life as well as the ability to blend in. Jepson outlined that they should have 'physical courage and sufficient intelligence combined with just enough leadership to enable them to carry out one simple and specific job'.[13] Above all, the women had to have a willingness to entertain the possibility of working for SOE and take on the underground work.

The reasons for such willingness varied greatly. Women were attracted to resistance work for many reasons: to fight the regime, to protect the future of their families or to avenge a loved one's deportation or death. Yolande Beekman's motives for joining SOE were 'idealism, the "good of the cause" and devotion to duty'.[14] Pearl Witherington had served with the office of the British air attaché in Paris since 1933 and escaped to London after the occupation, arriving in July 1941; she wanted to find a way to join the fight against the occupiers. Nancy Wake had already worked with the resistance and wanted to go back; F Section heard of her work and admired her courage. Phyllis Latour, the daughter of a French doctor, wanted the opportunity to make her mark against the Germans in revenge for their shooting of her godmother's father, whom she looked on as her own grandfather, and her godmother's suicide after being imprisoned by the enemy.[15] Interestingly, one woman's motive was another woman's obstacle. Children, for instance, could be a critical issue: Odette Sansom said 'I felt terrible. Then I thought, I am in the safety of beautiful Somerset, but am I going to accept, just like that, the fact that other people are going to suffer and get killed, let's face it, to get freedom for my children? Would I be satisfied not to lift a finger?'[16] Jepson recognised that the agents he recruited had many different motives: 'There were those seeking escape or relief from domestic pressure. An unhappy marriage, loss of a loved one that might be assuaged by devotion to a cause; perhaps the loss had been through the war simply to carry on where the dead had to stop. Above and beyond these personal motives one has to remember the basic fact that of all stimuli, war is the strongest, enough to deny self in a common need to defeat the enemy.'[17]

It was Jepson's job to establish, during the interview, what a woman's motive was and if she was suitable for recruitment into SOE. The initial interview was generally conducted in central London, at the former Hotel Victoria in Northumberland Avenue, or at Horse Guards. If successful, subsequent interviews might be at Orchard Court; there, F Section had use of an impressive apartment, complete with a black marble bathroom. For some women, arriving for interview would be the first time that they had even contemplated war work, while for other more experienced hands it would signal a welcome return to resistance activities. For some recruits it was a break from the monotony of a desk job in the WAAF or other services, and for several women it meant leaving behind their children in an attempt to secure their safety and the hope of a brighter future. Anne-Marie Walters recalled that at her interview she was asked, 'Can you speak French?' When she answered in the affirmative she continued to be questioned: 'How is it that you speak French so fluently? Are you ready to leave England? Are you ready to do anything we may ask you against the enemy? Can you ride a bicycle?' Her brief recollection rolls several interviews into one, but does indicate the type of questions asked and the rigorous way in which they were fired across the table, without hesitation or preamble. The recruiting officers had clearly been briefed on exactly what was required of an F Section agent.[18] Odette Sansom's reflections of her experience of interview are somewhat different, perhaps because she was a housewife, not a WAAF. She was called for interview to talk about some photographs of France she had mistakenly sent to the War Office instead of the Admiralty as the result of an appeal on the wireless. She received a letter asking her for interview and assumed it was about getting the photographs back. Odette, who had not anticipated what would be asked of her, was taken aback and once she had left the interview room tried to forget that it had ever taken place.[19] However, when she received another letter asking her to go back, she did. This time she was given much more information about what they wanted. She was told: 'we train people here, you may not know that but we do and we send them to the country of origin, or if they speak a foreign language very well, we send them to that country where they can use it, and they are extremely useful in the war effort'. When they asked if she would like to join she said it was 'impossible'. And yet, after giving it some more thought, she later agreed to undertake the training.[20]

Jepson used the interviews to glean information, and only once he was convinced by a recruit's potential did he tell them the precise details of the nature of the work involved, including the dangers and the chances of survival. He then waited for the candidate's reaction – he was wary of initial bursts of enthusiasm, which could indicate a misconceived notion about war work. Some of the women he interviewed, like Odette, were initially surprised by his proposal, while others rushed at the opportunity – Violette Szabó said without hesitation that she would do it. Her husband of only a few months, Étienne, had been killed serving in the Free French forces at El Himeimat, south of El Alamein, and had never seen his daughter Tania. Violette's reaction to the work took Jepson by surprise and he sent her away to give himself time to think as he did not wish to send out someone who may have been made 'unstable by grief'. But Violette's bravery and determination shone through and Jepson decided she was suitable for training.[21]

The training programme which a student-agent had to complete had been initially compiled by Major Tommy Davies in the autumn of 1940. Designed for all recruits, regardless of their sex or the country section for which they would eventually be working, the programme usually included four stages. Initial training was at a Preliminary School, the aim of which was to identify unsuitable recruits and reject them as soon as possible. If the recruit successfully passed this stage they would move on to paramilitary training in Scotland, followed by Parachute School at Ringway aerodrome near Manchester. Finally, there was a Finishing School, where agents would receive training in field craft to prepare them for the reality of life in occupied territory. Recruits who were selected to be wireless operators would also have an additional course to hone their wireless skills and perfect their Morse code.

Although a structured training programme was in place, the sequence in which training was undertaken was not always clear-cut and straightforward; there were always exceptions to the rule, and the details outlined above were not always adhered to for a variety of reasons, such as time limitations, a trainee's ability (or lack thereof) or an agent's previous experience in the field. And not all recruits undertook the same amount of training: though the training was intended to last six to nine months, if an agent was desperately needed in the field, or proved unusually competent in the use of the wireless set, then the training period could be cut short. The training programme was therefore quite flexible, and could be adjusted to meet the needs of the organisation, or to reflect the talents – or limitations – of the agent in question.

In the earliest days of the training programme, women trainees received neither preliminary nor paramilitary training. Thus, those agents recruited in the summer of 1942 – Yvonne Rudellat, Andrée Borrel, Lise de Baissac, Blanche Charlet, Mary Herbert, Odette Sansom, Marie-Thérèse le Chêne and Jacqueline Nearne – went straight to the full training course at the Finishing School at Beaulieu. Later, as women were trained as wireless operators as well as couriers, they first went through Preliminary School with the men, receiving basic paramilitary training, but not continuing to the full course in Scotland. Only after the introduction of the Students' Assessment Board in mid-1943 was it usual for women trainees to undertake the Arisaig area paramilitary course. However, some women, like some men, did not undertake parachute training, and for a variety of reasons, from the personal (previous injury or simply fear) to the operational: sometimes there was a specific need to deliver the agent into the field by small aircraft (such as Lysander or Hudson), felucca or motor gunboat.

Usually the preliminary course lasted for two to three weeks, and until the summer of 1943 was held at STS 5, Wanborough Manor, near Guildford in Surrey. Much to the amusement of F Section recruits, most of the Special Training Schools (STSs) were requisitioned manors and estates, and so it became a standing joke that SOE stood for 'Stately 'Omes of England'.[22] From June 1943, the Preliminary School syllabus was replaced by a shorter one-week Students' Assessment Board at STS 7 – Winterfold, Cranleigh, also in Surrey. At Preliminary School, recruits took tests to help determine their potential and to highlight their strengths and weaknesses; training included 'physical training, weapons handling, unarmed combat, elementary demolitions, map reading, field-craft and basic signalling'.[23] This course was conducted under 'Commando cover', and if locals questioned what was happening they were told that the Commandos were training there.

In her memoir *Moondrop to Gascony*, Anne-Marie Walters recounts how 'if anyone had told me that I would spend the summer of 1943 being timed on assault courses, tapping Morse messages on a dummy key, shooting at pieces of moving cardboard, crawling across the countryside and blowing up mock targets, I would have shrugged my shoulders in disbelief'.[24] At times, some women also found the physically trying nature of the work difficult to bear. Speaking of her time at Winterfold, Nancy Wake explained how her physical training (PT) course prepared them for life with the resistance and to think on their feet: 'there were trees to be climbed, gaps to be jumped, high slack ropes to be crossed with only another slack rope above to be used as a hand hold, difficult walls to be scaled, a seventy foot rope to be slid down, a dizzy platform off which one must jump to catch a rope six feet away and so slither down to safety'.[25] Nancy had spent two and a half years working in the resistance before she arrived in England and had never, she pointed out, been required to scale a 50 foot fireman's ladder.[26] But this was a course requirement if she wanted to move on to the next part of her training. The initial stage of the course was evidently designed to test a recruit's courage, physical strength and ability to think on their feet.

At Wanborough and Winterfold students were encouraged to work together and perform tests that required a high level of enterprise and coop-eration among the team members. Trainee agents received theory classes conducted in French and were known only by code names, and not permitted to talk about their outside lives.[27] This helped to instil a security routine from the outset. Free time was also closely monitored and recruits were actively encouraged to drink, so that the instructors could see how good they were at keeping a secret.

Not all recruits were successful in the first stage of training, including Joyce Hanafy, who was described by her instructors as being 'spoilt, affected, greedy for admiration and vain and superficial'; her file was marked 'Not recommended'.[28]

Joyce was sent home, but some other failed recruits were not permitted to leave. They could not be returned to civilian life or to their former job within the military as they might already have known too much in terms of intelligence or simply because they were now aware that an organisation like SOE existed at all. They were sent to various institutions, sometimes the SOE 'Cooler' in Inverlair, in Inverness-shire, Scotland, until their newfound knowledge became less significant and they could return home; it was like a wartime version of gardening leave.

From the summer of 1943, after Students' Assessment Board, successful recruits were sent on their paramilitary course, held at several shooting lodges in the Arisaig and Morar areas of Inverness-shire (STS 21 to 26c). This second course lasted for three to five weeks and recruits learnt 'physical training, silent killing, weapon training, demolition training, map reading and compass work, field-craft, appreciations – planning and reports and orders, raid tactics, elementary Morse, schemes and exercises designed to bring out the lessons taught in the forgoing subjects, para-naval training and boat work'.[29] No matter how physically onerous these tasks, no distinctions were made between male and female trainee agents. Major Aonghais Fyffe (security liaison officer for the training schools in Scotland) said:

> there was no distinction between the sexes and all suffered the same rigours of physical training in the early hours of wintry mornings, the same mud, muck soakings in peat bogs on fieldcraft and the same sore muscles and aching joints from the Arisaig form of unarmed combat. After all, when they were crawling flat to the ground over the peaty marshes of Loch nan Uamh, they were all just bods in battledress.[30]

Some aspects of the training were new to everyone, such as 'Silent Killing', 'an aggressive form of unarmed combat including the methods of defence against knife and other attacks (such as using stiffened rope as an offensive weapon), as well as the latest methods of attacking and killing sentries and other enemy troops quietly'. It had been developed in the 1930s by William Ewart Fairbairn and Eric Sykes, two former Shanghai policemen, as an unorthodox way of dealing with the city's criminal underworld. The recruits practised on straw dummies as well as on each other with the aim of becoming 'attack minded, and dangerously so'.[31] Silent Killing was added to the SOE syllabus in June 1942, when Fairbairn and Sykes were employed to instruct their own course. Fairbairn recognised that some people would perhaps be shocked by this form of combat, but he believed it to be a necessary and efficient tactic. The instructors taught that how hard one hit an opponent was of little consequence, it was *where* you hit them that was significant. At 11 stone and 5'7" tall, Nancy Wake was not terribly strong, but 'her instructors assured her that if she hit exactly the right spot she could still be effective enough to kill someone'.[32] This was a lesson that, some sixty years later, Pearl Witherington recounted with a gleam in her eye, saying that even in her 80s she would still be able to kill someone using techniques she was taught by Fairbairn and Sykes.

As well as teaching the courses Fairbairn and Sykes devised a knife for use in close combat by SOE agents and Commandos. The FS knife, also known as the Commando dagger, had a double-edged blade that was seven and a half inches long, the hilt was four and half inches long and was inscribed with the initials of its inventors. For SOE, the knife was intended to be concealed on the wearer, either in a trouser pocket or in the folds of a skirt. The knife was held in the flat of the hand and could be used in a swift stabbing motion or an upward thrust; it could also be used for cutting or slashing. Although it could be done, a downward blow was considered to be less effective.

When learning how to use her FS, Virginia Hall practised with a dummy knife smeared with red lipstick so she could see how accurate she had been against her target. Once she had succeeded in this she graduated to working on another recruit. She was to sneak up behind him and slit his throat. Virginia accomplished the task but was shocked when the man turned round and she saw the lipstick smear on his throat. The reality of what she was training to do had sunk in.[33]

The reality of training with an FS knife was a struggle for some recruits, but others seemed to come into their own when training with it. For instance, Yvonne Rudellat was said to be 'far more skilful at using a knife than most of the men'.[34] Nancy Wake admitted that Silent Killing taught her to kill someone in a cold-blooded fashion, and she 'concentrated as hard as anyone on those lessons, against the day I might have to use it'.[35]

In addition to Silent Killing and knife training, an SOE recruit was taught how to use various firearms including the Sten gun, Bren gun, Thompson submachine gun, PIAT (Projector, Infantry, Anti-tank) and hand-held pistols such as the Colt .32 and Colt .45. The agents were also trained in the use of various foreign weapons such as the Mauser, Browning and Flaubert. As with Silent Killing, the aim was that use of the firearms should become instinctive and the idea was that trainees should be comfortable shooting as many types of weapon as possible because they never knew what weaponry they might come across in the field and be able to put to good use.

Some female recruits were already accustomed to using firearms and many excelled in their use. As previously mentioned, Virginia Hall was an accomplished and experienced game hunter who used firearms. She was provided with a Browning repeater as it was the lightest gun available at the time and believed to be suited to her. Violette Szabó was reputedly the 'best shot in SOE', having learnt to shoot as a child.[36] Nancy Wake also achieved a reputation for being a 'crack shot' because her shots never went too high – shooting high being a problem often faced by users of the Sten gun.[37]

However, other women struggled. Yvonne Rudellat found the standard Colt pistol too heavy and was issued a .32 short-barrelled Colt, weighing just one and quarter pounds, which she still found to be 'remarkably heavy'.[38] Some agents did not like shooting at all: Noor Inayat Khan's training report states that she was 'pretty scared of weapons but tried hard to get over it'.[39]

At the end of this firearms course, recruits trained with and became accustomed to various handguns; if they favoured a particular type of weapon they would be issued with one. If they chose to, they could take this gun with them into the field. However, SOE advised recruits to seriously question doing this: 'Do you need a gun? It is generally only helpful when you are engaged in an activity for which there can be no cover story: e.g. landing by parachute. At other times it is likely to be an embarrassment. If you take one, decide what to do with it after landing.'[40] There were almost no reasons that were acceptable in occupied territory for carrying a gun; having one would arouse suspicion and heighten the risk of arrest.

Students also learnt how to use hand grenades, but Nancy Wake was particularly averse to this weapon: 'she loathed the rigid over-arm throw'[41] and seemed determined to make a spectacle of herself at training. The drill required that the class should sit in a trench; one by one the recruits got out, removed the pin from their grenade, threw it in the opposite direction and leapt back into the trench. Nancy asked her instructor what she should do, he sarcastically replied that she should: 'pull the pin, throw the grenade into the trench and run ... with a dead pan face Nancy pretended to believe him. The class in the trench – including the sergeant instructor – were last seen fleeing for cover!'[42]

Recruits were also instructed in the use of plastic explosive. Although sabotage was not typically work undertaken by women, many received training in it regardless and put it to good use in the field. The demolitions courses lasted twenty-four hours, usually in the form of one-hour lectures. Students were taught about the different types of fuses and the type of explosive used, which varied from Nobel 808 (a volatile, rubbery substance that smelt strongly of almonds) to plastic explosive (PE2), which was much safer to handle, had no smell or taste, and could be moulded into a variety of shapes such as cow dung, fruit or even logs.

Recruits at the Preliminary School and at Arisaig were taught how to blow up targets using these explosives and the training was kept as realistic as possible, meaning that sometimes objects that were only meant for practice were actually destroyed including, in the Arisaig area, a bridge at Loch Morar and the pier at Swordland (STS 23b), also on Loch Morar. Recruits were taught that the demolition must never fail and they spent many hours of the day and night familiarising themselves with various gadgets including incendiary devices, Molotov cocktails and booby traps.

Recruits needed to be at the height of physical fitness for their new clandestine roles and PT was an essential part of the course, albeit an aspect that was either loved or hated by recruits. Nancy hated it – on one occasion she refused to get of bed for an early morning run, saying that she did not feel well with 'women's problems'. After three weeks a doctor was sent, but she made a miraculous recovery when the time of the run was changed from 6 a.m. to 9 a.m. Some recruits rose to the challenge and made the most of it, enjoying the chance to get fit and healthy. The outdoor life suited 45-year-old Yvonne Rudellat and 'years seemed to drop from her shoulders',[43] while Noor was said to be in 'in good physical condition' with 'a renewed purpose in her life' due to her newly developed fitness.[44]

Parachute training was neither for the fainthearted nor the physically unsound – recruits needed to be in good physical condition. On this course, which was held at RAF Ringway aerodrome (now Manchester International Airport), it was intended that all agents should complete four jumps, three from an aircraft and at least one from a stationary balloon. It was essential in this case that men and women worked on equal terms. Those who passed the course proudly received their coveted parachute wings – in theory. In practice, both Pearl Witherington and Odette Wilen were only presented with them, by the RAF, in their later years.[45]

Yvonne Baseden recalled that she found parachute jumping 'terrifying, but it was always terrifying you know, you think oh I've done it once it will be fine. Mind you I had five jumps as part of the training and they were all just as unnatural if you like as the first one.'[46] Fortunately for Yvonne she was not required to jump from the balloon due to bad weather; many thought that this static jump was far worse an experience than the leap from an aircraft. Nancy Wake did undertake the jump and was reputedly terrified, thinking 'this is awful, I'll be killed, you know. I'll never do it again.'[47] The inclement weather ensured a repeat performance was not necessary. Another parachutist, Anne-Marie Walters, said that 'when I arrived at parachute school, I had realised that I never really believed it would happen. And if I had jumped, it was only because the boys expected the girls to be scared and refuse.' Anne-Marie was taunted and mocked by the men on her course. But she soon realised that the men were just as scared as she was, and that she had made herself equal to them by performing the jump.[48]

Some agents did not do the parachute training course: Virginia Hall was exempt on account of the fact she had a false leg (although Polish agent and Krystyna Skarbeks's lover Andrzej Kowerski, who also wore a prosthetic limb, became a parachute instructor), while other trainees could claim a fear of heights or were even deemed unsuitable, as was the case for Noor Inayat Khan. Injuries were commonplace too: Violette Szabó twisted her ankle badly on landing and took several weeks to recuperate, while Odette smashed her face on the side of the hole in the aircraft floor – an event known as 'ringing the bell', which could result in broken noses, black eyes and concussion. Odette also wrenched her ankle and suffered concussion and facial swelling, requiring treatment by an ophthalmic specialist as well as a brief spell in hospital. In spite of these mishaps many female agents did their required number of jumps.

After parachute training, agents were separated into various groups depending on what type of work they would be doing once in the field. Wireless operators were sent away on a course that would help to perfect their skills, usually held at STS 52, Thame Park in Oxfordshire. Many agents had to start their wireless operator training from the very beginning. They started by learning Morse code and gradually worked their way up to speeds in excess of 22 words per minute (at this time the average speed of a General Post Office (GPO) telegraphist was 12 words per minute). Most operators were graded for send and receive, and it was normal for these to be different. For example, a recruit might send at 20s but only receive at 18s. During her time at RAF Abingdon, Noor Inayat Khan had quickly been chosen for training as a wireless operator as she was already capable of 22 words per minute when she started training but was required to reach 24. In training, agents were expected to practise until they were perfect and to be perfect every time.

Recruits spent many hours learning the skills of transposition into cipher (according to their period of training several methods of encryption were used). They also learnt about atmospherics, wavelengths, oscillation, static, skip, dead spots, jamming and aerials, as well as ways of hiding sets and security. They were taught the composition of their wireless set, how to diagnose faults and how to repair it. Recruits learnt to incorporate predetermined security checks in their messages so that the listening posts in Britain could establish whether the messages were genuine, being sent under duress or even being sent by the Nazis. They were made aware that once they were in the field their messages would be sent to a particular receiving station in Britain where hundreds of men and women (often FANY) would be constantly listening out to receive and reply to their wireless messages.

In addition to the extensive wireless training, which sometimes totalled 40 hours a week, agents were also engaged in 'schemes', some lasting up to 96 hours. They were often sent on clandestine exercises with their wireless sets during which they had to go to a specified location, find an area from which to transmit and send pre-arranged messages to a home station. Often they were sent to locations where trees, mountains or tall buildings impaired their ability to transmit clearly. Occasionally SOE training officers trailed them and they had to attempt to lose them. Sometimes the local police were issued with a description of recruits and told that they should be brought in for questioning if they were seen. The aim was twofold: to make the training as difficult as it could be to test the recruit's resourcefulness and skill, and to prepare them for life in the field as a wireless operator.

Noor Inayat Khan undertook one such scheme in May 1943, having arrived some two months earlier as the first woman agent to be selected for intensive wireless training. A detailed report is given on her SOE personnel file of her ability to conduct herself as a secret agent, albeit in the surroundings of Bristol. For the scheme, Noor was required to stay in a safe house, make a number of rendezvous and be subjected to a police interrogation. The report states that 'she made several stupid mistakes' and 'always volunteers too much information when being questioned'.[49] So much information in fact that Marks, the head of SOE Codes section (who assisted in briefing agents), said that 'she was cycling towards her safe house to practise transmitting when a policeman stopped her and asked what she was doing. "I'm training to be an agent" she said "here's my radio, want me to show it you?" The officer who conducted her interrogation said that "if this girl's an agent I'm Winston Churchill".[50] The conclusion was that Noor needed to learn the art of discretion.[51]

This report does raise the question of why Noor continued her training, and indeed why she became an agent at all. The answer is simply that F Section was always chronically short of wireless operators and indeed wireless sets. The role was recognised as one of the most dangerous and vulnerable in the field and it was stated clearly that the wireless operator must never be used for other work. In fact wireless operators were so valuable that they were usually kept in hiding and were only permitted to send and receive messages. As such they might go for weeks without any human contact and were not permitted to engage in any courier or sabotage work. Of course, these rules were sometimes broken, but they suggest that a wireless operator had to be resourceful, independent and mentally strong.

The final training for all the women recruits, whether wireless operator, or courier, was at the SOE Finishing School at Beaulieu in the New Forest. Beaulieu was the place where agents learnt the skills of how to survive in occupied France and what being a secret agent really meant: 'they were taught the elements of clandestine techniques and security; above all the importance of looking natural and ordinary while doing unnatural and extraordinary things'.[52] This course was aimed at making the recruits familiar with the facts of daily life in France, training them to think and behave as if they were actually French, and highlighting the implications that simple mistakes could carry. Many changes had occurred in France during the occupation; for instance, women were not given a cigarette ration, so smoking in public could draw unwanted attention. Coffee was only available without milk – so asking for a *café au lait* would raise a few eyebrows, and certain food and alcohol were only available on set days of the week. Agents had to be aware of these changes, which would be second nature to a French civilian – the smallest of errors could mark them out as different and potentially cost them their lives.

Other mistakes that could be ironed out at Beaulieu included teaching an agent not to put milk in her teacup first, as this automatically gave her away as being English, to look right and not left before crossing the road, and to cycle on the correct side. Recruits were also taught about the differences between the occupied zone, Vichy (the free zone) and the demarcation lines. They learnt the importance of updating and checking their false documents, papers and cover stories. They practised recognition of the various uniforms they would encounter in France, and the responsibilities held by those who wore them. German services ranged from the army's Abwehr (Military Intelligence), Geheime Feldpolizei (Secret Field Police) and Feldgendarmerie (Military Police) to the Nazi Party's Sicherheitsdienst (Security/Intelligence Service), Schutzstaffel (Guard Unit) and Geheime Staatspolizei (Secret State Police). Among the French services, the Milice (the Vichy government's paramilitary force) was to be most feared, while the gendarmerie and local police implemented government instructions as a matter of course and duty. During the Nazi occupation there were collaborators in France, and agents were taught that no one could be trusted until their bona fides were established.

Another vital element of training at Beaulieu was the art of secrecy. Agents were taught various methods of contacting one another through the use of 'letter boxes', 'cut outs' or 'dead drops' – hidden places where messages could be left, such as in church Bibles, underneath a pre-arranged stone or in between the bricks of a wall. They were taught to write messages on cigarette papers and onion skins, and to pass them along in hollowed-out corks, cigarette packs or newspapers. It became second nature to the agents to use passwords when meeting with strangers, and they were drilled to leave a rendezvous if they sensed danger.

Agents were also trained at Beaulieu to be prepared for capture and its possible consequences by undergoing mock interrogation. The SOE syllabus stated that 'If you are arrested by the Gestapo, do not assume that all is lost; the Gestapo's reputation has been built up on ruthlessness and terrorism, not intelligence. They will always pretend to know more than they do and may even make a good guess, but remember that it is a guess; otherwise they would not be interrogating you.'[53] However, agents were still dragged from their beds at any time of the night and forced to withstand a Gestapo-style interrogation to determine their ability to stand up to interrogation techniques and test their familiarity with their cover story. Noor did not fare well in these episodes. Her escorting officer 'found Noor's interrogations almost unbearable'. Noor was 'terrified' especially by the bright light shone in her face which 'hurt her' and the officer's voice when he shouted. She was so 'overwhelmed she nearly lost her voice' and could barely be heard. When she left the room she was 'trembling and quite blanched'.[54]

Despite all the strains and rigours of the final stages of SOE training, Beaulieu was a place of calm and tranquillity. Many agents said it was a piece of England that made them remember what they were fighting for. Agents found time for contemplation in the grounds of the old abbey, and a monument is placed there today to remember the estate as the site of SOE's Finishing Schools.

Once the agents had finished their training it was the instructors' reports and a decision from HQ at Baker Street that determined whether they would go on to work in the field. The decision was not always easy. Violette, for example, was a very popular recruit with a complex character and motive, as was noted by her instructors:[55]

I consider that owing to her too fatalistic outlook in life and particularly in her work [and] the fact that she lacks ruse, stability and the finesse which is required and that she is too easily influenced, when operating in the field she might endanger the lives of others working with her. It is very regrettable ... with a student of this type who during the whole course has set an example to the whole party by her cheerfulness and eagerness to please.[56]

Nevertheless, Violette was invited to the next stage of training.

Yvonne Cormeau's instructor's comments were also uncomplimentary, stating that she had 'very little personality or aggressiveness', that she was 'intelligent and quick-witted without being intellectual' and she 'seems to live on her nerves and might become rattled in a difficult situation'. In spite of this, SOE decided to give Yvonne the benefit of the doubt and she went on to become their most successful wireless operator.[57] Madeleine Damerment's report was much more straightforward, describing her as 'intelligent, practical, shrewd, quick and resourceful'. She was deeply attached to her friends and 'should make a satisfactory subordinate under a strong leader, but would need careful handling'.[58] Yolande Beekman was described as having a 'ready sense of humour without being witty; more common sense then intellect; more reliability than initiative. She shows any amount of determination in mastering the intricacies of W/T and gives the impression that although she expects to learn slowly and with pains, it never occurs to her that she will not get there in the end.' However, not everyone saw her ordinariness as an advantage and one particular instructor was very disparaging about her, saying that she was 'a nice girl, darned the men's socks, would make an excellent wife to an unimaginative man, but not much more than that'. A training summary considered that she 'was not a sufficiently strong personality to be a leader but should make an excellent subordinate or W/T operator'.[59]

The man who had final say over an agent's destiny was Maurice Buckmaster: in his words, agents 'did not go unless [F Section staff] were completely satisfied that they were alright'. According to Buckmaster, F Section did not make 'any serious mistakes ... we did nothing that led to tragedy, I think that in one or two people we were somewhat disappointed and had to, not cancel their job but put them onto something else. We had to be very tough about it because other people's lives were at stake.'[60] Yet Buckmaster did send agents who were either unsuitable in training or proved to be so once in the field. Odette Wilen was infiltrated not knowing her codes properly and had to be sent home with great difficulty and expense to SOE. The issues raised in Noor Inayat Khan's training reports and the doubts about her suitability for secret operations were deemed as acceptable risks; yet, as we shall see, because of her failing to maintain security measures seven people lost their lives. And, though her instructors reported that Odette Sansom was 'impulsive and hasty in her judgements and has not quite the clarity of mind which is desirable for subversive activity', they also recognised her 'enthusiasm, intelligence and patriotism' alongside her knowledge of France and its language, her steely resolve and her willingness to undertake a dangerous role. Buckmaster was convinced of her abilities, and Odette was sent into the field.[61]

Buckmaster overrode reports time and time again. That said, he also overrode poor reports for women who turned out to be exceptional agents, such as Jaqueline Nearne, who was said to be 'mentally slow and not very intelligent' and 'a very simple person' who 'could not be recommended'.[62] She proved them wrong, and after her mission was described as 'one of the best we have had'.[63]

Overall, the training undertaken by female recruits for F Section seems to have been a success. Although for some agents training was much briefer than for others, those who undertook it inevitably learnt skills that they had not previously possessed and which would equip them for work in the field. Perhaps some women who were sent should not have been, and perhaps the training reports should have been taken more seriously: it would appear that when the need was highest, standards were lowered. However, of the seventy-three female recruits who started their training, thirty-eight passed and went on to become couriers, wireless operators and even, in one case, a circuit leader working behind enemy lines.[64]

Virginia Hall's debut operation was the first 'mainstream' F Section operation in France to involve a woman agent from the United Kingdom. But her arrival in France was delayed. In May 1941 she applied to the US embassy in London for a visa that would enable her, as a citizen of the US, at that point a neutral country, to travel through France, Spain and Portugal. She also applied for permission from the *New York Post* for her cover as a journalist; as an American she could work openly in Vichy France, reporting freely and with her articles uncensored, while being the 'eyes and ears' for F Section. Her wait was long and drawn out, and, with her nights in London restricted by the blackout, she spent her daytimes working on a code that could be used in her newspaper articles. Even though her name was on the embassy's 'priority list', it was just one long waiting game, which was tormenting for a woman with Virginia's enthusiasm and motivation. Her frustration at the situation grew and grew.

Meanwhile, the war took a major turn. On 22 June 1941 Operation 'Barbarossa' was launched. At 3.15 a.m. 3.2 million German troops invaded the Soviet Union across a 1,800-mile front, taking their new enemy by surprise. At 7 a.m. that morning, Hitler made a radio broadcast to the German people which announced: 'At this moment a march is taking place that, for its extent, compares with the greatest the world has ever seen. I have decided again today to place the fate and future of the Reich and our people in the hands of our soldiers. May God aid us, especially in this fight.'

To Virginia's surprise the invasion of Russia brought two benefits: it lifted the morale of the British as they no longer felt so isolated in their fight against the Germans; and in France it spurred the communists, who had not hitherto engaged in resistance work, to form and seek out resistance groups with whom they could work as allies. It made Virginia even more impatient to get to France and do her bit for the resistance.

At last, in early August, Virginia was called for a meeting at the former Hotel Victoria in Northumberland Avenue with Vera Atkins and Selwyn Jepson. It was explained that the delay had not just been due to her papers, but that F Section agent Jacques de Guélis had parachuted into Vichy France a few weeks earlier and since then had been busy recruiting resisters, identifying landing strips for aircraft, collecting documents that could be forged, and, most importantly for her, setting up contacts and paving the way for her cover story. The scene was set, the resistance in Vichy France was ready to receive their first female agent – and she was more than ready to go.

2
TRAILBLAZERS

I'd give anything to get my hands on the limping Canadian bitch.

Klaus Barbie, Head of Lyon Gestapo, about Virginia Hall[1]

On a hot summer night in late August 1941, Virginia Hall boarded a ship bound for Lisbon. Crossing the Channel before heading out into the open Atlantic, the risks from mines or detection by an enemy ship were still great, even for a passenger vessel. On reaching the port safely, Virginia made her way to the railway station and took the train across Portugal through Spain and into France. Under the cover name 'Brigitte Lecontre' and with the field name 'Marie', Virginia arrived in Vichy, some 400 km from Paris, on 23 August 1941, wearing two money belts strapped round her waist stuffed full of French francs with which she could build her resistance network, finance bribes and fund her own living expenses.

Once a holiday resort, the small picturesque town of Vichy had become the administrative centre of the unoccupied zone on 22 June 1940, its government headed by Marshal Philippe Pétain, a highly decorated Great War veteran who acted as a figurehead for the state's collaboration with the Nazis. Virginia's first port of call was the US embassy to register so she would be able to travel and work freely. She then went to the Vichy gendarmerie, where, fighting her contempt for the men who had so readily collaborated, she answered their questions politely and in full. Virginia took up residence in a basic but cosy hotel on rue Jardet, where, from her third-floor window, she had an excellent view of the street. She could observe the life of ordinary French people who had been thrust into this most extraordinary situation.

Virginia soon came to realise that the France she had left only eighteen months before had all but disappeared. In a story wired via Western Union to the *New York Post*, dated 4 September 1941, she wrote:

> The years have rolled back here in Vichy. There are no taxis at the station, only half a dozen buses and a few one-horse shays. I took a bus using *gazogène*, charcoal instead of gas, to my hotel. Vichy is a tiny town used once by summer visitors to take the cure. It is an infinitesimally small place to accommodate the government of France and French empire which has commandeered most of the hotels.[2]

At the forefront of everyone's mind was food, or to be more precise the shortage of it. The majority of France's produce, including meat, wine and champagne, had been taken by the Nazis. A bar owner told her that the promised extra ration of sugar with which to make jam had arrived too late and the strawberries had spoiled, and that when the winegrowers had needed pesticides to control their crops, these too had arrived late so that the crops were ruined.

Food rationing in France had started in September 1940 with meat and bread and had resulted in stock piling and food shortages. Having grown used to British rationing, Virginia was surprised to learn that she was now only allowed 10 ounces of bread per day and then a monthly allowance of '2 ounces cheese, 25 ounces fats, 20 ounces sugar, 10 ounces meat and 6 ounces coffee'. She added that the majority of the coffee allowance was ersatz, made from acorns or grilled barley, also known as Pétain coffee; it was foul and no substitute at all for the real thing. Rice, noodles and chocolate were reserved for colder months. France, she said, 'would be a paradise for a vegetarian if there was milk, cheese and butter, but I haven't seen any butter and there is no milk . . .'[3]

So, French cuisine, made famous the world over for its fine ingredients and rich flavours, was reduced to the basics and, even then, only when they were available. People were literally starving and the food shortages quickly affected people's health, physical fitness and mental well-being. Virginia observed that 'the average weight loss today is 12 pounds per person not only from lack of food, but increased physical activity and mental strain ... people are separated from their loved ones ... prisoners of the Germans.'[4]

Virginia spoke of clothing shortages, saying: 'I also see little clothing in the shops and that is extremely dear. Shoes, however, are abundant and gay with their cloth or crocheted uppers and painted wooden soles.' Nonetheless magazines encouraged women to keep up their standards for the men's sake and 'stay how they would like to see you'. Make-up companies promoted their products to boost self-confidence and optimism, while articles were published on knitting jumpers and balaclavas, as well as how to revive old dresses into this season's fashions.[5]

Virginia's observations of life in Vichy France were crucial, not only because they were printed in the *New York Post*, but also because they provided F Section with vital insight into how the French people were coping and what life under Nazi rule was like. Such knowledge would allow them to target resistance networks with up-to-date propaganda and help them to win the support of the average French person with promises of supplies and money that would make a tangible difference to their lives. For example, Virginia noted that smoking, which was very popular among women, had all but stopped due to the fact that they no longer received a ration and therefore were not entitled to buy cigarettes, and men were rationed to two packs a week.[6] This was of huge significance for those back at F Section, and female trainees were told they could not smoke quite as freely as they might have liked as it might attract unwanted attention.

Shortly after her early articles were sent to New York, Virginia met with F Section agent Jacques de Guélis, the man who had helped prepare for her arrival, to discuss her role within F Section. She was to go to Lyon, 120 km away, where she could make contact with de Guélis's resistance colleagues, whose names and addresses she had memorised. Her first contact was a gynaecologist named Dr Jean Rousset. After she arrived in his office he told her that he had been busy since de Guélis had visited him and had made the acquaintance of several people who were willing to help the cause of the resistance. He had also been doing sabotage of his own, by deliberately infecting German soldiers with gonorrhoea and syphilis, while giving the all-clear to prostitutes who carried a variety of infectious sexually transmitted diseases.[7] He told her that he was grateful for the risks that she was prepared to take, and put himself and his office at her disposal. Later that day Virginia made her way to the Café de la République where she dined on black market cuisine with several would-be resisters, one of whom was hiding a downed British airman in his house and wanted her help to get him home. There, at that table, were the beginnings of a ready-made resistance circuit.

Virginia also made the acquaintance of a brothel Madame, who, as a devoted Gaullist, not only offered to help find extra clothing and food from her black market contacts, but gathered intelligence where she could from 'her girls', who were privy to all sorts of information that their customers let slip.

With the backing of the locals and the knowledge that she could, as far as possible, trust them, Virginia was able undertake her role as organiser of her new HECKLER circuit. Providing intelligence reports about the conditions in France as well as developing her various contacts with a view to building up the resistance, Virginia worked tirelessly and effectively. Her SOE file praises her 'high degree of organising ability and a clear sighted appreciation of our [F Section's] needs'.[8] She acted as a go-between, carrying instructions to F Section personnel, and generally taking care of them by seeing to their everyday requirements. She met practically every F Section agent sent to France during this period and helped them in any way possible: she provided papers and cover stories, looked after them when they were in difficulty, did everything she could to get them organised.[9]

Most agents came to know Virginia as an affable and approachable person who took to her role with skill and efficiency, which instilled in them a sense of confidence and calm. She was there for anyone who needed her, and could help with practically any eventuality, from low morale to getting a desperate person out of danger and across an escape line. Her home was welcoming and friendly; F Section agent Ben Cowburn said that 'if you sit in

[her] kitchen long enough you will see most people pass through with one sort of trouble or another which [she] promptly deals with'.[10] She was admired and trusted.

But in October 1941 the unthinkable happened: twelve SOE agents were arrested when a meeting in Marseille was raided by French police. Virginia had been invited to the meeting, but had declined the invitation. The arrested agents were taken in for questioning, leaving Virginia as one of the few F Section agents still at large in France, and the only one with a means of getting information to London.

But Virginia was not prepared to leave her colleagues to fester in a French jail. She found out where they had been taken, and a few days later learnt that the prisoners were being moved from Périgueux prison to the Vichy internment camp of Mauzac near Bergerac. Virginia recruited Gaby, the wife of Jean-Pierre Bloch, one of those arrested, in order to plan their escape.[11] The imprisoned wireless operator Georges Bégué – the first F Section agent in France – managed to smuggle letters out to Virginia and thence to London via Gaby, who visited the prison frequently to bring food and other items to her husband; these included tins of sardines, which Bégué used to make a key to the door of the barracks where the prisoners were kept. Virginia organised transport and helpers to get the agents away from the prison and safe houses in which to hide them.

At 4 p.m. on 15 July 1942, an old woman walked past the camp: this was the signal to the prisoners confirming the escape was on – an old man would have meant the mission had been aborted. That night, at 3 a.m., they drugged their guard with a sleeping draught, unlocked the door of their hut with their duplicate key and escaped through the wire into a waiting lorry which drove them to a forest hide-out. They waited there a week while an intense manhunt ensued. Leaving in twos and threes, it was not until mid-August that all of them met up with Virginia in Lyon. She saw them onto an escape line which brought them across the mountains, into Spain and then on to England. The escape was 'one of the war's most useful operations of its kind'. Bégué became F Section's signals officer and several of the prisoners returned to France as agents.[12]

Virginia continued her work as a 'stringer' for the *New York Post*, her stories not only lending credibility to her cover but also giving vital information to SOE HQ about life in France. Her missive of 24 November 1941 highlighted the stark reality of life with collaborators and Vichy's own anti-Semitic policies:

> A law forbidding acquisition of stock by Jews without special permission has just been passed ... Jews are not permitted to be bankers, publicity agents, merchants, real estate agents or owners, owners of gambling concessions, nor are they allowed to earn a living by working in the theatre, movies or for the press.[13]

She went on to say that banks, movie companies, textile, gas and iron companies and one newspaper were due to be liquidated or put under Aryan control. The world in which she lived was becoming ever bleaker, and more dangerous for those around her.

The collaborators also made it clear that anyone working with the resistance would be severely punished. Secretary-General René Bousqet, who oversaw the Vichy police, hunted resisters, communists, Jews and those who hid them with unbridled enthusiasm. The regime announced that anyone helping Allied airmen would be severely punished: men would be shot and women deported to concentration camps in Germany.

Despite the dangers and threat of arrest, Virginia continued providing reports to the press, but in SOE matters she sometimes found herself rather lonely and cut off. Things did not run as smoothly as perhaps they could have. Ideally, Virginia would have had her own wireless operator, but two of the four who had been sent from England had been captured, which restricted her ability to contact F Section and was a hindrance to all agents for whom communication was vital. Also, while her cover as a journalist provided her with a great deal of freedom, it meant that she could not 'pass around France anything more bulky than money and messages'.[14]

Unfortunately, by the end of the year, and in spite of her best efforts, a third of all the agents who had entered France were in prison and the rest were in hiding.[15] But it was early days for F Section and Virginia had done her utmost to help set things out and prepare the ground for incoming agents. She was greatly esteemed: her SOE file states that 'she acted as a universal aunt to all our people who were in trouble and anyone in difficulties immediately called upon her for help. Many of our men owe their liberty and even their lives to her assistance.'[16] She carried out these tasks with utmost efficiency and devotion for a further fifteen months.

It was while Virginia was still active in the field that the groundbreaking decision was made by SOE F Section to use women as agents, and that the ad hoc fashion in which she and Krystyna had been recruited and prepared for their active roles became formalised through an interview process and training programme. It appears, then, that Virginia's deployment for F Section was an experiment; she was an unusual case, not conforming with any policy or decision that was made with regards the recruitment, training or deployment of other women for F Section.

After this the recruitment and training of female F Section recruits began in earnest. The first group (party 27 OB, sent to 'Boarmans' at Beaulieu) to undertake training were Andrée Borrel, Marie-Thérèse le Chêne, Blanche Charlet, Lise de Baissac, Mary Herbert, Odette Sansom, Jacqueline Nearne and Yvonne Rudellat (who was the first to receive a commission in the FANY).

Forty-five-year-old Yvonne was born on 11 January 1897 in 22 rue de Paris in Maisons-Lafitte to parents Henri Firmin Cerneau and his wife Alphonsine Matilde (née Cogneau). Her father worked buying and selling horses and as a child she often accompanied him, visiting horse fairs all over the region. It is believed that he died after catching pneumonia trying to save his horses from the great flood of the winter of 1909/10. After her father's death, Yvonne took a job in the Galeries Lafayette on Regent Street in London, where she met Matteo Alessandro Rudellat (Alex), who worked as a waiter at the Savoy Hotel, and who, some claim, was an undercover spy.

The two fell in love and were married at St Giles registry office in October 1920. The following year, Yvonne gave birth to a baby girl and named her Constance Jacqueline. When the child was 7, Yvonne and Alex separated, but remained friends, and shared time with their daughter.[17]

Ten days after the declaration of war in 1939, Yvonne's 17-year-old daughter joined the Auxiliary Territorial Service, and later married a sergeant. By now, Yvonne was working as club secretary at Ebury Court, a London hotel and private club. With its bright and cheerful atmosphere, Ebury Court was a substitute home for those who had either lost theirs or were home on leave. However, unbeknown to the management, the staff or even most of the guests, Ebury Court was also home to a diverse group from all walks of intelligence who used its unassuming and modest atmosphere to their advantage. It was estimated that at least fifteen men (if not more) who had connections with naval or military intelligence, espionage, counter-espionage and SOE were among the hotel's visitors, club members and regular guests.

As club secretary, Yvonne met everyone who came through the doors and she was well liked. She had a knack for being unobtrusive, which members noted and appreciated. She 'never stood out in a crowd' remaining unnoticed 'unless attention was drawn to her' yet all the while remaining attentive and eager to assist.[18] When SOE agent Jacques de Guélis (who had assisted Virginia) came into the club and met Yvonne, he saw something in her, and, believing her to possess the necessary qualities to work for SOE, introduced her to the organisation.

She subsequently passed through the interviews and completed the training programmes. On 17 July 1942 she was landed by felucca (a traditional wooden sailing and fishing boat, not uncommon in the Mediterranean) in the south of France and from there travelled north to Tours in the Loire valley.

Like Virginia before her, Yvonne arrived in a France that was very different from the one she fondly remembered. The country had been under German rule for over two years and life during the occupation was harsh, with rules that affected every part of daily life: permits were needed to drive vehicles, and special permission had to be sought to drive a petrol-powered one. Identity papers had to be carried at all times, rationing was in full force, curfews were in place, listening to BBC radio broadcasts was forbidden, maps and compasses were banned and various restaurants, cinemas and cafés were out of bounds to ordinary French people. Food, clothing and fuel shortages remained something of a national preoccupation and people sought ways to find alternatives: ersatz coffee was made from acorns, women used cork to resole their shoes and wore their husbands' clothing when their own garments became threadbare, and cars were converted into the *gazogènes* which Virginia Hall had written of in 1941 and which ran on charcoal.

In an attempt to humiliate the country still further the Germans demanded that the Vichy government pay 400 million francs a day to defray the costs of the occupation. The payments, which started in August, were backdated to June; they were reduced to 300 million francs between May 1941 and November 1942, but then raised to 500 million until the end of the occupation. This was an ironic twist on the reparations that France had made Germany pay at the end of the First World War, resulting in France paying nearly 60 per cent of its national income to the Reich.[19]

Resistance was stamped out wherever it was found. Printing materials were restricted to prevent people forging ID cards, printing underground newspapers or producing propaganda. The rules were regularly changed at very short notice (for instance, new ID cards would suddenly be issued in an attempt to catch out those who had forged ones). The inhabitants of occupied France felt the full force of the German occupation and collaborators weighing down on every aspect of their existence; the grind of daily life was closely monitored and constrained.

Nonetheless, a nucleus of resistance was emerging among those who were resentful of the restrictions that had been put on them and who felt betrayed by Pétain's armistice with Germany. On 14 July, a message was broadcast via the BBC calling for a show of resistance from the French people: 2,000 people gathered at the Barbès monument in Carcassonne, and crowds also gathered in Perpignan and Marseille, where shots were fired. The French were starting to stir. They felt that France should unite against Germany and drive out the occupiers. The loss of friends, family and loved ones motivated many to join as well as a sense of patriotism, a hatred of Nazi rules, forced labour and extreme anti-Semitism, and the humiliation of the occupation. Some were haunted by memories of the Great War, and they felt determined that history should not repeat itself. It was in an attempt to help nurture, develop and assist these growing resistance networks that Yvonne was set to work as courier to the MONKEYPUZZLE network.

MONKEYPUZZLE had the task of finding suitable drop zones (DZs)[20] where Special Duties squadrons could deliver supplies and agents who would then organise and equip resistance members, helping them to blow up road, rail and communication networks and to locate ammunition dumps. The organiser of MONKEYPUZZLE, Raymond Flower, was 'brave and cheerful enough, but undistinguished for security sense or forethought'.[21] Flower took an instant dislike to Yvonne and left her to her own devices, making her find her own safe house and process her own papers. He sent reports back to Baker Street and in one of them sarcastically described how she had 'acquired a bicycle and was busy riding around Tours carrying packets of 808 explosive. She had found a good hiding place for her lethal packages. She concealed them by tucking the parcels into the legs of her hated bloomers.'[22] Flower's derogatory report was greeted with much amusement by F Section, but Yvonne's initiative and resourcefulness also impressed them, and they lauded the fact that she had not only risked her life but her actions had directly helped to blow up a power station and two locomotives. Yvonne's success validated the decision that SOE had made some months before by proving that women could do the work, as well as take the risks that a life as an agent in the field demanded of them.

There were many risks for agents, but for Denise Bloch, a 26-year-old Jewish Parisian, the stakes were particularly high. Not only had she put herself at risk of arrest by becoming involved in clandestine activities but, as a Jew, she was especially vulnerable. There is very little early information available about Denise. Born on 21 January 1916, she was the only daughter of Parisian Jews Jacques and Suzanne Bloch. She had grown up in Paris with her three brothers, and when war broke out her father and two of her three brothers joined the army; her father and one of her brothers were captured, while the other escaped and joined the resistance.[23]

By the summer of 1942, life in occupied France had become unbearable for the Jewish population. The Germans were steadily tightening restrictions on the community. On 7 June, all Jews over the age of 6 in the occupied zone were forced to wear a Star of David and on 2 July the Gestapo ordered French police in Bordeaux to proceed with the deportation of all Jews aged between 16 and 45. Denise and her family became aware of the increasing danger and fled Paris just in time to avoid the round-up of Jews in the city which became known as the *Rafle du Vél d'Hiv*. The French authorities had been given a quota from the Germans to round-up 28,000 foreign and stateless Jews in the greater Paris area. For 'humanitarian' reasons it was decided that children should be arrested with their parents, unless a family member remained behind to care for them.

Starting early on 16 July and lasting until the following evening, the French police (with no German participation) rounded up thousands of Jewish men, women and children. In order to maintain a detailed record of the round-up, the police were to report the number of people they arrested each hour to their local prefecture. By the end of the first day, 2,573 men, 5,165 women and 3,625 children had been taken from their homes. Approximately 6,000 of those rounded up were taken to Drancy, an internment and transit camp located in a housing development in the poorer northern suburbs of Paris. The rest were taken to the Vélodrome d'Hiver (Winter Cycling Track), in Paris's 15th arrondissement near the Eiffel Tower.

The Vél d'Hiv had been used to intern German nationals and refugees at the beginning of the war, and the French were under no illusion about how deplorable the conditions were, nor how unsuited the building was as accommodation for human beings. Below the huge glass ceiling, 4,115 children, 2,916 women and 1,290 men were imprisoned. By day the atmosphere was stiflingly hot, especially since all other means of ventilation had been sealed to prevent escape. But at night, after the sun went down, the temperature plummeted. Those inside, wearing only the summer clothes they had been arrested in, struggled to stay warm.

There was nowhere to lie down, and only hard wooden benches on which to sit. There was no food, water or sanitary provisions and the place soon reeked of sweat, urine and excrement. There were only two physicians per shift permitted to treat the thousands of internees who began to suffer and die of dehydration and exhaustion. There were several suicides as desperate people who could take no more deprivation or abuse hurled themselves from the balcony seats onto the cycling track below.

After five days, the Jews incarcerated were transferred to the transit camps outside Paris – Drancy, Pithiviers and Beaune-la-Rolande – where they were closely guarded by French police until they were transported. At the end of July, the remaining adults were separated from their children and deported to Auschwitz. The 3,000 children left behind remained interned with no adults to care for them or offer a soothing word – the older children tried their best. The shouts of the guards and deprivations in the camp became normal, until these children too were deported to Auschwitz. Very few of the Jewish deportees from Paris ever came home.

Terrified by the news of these events and determined to escape any further round-ups, Denise's immediate family adopted the surname Barrault and began a new life in Lyon, where, shortly after their arrival, Denise met Jean Aron. A Jewish Citroën engineer, Aron was involved with F Section's VENTRILOQUIST network, which operated in the Orléans/Blois area, where they received incoming agents and built lines of communication between various groups from Le Mans to Marseille under the leadership of Philippe de Vomécourt.

VENTRILOQUIST was a strange network as it seemed that no one really liked each other, let alone trusted one another. In spite of this distrust, Aron asked Denise if she would join them as they needed a courier and someone to deliver messages across the network. It was a tiring, dangerous role, which Denise bravely undertook with no formal training in August 1942.

In mid-September, Denise was joined by two new agents from England, wireless operator Brian Stonehouse and Blanche Charlet. Blanche was another acquaintance of Jacques de Guélis, who had recruited Yvonne Rudellat a few months before. Blanche, two years younger than Yvonne, had been born on 23 May 1898 in London to Belgian parents. She had lived in Brussels where she managed the Le Centaur art gallery until 1932, when she moved to France and worked as a newspaper reporter for a press photographic agency in Paris. Blanche met de Guélis when he came to France in August 1941 on the first reconnaissance mission for F Section, during which he looked for suitable drop zones near the Rhône, recruited several agents and prepared the way for Virginia Hall's mission by scouting out contacts for her.

Blanche left France and sailed from Lisbon, via Gibraltar, arriving in England in December 1941. She found work writing reviews of London art exhibitions for a monthly English-language cultural magazine published by the Belgian embassy. Blanche and de Guélis bumped into each other again in London, and he introduced her to his friend Ernest Biggs at a party at the Studio Club, a popular stomping ground for artists in London. Biggs, who had been an art critic in Sweden, had joined Section D shortly before the outbreak of war and had spent eighteen months in a Swedish prison convicted of espionage. Returning to London to recuperate, he had run into his old friend de Guélis, who invited him to his club at Ebury Court, where the two frequently met over the next few weeks. As Biggs got to know Blanche better he offered to help her write her art articles and correct her far from perfect English.[24] He saw the potential in her as an agent and soon passed her name on to SOE.[25] F Section called her suitability into question when rumours that Blanche was a political agitator with connections to anarchists in Paris came to light, but, when interviewed on the matter, she said nothing to 'support the theory'; while she was considered to be 'worth watching', she had been permitted to undertake her SOE training in May 1942.[26]

Just a few months later, arriving in France by felucca on 1 September, Blanche's role in the field was essentially to take over from Virginia Hall: she was to arrange contacts, recommend who to bribe and where to hide, soothe the jagged nerves of agents on the run and supervise the distribution of wireless sets.[27] It was a tough task as VENTRILOQUIST was a very unsettled circuit and there were huge personal differences between colleagues. Blanche and Denise Bloch met every day for lunch to chat and plan work, yet Blanche secretly harboured the belief that that Denise was a bad influence on Jean Aron. Denise, for her part, did not like fellow agent Brian Stonehouse, who had arrived at the same time as her, but who, she felt, was too lax in his security, particularly when he stopped her in the middle of the street and in English declared: 'After the war you must come to Scotland to see my house.'[28]

Just days after Blanche arrived in France, the 'Law of 4 September 1942 on the use and guidance of the workforce' was passed, and a census was carried out among its citizens; men aged between 18 and 65 and single women aged 21 to 35 had to make themselves known in preparation for the implementation of STO, the forced labour programme, to help meet the German requirements for manpower in the war industries

Eligible candidates would be taken away from their homes and 'be subject to do any work that the Government deems necessary'. At first men aged 18–50 were taken, but as the war progressed the rules constantly changed.[29] Those who refused were arrested and those who shirked it fled to the countryside and mountains to join the Maquis (literally translates as shrub or bush), planned guerrilla attacks and formed pockets of resistance.[30]

The STO had a huge impact on the work of the resistance and SOE. There was much hostility towards it, which encouraged many men to engage in resistance activity. In the event, only men were taken under the STO, which meant that women became even more useful to the resistance as there would be more of them available to travel from place to place as couriers and carry messages or materials, and they would raise less suspicion than men. This was the type of work that Denise and Blanche were already doing, but it meant that many more women would go on to be infiltrated and undertake the same tasks. Indeed, in early November a felucca arrived carrying three more female agents: Mary Herbert, Marie-Thérèse le Chêne and Odette Sansom.

On the evening of 24 October, after working for several weeks in the field as a courier, Blanche turned up for a pre-planned meeting with Stonehouse, who, unbeknownst to her, had just been tracked down by a direction-finding (D/F) van and arrested.[31] She was greeted by the German police, who took her to the police station and interrogated her. Playing innocent when asked if she knew the wireless operator 'Celestin' (Stonehouse), she replied that she did not even know what a wireless operator was. After refusing to give her address (in the hope of preventing her landlady from being arrested) and telling a convoluted story of lovers and family and her desire to avoid scandal, Blanche was incarcerated. She was kept on a different floor from Stonehouse, but when she was allowed out into the courtyard for a walk, she was able to talk to him through a window and each was able to find out what the other had said and to see if their stories matched up.[32]

On 2 November, several more agents were arrested, including Aron, who was captured at Lyon railway station. Denise took a different exit and escaped unseen, but when the network leader Phillipe de Vomécourt was taken into custody the circuit was effectively finished. Denise lay low and moved to a safe house in a fishing village just east of Nice; there she kept herself to herself, only venturing out to the hairdresser to get her hair dyed (as she was afraid the police had her photograph and would be looking for her). She then moved to Toulouse, where a new F Section agent, George Starr, had begun to form WHEELWRIGHT. Starr had no wireless operator and relied on help from the neighbouring PRUNUS circuit in Toulouse, run by Maurice Pertschuk, who also helped out with money. Starr needed a courier and asked Denise to join him in Agen, where she continued her work.

On 10 November 1942, just days after Mary, Odette and Marie arrived, France was occupied in its entirety. German troops marched in their thousands over the demarcation line, while the Italians moved into the Côte d'Azur. This was the direct result of Allied military action in French North Africa. On 8 November the Anglo-American First Army had successfully landed on the beaches of Algeria and Morocco (French North Africa). Vichy French troops failed to stop the invasion, which allowed the Allies to quickly make their way to the western border of Tunisia.

With the German seizure of the previously unoccupied zone of France, the demarcation line was abolished and Vichy's 'Armistice Army' disbanded, and with it the last remnant of independence. In spite of this, Marshal Pétain remained as head of state, still based at Vichy, while de Gaulle continued to mount his challenge from London.

During all of this Virginia Hall continued to work as diligently as ever, aware how easily she might be seen as a 'spy' by the Germans. F Section HQ soon decided that her work was far too dangerous to continue; her cover could easily be blown, which would risk the safety of everyone with whom she had been in contact. Virginia made the decision to leave France while she still could, but before she left she made a note of what all of her associates were doing and what they needed in terms of finance or support. These notes became comprehensive reports that helped SOE once she had returned from the field.

Virginia made her way by foot across the Pyrenees into Spain, escaping just in time. The head of the Lyon Gestapo, Klaus Barbie, said that he 'would give anything to get his hands on that Canadian bitch'.[33] She did not give him the opportunity. Yet crossing the mountains in the dead of winter caused additional problems arising from her disability. The route was tough, even for the fittest person – the combination of difficult terrain, freezing conditions, ice, wind and snow, as well as the fact that she had little or no specialist clothing or shoes made the journey a true test of Virginia's grit and determination.[34]

Despite her physical handicap, Virginia trudged on. She was resolute that this would not be the end of her resistance career and that she would overcome these problems through sheer determination. In a message transmitted to SOE headquarters in London, referring to her false leg, she said, 'I am having trouble with Cuthbert, but I can cope.' The reply, from a seemingly unversed colleague, came back, 'If Cuthbert is giving you difficulty, have him eliminated ...' Virginia and Cuthbert arrived in Spain together. However, Virginia did not have the required entry papers and was arrested at the border town of San Juan les Abadesas and then incarcerated in Figueres prison. Her cellmate was a Spanish prostitute who, upon her own release, smuggled out a letter from Virginia to the US consul in Barcelona. After six weeks she was released, and reported to SOE contacts in Madrid.[35]

Virginia then transferred to DF Section (the North West Europe escape section of SOE) and worked in Madrid, also being available to work with SOE's H Section, which covered Spain and Portugal. Her cover was once again as a journalist, this time for the *Chicago Times*. As before, she identified suitable safe houses for agents and sought out possible personnel for future recruitment into DF Section, a job she undertook with great success.[36] Madrid itself was a hotbed of intrigue, clandestine manoeuvres and strategic operations between Allied and Axis operatives. It was dangerous and exciting, but instead of revelling in the atmosphere Virginia found her work frustrating and unfulfilling. After four months she requested a transfer back to F Section. In a letter to Buckmaster she wrote: 'I thought I could help in Spain, but I'm not doing a job . . . I am living pleasantly and wasting time. It isn't worthwhile and after all, my neck is my own. If I am willing to get a crick in it, I think that's my prerogative.' Buckmaster refused, however, and grudgingly she spent the next few months living and working in Spain.[37]

While Virginia had been crossing the Pyrenees, the three women who had arrived by felucca in November had settled into their work as agents. Mary Herbert became courier to Claude de Baissac in the SCIENTIST circuit in Bordeaux, Odette Sansom was destined for Auxerre where she was to 'start up a circuit',[38] and Marie-Thérèse le Chêne joined the PLANE circuit in the area around the industrial town of Clermont-Ferrand, in Auvergne, to work alongside her husband Henri and his brother Pierre, who had both joined SOE in late 1941.

Marie-Thérèse was born at Sedan in the Ardennes in 1890 and was the eldest of a family of three. She spent much of her life in London with her husband, Henri, who was a British subject and a hotel manager. It is not clear whether Marie-Thérèse came to the attention of SOE through her brother or her spouse – or both – but she refused to join de Gaulle's RF Section and insisted on joining F so that she could go to France to work for Henri once the circuit was established.[39]

When he was ready, Henri requested that his wife join him (although some say he went to France to get away from her). Described as 'very intelligent and quick thinking' as well as 'shrewd and experienced', 51-year-old Marie-Thérèse was given various tasks by her husband, including distributing propaganda leaflets to factories and tram sheds.[40] Some of these encouraged factory workers, such as those at Michelin, to sabotage their goods by turning out inferior products, for example car tyres of such poor quality that they needed constant repair. This slowed down the German war effort but also kept local men employed and held off their deportation on the STO. In her time as a courier Marie-Thérèse made contact with a staggering twenty to thirty agents across ten networks – a huge area to cover for just one agent. But her operational activity was limited.

In December 1942, her brother-in-law Pierre, who was the circuit's wireless operator, was arrested by the Gestapo while at his wireless set. Several more arrests followed until the whole network was 'blown'. Henri decided to fold everything and to get out with Marie-Thérèse while they still could. The plan was to escape across the Pyrenees, but Marie-Thérèse refused, believing the journey to be too long and hard, with no guarantee of success. Instead, she found a safe house where she sat it out with friends until she could arrange a pick-up. Henri made it across the mountains, but then spent four months incarcerated in a camp in Spain. Meanwhile, Marie-Thérèse simply bided her time until eight months later, 20 August 1943, she departed for home aboard a Hudson aircraft. The welcome she received at SOE HQ a week later was not a happy one. Accused of a breach of security and the Official Secrets Act, having reputedly told someone that she 'worked for the Secret Service in Baker Street and that she was sent to France on a destroyer and has recently returned from that country', the SOE interviewer did not believe her version of events – that 'wicked people had a down on her and had invented this clever story in order to put her into prison' – and concluded that she would never work for SOE again.[41]

Odette Sansom was a French-born mother of three. Born in Amiens on 28 April 1912, her father was killed at Verdun just before the armistice. In childhood Odette suffered from poliomyelitis, which left her blind for three and a half years and paralysed for one.[42] When she was in good health she attended a convent school in Amiens and in 1926 moved to Boulogne with her mother, where she later met an English hotelier, Roy Sansom. They married in 1931 and had their first child, Françoise, before moving to London where they had two more daughters, Lili in 1934 and Marianne in 1936.

Roy joined the army in 1939 while Odette and the children stayed in London, moving after the Blitz began to the safety of Somerset in October

1940. In spring 1942, Odette came to F Section's attention: she had heard an appeal on the BBC asking listeners to send in old photographs of the coastline to help with the planning of the Allied invasion. In her enthusiasm she sent her photographs not to the Admiralty as requested, but to the War Office, and shortly afterwards received a request to attend an interview in London. Leaving her daughters in a convent school, Odette began her SOE training in July 1942.

Said to possess determination, patriotism and a 'keenness to do something for France', Odette set sail for her motherland, arriving on 2 November 1942. Her original mission was to set up a circuit in Auxerre. However, some of her papers were delayed and, while waiting, she undertook some work for Peter Churchill, leader of the SPINDLE circuit in Cannes. Her first task on his behalf was to take a case of money to Marseille and to collect detailed maps of French ports (which later proved crucial in planning the August 1944 Allied landings in southern France). This job was dangerous, not only because carrying such large amounts of cash was extremely hazardous but because Marseille itself was a hotbed of illegal activity: prostitution, forgeries and the black market were rife. Odette met agents Marsac and Muriel at the train station café at 6 p.m., but Marsac had been unable to find the case containing the plans. Odette refused to hand over the money until it was found, which it eventually was more than two hours later, by which time she had missed her return train. Worried about being stuck out after curfew she ran through her options. There were no hotels in the area available. She could sleep at the railway station, but this brought the risk of spot checks, round-ups and even deportation. A contact gave Odette the address of her only other option: a brothel. When she got back to Cannes Churchill was so impressed with her skill and resourcefulness that he asked her to stay and work for him instead of going to Auxerre, and, with F Section's permission, she became courier to the SPINDLE network.

Odette's work involved travelling along the coast to various towns with messages and codes, as well as to contacts in both zones. Her time in Cannes was fraught with danger and the apparent lack of security troubled her. Agents dined in black market restaurants while chatting loudly in English, and members of the resistance did not take things seriously; some, she said, were 'too ostentatious and flamboyant ... Cannes was not a place that lent itself to that kind of Resistance work. It's a playground'.[43]

SOE's hopes that SPINDLE was destined to be a great circuit did not come to fruition. The idea had been that it would work alongside CARTE, but political infighting within the latter network caused many security problems. CARTE's leader, André Girard, claimed to have links with senior members of the French Army and access to over 300,000 resistance fighters. But he proved to be a power-crazed fantasist whose network, it transpired, was largely a figment of his imagination. Girard's promised support and men never materialised and Churchill ended up being his go-between rather than equal, with little choice but to communicate CARTE's increasingly bizarre demands to F Section. It was also through the carelessness of one of Girard's men that a list of some 200 agents fell into German hands and the ensuing row between Girard and his chief of staff, Henri Frager, led to a rift within the circuit.

Girard moved to Arles and made several failed attempts to arrange a pick-up for himself and Churchill out of France. With each failed attempt the risk of capture increased. One night the Germans overran their landing ground. Odette, Churchill and Girard got away but had to flee the area. Churchill relocated the remains of SPINDLE from the Riviera to Saint-Jorioz on the shores of Lake Annecy in the Haute-Savoie. Girard returned to London by a clandestine air operation on 20/21 February 1943, and Churchill flew on 23/24 March 1943 with Henri Frager. Francis Cammaerts, head of the JOCKEY network, was a passenger on the latter incoming flight to France.

Cammaerts was due to meet with André Marsac (a member of their former resistance group CARTE in Cannes who had been on his reception committee), but Marsac never arrived – he and his secretary had been arrested by the Abwehr and taken to Fresnes prison in Paris. There they received a visit from Hugo Bleicher, a member of the Abwehr, who claimed to be anti-Nazi.[44] He told Marsac that if he gave him the name of someone who could assist in getting him to England to discuss ending the war, Marsac could go free. Marsac believed Bleicher to be genuine and passed on the details of SPINDLE.

Meanwhile, Cammaerts was dismayed at the lack of security he encountered in Saint-Jorioz. He said he was met by 'a lot of very brave young men

... dressed like young resistance people' who took him to a building that, he said, may as well have had a sign above the door saying 'Resistance Clubhouse'.[45] Matters were compounded when a young resistance leader got wind of Cammaerts's criticism and threatened to shoot everyone. In the midst of all of this chaos in Saint-Jorioz, a letter arrived from Marsac introducing Bleicher, or 'Colonel Henri' as he now called himself, who wished to be flown to London for talks about ending the war.

The SOE training taught that 'should enemy agents or informers present themselves to try to win your confidence they must be killed'. But Bleicher, who came to Saint-Jorioz to discuss things in person, was convincing in his story. Arrangements were made that a Lysander due to land nearby on 18 April 1943 would take them to London on its return.[46] Cammaerts, who felt this was all an 'impossible fantasy', left that night to set up his own circuit further south.[47]

Odette instructed SPINDLE's wireless operator Adolphe Rabinovitch to send a message to Baker Street informing them of the meeting with Bleicher and all that had passed between them. London's message came back almost immediately: 'Henri highly dangerous ... you are to hide across lake and cut contacts with all save Arnaud [Rabinovitch] ... fix dropping ground your own choice for Michel [Churchill] who will land anywhere soonest'. In other words, she was to cut all contacts with the now compromised Annecy and Saint-Jorioz groups, go into hiding on the other side of Lake Annecy, and find a suitable drop zone for Peter Churchill who was to return imminently. Feeling the urgency of securing the DZ in a remote place, given the current security issues, Odette and Rabinovitch fixed on a small, mountainous plateau a few miles south-west of Saint-Jorioz and sent the coordinates to London. Odette also relocated her colleagues.

On 14 April 1943, the signal came through on the BBC *Messages Personnels* that Churchill was due to land.[48] Knowing that Odette was compromised, F Section had told Churchill to avoid her 'till she had broken with Bleicher'.[49] But when Churchill touched down from his parachute drop on 15 April, Odette was in the reception committee. They made their way back to Saint-Jorioz and the same hotel that Odette had been staying in previously, where, Cammaerts said, they 'lived as man and wife', thus according with their cover story.[50] Odette believed that Colonel Henri would not return until the 18th, the date of his flight to London, so there would still be time to move their location. Unfortunately, Bleicher would make a much swifter and more devastating appearance that night. As Odette recounted:

> Henri [Bleicher] offered his hand to me but I did not take it. He said 'I think a lot of you' but I replied I did not care what he thought. He told me that I nearly fooled him. He said that this was not my fault because my people were bad (meaning that the French people had talked and been careless). He said he knew Raoul [Churchill] was here and asked me to show him the way; I did not for a minute and a gun was stuck in my back.[51]

From her later testimony, it is clear that Odette believed a courier called Roger Chaillan had betrayed them. Chaillan knew that Churchill was due to return by 14 April and had also been told that Colonel Henri's exfiltration might not take place, something he was furious about as he had complete confidence in him. Chaillan's revelation of this information to Bleicher would explain both the German's early appearance in Saint-Jorioz and his certainty that Churchill was at the hotel. In Odette's opinion, Chaillan was either 'extremely stupid or a traitor, and he was not the kind of man one would regard as stupid'.[52]

Reluctantly, Odette led Bleicher and his party to Churchill. Displaying some quick thinking in the midst of a terrible situation, Odette switched Churchill's jacket when no one was looking, as she knew the one he would otherwise have put on had incriminating messages received that afternoon in its pocket. She also slipped his wallet up her sleeve, later depositing it under a car seat, hoping it would not be found for several days and give the others time to get away. Nevertheless, inevitably, their capture and the destruction of SPINDLE in Saint-Jorioz sent shock waves across the whole area and arrests were made in Marseille, Toulouse and Lyon.

In France the occupation had split both the country and its loyalties, and, as well as those who were prepared to resist, there were also those who were prepared to collaborate. On 31 January 1943, the Milice Française was formed with Pierre Laval as president and Joseph Darnand as secretary-general. The Milice was a paramilitary organisation which was made up of approximately 35,000 collaborators who worked predominantly in their home towns or in areas that they knew well. They proved to be a great threat to the resistance. If a suspect, or a suspect's family member, was caught they had free rein to interrogate and torture them. The Milice were also complicit in multiple round-ups of Jews across France and acted without German assistance. France was blighted by collaborators and the resistance needed a boost; in Britain the SOE were ramping up their operations in order to assist as much as possible. In February 1943 Cicely Lefort, Noor Inayat Khan, Yvonne Cormeau and Yolande Beekman began their training to become secret agents.

While they were practising blowing up dummy targets in the English countryside, in France Yvonne Rudellat had moved on to the real thing. In March 1943 she was involved in the derailing of two locomotives, the main goods trains between Tours and Blois and between Tours and Vierzon. Cycling out under cover of darkness, Yvonne had assisted with laying charges which, when detonated, blew a gap in the track, making the oncoming train derail and causing mayhem to the rail service and the deaths of some of those who were on board. Such derailments disrupted the German war effort by slowing down the movement of troops and goods on their way to various destinations. They were a popular and successful means of sabotage.

Yvonne was also involved in attempting to blow up a railway tunnel at Montrichard, but when it came to it the damage was insufficient to cause any real problems. 'The plastique and 808 went off in a shattering explosion, capable of crushing steel within a short radius, but not enough middle or long distance. What we needed was a product less powerful but with a longer shock wave,' reported locally recruited agent Pierre Culioli, who led the sub-circuit in which Yvonne served and was also involved in the sabotage.[53] Although the effects were not as successful as hoped, Yvonne's active engagement in sabotage, and her success in fulfilling her mission with skill and resourcefulness, had proved that women could indeed make successful agents.

One woman determined to prove her worth and undertake formal SOE training arrived in England on foot. On 29 April 1943 Denise Bloch set off for the border town of Cier-de-Luchon where she met two guides. Her mission was to cross the Pyrenees into Spain and get financial help for George Starr of WHEELWRIGHT, who had lost his main benefactor when Maurice Pertschuk was arrested on 12 April. Since then Starr had been penniless and was now desperate for help.

The conditions on the mountains were harsh and cold, but Denise was determined and, despite being both ill-dressed and ill-equipped for the journey, she arrived seventeen hours later in the Spanish village of Bausen. After being questioned by the local police (who confiscated the report that Starr had written for SOE), Denise's own papers were given to the British consul who, rather than interrogate her, invited her for dinner and unexpectedly gave her authorisation to travel to Madrid and then Britain.

This was not what Denise had had in mind, but she took the opportunity and, after twenty-two days of travelling, arrived in London where she managed to convince F Section that Starr needed help. She also requested to return to France as an agent. Jepson was concerned that Denise was too 'blown' to return to her former network, believing that she would not only endanger her own life but those of everyone who knew her if she went back. Frustrated by the delay, Denise told him that she had been living under a cover name until very recently and that the Gestapo had shown no interest in her at all, besides which, she added, Starr's French accent was so bad that he needed her help; he couldn't be left to fend by himself. After another month Jepson finally agreed that she could undertake training: if she had been known to the Gestapo, they would possibly have forgotten all about her by the time of her return.

Denise did not have a good opinion of SOE as an organisation; her initial welcome had been lukewarm and their insistence that they knew better than she did riled her. F Section's reluctance to send her back to France had slowed everything down, meaning that her circuit had lost the momentum that it had built up so successfully with her at the heart of it. A fellow SOE recruit said that Denise did her work in the field to the best of her ability, in the hope that she will live through it and tell us all, afterwards, what she thinks of us'. But first she had to complete her training and get back to the field.[54]

By now the STO had taken a firm hold of the population and increasing numbers of men from all walks of life were receiving their orders to pack up and leave: farmers, teachers, clerks, professionals and civil servants alike. As a result, the Maquis was growing: many men chose to become Maquisards rather than undertake forced labour for the enemy. By the summer of 1943 SOE leaders actively sought out their local Maquis to forge alliances and partnerships, which would prove vital in the months ahead.

In spite of the wave of arrests that seemed to be plaguing the resistance and F Section agents, the work that they undertook in the field was clearly considered to be valuable and successful by those at the top. As such they continued to recruit and train potential agents and, in the summer of that year, Anne-Marie Walters, Denise Bloch and Violette Szabó began their training as SOE operatives.

In July 1943, Virginia Hall returned from her mission safely and was awarded the MBE. She asked if she could train as a wireless operator in order to return to France for another mission with F Section, but was turned down by Buckmaster. With that, her involvement with F Section was over. But he praised her contribution in a letter:

> what a wonder you are! I know you could learn radio in no time; I know the boys would love to have you come into the field; I know all about all the things you could do, and it is only because I honestly believe that the Gestapo would also know about it in a fortnight that I say no, dearest Doodle. You really are too well known in the country ... you do realise don't you that what was previously a picnic, comparatively speaking, is now real war.[55]

Eliane Plewman realised that life as an agent was 'no picnic' when she landed awkwardly after her solo parachute jump on the night of 13/14 August. Born in December 1917, Eliane was the daughter of Eugene Henry Browne-Bartroli, an English manufacturer based in France, and his Spanish wife Elisa Francesca (née Bartroli). She lived a cosmopolitan life, and was brought up in Marseille, receiving her schooling first in England and then at the British School in Madrid. She had two elder brothers, Albert and Henry, the latter of whom died suddenly aged 24 before the war broke out.

When she finished college Eliane moved to Leicester to work for a clothing and fabric import-export company, where she used her extensive language skills in English, French, Spanish and Portuguese. It was there that she met and fell in love with Tom Plewman, but she moved abroad again to work for the British embassy in both Madrid and Lisbon. In 1942 she returned to England, took a job at the Ministry of Information and married Tom that summer. In February 1943, F Section acted on a tip (that came from the Ministry of Labour or possibly from her elder brother Albert Browne-Bartroli, who was already an F Section agent) and called her in for an interview.[56]

Described as 'a great asset to the gaiety of the party', during her SOE training Eliane sometimes took fellow recruits to her club and 'round to her flat where they met her husband'.[57] Yet she passed her training and was security cleared, described in her reports as being 'calm, efficient and conscientious, and with admirable composure'.[58] SOE agent Bob Maloubier described Eliane as:

> the live wire of the team, always ready for anything thrown at her by the pitiless SOE instructors who don't do their 'students' any favours. She knows how to stand up to them when necessary. She seems to be preparing, enthusiastically, for some mortal challenge she is going to throw down 'to the Huns' who are making a martyr of France, but from which she is sure to emerge the victor. . . . Nobody can break Eliane.[59]

As Eliane was descending over France, on 13/14 August 1943, she began to realise that things were not as they should be. There was none of the paraphernalia that there should be at a drop zone: no lights, no bonfires and no reception committee. Eliane came down over a farmhouse with a dog that barked and snarled at the descending intruder; she landed in nearby fields and sprained her ankle, which made walking difficult and painful. Luckily her briefcase containing a substantial amount of money had landed nearby, but she thought better of taking it with her for the time being, leaving it in some thick bushes so she could come back for it. Having buried her parachute she made her way painfully slowly towards the road – she had no idea where she was, just that she was not where she should have been.

Eliane attempted to make contact with the people in the safe house that she had been given by SOE, but there was nobody there. She was told by neighbours that they had been arrested and that the Germans could be back at any moment to see who else turned up there, so it was too dangerous to stay. Eliane made her way to her destination, Marseille, but it took her two months to get there, during which time, according to her file, 'she showed outstanding initiative and made several useful contacts of her own, which were later of considerable use to her circuit'.[60] She never managed to recover the briefcase: a courier was sent to get it, but all he found was the empty case, the million francs that had been in it was gone.

By 1943, Marseille was a hotbed of activity. As it was both a port and directly across the water from North Africa (which had been under Allied control since 1942), there were constant comings and goings by all sorts of people. The city itself was well known for its underworld of rackets and organised crime, and many of the men involved now collaborated with the Germans, thus strengthening the substantial Sicherheitsdienst (SD), SS security and intelligence secret services presence, as well as swelling their own ranks and pockets. The city was swarming with Germans who put their mark on the place by strengthening the existing fortifications and putting in roadblocks.

Eliane arrived there in October 1943 and, once established in her safe house, began her important role as a courier to MONK. Her schedule was punishing and fraught with danger since her main role was to provide a continuous link between Charles Skepper, her circuit leader in Marseille, and other members of the circuit in Roquebrune. Eliane was incessantly on the move, back and forth between the two towns, carrying messages and occasionally equipment. Sometimes she used a van which had been specially installed with a false gas converter (complete with red lamps to simulate the heat source, so as not to attract attention), even though the van ran on petrol bought on the black market. By driving, she ran the risk of security checks, roadblocks and questioning if stopped, and the exhausting work played on her nerves and strength. So, on occasion, while waiting for a message from F Section, she would spend a day or two resting at the villa where Arthur Steele – MONK circuit's wireless operator was based.

In the New Year, Eliane and her brother Albert – who had followed her into the field in October 1943: he headed the DITCHER network – had a brief reunion, and together were involved in a major act of sabotage. Just after 2 a.m., and in between two German patrols, they laid explosive charges under a railway line. Once they had activated the time pencils (which allowed the explosion to go off on a delay) they retreated to a nearby house. It was a cold night and so the explosions took longer than expected, but the damage was vast: some 30 locomotives were put out of service, causing a huge blow to the German war effort by hampering the movement by rail of troops and supplies.

After Albert had taken his leave, the circuit also blew up a train in a tunnel and set off a second charge which derailed the salvage train – it took the authorities four days to clear the line.[61] During these operations, Eliane was responsible for carrying the explosives to the locations where the sabotage was to take place, but it took its toll on her, and to those around her she seemed tired. The circuit was also being watched: one of the women resisters in MONK was living with a Gestapo agent and told him everything. In spring 1944, he managed to infiltrate the group and, just as MONK were planning another spate of activity, he closed his net around the unwitting agents.

A week after Eliane's arrival in August 1943, Yvonne Cormeau parachuted onto a plateau at Saint Antoine du Queyret, 120 km north-east of Bordeaux, to work as the much-needed wireless operator for George Starr's WHEELWRIGHT circuit. Yvonne had been born in Shanghai in 1909 to a Belgian Consular Official and a Scottish mother, and educated in France, Brussels and Scotland. She grew up with a French governess and, although she regarded English as her mother tongue, most of her education was in French. She also spoke some German.[62] After leaving school aged 18 she became a barrister's secretary.

In 1937 Yvonne married an accountant, Charles Edouard Cormeau; they lived in London and had a daughter named Yvette. As soon as war was declared, Charles enlisted in the Rifle Brigade and Yvette was sent to the countryside. In 1940 he was wounded in France and sent home on sick leave, during which time their house was hit by a bomb during the Blitz. Yvonne is said to have escaped because a bath fell over her head and protected her, but her husband was killed.

Devastated by Charles's death, Yvonne decided to 'take her husband's place in the Armed Forces' so she could 'do something and save France from the Nazis'. In November 1941 she joined the WAAF as an administrator, and worked at RAF Innsworth before being posted to RAF Swinderby, where she noticed an appeal for linguists pasted on a noticeboard and applied for the role, not really knowing what it was. Her CV detailing her language skills and knowledge of France was quickly handed over to F Section and she began training as a wireless operator on 15 February 1943, achieving the rank of Flight Officer. Yvette was placed in a convent school in Oxfordshire where she stayed for the duration of the war.[63]

With Yvonne's help, WHEELWRIGHT became one of the most active and important circuits in France and for the majority of this time Yvonne was the only wireless link with London, even training a locally recruited operator to help her.[64] Yvonne was held in incredibly high esteem by all who knew her, and was described as: 'a perfectly unobtrusive and secure crafts-woman', 'a first class operator' and 'a quite remarkable woman'.[65] During the next twelve months she never took a day off and sent over 400 messages without a single miscode. As a result of these flawless wireless messages,

WHEELWRIGHT received approximately 140 arms drops and Yvonne was part of the reception committee for several of them. Her circuit also cut power and telephone lines, resulting in the isolation of the Wehrmacht Group G garrison near Toulouse.[66]

In spite of being involved in these dangerous activities, Yvonne was very security conscious, even in the more mundane aspects of life in France. She took great care with her appearance, dressing and doing her hair and make-up like the locals. She even made sure she obtained some large gold hooped earrings that were fashionable in the town where she resided so she did not stand out.[67] Yvonne chose her safe houses wisely, one of which had a long garden and a window so she could spot anyone approaching the building as she worked. There was no running water in the house nor in the entire village and, while the Nazis knew there was a British wireless operator somewhere close by, they never thought of looking for her there as they did not believe an English woman could survive without basic amenities. She continued to operate for the next few months, constantly on the move using cafés, car repair shops and farms from which to operate her wireless.

The last female agent to be sent to France in 1943 was US-born Elizabeth Deveraux Rochester, who had been recruited in June. Elizabeth's father was fighting at the Western Front when she was born in 1917, in New York. When war ended her parents divorced and, although she never knew her father, she grew up surrounded by war stories and the aftermath of the battle of Verdun. Aged 11, she began her education in England; later she made France her home but travelled widely through Europe to Bavaria, Budapest, Vienna and Greece, where she was the day war broke out.[68] Returning to Paris she worked for the American Hospital Ambulance Corps and became involved in anti-German activities such as taking food to POWs. In late 1942, she narrowly missed being interned because she was a US resident; burying her US passport, she fled across the demarcation line into the unoccupied zone.

After a failed attempt to get to Britain she went instead to Switzerland, where she became involved in the escape lines, and her potential as a courier was recognised. She also became involved with a Maquis unit that eventually helped her across the Pyrenees and, after spending some time in Spanish detention camps, she finally made it to England. Having been cleared by MI5's London Reception Centre (at the Royal Victoria Patriotic School), the US embassy and the War Office, she was approved for training with SOE.[69]

Described as being 'of very poor intelligence. Easily muddled and confused' and 'continually in a state of emotional tension' verging on a nervous breakdown, Elizabeth was continually losing and misplacing things. She was used to having everything done for her, was moody and 'fond of drinking', but she was extremely keen to go into the field and 'was perfectly capable of doing any work required'. She told her instructors that she was homesick, missing 'the smells and the sights' she knew and said that she felt like 'a fish out of water in England'.[70] She also had several existing contacts in France which could be beneficial to F Section as contacts or safe houses. She certainly had the motivation to go into France and assist with the resistance, but her instructors did not share her confidence in herself, saying she 'would NOT be suitable to work with'. Despite this, she was sent to France almost immediately.[71]

Parachuting into a field near Lons-le-Saunier in the Jura department of eastern France, she deposited the wireless set she had brought with her and proceeded to Annecy. Her achievements while working as a courier to Richard Heslop – head of MARKSMAN – included assisting George Millar to escape across the Pyrenees, instructing Maquisards in the use of explosives (though she regretted not getting to use them herself), working with local espionage groups and acting as Heslop's liaison officer in Haute-Savoie. Life in Haute-Savoie was extremely hard as the Germans were clamping down on the area and making travel as difficult as possible – in order to travel in the area one had to have a special pass. There was 'very severe control of identity papers, close check on circulation permits and roads'; meanwhile, the Milice attacked and cleared the Maquis camps in the area.[72]

In March 1944, Heslop made the decision to send Elizabeth home. He had several concerns about her, one of which was her appearance: she 'looked so like an English girl' wearing a tweed suit, carrying 'a knapsack on her shoulder' and striding through the countryside. Others also noticed how she didn't quite fit in and looked too English for comfort. He felt it wise to send her back to England 'partly for her own sake and partly to relieve the minds of those she worked with, who were anxious lest their activities be compromised if the girl was captured'.[73]

Heslop was reluctant to dismiss her, saying that he 'did not have the heart to do it' and anyway he had always found her to be a keen worker and 'of great assistance' to him, recalling that 'she never liked to sit about and if she had to stay in the command post for any length of time she would pester me to give her a task to get her moving again'. But in spite of this he felt that she had to go, so he took 'the coward's way out' and asked London to recall her and gave his reasons.[74]

Heslop recalled that she was very upset when the recall arrived and when she asked him why she had to leave, he was 'evasive and embarrassed and made some poor excuse'. She begged to stay but he told her it was too dangerous, especially as he believed that 'her mother would be under constant surveillance by the Gestapo and French police as she was known to be a foreigner'.[75] However, Elizabeth agreed that perhaps she was too compromised in Haute-Savoie and L'Ain, and arranged to stay in a safe house and there await her pick-up.[76]

Ignoring Heslop's warning, Elizabeth then made a foolish error when she visited her mother, whom she had not seen for two years. The pair had much to catch up on and, in spite of the dangers, Elizabeth arranged to dine with her mother again the day before she was due to leave Paris. They enjoyed a meal together and said their goodbyes, but on 20 March 1944, the day that Elizabeth was due to fly to safety, she was arrested under her real name and her real nationality as a US citizen. She was taken to Gestapo headquarters at the rue des Saussaies in Paris.

Virginia Hall's SOE career came to an abrupt end when Buckmaster told her categorically that she would not be returning to the field as an SOE agent.

Virginia then joined the US Office of Strategic Services (OSS) Special Operations Branch in 1944. The OSS was the forebear of the CIA and was formally established on 13 June 1942. Essentially the US equivalent of SOE, its remit was to collect and analyse strategic information, as well as undertake unconventional and paramilitary operations. The OSS sent agents worldwide and at its peak employed almost 13,000 people, 35 per cent of whom were women.

As an OSS agent, Virginia could fulfil her ambition of returning to the Haute-Loire. There, disguised as a middle-aged farm woman, complete with grey hair, shuffling gait and badly fitting clothes Virginia collected intelligence, organised safe houses and drop zones, and helped to train three battalions of resistance fighters. She also linked up with 'Jedburgh' teams, who were formed, trained and sent into the field under SFHQ (Special Forces HQ) auspices – usually a team of three men from the Allied nations of France, Britain and the US. While it had originally been intended that one representative of each country would serve in each team, this proved impossible. The composition of a team was therefore one man from the country in which it was operating (in this case, therefore, from the French forces), and two others, whether British, American or French, but one was a radio operator who parachuted in and liaised with SFHQ and aided the resistance fighters by giving weapons instruction or harnessing their combined strength to hinder the enemy.

In Virginia's final report, she stated that her network had derailed freight trains, severed a key rail line in multiple places and downed telephone lines. They had also destroyed four bridges, the demolition of one of which resulted in a German convoy being ambushed. During the fierce struggle that ensued 150 Germans were killed and 500 were captured.[77]

Virginia was a woman of great skill and fortitude. As the first female F Section operative operating in the field before SOE had even sanctioned the use of female agents, she set the standard, establishing safe houses, funding resistance groups and facilitating the use of escape lines for numerous stranded British personnel. Her work proved that women were trustworthy and capable in the field, and she was a trailblazer for other women who would work for F Section.

PART II
WAR

3

THE FALL OF PROSPER

It is unique in the annals of this organisation for a circuit to be so completely disintegrated and yet to be rebuilt because, regardless of all personal danger, this young woman remained on her post, at times alone, and always under threat of arrest.

> Quote from Noor Inayat Khan's George Cross citation,
> by Maurice Buckmaster, 24 February 1944[1]

Early 1943 saw the closing days of one of the most pivotal battles of the Second World War. The previous year the Axis powers had launched a new offensive on the Soviet Union, and had attempted to take Stalingrad, on the banks of the Volga River. Stalingrad was a huge industrial city producing armaments and agricultural equipment and it bore Stalin's name – for these reasons the Germans were ordered to take the city. A victory here would be a great propaganda boost for the Germans.

By mid-September the Germans had fought their way into Stalingrad and penetrated deep into the oil fields of the Caucasus. In November the Soviets had counter-attacked, breaking lines held by Hungarian, Italian and Romanian units in the north-west and south-west of the city, and trapped the German Sixth Army within the city itself. The situation was beyond hope for the Germans: the Volga River was frozen solid, and Soviet forces and equipment were sent over the ice at various points within the city. Hitler forbade his men to retreat or try to escape, and even promoted the German commander Paulus to the rank of Field Marshal (reminding him that no German officer of that rank had ever surrendered).

Seven Soviet armies closed in on the city and the Sixth Army as a part of Operation 'Ring'. On 31 January, Paulus, disobeying Hitler's orders, surrendered, alongside twenty-two generals. On 2 February the last of 91,000 frozen starving men (all that was left of the Sixth and Fourth armies) surrendered to the Soviets. The German mood was bleak, their morale was low and they took it out on the countries they occupied.

All over France F Section circuits had been formed to undertake sabotage and subversion. Each circuit was supposed to work as a self-contained unit with, as the norm, a leader, a wireless operator and a courier, but liaised with others if the need arose. The arrival of SOE agents contributed greatly to the morale of the French resistance by providing arms, financial support and expertise in preparation for an Allied invasion. One of the most important of these circuits was PHYSICIAN, better known by the field name of its leader, PROSPER – Francis Suttill – and operating from the very heart of France: Paris.

PROSPER was intended to take over from AUTOGYRO, a circuit which had been penetrated earlier that year due to its betrayal by double agent Mathilde Carré, which had resulted in numerous arrests. Also known as 'La Chatte', Mathilde had initially been employed in the INTERALLIÉ network that worked on behalf of the Polish Secret Service in occupied France. In November 1941, she and some other members of the circuit were arrested by the Abwehr, at which point she was 'turned' and became one of their most trusted agents. As a double agent, she undertook work for the Abwehr while still operating the INTERALLIÉ network's wireless, and was allegedly Hugo Bleicher's mistress. Mathilde provided the Germans with the names and locations of organisation members still at large, as well as acting as a decoy or as an *agent provocateur*, so they could be arrested by the Gestapo.

In October 1942, the PROSPER circuit was established by Francis Suttill, Gilbert Norman worked as the circuit's wireless operator and Andrée Borrel as the courier. Suttill made rapid progress and formed numerous F Section sub-circuits across much of northern France, his workload growing so large that, in December, a second wireless operator, Jack Agazarian, was sent to help. However, due to an acute shortage of wireless operators Agazarian often found himself handling traffic for several other circuits as well.

This was not the first time their courier, Andrée, had been involved with resistance work. She had spent two years working on the PAT escape line with her lover, Maurice Dufour. Together they helped downed RAF pilots (among others), maintained the escape line and rented safe houses where they hid fugitives. When the PAT line was compromised in 1941 it was no longer safe for Andrée to stay; in doing so she risked arrest and possible deportation. In the dead of night, February 1942, Andrée and Dufour took the escape route over which they had helped hundreds of people cross. Travelling via Spain and Portugal, they arrived in England a month apart.

Andrée was taken to the MI5 clearance centre at the Royal Victoria Patriotic Schools in south-west London where she was interviewed by government officials who wanted to know if there was anything suspicious about her, or if she could be useful to them. Her story was corroborated by Dufour and the interrogators remarked that she seemed 'perfectly straight-forward', an intelligent 'country girl who was a "keen patriot"'. They recom-mended that she should be released and sent to join the Free French 'Corps Féminin'.[2]

But the Free French did not employ people who had worked for the British unless they were willing to make a statement in which they gave the details of all their contacts and any useful information they may have had access to. While in the eyes of the Free French forces this proved loyalty to their country, it could endanger the lives of the contacts that the potential recruit had left behind. Both Andrée and Dufour refused to make the state-ment. There were many French collaborators, and they did not know how the information they provided would be used. Dufour was taken away and detained at the Free French HQ at Duke Street, where, denied food, water and sleep, he was beaten so badly that two of his teeth were broken. The interrogators threatened to gang rape Andrée if he did not speak out – his crime was that he would not betray British Intelligence.[3]

Andrée was refused entry to the 'Corps Féminin' of the Free French movement and was interviewed by F Section in May 1942. Her interviewer commented that she will 'make an excellent addition to our own corps feminine' and that 'she is perfectly willing to let us have the information she refuses to give the Free French.'[4] She became firm friends with Marie-Thérèse le Chêne, who thought that Andrée 'knew little of the world' and tried to help her find her way by attempting to improve her etiquette and behaviour, such as not smoking on the street while wearing uniform.[5]

When Andrée was briefed for her mission, her instructions upon arriving in France were clear: she would land and be met by a reception committee who would update her regarding 'local conditions' and house her for a couple of days. Then she was to travel to Paris to meet 'les Tambours' sisters, Germaine and Madeleine, two middle-aged women who had initially helped the CARTE network, but then, more recently given valuable support to PROSPER. Germaine had been one of Suttill's first contacts and had introduced him to many helpful people. The sisters allowed their apartment at 32 avenue du Suffren to be used as a safe house and a letter drop for resisters and agents.[6]

Andrée tried to fight her nerves as she boarded the aircraft on the autumn evening of 24 September 1942. Lise de Baissac was by her side and the two got on well: Lise said she appreciated Andrée's 'manner, her character. She was quick, determined, and ready to face any situation.'[7] As the aircraft began its approach to the drop zone, the pair sat silently waiting for the dispatcher's green light. It never came: the signals on the drop zone were incorrect, and the pilot did not want to risk dropping them into the middle of a German trap. The women were both immensely frustrated, but understood that if anything was out of order the mission had to be aborted. They sat uncomfortably for the several more hours it took them to return to England and then, disappointed and drained, were taken to a holding house where they spent the next few hours.

The next night they tried again. This time all went well – and as they jumped they made history by becoming the first two women agents to parachute into wartime France. Upon landing they buried their parachutes and pistols and went in search of their safe house. It was soon time to go their separate ways. Lise headed to Poitiers, while Andrée made her way to Paris where she successfully made contact with 'les Tambours' and, after his arrival on the night of 1/2 October, with Suttill (who had waited for her for five minutes every day at a set time outside a café on rue Caumartin). She then began work as Suttill's courier. Andrée's intimate knowledge of Paris and her 'cool judgement' helped her undertake her 'delicate and dangerous work' with finesse. Suttill was so pleased with her that he sent a message to SOE thanking them for sending her to him. 'She is the best of us all,' he said, 'she has a perfect understanding of security and an imperturbable calmness.' He trusted her so implicitly that he made much more use of her than just as his courier, calling her an 'able and devoted Lieutenant'.[8] She acted as an intermediary and his 'cut out' for receiving and passing messages to avoid him coming into contact with too many people.

At first, however, Suttill had hoped he would not be teamed with Andrée at all. He had met her before, during his training, and was drawn to her. He told a fellow trainee that he 'found her attractive, so much so that the prospect of working long months with her at his side, once they were in France, to some extent troubled him, in as much as he was a married man and might find the enforced proximity a strain'.[9] But the two enjoyed a purely professional relationship in which they admired and respected one another. Andrée did, however, reputedly have a romantic liaison in the field with Gilbert Norman, the wireless operator for the PROSPER circuit, and they would often spend the night together.[10] Romantic or sexual relationships between agents were not encouraged as they compromised the circuit's safety and anonymity, as well as distracting agents from their mission, but they were far from uncommon.[11] Buckmaster said that agents were organised into groups that would 'get on well together, but not too well . . . in other words, that the organiser wouldn't want to go to bed with the courier the whole time'.[12]

Described as 'a brave woman who always volunteered for the most dangerous tasks', Andrée was also 'given the task of organising parachute dropping operations' for PROSPER and, during the moon period of November

1942, led a reception committee that consisted of Norman, Suttill and Yvonne Rudellat.[13] The group made their way to the drop zone where they waited in silence, unable to move or even light a cigarette for several hours so as not to attract unwanted attention, until they heard the drone of the aircraft's engines. If the drop was successful the containers and their contents had to be hidden before dawn. This was usually done on foot as motorised vehicles would have drawn too much attention since gasoline was hard to come by.

These night-time drops were tense for everybody concerned and were highly dangerous, as the committee could be denounced or the DZ overrun by the Nazis, but Andrée remained cool and efficient throughout. In the containers dropped that November night was a wealth of much-needed arms and equipment, including '88lbs of plastic explosive, 24 Sten guns, 34 revolvers, 46 grenades, 15 clam mines and 50 incendiaries' – an arsenal that would aid their fight against the Germans, when the time came. They hid the containers in a barn to await distribution and further use. A further 240 containers full of guns and explosives were dropped over the next few months to PROSPER, with Andrée very much involved in organisation and planning.[14]

Agents also came to the circuit by parachute and, on 22 January 1943, two men landed near Chartres. Jean Worms went on to set up the JUGGLER circuit, a sub-circuit of PROSPER. The other, Henri Déricourt, an ex-French air force pilot, who, after passing the Royal Victoria Patriotic School's vetting process, had joined SOE to find suitable landing grounds and assist in infiltrating agents by air. His mission included facilitating the entire PROSPER circuit, and, some would argue, bring about its eventual downfall.[15] Over the next few months he arranged the transport by plane of some sixty-seven agents, including Noor Inayat Khan, Vera Leigh, Yolande Beekman, Eliane Plewman, Diana Rowden, Jack Agazarian, Francis Suttill and Pearl Witherington. Déricourt's web spread far and wide, even as far as Poitiers where Lise de Baissac was courier and liaison officer for the SCIENTIST circuit led by her brother, Claude, who communicated with PROSPER and BRICKLAYER, led by France Antelme.

Lise de Boucherville Baissac was born on 11 May 1905 on Mauritius and was completing her education in Paris when the Germans invaded. She moved to Dordogne in the free zone and then on to Gibraltar. In Gibraltar she was reunited with her brother, Claude, who had just been released from a Spanish jail. He was keen to go back to France and assist with the resistance, so he secured a role within SOE and, as soon as the organisation started recruiting women, he saw to it that Lise was interviewed and accepted too. Lise de Baissac was trained in the second intake of SOE's women agents, and in 1942 was granted a commission in the FANY.

Her mission was to establish a safe house in Poitiers and form a new circuit named ARTIST that was 'mainly for the reception of material but otherwise not operational'. It would be a 'new centre to which members of the organisation can go for material, help and information on the local condition' and to organise the arms drops from the United Kingdom to assist the French resistance.[16] Using a variety of code names (including 'Odile', 'Marguerite' and 'Adèle'), Lise's cover story was that she was a poor widow from Paris named Madame Irène Brisse who was seeking refuge from the tensions and food shortages of the capital.

Lise became acquainted with the local Gestapo chief, Grabowski, and she even moved into an apartment near his Gestapo HQ. It was a private flat on the ground floor off a busy street where there was no concierge. This meant she could bring people in with relative ease and, if necessary, hide them without being asked awkward questions. She needed the freedom for people to come and go and, to keep the neighbours at bay, she made friends with as many people as possible and frequently asked them for dinner at her flat, the idea being that if she constantly had people at the flat no one would pay too much attention. She also became very friendly with a local family, which made it easier for her to be accepted. Her role, as she saw it, was to 'receive agents from England when they first arrived in the field, arrange liaison for them, give them information about the life, and encourage them if they were nervous'. Lise effectively reproduced in Poitiers what Virginia Hall had created in Lyon. No one, she said, seemed to suspect her.[17]

Lise felt that she fitted in well in the quiet town of Poitiers, which she described as a town with no industry or factories and with 'a quiet ... ecclesiastical air'. But the town had its fair share of troubles, and not only from the Germans. She recalled that 'a newspaper seller who had been informing for the Germans was shot near [her] flat one evening a few minutes before curfew. Another collaborator was the director of a newspaper, and he was disposed of by means of some 30 wounds inflicted with a large file.' The Germans themselves were relatively polite and sober, but if rules were broken (such as breaking the curfew) they would 'shoot at sight and without warning' and make use of their dogs.[18]

In the first weeks of her mission Lise cycled 60 or 70 km a day, often carrying compromising materials on her person, such as wireless messages or documents, which, if discovered, would have meant arrest or even summary execution without a trial. Undeterred, she often cycled through country lanes looking for possible drop zones or landing fields, and building up contacts who would be prepared to help her. As Lise did not have a wireless set or operator, she had to travel to Paris or to SCIENTIST in Bordeaux to send and receive messages or pick up supplies of cash. While in Paris, she assisted in reactivating circuits that had been badly damaged by betrayals of agents.

Lise was not keen on attending parachute drops. It was rather incongruous, she said, 'for an apparently ordinary citizen to be rushing about in the middle of the night', and she worried that the Gestapo were on the look-out for anything out of the ordinary. She preferred to focus on carrying messages on her bicycle, modes of transport which she explained were 'very much used by everybody, especially in the country. You are not supposed to ride one unless it is necessary to reach your work that way. One is frequently stopped in town but never in the country.' Occasionally she had a car at her disposal.[19]

Lise attracted much praise from colleagues, particularly from her circuit leader and brother Claude who valued her skill, saying she was 'one of our most successful girls . . . a good organiser and administrator . . . popular with contacts and much loved in the region'. Claude sometimes sent her on missions to Paris carrying incriminating plans or wireless crystals. On one occasion, she was arrested and searched by the Germans and only 'got out of [this] hole because of her great calm and *sang-froid*'. Her actions enabled the SCIENTIST circuit to keep in contact with F Section 'at a crucial moment'.[20]

Claude's other courier was Mary Herbert who, since her arrival, been carrying out her duties 'with great tact and discretion'. She was very security conscious and 'had a rule that she kept very strictly, of never talking to Claude if she saw him in conversation with someone she did not know'.[21] Her coolness towards him in public gave way to a love affair when in private, in spite of the SOE regulations that agents should not become involved with one another. Not only did Mary have a relationship with Claude, she also became close to his sister Lise, and, on her visits to Poitiers to exchange information or take messages that had come for Lise over the SCIENTIST wireless set, the two would spend time together for pleasure and relaxation as they 'liked and trusted one another'.[22] This too would have been frowned upon by F Section staff: agents were supposed to keep each other at arm's length, because if one of them was compromised they would both be at risk.

In the late spring of 1943, Mary discovered that she was pregnant with Claude's child. According to Lise, this was not an accident: Mary had asked Claude to give her a baby – 'a very dangerous thing to do'.[23] Perhaps, as she was about to turn 40, Mary decided this was her last chance to have a child. The timing was somewhat unorthodox, especially with regard to Mary's F Section role and mission; indeed the situation could not have been more dangerous and was certainly an extraordinary breach of SOE rules, but there was nothing that could be done about it. The couple had choices to make and they eventually decided not to marry (although Claude would have willingly done so) in case their forged papers gave them away and led to their arrest. Instead Claude signed a document stating that he was the baby's father to try, at least, to give Mary some peace of mind.[24] Pregnancy in wartime France would have been a difficult enough experience for the mother-to-be due to food shortages and the pressure of life in an occupied country. For a young woman who only occasionally saw her lover (who led one of the most active resistance circuits in France), and was running the risk of arrest herself by her day-to-day actions, Mary's pregnancy must have been a fraught and difficult time emotionally and physically. She continued to work in Bordeaux for as long as was practicable, riding her bicycle over long distances, but as her pregnancy progressed and she could no longer cycle she resorted to trains and buses. SCIENTIST and PROSPER were beginning to break apart and the situation was getting increasingly dangerous. Claude made sure that Mary was safe and found her a place at a private nursing home in la Valence, a suburb of Bordeaux. He visited whenever he could and took her money and supplies. His last visit was on 30 November; the following day he escaped across the Pyrenees. Mary severed all ties with the resistance and awaited the arrival of her baby. Their daughter Claudine was born in December 1943 by C-section.

Since his infiltration in January, Henri Déricourt had sought out several suitable landing strips for the incoming Lysander and Hudson aircraft, and had become reacquainted with a French woman by the name of Julienne Aisner. Born in 1899, before the war Julienne lived in the US with her first husband, a lieutenant in the United States Marine Corps, and their son Louis. When her husband died after just three years of marriage, she moved to Lebanon and then Hanoi with her parents. Returning to France in 1933, she worked as a scriptwriter at a film studio and married Robert Aisner in 1935, divorcing some six years later.

At the outbreak of war Julienne remained in France, but sent 14-year-old Louis to live with his aunt in the US, fearing his US nationality might get him interned as an alien by the Germans. He departed on the last ship to leave the country after the fall of France and did not see his mother again until after the war. In mid-1941 Julienne was released from Cherche Midi prison in Paris where she had been incarcerated for two months for slapping the face of a German officer who had indecently propositioned her. While incarcerated Julienne and other women were injected in the breast with an unknown substance, an incident that would greatly affect her a few years later. A few days after her release she received a visit from Déricourt, who brought with him a telegram from her son which had been sent to him in London. Julienne had not heard from Louis since he left for the US, and his brief note stating 'I am well' brought her great relief.[25] Déricourt quickly burnt the note, which proved to Julienne that he was trustworthy. That night they decided to work together, and began a love affair.[26]

Julienne's work for Déricourt involved finding safe houses in which to hide incoming agents as well as those who were known to the Gestapo and therefore in danger. She also sorted out their various papers, including identity cards, ration cards and work permits, which she acquired from a local town hall. Soon, she had all the papers she needed, and several apartments were prepared for the incoming agents. During the March 1943 moon period, Déricourt and Julienne prepared for their first reception together. They travelled to Poitiers where they stayed in a small hotel, and, every night, they listened to *Messages Personnels* on the BBC:

> For this, we had a precarious arrangement. No power plug, only a light socket from the ceiling. We had to put a chair on the bed, remove the bulb and plug in the set; to make it more secure I stay perched on the chair and hold everything together. Henri keeps his ear glued to the loudspeaker to avoid any sound being heard. For several days nothing for us . . . but finally one night we are rewarded. . . . Henri jumps up: 'That's it you heard it: The wind from the sea. . . . It's for us.' I never heard the end of that message.[27]

That night Francine Agazarian arrived by Lysander to work for PROSPER with her husband, Jack, who had been taking on more and more work to assist Suttill. Unfortunately, there is little documented about Francine's early life except that she was born in May 1913 to French parents in Narbonne. She was working as an English-speaking secretary when war broke out and, following the fall of France, was so desperate to leave that she 'contracted a marriage of convenience' with a Sergeant in the Royal Signals, who claimed to be an escaped POW. When they eventually got to Britain in September

1941 she made a few enquiries about him and discovered that her new husband was in fact already married and her marriage was null. However she had got what she wanted from it, she was out of France and was apparently not too concerned by the betrayal as she began the hunt to track down a former fiancé, Charles Stanmore Agazarian (known as Jack), whom she found and married in late 1942.

Jack was already in training to become an F Section agent himself, and Francine received MI5 clearance to undertake her own SOE training, which she started in December 1942. A training report stated that she was 'quite at home with the others; popular, genuine, full of interest in everything' and would make 'une excellente camarade'.[28]

She hoped that she would be able to take the pressure off Jack by assisting with the coding and decoding of messages, and by carrying messages and crystals, all of which would leave him to concentrate on his own role. Although they were married, Francine and Jack saw little of one another in Paris, only occasionally rendezvousing in cafés. Security was paramount, and Francine was tasked with 'keeping contact between the scattered groups of the circuit' so that Suttill did not become too widely known. The role involved 'continuous travelling throughout an area where police and Gestapo activities were intense and travel checks an everyday occurrence. Francine conscientiously undertook all of these tasks, and with great success.'[29]

Francine's work in the field suited her: she had carved a niche for herself which enabled her to flourish both practically and personally. Her comrades described her as 'a pleasant person' who was 'courageous and intelligent'. She liked working under Suttill's instruction and 'enjoyed the small challenges' he gave her, which were varied and included visiting the town halls of Paris to exchange the circuit's expired ration cards (fakes, manufactured in London) for new ones, delivering messages and distributing sabotage material that had arrived from England. On one occasion, she carried a shopping bag full of hand grenades on a busy train; another time she wore a wide cloth belt concealing a vast amount of bank notes, several blank ID cards and some ration cards. Meanwhile, tucked into her coat sleeves she carried the crystals for PROSPER's wireless sets, with a .32 revolver and its

ammunition in her suitcase. 'The ridiculousness of it all somehow eliminated any thought of danger.'[30]

The explosives that she carried were put to good use when PROSPER
members attacked the power station at Chaigny near Orléans, cutting off the
power supply completely. Though the power cut was relatively short-lived
and the severed cables on the pylons were replaced quickly so output
resumed after only eleven hours, that was enough to significantly slow down
the factories and railways that bolstered the German war effort, and the
sabotage was deemed to be a success by PROSPER and F Section HQ.

On occasion, the circuit came together. While Francine decoded
messages, they would all sit around a table 'hoping to read the exciting
warning to stand by, which would have meant that the liberating invasion
from England was imminent.'[31] But, despite this image of unity, relations
within the circuit were not nearly as happy as they could have been. Jack's
report highlights tensions within the circuit which seem to have gone unresolved. Suttill had told Jack that 'I don't want you … I never asked for a
wireless operator'. Jack felt that he and Francine were treated as outsiders;
that Suttill made excuses to try and get rid of them, such as saying Francine
was too ill to work, that she acted above her station, considered herself
outside his authority and that she had never 'been able to fit into the picture'.
Jack retorted that they had never been invited into it.[32]

Life became unsettled and awkward for them both. Suttill evidently did
not want either of them in his circuit and was reluctant to keep them longer
than he had to. As a result, Francine's mission only lasted ten weeks, the official line given was that 'she was unfit'[33] and that Jack was 'so badly compromised that he had to leave France'.[34] However, it was apparent that neither
were welcome in the tight-knit PROSPER circuit of Suttill, Andrée and
Norman, and it was prudent to get out rather than continue fighting an
internal battle. But they had to wait for Déricourt to arrange a Lysander to
get them back to England.

Déricourt, who had been working closely alongside Julienne Aisner, realised that she was a true asset and insisted that she be sent to England for
formal SOE training. This way she would be officially recognised by the

organisation and could acquire the skills she needed to undertake the various roles he had in mind for her.[35] On 15 April 1943, she left for London as the lone passenger aboard a Lysander. Her previous experience impressed SOE who kept her training to a bare minimum and she was back in France within a month.

PROSPER had grown considerably during the first half of 1943. The circuit covered a large part of northern France and had a huge number of locally recruited agents. There were two main clusters: one in the Vernon–Beauvais–Méru triangle to the north-west of Paris and the other in the Tours–Orléans–Vierzon area, between the Loire and Cher rivers. In June 1943 alone, sixty-eight supply operations were flown to these groups. Furthermore, due to a shortage of wireless operators, PROSPER dealt with most of the wireless traffic for the rest of northern France in those few months. Such a busy circuit needed more agents and Déricourt ensured that plenty more arrived at his landing grounds.

The night of the next organised landing on 15 May was clear and bright. There were German night-fighter patrols in the area but the pair of Lysanders skilfully avoided them. On board the aircraft were Vera Leigh, Julienne Aisner, Sidney Jones and wireless operator Marcel Clech, alongside fourteen packages. They landed just east of Tours in the Cher valley in the early hours of the morning. After they were safely on the ground, Suttill emerged from the shadows and boarded one of the homeward bound Lysanders, having been recalled to England to deliver a report. The newly arrived male agents cleared away the suitcases and departed on bicycles while Julienne and Vera walked 10 km cross country to the railway station. They took the train to Paris the next morning and arrived safely.

Vera Leigh, known as 'Simone', was 'a very smart business woman'. Her cover story as a milliner's assistant suited her well, as before the war she had run a boutique fashion business, Rose Valois, with two friends. Vera's life was a tale of rags to riches: born in 1903, she was abandoned as a baby in Leeds and subsequently adopted by Eugène Leigh, a wealthy American racehorse trainer who had stables in England and at Maisons Laffitte, near Paris. Vera dreamt of being a jockey, but on leaving school she took up dress design and established a shop in Place Vendôme in Paris. After the occupation, she left Paris to join her fiancé in Lyon where she became involved with the resistance and escape lines, guiding fugitive Allied servicemen out of the country. In 1942, she left France along the escape route with which she was so familiar, and on arrival in England volunteered to join the FANY, through which she was recruited into SOE.

Vera was courier to the INVENTOR circuit, a sub-circuit of PROSPER, and her main role was to carry messages from her organiser, Sidney Jones, to his wireless operator and to provide courier duties to Henri Frager, head of the DONKEYMAN circuit. She carried out her work with diligence and was well respected among her colleagues, earning her 'high praise from her superiors in the resistance'.[36] But it was difficult for Vera to come to terms with seeing her native Paris under Nazi control – the city of fashion, where she had once felt so at home, now a city of old clothes and wooden-soled shoes.

Agents were taught, as part of their security training, to avoid old acquaintances, friends and places. Since she had no idea if they were still a friend or now sided with the occupiers, Vera needed to consider how she would react if she saw an old friend in the street. Whom could she trust if she needed help? In spite of herself, Vera felt dragged back into her old life in the city. She went to her pre-war hairdressers, and even bumped into her brother-in-law on the street, at first pretending not to know him. He eventually managed to convince her to help him by guiding downed airmen through the streets from one safe house to another. Another piece of SOE advice that she disregarded was that she should not be seen with or spend too much time with fellow agents, yet Vera frequently rendezvoused with other agents at a café on Place des Ternes where Julienne Aisner and others were to be found.

For her part, Julienne had got back to work quickly and effectively after her brief sojourn in England for training. She provided 'safe houses, papers and contacts for a number of agents' as well as sending documents and ration books back to England for copying, which were also a valuable source of information. Her knowledge of official documents was utilised when she forged papers for Jack Agazarian (who helped her as a wireless operator) as well as tampering with X-rays so it appeared that he had stomach problems that would exempt him from the STO.

Julienne also renewed contact with Jean Besnard, an old friend with connections in 'the most varied circles' and who was 'an inexhaustible source of highly important information'. He had rented a house in the Paris suburbs for use as a safe house when required.[37] She also rented two flats and a bistro where agents could make contact with one another, and 'ran a *bôite*' – a letter box used for rendezvous – which she personally attended daily. She worked with 'efficiency and discretion' and ensured the 'smooth infiltration and exfiltration of a very great number of persons'.[38]

On 17 June, another double Lysander mission arrived at one of Déricourt's landing grounds 12 km north-east of Angers in the Loire valley. One plane carried Cicely Lefort and Noor Inayat Khan; in the other were Charles Skepper and Diana Rowden. Time was of the essence – the longer the Lysanders were there the more chance there was of them being spotted by the enemy and the landing ground being compromised. The arriving agents hurriedly climbed down from their aircraft and collected their luggage, and then two agents, Francine and Jack, quickly boarded one of the planes. Jack was among several agents, including Cammaerts and Suttill, who were increasingly concerned about where Déricourt's loyalties lay, a worry that was intensified when it was discovered that he was living in Paris in a flat next to one rented by Hugo Bleicher of Abwehr. Once back in England, Jack relayed his fears to the leadership of F Section. Fatefully they remained unconvinced and refused to recall Déricourt to Britain.

Another F Section agent, Henri Frager, told Nicholas Bodington when he visited occupied France in July 1943 of his fears that Déricourt was a German spy. Bodington dismissed the idea: Déricourt had arranged his journey to France and he had not been arrested. When Bodington refused to take action some agents began to think that he was also a double agent. Soon afterwards Maurice Buckmaster was told that a Frenchman in charge of air operations in the Paris and Angers districts was working for the Abwehr. Buckmaster dismissed the rumours and Déricourt was allowed to continue his work in France until February 1944.

Newly arrived agent Diana Rowden was described by her mother as a 'turbulent tomboy' who found it difficult to conform and do what was expected of her.[39] Born in 1915, she had a sense of adventure and fun, spending most of her time as the 'boon companion of two brothers, living a beach combing life along the Mediterranean coast'. Diana was clever and received an advanced certificate in Italian grammar and literature from her school at Hadlow Down, near Mayfield, and later became an associate of the Institute of Linguistics. Despite being extremely intelligent she hated school and studying, much preferring the sea where she could sail, fish and enjoy the sun.

In the early days of the war, Diana and her mother were in France. Diana joined the French Red Cross and, in those desperate weeks of 1940, became separated from her mother, who eventually reached Britain in a coal boat. Diana stayed on, believing it was her duty to continue her war work, but in 1941 she too fled. She was reunited with her mother and they shared a flat in Kensington, but she wanted to go back to France. She looked for work where her knowledge of French and France would be useful. Having joined the WAAF, she was disappointed that they seemingly did not need these particular skills – but they were soon noticed and she was passed over to SOE, where the work would be more in keeping with her adventurous nature and her abilities. Her personnel file says that 'she is very anxious to return to France and work against the Germans. She should prove valuable to this organisation after training.'[40]

She entered the field as courier for John 'Bob' Starr and the ACROBAT circuit in the Jura. Diana was to meet with her new boss and give a set phrase to ensure she had the right man: '*La pêche rend-elle par ici?*' (Is there any fishing round here?) to which the reply was '*Oui, j'ai pris "x" poissons la dernière fois que j'y suis allée*' (Yes, I caught 'x' fish the last time I went there). The

number of fish depended on which day of the month it was.[41] She successfully met Starr, who in turn introduced her to John Young, his wireless operator, who used a nearby château as a base from which to transmit. While he
made an excellent wireless operator, Young's poor grasp of the French
language let him down and he could not really move about without someone
who could do the talking for both of them – Diana was now that someone.

She took a room in the Hotel du Commerce in Saint-Amour with a
window that gave onto a rooftop for ease of escape. Sometimes her courier
work took her as far afield as Marseille, Besançon, Montbéliard and Paris.
On these longer train journeys, she did her utmost to avoid security checks
and once locked herself in the train toilet until the guard had passed. She
also took part in reception committees which, in addition to money and
equipment, brought the circuit explosives.

On 18 July, Starr was arrested and taken to a Gestapo prison. Diana and
Young hoped that he would hold out under interrogation and not give away
their names, but they went on the run regardless to avoid being arrested
themselves. At first Diana took shelter in a bistro just a few kilometres up the
road from Young's château, then, after three weeks, they went to stay with the
Juif family, who had been letting Young transmit from their house since
April 1943.[42]

Diana reinvented her appearance by dyeing her hair a different colour
and changing her clothes. Her name was now 'Marcelle' and, according to
her new cover story, she had come to the town to recuperate from a serious
illness. She lay low at first but gradually started to take walks outside,
becoming involved with the life of the house and well liked by the family.
Madame Juif said that Diana was 'as tough as a man and as tireless as a
child'.[43] She remained with the Juifs until November, when her world would
turn upside down.

Diana was infiltrated at the same field as Cicely Lefort, who was born in
1900 in London – the child of a scandalous *ménage à trois* and a protracted
custody case.[44] Cicely moved to France with her mother when she was 6
years old. During the Great War she worked as a nurse and it was while she
was treating wounded French soldiers that she met Dr Alix Lefort, at that

time a soldier, who was suffering from tuberculosis. Despite a ten-year age gap the two fell in love and were married in 1924. Taking French nationality, Cicely worked as her husband's receptionist at his part-time doctor's surgery. The couple divided their time between their Paris apartment and La Hune, Alix's villa on the cliffs of the Brittany coast near Saint-Cast. Here the couple indulged their passion for sailing and spent time on their private beach below the villa. In 1939, Alix was called up to join the French Army's medical service and he insisted that Cicely go to England, fearing she might be interned by the Nazis on account of her English background. She was reluctant to do so but saw an opportunity to help the war effort and on arrival in Britain (via Jersey) in 1940 she enlisted with the WAAF, with whom she served for about a year. Her background and knowledge of France, as well as her fluent (if accented) French, caught the attention of SOE; even before she got back to France she had helped DF Section with a new escape line project, and had volunteered her villa at Saint-Cast as a safe house and the secluded beach in the Baie de la Fresnaye not far from her house as a landing place for arriving SOE agents.[45]

Cicely was recruited by F Section on 30 January 1943. She was described as 'spinsterish but kind' and 'very ladylike, very English', in spite of her largely French background. She was, however, 'inclined to blurt out things in a rather embarrassing way, which she probably would not have said if she had thought first'.[46] Despite her rashness and the disadvantage of seeming so English, SOE thought Cicely could be useful due to her wide circle of friends and acquaintances.[47] Her code name was 'Teacher', which was the profession of her false identity.

Cicely went straight to Paris, where she may have taken the opportunity to see her husband, and then travelled south, eventually reaching Cammaerts in Italian-occupied Montélimar. In his official report Cammaerts said that he liked Cicely as she was 'very useful' with 'exactly the right temperament'.[48] However, after the war he expressed a rather different view of 'a shy woman who was just completely lost', whom he believed 'looked forward with terror to the next day'. Baker Street, he said, 'made mistakes and she was one of the most serious', but he worked with her in the hope that things would improve, and felt unable to ask her to leave as she was several years his senior 'with a lot more experience of France' than him.[49]

Cammaerts was head of JOCKEY, which covered the Rhône-Alpes, Drôme and Montélimar areas of France, and was in the process of building up teams for sabotage work. The circuit was very active in arming and training résistants and guerrillas ready to commit acts of sabotage on the railways, oil and fuel depots, factories and locomotives. They blocked roads, caused general mayhem and harassed German troops retreating through the Alps. During Cicely's time with the circuit, the hydroelectric station in Durance was put out of action, which in turn interrupted power supplies to the plants turning out aluminium for the Luftwaffe. Railway turntables and locomotives were also sabotaged, and communication pylons put out of use. The aim was to cut off the local Abwehr from their HQ ahead of the Allied invasion.

Just three months after her arrival in France, Cicely was arrested in Montélimar, at the home of local resistance leader Raymond Daujat. Cammaerts had advised her to go to Daujat's office and stay away from his house at all costs, but she had turned up on his doorstep at 4 a.m.; her 'need for simple human contact might have been the reason for her going against' the advice, her file suggests.[50] Daujat was 'obliged to put her up for the night'. All too predictably, at 8 a.m. the Gestapo arrived. Perhaps they had followed her from the station, or perhaps Daujat had been denounced. He managed to make his escape through a window, taking most of the compromising material with him. But in her panic Cicely hid in the coal cellar of the house next door, rather than secreting herself in one of several safe houses available to her. She was soon discovered and arrested. In her bag was a small but 'incriminating' piece of paper. Cammaerts was certain that it did not contain names or addresses of fellow résistants as her security had always been very good, but he had no idea what was on it. He later stated that he wanted her to 'admit that she is English, as her appearance and accent are definitely so, but, if she sticks to a story that she has been in France since before the war ... she had a chance of being released'.[51] Cammaerts said he thought the arrest 'may have been a consequence of the arrest of xxx's [blanked out in file] courier or of denunciation by a personal enemy known to have been intimate with the Gestapo recently. This man has been "dealt with".'[52]

Cammaerts was committed to keeping a close eye on where Cicely was taken by the Gestapo and sought out contacts inside the Gestapo prison. He also said he regretted her arrest as she had 'worked well', but she had not followed the security measures he had put in place and had sadly placed herself in the worst possible position. One small consolation was that 'unless she has some direct evidence on her . . . they have no means of knowing who she is'. Cicely was first taken to a Gestapo prison in Lyon and then was moved to 84, avenue Foch in Paris, until she was deported with several other SOE women in 1944.

Noor Inayat Khan had arrived by Lysander the same night as Diana and Cicely, and was the first female wireless operator to be infiltrated into France. Born in Moscow on New Year's Day 1914, her mother was American and her father an Indian Sufi priest – her name meant 'Light of womanhood'. Many sources state claim that Noor was a devout Muslim or indeed a princess, and these claims need to be addressed.

Noor and her siblings were direct descendants of Tipu Sultan, the eighteenth-century Muslim ruler of Mysore in India, which technically made her a princess. Nevertheless, Noor and her family never referred to themselves by their ancestral title. It is only in recent years, since Noor became a public figurehead and icon, that it has begun to be used.[53] Also, while Noor's 'father was raised a Muslim', he was 'equally respectful of Hindu culture and, like his own grandfather, performed the music of both these traditions. When her father came to the West he promoted a universal Sufism based on respect and tolerance of all traditions. His teachings honoured all the sacred traditions and the children were not raised with solely Islamic practice, 'they were equally at home with all forms of worship'.[54]

At the outbreak of war, Noor's family had been living in Bordeaux but escaped to England, where Noor wanted to get a job as a nurse. Instead, she enlisted in the WAAF as her brother Vilayat was applying for the RAF, and she wanted to be in the same service, but Vilayat's eyesight was not good enough and, therefore, while Noor continued in the WAAF, he joined the Royal Navy. Noor attended a wireless course in Harrogate, and a month later was sent to 34 (Balloon Barrage) Group, RAF Balloon Command, in Edinburgh to train as a wireless operator for six months. In May 1942 she attended a course for advanced signals and wireless training at Compton Basset in Wiltshire and, following a promotion to Leading Aircraftswoman in December 1942, Noor applied for a job in intelligence.

At a time when F Section was desperate for wireless operators, Noor's advanced wireless skills got her an SOE interview. PHONO, a developing circuit, was without a wireless operator of its own and Noor fitted the bill in more ways than one. But her training reports were poor (see Chapter 1). The head of the Finishing School at Beaulieu wrote that she was 'not over burdened with brains' and was temperamentally unsuitable for her proposed role.[55] He felt so strongly about this that he sent a copy of his report to SOE's head of operations, Major General Gubbins. Buckmaster was furious that 'that bastard Spooner' had 'taken against her' and that the 'damned busy-body' had gone above him and sent his report to Baker Street; in the margins of her report Buckmaster scribbled 'we don't want them overburdened with brains' and 'makes me cross'.[56] He went on to say that the reports were 'absolute balls' and called the instructors 'a mob of second-raters'.[57] Overriding the report, Buckmaster sent Noor to Leo Marks to test her coding ability in an 'extended briefing' to ensure she 'understood her code conventions' and would remember them when in France. Marks was very fond of Noor but wondered 'what the hell she was doing in SOE'. Nevertheless, he put her through her paces and she passed the tests he set her.[58] She was told to prepare to go to France.

Noor's unsuitability for work in the field had attracted the concern of two other agents, who wrote to Vera Atkins at F Section saying that they 'did not think she was the type to be sent'.[59] When the letter was brought to Noor's attention, she was 'shocked and hurt', insisting that she was 'the proper person for the job'.[60] Vera gave her the option to withdraw from her mission, adding:

'for us there is only one crime: to go out there and let your comrades down'.[61] Noor insisted that she wanted to go and was competent enough to undertake the work. Her primary concern was her family, and she found saying goodbye to her widowed mother the most painful thing she had ever had to do. She told her mother a half-truth, saying she was going abroad, but to Africa; she had found maintaining the deception cruel.[62] Vera asked Noor if there was anything she could do to help with family matters, and Noor replied that, if she went missing, SOE should as far as possible avoid worrying her mother.

Noor's 'dreamy' nature and inability to lie had been raised, alongside other security issues, by nearly every member of staff who came into contact with her.[63] Quite simply, Noor was not felt to be suitable agent material, but was the product in a chain of human supply and demand, evidenced by the fact that Buckmaster overrode the instructors. He had known from the moment he took her on that Noor had the wireless skills and knowledge of France that he required. From Buckmaster's perspective, any wireless operator was better than no wireless operator.

After landing by Lysander in the Loire valley, Noor was to become known by her false identity of Jeane-Marie Regnier, her codename was 'Nurse' and her field name to her colleagues in the circuit was 'Madeleine' (and later 'Rolande'). During her first few days, Noor met her organiser, Émile Garry, but she did not move out to her original destination of Le Mans; Garry was spending part of his time in Paris with his fiancée, so Noor also stayed there. Noor's first wireless transmission on behalf of PHONO was received in England on 22 June 1943, but, just days later, Noor stood by as much of PROSPER, 'parent' circuit to PHONO, fell apart around her.

The disaster had started on 15 June. Yvonne Rudellat and Pierre Culioli of PROSPER received two Canadian F Section agents, John Macalister and Frank Pickersgill. The following night, Noor, Cicely and Diana arrived in the area, which was fraught with tension and enemy activity. The agents kept their heads down and tried to remain as safe as possible. However, it was not that easy for Yvonne and Culioli. On 19 June, they picked up the Canadians in a car, their mission being to take them to Beaugency station, and then on to Paris by train where they would meet Francis Suttill, Andrée Borrel and

Gilbert Norman at Gare d'Austerlitz. The car also carried a parcel containing radio equipment that had been brought by the Canadian agents, as well as a pile of messages addressed to members of the PROSPER circuit by their code names. While the package was disguised as a Red Cross parcel and was even addressed to a fictitious POW, everything in the car was illegal and would be horribly incriminating were it to be discovered. At Dhuizon, the car was stopped at a roadblock. Checkpoints had been set up a short while before in an attempt to close the net on resistance activity in the area. Culioli was ordered to park the car outside the town hall, where all four agents were ordered inside to have their identities checked.

There, it seemed that fortune was smiling on them: Yvonne's and Culioli's papers passed inspection and the parcel was initially all but ignored. They were told they could leave and, returning to the car, they moved off just a few yards and waited, engine running, hoping that the two Canadians would follow them out of the town hall. Something had alerted the Germans' suspicions, however – either the Canadians' POW parcel or their accents – and a soldier was sent outside to bring Culioli and Yvonne back in.

Hearing the shouted command from the soldier to come back, Culioli slammed his foot on the accelerator and the couple sped away, pursued by three German cars. Stopping for nothing they drove straight through a barricade which shattered the windscreen. Shots were fired at their car and, while Yvonne was keeping an eye on the danger behind them, she was hit in the head by a bullet. Assuming that she was dead (and knowing he did not have an 'L' pill) Culioli either lost control on a bend or, as he stated later, tried to kill himself by crashing into the wall of a house. Still alive, he jumped out of the wreckage and tried to make a run for it but was shot in the leg and fell to the ground. Yvonne was still alive too. Culioli was taken back to the town hall, where the parcel had been opened, revealing two small radios, crystals and messages or packages for 'Archambaud', 'Prosper' and 'Marie-Louise' (de Baissac's courier). Equally incriminating was the large sum of money found in the belt around Macalister's waist. Yvonne and Culioli were taken under German guard to the hospital in Blois to be treated for their injuries, while interrogation began of the two Canadians.

Andrée and the others waited for the foursome to arrive in Paris but they never turned up. Unaware of events, they aborted the rendezvous and prepared themselves for handling a reception committee which was to take place that night. The next day, Suttill slept late, and then lunched with friends in Montparnasse before going to Gisors for a rendezvous. The following evening, on 23 June, Andrée and Gilbert Norman dined with some acquaintances at their home in Montparnasse, leaving around 11 p.m. and making their separate ways to the flat of Nicholas and Maud Laurent in the 16th arrondissement where Norman was living. Once inside, despite the late hour, they began coding some messages in preparation for transmission. Just after midnight there were bangs on the door and shouts of 'police'. Madame Laurent opened the door and the Gestapo burst in shouting and pointing their guns at everyone inside. Not only did they arrest everyone there, they also found Norman's wireless set and his horribly incriminating codes. They were all taken directly to 84, avenue Foch, where Andrée 'maintained a silence so disdainful that the Germans did not attempt to break it'.[64] Suttill returned from Gisors early in the morning on 24 June, having rushed back to prepare for another meeting with Claude de Baissac. Upon entering his hotel room he was confronted by German agents and promptly arrested. The entire PROSPER circuit was doomed.

Noor reported back to London that contact had been lost with the leadership of the group and they were assumed to be in Gestapo custody. However, F Section was still receiving messages from Norman's wireless. Leo Marks believed that the messages were being sent under duress and that Norman was in fact in Gestapo hands; but Nicholas Bodington disagreed and managed to persuade Buckmaster to let him go to France to find out what had happened. Jack Agazarian was recalled from leave and the two men were flown into France on 22 July. Once in Paris, it was agreed that an attempt should be made to contact a helper of Suttill, Madame Filipowski. According to Bodington, they tossed a coin to decide who should go. Agazarian lost and, even though he was convinced it was a trap, went to Filipowski's flat – where he was immediately arrested.[65]

Julienne had been due to meet Agazarian at 10 p.m. that evening but he did not turn up. She waited again the next day, to no avail, and eventually found out that he had been arrested and interrogated. For the next six months he was kept at Fresnes prison and subjected to regular interrogation by the Gestapo.

Miraculously, Noor managed to escape the wave of PROSPER arrests. As a result of the collapse of the circuit, 167 people were arrested and deported, of whom just over half survived the war. A futher 3 were shot when the Germans tried to arrest them; 2 died in France as a result of maltreatment in prison; and 2 escaped from a train taking them to Germany.[66]

Noor believed her work to maintain wireless contact with England was more important than ever; she was a lifeline, but she was also a livewire. Her security, or rather lack of it, was a major cause of concern, especially in these times of heightened risk and danger. Within the first few days of her mission beginning, Noor went to visit several members of the circuit. She immediately made several mistakes that gave her away as English, such as pouring 'the milk into the cups before the tea' and toasting 'before the fire some slices of bread she had brought in'.[67] She was told off for her errors as these things 'would be suffi- cient to betray her'.[68] Noor also contacted people that she had known in pre-war Paris. She asked old acquaintances if she could use their residences as safe houses and transmitting places, telling them that she was an English agent; she even allowed a friend to help her code and decode messages.[69] She left packages with her landlady, instructing her 'to give them to whoever called for them'. By doing this she was potentially endangering the lives of fellow résistants and friends as well as her own. More than once she left her codes lying around. A friend tried to shake her up a little by saying to her: 'What reason do you have to suppose that I am to be trusted ... that I am not a double agent ...?'[70]

Another of Noor's acquaintances, businessman and member of the resistance Pierre Viennnot, said that he felt 'a little more familiar with its [the codebook's] appearance than he liked to be', asking Noor to burn the book as well as each message she sent. She refused, insisting that London had told her to 'be extremely careful with the filing of your [her] messages' and would not part with her notebook.[71] SOE meant for her to burn her messages once they were finished, known as 'filing'. However, Noor believed that she should keep a record in code of every message she transmitted and received. Since she was not allowed to leave it on the kitchen table, she carried every incriminating word with her instead. Viennot was also concerned about Noor's appearance, with her bleached-blonde hair and very English-looking mackintosh. He said that 'she seemed ... typically English, in her walk, in her manner, in everything'.[72] To rectify the situation, he bought her new French clothes and insisted that she dyed her hair to a natural brown colour. 'With her new and more soberly coloured hair, and these new clothes, she looked to his eye like a French girl.'[73] At least some things could be done to lessen Noor's chances of being caught.

According to Francis Suttill's son, Noor also developed a close friendship, if not a romantic liaison, with France Antelme. Now on his second mission to France, Antelme carried messages to former French prime ministers, inviting them to come to England. But when PROSPER collapsed he went on the run. He and Noor had been thrown together on more than one occasion; they stayed in Garry's flat together, and when that was raided they stayed at another. They travelled to Angers with Déricourt and stayed with the leader of the CLERGYMAN circuit, Robert Benoist. Antelme was romantically attached elsewhere, and Noor is said to have been in a relationship with someone from the War Office according to her biographer Shrabani Basu. Given the number of other in-the-field relationships it is not at all improbable that they had an affair, although some argue that Antelme's interest in her was paternal. When he flew back to England, he asked Noor to go with him; she declined, and unwittingly became instrumental in his downfall when he returned to France some months later.

At the end of June, Garry married his fiancée, Marguerite, with Noor in attendance. The blown circuit was incapable of engaging in any kind of subversive activity. Noor and Antelme had spent a few days with a surviving circuit near Paris called CHESTNUT but by the end of July its agents were also arrested and Noor fled back to Paris. In August, Bodington found her and asked her to temporarily become his wireless operator after the arrest of

Agazarian. He told her that he would help her to find a safe address before he returned to England.

The shock waves of the arrests in PROSPER had far-reaching effects and anyone who knew or was involved with the man or the circuit was now in danger. The news trickled down to Bordeaux and Claude de Baissac who, via his own links with PROSPER, now realised he was in danger, as was his sister. But Lise, who was still in Poitiers, continued her work as a liaison officer for many months, ensuring that new agents had a safe arrival and passage and everything required for a successful mission (for example, replacing lost wireless sets). It was work that she described as being 'very, very lonely. You grew to know very well what solitude was. Because you are alone; you have false papers; you never have a telephone call; you never get a letter.'[74] To alleviate her boredom she took Spanish lessons and became friendly with the teacher, but she always had to maintain her cover; she could never talk about her home life, nor, obviously, her resistance one. She was unable to let her guard down at any time, which was mentally and emotionally exhausting. Then, one of the French leaders with whom the agents had worked was turned by a German officer. The former résistant told the Germans where to find SCIENTIST's arms dumps and subsequently another series of arrests began.

In the summer of 1943, Baker Street decided that both Lise's and Claude's safety was compromised owing to the fact that they had contacts with PROSPER. Their departure was organised by Henri Déricourt, who had used Noor to send the message to F Section. On 16 August 1943, they boarded a plane and returned safely to England to be debriefed. Lise gave a comprehensive report of life in occupied France, then continued to work, guiding agents through their training. It was always intended that she should return to operational work in France, but a broken leg sustained while helping with parachute training temporarily put paid to her plans.

Despite the strain she was under, Noor had sent an enthusiastic letter to Buckmaster in which she wrote: 'Thanks a lot, it's grand working [with] you ...'[75] Noor was unaware of just how much danger she was in. Before Buckmaster had even laid eyes on this letter, Déricourt had handed it to the

Gestapo, who photographed it. Noor was now transmitting from three different addresses, one of which was a flat on rue de la Faisanderie in the 16th arrondissement. Baker Street was extremely concerned for Noor's safety and sent her a wireless message saying it was too dangerous for her to continue her work and that she must return to England. Noor refused: she wanted to stay and, believing that she was the only link between Paris and London, considered she was crucial to SOE. Buckmaster 'knew that Noor's life was in danger and it was only a matter of time before she was arrested. But *Poste Madeleine* was now the last link with Paris and it had a crucial role. He accepted her offer as the sacrifice of a soldier and allowed her to remain.'[76] Noor was advised to lie low: she could receive wireless messages but was not allowed to transmit them as the D/F units could trace her signal and find her. Noor agreed, but within two days had started transmitting again.

Buckmaster knew that it was dangerous and that he should withdraw her; he had told others to leave and they had gone, so why was Noor disobeying orders? Allowing Noor to remain in Paris was essentially a death sentence for her, and a major security risk to those agents still working there.[77] Noor again refused to leave, reiterating that she believed that she was the only means by which Baker Street could still communicate with Paris, that she could help rebuild the PROSPER circuit and as such she was still vital.[78] She knew the dangers and decided to face the inevitable, while maintaining wireless contact for as long as possible. Unfortunately, the wireless contact went on for longer than she could have ever imagined.

The Gestapo had been making enquiries about a British wireless operator and, although they did not know who it was, they were now able to recognise her 'fist' and knew that she worked alone. Noor was put on the wanted list, with a substantial price on her head. But when the betrayal came, it was for just 100,000 francs. The Gestapo were prepared to pay ten times that much to get their hands on her.[79]

One reason Noor remained in the field as long as she did may have been that, in spite of being known by the Gestapo, she worked for Henri Déricourt, who at one time had no other wireless operator. London told her that a replacement wireless operator was on the way to assist Déricourt and would arrive on 16/17 October, so she would be free to leave around then. Her own departure would be by Lysander on 14 October.

In mid-October, as Noor was walking towards her 16th arrondissement apartment, she saw two Gestapo men standing outside it waiting for her. She managed to flee before they saw her, but knew she would have to return eventually as one of her wireless sets, and all her neatly recorded messages, were still inside the flat. When she thought enough time had passed and it was safe to return, Noor went back, but the Gestapo had left a man there and, as she turned the key in the door, she was arrested. It is likely that Émile Garry's sister, Renée, betrayed Noor by contacting the Germans and giving them Noor's safe house address in rue de la Faisanderie.[80] Renée had reputedly been in a relationship with Antelme and when he shifted his affections to Noor, she had grown jealous and sought revenge. Both Ernst Vogt and Josef Goetz of the Paris Gestapo told Noor that a Frenchwoman had been responsible, and Renée was the chief suspect when the matter came to trial after the war.[81]

Even though she was captured, Noor's wireless continued to send messages to England and, as late as February 1944, London still believed they had contact with her. A memo dated 2 February 1944 stated: 'according to telegrams from MADELEINE, this equipment has not yet arrived and the BELLIARD address is no longer safe …'[82] The BRICKLAYER team of Antelme, Lionel Lee and Madeleine Damerment was still sent to a supposed safe reception on the night of 29 February 1944, organised over Noor's set. By this date, Noor had long been in captivity and the Gestapo had been playing back her wireless to England for three and a half months, confirming all the security fears which some in SOE had had and which, without their knowing, had been comprehensively exploited by the enemy.

4

THE ARMY OF SHADOWS

Throughout her long tour of duty F/O Pearl Witherington showed outstanding devotion to duty and accomplished an important task. Her control over the Maquis group to which she was attached . . . was accomplished through her remarkable personality, her courage, steadfastness and tact.

Recommendation for the award of OBE to
Flight Officer C.P. Witherington[1]

A sense of expectancy and optimism permeated Europe in the spring of 1944 as the promise of an Allied invasion and the liberation of Western Europe grew ever closer. On the Eastern Front the Red Army advanced from Ukraine into Romanian and Polish territory, and made preparations for their most ambitious offensive yet: Operation 'Bagration', which would launch on 22 June (the third anniversary of the German invasion), sending 1.2 million Soviet troops into Belorussia and taking Hitler completely by surprise. That spring, one of the bloodiest campaigns of the Second World War – the four battles of Monte Cassino – was fought in Italy. By mid-May the Allies had broken through German lines and a few days later were joined by forces who had pushed through the Anzio beachhead; together, they took Rome on 4 June.

Meanwhile, preparations for D-Day were well under way. It was intended that the Allied invasion would begin on the eve of the invasion with para-troopers dropping into enemy territory to capture key bridges and roads to prevent German movement towards the beaches. The British, Canadian and

American troops would assault five beaches in Normandy and then begin the fight inland. However, the German high command had no idea where the landings would take place, and the Allies successfully deceived them into believing that the invasion of France would happen in the Pas-de-Calais (at the narrowest point of the English Channel). As part of Operation 'Fortitude South', the fictitious First US Army Group (FUSAG) was created. Fake radio traffic and decoy equipment such as inflatable tanks and dummy landing craft mimicked FUSAG preparations for a large-scale invasion aimed at the Pas-de-Calais. Double agent Juan Pujol Garcia ('Garbo') oversaw a network of imaginary agents that fed the Germans false information on Allied plans.

As plans were made for the invasion, preparations continued in the interior of France so that, when the time came, the resistance could offer assistance and fight back against the occupiers, putting to use all the training and assistance they had received. Supply drops increased and more agents were sent to France to support the eventual Allied attack and contribute to the long-hoped-for liberation. The resistance planned to carry out several distinct initiatives in support of D-Day. The operations were coded and included 'Vert' (green), sabotaging the railway system; 'Tortue' (turtle), attacking the road network; and 'Violet' (purple), destroying telephone lines. There were also plans to destroy power supplies and to attack German ammunition dumps, fuel depots and command posts. Some of these plans went active in the weeks leading up to the invasion.

As the anticipated Allied invasion approached, more and more French citizens listened to the radio news in the hope of hearing the message that would change everything. Tuning into the BBC had been banned in the early days of the war by the Germans, but many Frenchmen still kept a set hidden away and listened to the news despite the Germans' jamming or disturbance of the frequency and the risk of arrest that tuning in brought. The famous first notes of Beethoven's Fifth Symphony (representing the Morse 'dot dot dot dash' of V for Victory) could still be heard through the worst jamming and gave hope to those waiting. The message would be the signal for the resistance to strike a series of pre-arranged targets including bridges, railways and roads. Their aim would be to slow and try to stop the German reinforcements heading to Allied landing beaches.

However, spring 1944 also brought news of a resistance defeat. The battle of Glières, which had consisted of several skirmishes, had ended – and the Germans had won. The mountainous Glières Plateau near Lake Annecy had been in a state of siege since January, and anyone found to be helping the Maquis or bearing arms risked arrest and execution. Several parachute drops containing Bren and Sten guns as well as grenades had been made, but it was not enough; in late March, 4,000 Germans armed with heavy machine guns, mortars and armoured cars took on the Maquis, who were outnumbered and overpowered. In the following days 121 Maquisards were found dead – killed in the skirmishes or executed by Germans. Those who were taken prisoner were either executed or deported. While the sad episode underlined that resistance groups were not strong enough to take on regular German forces and needed heavier weapons, propaganda turned the defeat into a victory, giving a much-needed boost to the reputation of the resistance for its bravery and devotion to the liberation of France.

In the run-up to D-Day, the indomitable Pearl Witherington and her Maquis undertook work of great value to the Allies, blowing up 800 stretches of railway lines and supply routes. As the Allies advanced out of Normandy after the invasion in central France, 18,000 Germans gave themselves up as POWs to the WRESTLER network, of which Pearl was the leader. She was a wanted woman, and such was her success that a 1 million franc bounty was placed on her head by the Germans.

Born in Paris on 24 June 1914, Pearl was the eldest of four daughters of an expatriate English couple. Her childhood was far from easy, and in 1930 her father succumbed to drink, meaning that Pearl had to go and work as a secretary to make sure the family had food on the table. She had been employed as a short-hand typist to the air attaché at the British embassy in Paris, but, when France fell and the diplomats departed, she was left with little work. By December 1940, Pearl and her family decided it was time to get out of France. The lengthy journey was demoralising. They spent three months in Marseille and three more in Lisbon, but Pearl's determination and drive ensured that they eventually made it to the United Kingdom on Bastille Day 1941, and she was anxious to do something worthwhile.

Pearl took a job at the Air Ministry in London, but found it tedious and dull, wanting instead to go back and help France. She recalled later that 'deep down inside me I'm a very shy person but I've always had a lot of responsibilities ever since I was quite small. So I thought, well, this is something I feel I can do . . . and anyway I didn't like the Germans. Never did. I'm a baby of the 1914–18 war.'[2] She was put forward for an interview with SOE and, after making quite an impression on Buckmaster (who said it seemed to be her who interviewed him), she was accepted and started training in April 1943, arriving in France five months later.

On the night of 22 September 1943, after two failed attempts, Pearl parachuted into the STATIONER network in the Valençay–Issoudun–Châteauroux triangle. She landed between two lakes and an electricity pylon, but her suitcase slipped beneath the water. She spent the next three weeks with hardly any clothes to wear, borrowing her colleague's pyjamas when she did her laundry.[3] Following this unorthodox start to her mission as courier to the STATIONER network of Maurice Southgate, Pearl was joined by her fiancé, Henri Cornioley, and they proved to be a formidable duo. Pearl's particular role was to act as liaison officer and courier to a Maquis group in the Puy-de-Dôme area, a role in which she faced unexpected challenges. On one occasion, she had to cycle 80 km to deliver a message, only to find on her return journey that one of the bridges she had to cross was heavily guarded; rather than risking going through the checkpoint, she waded across the freezing River Cher with her bicycle on her shoulders.

A part of Pearl's job was to share the workload of Jacqueline Nearne, who had been in the field since January 1943, also working as a courier for Southgate. Born in May 1916 in Brighton, Jacqueline was the eldest daughter and second of the four children of John Francis Nearn (later Nearne), a chemist's dispenser, and his wife Mariquit (née de Plazaola), a French national of Spanish descent.

In 1923 Jacqueline moved to France with her parents and siblings Frederick, Francis and Eileen; the latter two also joined SOE, though Francis did not pass his training. Educated in England until the age of 7 and then in France, Jacqueline became a travelling sales representative for an office equipment company based in Nice, and as a result saw much of the country.

In 1940, feeling upset and betrayed at France's surrender to the Germans, Jacqueline and her sister left France for Britain via Portugal and Gibraltar. Jacqueline attempted to join the Women's Royal Naval Service, but was disappointed to find out that they only needed drivers, and as she had never driven in the blackout she did not have the right experience. In June 1942 she received an invitation for interview from Selwyn Jepson; she was taken on by SOE and joined the FANY.

Jacqueline had lived in Nice and Pas-de-Calais before the war, but this time she was bound for the STATIONER circuit, where she landed on 25 January 1943 alongside her circuit leader Maurice Southgate. This circuit covered the south and centre of France, from Châteauroux to the foothills of the Pyrenees. Her field name was the same as her own, Jacqueline, and her cover story was that of a chemist's representative of no fixed abode. Times were hard in occupied France; people were wary of strangers and as such Jacqueline found it difficult to get a room in which to live. First of all she went to Clermont-Ferrand, where she used the home of the Nerault family in the rue Blatin as her base for five or six months, but spent a great deal of her time travelling. She stayed for a few days in a hotel in Châteauroux, where the circuit's radio operator was based, and by August she had settled in a room in the town of La Souterraine.

Jacqueline's work involved liaising with people across a very wide area so she frequently travelled by train via Paris as well as directly to Châteauroux, Tarbes, Clermont-Ferrand and Poitiers. She reported that some lines were more straightforward to travel on than others; for example, the Paris line was 'easy', but one had to be on one's guard if travelling to Poitiers as the Germans would often 'choose one person in each compartment who has to be searched'.[4] On the occasion of one search she saw a woman handing over her bag and knew from then that she had to be especially careful, advising others 'not to carry papers etc. in their wallets, as they are likely to be searched when they are not expecting it'. Jacqueline was renowned among her resistance colleagues for being bright and quick-witted. She evaded these checks time after time, displaying her 'coolness and courage', but it must have been a nerve-wracking experience watching someone being scrutinised and searched, knowing all the while it could have been her.[5] At least Jacqueline could be assured of one thing: her papers were real and, should she ever be stopped, she would have confidence in them.

Jacqueline was never questioned or arrested by the Germans but she was interrogated by a French police inspector, who came to her hotel room in Châteauroux three weeks after her arrival in France: 'an inspector came to the hotel at 12 a.m. ... and asked her for her papers'. Fortunately she had obtained her genuine card the previous day. She said she was en route from Toulouse to Clermont-Ferrand and had stopped at Châteauroux to visit some friends. He did not press the point but instead asked her about Southgate; she told him Southgate's cover story and he went away. The following day at 6 a.m. another French inspector came; this time Jacqueline pretended to 'be very sleepy' and he left her alone. Jacqueline warned Southgate that someone had been asking after him and he stopped using the hotel in case they should come back for him.[6]

Both Jacqueline and Southgate were well known for being security conscious, particularly when in the presence of the Germans. A growing concern was the rise in the number of *rafles*, or round-ups. Jacqueline reported that agents should be very careful, especially in cafés when their guard was down and they might be inclined to forget the security measures. There were a good number of informers and no one could ever be sure in whom they could put their trust; for the right money, an agent could be turned over to the authorities in an instant.[7] Her attention to security and to detail was exemplary and it was said that she 'ensured perfect liaison in her large and important circuit and at no time endangered its security'.[8]

She was also involved in parachute drops, which showed Southgate's immense trust in her. He was very particular about who he would and would not use on these hugely risky nights; he only made use of people outside the organisation when it was necessary, and not at all if the reception was a small one.[9] Jacqueline did not experience many difficulties with receptions, although on one occasion they were expecting three containers when four arrived, meaning that one had to be left behind as there were not enough people to help move it. Unfortunately, the committee discovered that it had been picked up by the Gestapo when they returned to collect it the following month; luckily, they were not caught, but the ground was *brûlé* (burnt) and unusable from then on. This meant yet another task for Jacqueline: finding new drop zones, which was both time-consuming and frustrating. Although her work was varied, it could be tedious and it could be dangerous, yet she always buckled down to the job in hand.

As the heavy workload and constant travel across the huge geographical area of STATIONER began to take its toll on Jacqueline, Pearl arrived to share the courier responsibilities. The arrangement worked well until 9 April 1944, when Jacqueline returned to England to recover from exhaustion after fourteen months in the field. Two days later the circuit received a new wireless operator, Odette Wilen.

Odette Victoria Sar was born on 25 April 1919. Her mother was French and her father was Czech, but she became a naturalised British citizen and subsequently joined the RAF. In June 1940 Odette married Dennis Wilen, a Finnish RAF pilot instructor, but he was killed only two years later aged 27 in a flying accident. It was as a war widow that Odette had begun her work for F Section in April 1943, serving as a conducting officer to four FANY students. She also undertook wireless training in addition to her own duties. In February 1944 she volunteered to become an agent in the field, possibly to avenge the premature death of her husband, and underwent the relevant training. But her French was poor: although she had a sound knowledge of the language, she spoke it with an English accent and had a tendency to mix up her vocabulary and genders. Her lack of language skills was made up for by her intelligence and patriotism, although she was reputedly terrified at the prospect of going to France – perhaps rightly so: the odds seemed stacked against her as she received approximately half of the training she should have had as she was so urgently needed across the Channel.

She landed in the Auvergne, in the south-west of France, where she soon confessed to Pearl, with whom she done some of her training, that she did not know her codes. Pearl was furious and told Southgate 'you can't keep her, it is too dangerous'.[10] On her first night they put her to the test and 'she proved to be useless as a wireless operator'.[11] Southgate sent a report to F Section, saying it was impossible to keep Odette in their circuit; her inexperience and lack of training meant that she was unsuitable as a wireless operator and they had neither the time nor resources to invest in her. London decided that she could be courier to the LABOURER circuit near La Châtre, south of Bourges.

It is probable that this transfer to LABOURER was Odette's own suggestion, since she and LABOURER's circuit leader, Marcel Leccia, had met at an SOE Finishing School and had immediately struck up a romantic liaison. Once reunited in France they became engaged within days. But tragedy was to strike when Leccia and his two comrades were betrayed by a Nazi sympathiser. They were arrested by the Gestapo and Leccia was tortured. He was eventually murdered at Buchenwald concentration camp in September 1944. Leccia's sister, Mimi, was able to prevent Odette from being arrested: she ran to Odette's safe house and led her to safety just moments before the Gestapo arrived.

Odette contacted Virginia Hall for help, but she 'had no use for her in her circuit' and so Odette began the long journey home, on foot.[12] She crossed the Pyrenees with the help of escape line guide Santiago Strugo Garay, on whom she made quite an impression. Arriving back in England via Gibraltar, Odette found she was no longer needed by F Section, although Buckmaster said that she had 'at all times proved extremely reliable and hard-working'. He released her to work for the FANY and she ended the war working in Belgium.[13]

Meanwhile, Pearl and Southgate had continued to work well together. With D-Day only a few months away, the risks of capture were greater than ever, especially as Southgate now had a price on his head. The workload was vast and Southgate found himself having to arrange numerous reception committees, fetch and relocate other agents, keep in close contact with his lieutenants and equip Maquis units in anticipation of the Allied landings. In April, Southgate reported having 2,500 men under his control. Then, on

1 May, while visiting his new wireless operator, René Mathieu, in Montluçon, Southgate missed the prearranged signal showing that the house was unsafe. Exhausted by the demands of his responsibilities, he walked straight into a Gestapo trap and was arrested.

It was also in preparation for D-Day that 21-year-old Anne-Marie Walters was dropped into the Armagnac region on 4 January 1944, becoming one of SOE's youngest and brightest agents. Born on 16 March 1923 in Geneva, her father was in the secretariat at the League of Nations and Anne-Marie was educated at Ecole Guibert and then the international school (Ecolint) in Geneva, where she played an active part in school life, including editing the Ecolint journal.

Once war had broken out, the sense of danger became more imminent and the family decided to leave Geneva on 25 May 1940 and make their way to England. The whole family, along with their pet dog, Micky, got as far as Hendaye in south-west France, where they waited several tense days for a ship to take them away from continental Europe. Eventually, they managed to board a liner that been diverted from its journey to India to pick up refugees; no dogs were allowed, however, and Micky was left behind as the ship pulled away and the Walters made good their escape.[14]

Although still only 17 years old in 1940, Anne-Marie immediately volunteered for the WAAF, and was accepted, serving as a plotter in Fighter Command's headquarters at Bentley Priory in Middlesex. A year later she was recruited by SOE and by November 1943 she was waiting for the next full moon to take her to France.[15] In December 1943 Anne-Marie's first attempt to parachute was aborted due to inclement weather. On returning to England the aircraft crash-landed, killing three crew members and injuring three others; Anne-Marie suffered a minor head injury and her companion Claude Arnault emerged from the wreckage unhurt but undoubtedly very shaken up. The fact she was prepared to try again a month later was a credit to her bravery and *sang-froid*. Fortunately, the second flight was successful and, in January 1944, she and Arnault parachuted into the Armagnac area of south-western France where she became a courier to the WHEELWRIGHT circuit, working for George Starr alongside his wireless operator Yvonne Cormeau. Her instructions from F Section were that her work must be straightforward and limited to tasks that would not affect anyone else's safety or security. These were adhered to, much to Anne-Marie's disdain.

Her post-operation report states that 'as a rule [she was] not allowed to act on [her] own initiative', that her work was 'not particularly difficult nor particularly interesting' and that Starr 'objected to sending her on "risky jobs"'.[16] Her attitude towards her work becomes clear as the report develops. She was unimpressed with the mundane nature of her role and clearly felt that she was being under-utilised: 'I kept on travelling at irregular intervals to the different sectors of my circuits; Dordogne, Lot et Garonne, Gers, Hautes Pyrénées and Haute-Garonne. I carried London's orders to the various regional chiefs under Starr – also BBC messages, D-Day action, demolitions orders, A and B messages, money, letters etc. I travelled by bus, train, bicycle or taxi . . . the main fighting I did was getting onto buses, which was no small enterprise.'[17] Anne-Marie's dissatisfaction with her work is evident: she clearly felt that she should have been given more to do and been allowed to work on her own initiative.

Eventually, she impressed Starr just enough that he gave her more independence, allowing her to work with his assistant Claude Arnault in the Pyrenees sector. There she assisted with 'fixing up depots, instruction, carrying explosive around', as well as assisting on a local escape line, getting people known to the Gestapo and Allied airmen out of danger.[18]

Starr was critical of Anne-Marie and clearly did not like her, accusing her of wearing 'high Paris fashion' that made her stand out, when he believed a courier should be inconspicuous.[19] On 31 July Starr sent a message to SOE HQ: 'Have had to send Colette [Walters] back because she is undisciplined in spite of my efforts to train her since arrival. Most indiscreet. Very man-mad, also disobedient . . . totally unsuitable for commission, she must never be sent back to France to work for our organisation.' He did also say that she had courage and never hesitated to undertake any mission on which he sent her.[20] She left France and travelled through Spain to Algiers, where it was proposed by SOE's 'Massingham' mission that she should return to France to work with for Operation 'Jedburgh'. SOE refused to allow her to return to France and ordered her back to London.

On her return she was interviewed by Vera Atkins, who found her to be 'in a highly excitable and unsatisfactory frame of mind. She seems to have an idea of the unfavourable reports received by us and is in a most aggressive mood.'[21] She also wrote a report in which she said that Starr had accused her of having an affair with a member of the circuit and of spreading stories that he was having an affair with a female SOE agent. He also had her thrown into prison 'with captured miliciens and collaborators (including their fleas and lice) and a guard was ordered to sleep by my side . . . the whole Maquis knew of this and decided I must be a Gestapo double agent.'[22] She added that Starr had a Russian bodyguard who 'carried out absolutely horrible tortures on captured miliciens', which, she said, lowered them to the same standards of the Gestapo.

In September 1944, Starr returned to London and in a lecture that he gave to an SOE training establishment in October/November 1944 he recounted 'with relish' an incident of torture in which he had been involved. The allegations that he had boasted about acts of brutality being carried out by his group caused consternation to his SOE contemporaries, but they concluded that he could not be blamed for acts committed by the French resistance. Anne-Marie's additional accusations of mistreatment led to an inquiry in February 1945, with testimony from Anne-Marie, Starr and others. The conclusion, on 28 February, of the 'rather perfunctory court of enquiry' was that 'there is no justification whatever for any imputation against Lt. Col. Starr of inhumanity or cruel treatment to any prisoner at any time under his control or under the control of troops or resistance forces under his immediate command or control.'[23] The matter was closed and Anne-Marie only returned to France in 1946 to marry her childhood sweetheart.

In the spring of 1944, Julienne Aisner, Jean Besnard and their wireless operator, André Watt, became aware that they had been compromised and needed to get out of Paris. It was too late to leave that day and so they waited until 'early the next morning, we hear five o'clock strike with relief', she said, each 'leaves on his own, without luggage and will meet that evening in a safe house in the suburbs'.[24]

They all made it safely to the rendezvous, which was the home of Julienne's cousin. At 6 a.m. the next morning they met at the Gare de l'Est in a state of high alert, all believing that they had been followed several times. They made it safely out of Paris and were put up in a safe house in Troyes which was being used as an arms cache. There were 'grenades on the night stand, [a] revolver in the drawer, a sub machine gun under the bed and a basement stuffed with munitions', Julienne later remembered.[25] Watt made contact with London, and they were advised to travel to Amboise and be ready to leave by Lysander in the April moon period. They travelled in a fifth-class compartment equipped with several bottles of wine and three dozen hard-boiled eggs, so as to avoid unnecessary stops in cafés or restaurants. On the night of 5/6 April the coded confirmation message was received via the *Messages Personnels*: 'Message from Colonel Ronchonneau: when three firemen meet two artillery men.'[26] This signalled the arrival of two Lysanders bearing four agents into the field. Julienne, Besnard and Watt left France safely and, just three weeks later, Besnard and Julienne were married. Despite her wish to return to France, Julienne accepted that they were *brûlé* and all they could do was wait for the liberation.[27]

As France prepared itself for the Allied invasion, Yvonne Fontaine, Lilian Rolfe, Violette Szabó, Maureen 'Paddy' O'Sullivan and Eileen 'Didi' Nearne were infiltrated. Born in 1921 and educated in a French convent school, Eileen was a devout Catholic and wanted to train to become a beautician. She was also the sister of one of SOE's most respected women, Jacqueline Nearne, but was five years younger and had a very different personality. She liked to be with people but was equally content to busy herself in her own company and, although lively and enthusiastic, she also had a serious side.[28] Jacqueline had been very insistent that her sister should not join the SOE, telling her that there was an age restriction and she was too young to join; she then begged Vera Atkins and Buckmaster to promise not to take Eileen on. She stressed to them that her sister was immature and had led a sheltered life; she was unworldly as well as stubborn and lacked the experience necessary to be a good and safe agent. She thought that Eileen would see the role 'through rose tinted glasses and that when faced with the reality of the situation she might find herself out of her depth – and by then it would be too late'.[29] Jacqueline was far happier that Eileen stick to her role in the FANY at a listening station and see the war out safely at home.

However, Eileen was asked to attend an SOE interview. She soon realised that her sister had been asked to go back to France to undertake clandestine work and wanted to undertake the same role, demonstrating her knowledge of France and French. Jepson was reluctant to send her to France but offered her work as either a wireless operator or decoder working in England. In 1943 Eileen became a cipher clerk at Grendon Underwood, an SOE/FANY listening station for coded messages from British agents abroad, but she found the work monotonous and soon applied again to become an agent in France.[30]

Her application was timely as Buckmaster needed agents, and Eileen's knowledge of French, France and Morse code was exactly what was required. Unaware that her sister had asked Buckmaster to keep her in England, Eileen was finally accepted for training, some of which was undertaken at Beaulieu while the rest concentrated on wireless operation as well as the security aspects of her new role. Her sister's words were echoed when an instructor considered that she was not suitable for work 'in any capacity on account of her lack of experience'.[31]

However, against all this advice Eileen arrived by Lysander on 2/3 March 1944 to work as a wireless operator for the WIZARD circuit in Paris. She recalled the emotion she felt at seeing the lights of the reception committee: 'she then heard two voices speaking with Parisian accents asking "Are you OK? We have to move quickly to avoid getting caught."' They crossed the countryside by cart, pistols at the ready. She found a house in Bourg-la-Reine, south of Paris, for the radio transmissions, contacting WIZARD's circuit leader, William Savy, twice daily, a man she described as a 'plucky Frenchman' whom she was 'proud to work for'.[32]

Eileen was vigilant and constantly on the look-out for the Gestapo. If she believed that she was being followed she would about-turn or duck into a shop, and she tried to avoid places where she knew Germans would be. When travelling by train, she headed for compartments that were already full, rather than risk an empty one filling up with Germans who might quiz her or ask her awkward questions.

Savy was working tirelessly in readiness for D-Day, preparing messages for Eileen to send to England and trying to keep the circuit running financially and logistically. When he discovered the whereabouts of a large 'secret ammunition dump in the stone quarries at St Leu d'Esserent ... and its content: 2,000 V-1 rockets ready to fire', he requested to be sent to England in order to relay the information in person; it was too sensitive to be shared via wireless.[33] As a result of this information the site was attacked by RAF Bomber Command in July 1944.

Just before Savy left, another wireless operator, Jean Gerard Maury, had been dropped into the WIZARD circuit. With no circuit leader, there were no messages to send and, as a result, there was virtually nothing to do. After a few days Eileen and Maury were transferred to the SPIRITUALIST circuit (also in Paris) meaning there was minimal disruption to their routines. The circuit leader, René Dumont-Guillemet, was a man of action and he had been given several tasks, including arranging a mass break-out from Fresnes prison (which was eventually deemed impossible) and kidnapping a V-1 rocket engineer (who was relocated before they could get to him). Despite her move to a new circuit, Eileen had decided to continue transmitting her wireless messages from the same safe house she had used for WIZARD at Bourg-la-Reine. She had noticed a gradual rise in the number of Germans in the area, as well as an increase in D/F vans. Realising that she was in more danger than ever before, Dumont-Guillement found her new rooms in the western suburbs of Paris at Le Vésinet. Nevertheless, she continued to return to the old house, risking her own safety and that of everyone around her. By now, she had been operational for four months and had sent 105 messages, but her reluctance to move to her new safe house was to prove extremely costly.

Maureen Patricia 'Paddy' O'Sullivan was dropped to the FIREMAN circuit near Limoges a few weeks after Eileen's arrival on 22/23 March 1944. Born in Dublin in 1918, Paddy began her education at St Louis Convent. At 7 years of age she went to live with an aunt in Belgium, where she attended a convent school in Coutrain, then the Athénée Royal in Ostend.

At the beginning of the war she was working as a nurse at Highgate Hospital, London. She left to begin her WAAF service in July 1943 and was based at RAF Compton Bassett. F Section recruited her due to her fluency in French, and their instructors described her as 'pleasant' and 'intelligent' as well as 'more of a boy than a girl' and, somewhat crassly, as a 'tough type of woman' who was 'growing quite a successful moustache'.[34] Despite finding the going very difficult, Paddy worked hard at her wireless training and became a fully fledged wireless operator at a time when they were critically needed to maintain close contact with F Section in the run-up to D-Day.

She was dropped, along with two cases of personal belongings, two wireless sets and twenty-two containers, into the northern Creuse area near Le Bourg. Landing on her back, Paddy thought for a moment that she must have broken her neck and lost consciousness; she came to as she felt someone's breath on her face. In a panic, she believed it was a German looming over her and was relieved to discover that it was a friendly cow. Her fall had been cushioned by a money belt containing 2 million francs so she was not hurt too badly. Having landed half a kilometre from her correct drop zone, Paddy set off to find her reception committee – who were somewhat surprised to see a woman as, judging by her name, they were expecting a man. Any disappointment was abated when they found all the containers she had brought with her.

Her circuit leader, Edmund Mayer (known in the field as 'Barthélemy'), was not impressed that London had sent him a woman. He was 'dubious of taking the responsibility of hiding a woman and considered the job too tough for a girl'.[35] With her good looks, blonde hair and blue eyes he was concerned Paddy would not pass off as French. She told him they would just have to 'make the best of it'.[36] Based in Limoges, a town that was humming with German activity, the pair moved from safe house to safe house and travelled almost continuously for the next few weeks. The easiest means of transport in occupied France was the bicycle, but Paddy did not know how to ride one; 'she was obliged to learn' and did so 'in front of a squad of Germans who were drilling'. Two of her comrades sat her on the bike and pushed her off, and every time she fell off 'the Germans roared with laughter'.[37] Once she had mastered it she rode up to '50km every day collecting and delivering messages'.[38]

Mayer felt that Paddy's wireless work was not good enough; he believed that she had not been fully trained and was 'inadequately prepared for her role'. As far as he was concerned, 'the technical training she received was [also] very much below par and her knowledge even in simple matters ... was very scanty'. He also said that 'she had received absolutely no training in that all-important matter of security'. Paddy observed this too, saying that if it had not been for Mayer she would have slipped up many times. She was a heavy smoker and, given most French women in her area did not smoke, 'it would have looked very suspicious if informant [Paddy] had smoked too much in public places'. Her lack of security training was a 'considerable source of trouble and worry' for Mayer.

He was so concerned about her safety and reliability that he looked around for another wireless operator to act as a stand-by in case anything should happen to her. To add to his concerns, he also discovered that, before she had come to France, Paddy had been in hospital with lung problems, and continued to suffer, to some degree, with chronic bronchitis. It did not affect her work, but he rightly worried that she might fall ill and have to be hospitalised in France, which would have caused numerous security issues for all concerned.[39] Paddy's security improved considerably, however, and she proved so efficient that when, after six weeks, Baker Street sent a message saying they had two men available and Paddy could be sent home, Mayer replied, 'having trained her, I will keep her'.[40]

Paddy sent over 300 messages and, in the run-up to D-Day, sent up to seven skeds (scheduled transmissions) a day, using her code poem, which she had learnt by heart, as her cipher, making coding quicker and easier. She had seven wireless sets distributed in different houses, some of them buried or hidden under piles of sticks. She always used a look-out to make sure she was as safe as she could possibly be. In one house, the owner kept her own wireless on in the next room to drown out the tapping from Paddy's Morse key. In another house, La Fôret, the daughter of the owner would sing to warn of potential danger, and in yet another the gate was always on the latch so Paddy could hear it being opened.

Mayer changed his opinion of Paddy and was pleased with her work, writing that 'if communications have been so successful on the whole the credit is down to her patience and determination to make a success of the job, her untiring efforts and hard work'. Her 'willingness to take advice' saw her through and she became a 'first class W/T operator who could be entirely trusted to carry out her job thoroughly, and all the credit for that is entirely due to herself'. Paddy also found time to train two other locally recruited wireless operators and became a highly valued member of the team.[41] She said, 'I was terribly frightened at times, but there was a wonderful spirit of sharing danger with men of the highest order of courage, which made it a privilege to work for them.'[42]

On 25 March, two days after Paddy had been infiltrated, Yvonne Fontaine arrived by a Royal Navy motor gunboat on a Brittany beach. Born in August 1913, she was 'twice married, once divorced'; her second husband, an Italian, had disappeared, which 'she was not unhappy about'.[43] Yvonne had worked in the resistance before going to England to undergo SOE training, carrying out courier duties for SOE agent Ben Cowburn in the Troyes area since the autumn of 1942. She had helped organise the evacuation of twenty US airmen who had been shot down, assisted in providing safe houses for resistance workers and SOE agents, and allowed her flat to be used for meetings. She was also a courier for a circuit in the Aube department, one of the most effective groups in northern France, carrying compromising papers between members. She was employed as manageress of a dyeing and dry cleaning works that dyed the fabric for German uniforms, but when the Gestapo began to suspect her of clandestine work she rapidly found the means to leave France in November 1943. She then undertook formal SOE training, returning to the field on 23 March 1944.[44]

When Yvonne returned to France, she worked as part of the MINISTER circuit under the leadership of Pierre Mulsant, a good friend who had also worked for Ben Cowburn before leaving for training in England. Returning to France by parachute earlier in March, Mulsant had set about developing MINISTER south-east of Paris, in the Seine-et-Marne department, with Yvonne as his courier. In April and May 1944 five arms drops brought them sixty containers, the contents of which Yvonne then helped transport to safe places for storage and distribution when needed. She was also instructed in various sabotage techniques and undertook intelligence work in preparation for the forthcoming Allied invasion.

On another spring night in 1944 one of SOE's most famous female agents arrived in France. Violette Szabó was familiar with the country having spent much of her childhood there. Her parents had met while her father was serving in the British Army in France during the Great War. In 1931, the family, which by then included four brothers for Violette, moved to Brixton in south London. At the age of 14 Violette left school and, hating the job she found herself in, went to stay with her aunt in France. Upon her return she worked in various roles, including as a sales assistant at Woolworths. By 1939 Violette was working in the Bon Marché department store where she sold perfume. In 1940 she joined the Women's Land Army and then took work in a munitions factory in London.

That summer her mother asked her to go out and find a French soldier to come and spend Bastille Day with the family. While searching for a suitable candidate in the centre of London, Violette met Étienne Szabó, a sergeant major in the French Foreign Legion. After courting for just five weeks they married on 21 August 1940 and had only one week's honeymoon before Étienne was posted overseas. Violette took a temporary job as a Post

Office telephonist and waited over a year before Étienne returned to England on leave. Again, they had only a week together, but during that brief time Violette revealed that she wanted to join the women's forces and that she had set her heart on volunteering for the ATS, the women's branch of the British Army. Although Étienne would have supported her so she would not have to work, in September 1941 Violette joined the ATS with the rank of private.[45]

After training, in December 1941 Violette was posted as a gunner to a heavy anti-aircraft battery. But just a few weeks later, she discovered she was pregnant, and, released from the ATS, she returned to her parents' south London home before finding a rented flat in Notting Hill. In June 1942 she gave birth to her daughter, Tania, in a local hospital.[46] With a return to the ATS in mind, Violette left Tania in the care of her parents in Stockwell and a friend in Mill Hill, and waited for Étienne to come home again on leave to see his daughter. But in October the terrible news came that Étienne had been killed at Qaret el Himeimat, south of El Alamein. Violette was devastated; she and Étienne had still been in the heady early days of their romance and now would never have the chance to enjoy a happy, settled marriage. She was heartbroken, too, that Tania would never meet her father. It heightened Violette's desire to contribute to the war in order to avenge her loss – a desire already stoked by the fact that her grandparents and aunt were living under occupation in Picardy.

In 1943, at 22 years of age, Violette was invited to attend an interview at the Ministry of Pensions in London. Believing the meeting to concern her late husband, she soon realised that that was a cover to get her there. It was an interview for SOE, conducted by Jepson.

After her training, Violette was flown into France by Lysander on 5/6 April 1944, arriving near the village of Azay-le-Rideau.[47] She was with Philippe Liewer, also known as 'Staunton', who had already served in France. When his SALESMAN circuit was compromised in February 1944, he had managed to avoid the wave of arrests and had escaped to England. His latest mission, with Violette nominally working as his courier, was to investigate what remained of his earlier circuit in Rouen. The pair made their way to Paris, where Liewer remained, as it was too dangerous for him to go any further. Violette continued alone to Rouen, where she saw 'Wanted' posters with Liewer's image and a reward for his arrest.[48] She ripped one off the wall and hid it in her bag so that she could show him. Its presence would have been difficult to explain had she been searched at any point; luckily, she was not.

Violette's job was to follow the trails of those agents and resistance workers who had been arrested a few weeks before and to visit those who were still active, gathering what information she could.[49] For the next three weeks, she attempted to untangle the situation in Rouen, visiting numerous houses and apartments and trying to ascertain what had happened to their occupants. She soon came to the conclusion that nearly 100 resisters and agents had been arrested and that SALESMAN was *brûlé*. Among the arrested were Liewer's lieutenant, Claude Malraux, who had fallen into a Gestapo trap in February; his wireless operator, Isidore Newman, who had been arrested at the end of March; and Roger Mayer, who was severely beaten by the Gestapo but had not given away any names or addresses. All three men were subsequently deported to Germany.[50]

Having discovered everything she could, Violette travelled by train to Paris to rendezvous with Liewer and tell him all she had learnt. They returned to England by Lysander from a landing ground near Châteauroux on 30 April. The plane was piloted by Flight Lieutenant Robert 'Bob' Large and as it made its way over France it was hit by flak. Lysanders flew with specific weight restrictions and needed a great deal of fine tuning to fly well, and so now the aircraft became very difficult to control. Lurching and unwieldy, the engine grumbling, somehow Large managed to get the Lysander to the English coast and to land successfully. To Violette it felt like they had crash-landed. When she climbed out of the aircraft she was shaken and unsure of where she was. In the dark, she saw a man dressed in a uniform with a mop of blonde hair and assumed the worst: that he was German and they had been shot down over France. With a fire in her eyes, she rushed to attack him, realising at the final moment that he was wearing an RAF uniform and was, in fact, their pilot. With an affectionate twinkle in his eye, Large recalled that 'if she had had a gun she would have shot me'.[51] Instead, realising he was friend, not foe, she smothered him in hugs and kisses to thank him for his skill and courage at getting them home safely. Violette's first mission had been such a success that she was confirmed as an ensign in the FANY and asked to wait while preparations were made for her re-entry into the field.

Lilian Rolfe, who was infiltrated on the same day as Violette, began her mission as wireless operator to the HISTORIAN circuit, where her main task was to secure radio links in an area that covered Orléans, Montargis and Nangis. While awaiting her first orders she got to know the surrounding area by establishing her cycling routes and making contact with the local Maquis. Lilian possessed excellent wireless skills, and the sixty-seven messages she sent to England were consistently accurate, in spite of the fact that the area was constantly under the observation of the Gestapo, who were listening out for illegal wireless signals or unusual activity. Her messages enabled the Maquis at Loiret to receive substantial supplies of arms, ammunition, money and clothes which, in turn, enabled the organisation to build up to 'maximum strength and to carry out some important actions'.[52]

Wireless operators were crucial in the build-up to D-Day to maintain contacts with SOE HQ and organise the vital parachute drops. Another wireless operator, Muriel Byck, arrived on the night of 8/9 April 1944 to serve the VENTRILOQUIST circuit in the Orléans–Blois area, under the leadership of Philippe de Vomécourt. Born in June 1918 and of Jewish heritage, Muriel (who was fluent in French and Russian) was brought up in Germany and France before moving to England in 1930. She worked as a secretary in London as well as in a theatre, but when war broke out Muriel's strong sense of duty drew her to voluntary work in the Red Cross, Women's Voluntary Service and as an ARP (Air Raid Precautions) warden in Torquay. Muriel joined the WAAF as a clerk in December 1942, pending a commission. She was recruited into F Section in July 1943 because of her excellent French and began initial training in September 1943, during which time she became engaged to 2nd Lieutenant Maurice Martin, an American in the OSS.

As a wireless operator in France, Muriel undertook an extremely dangerous role, but as a Jew she was doubly at risk from the Nazis if either of her identities were uncovered. Her task was not only to act as HISTORIAN's wireless operator, but also to instruct on coding, supply London with the details of new recruits and establish 'post boxes' for contacts. VENTRILOQUIST had four transmitters in different locations covering a wide area which were constantly moved so as to avoid D/Fing. During her active service in the field Muriel sent twenty-seven messages and received sixteen. Her security was said to have been excellent, she never used the same set consecutively or at the same hour on any day, and could be seen 'rushing from location to location' where 'she would encode, send, receive and decode messages, always on schedule, and, on her own initiative, often do this for other circuits as well, so messages would not ever be delayed. She also acted as a courier, alerting sabotage teams over a wide area.'[53]

Unsurprisingly Muriel grew tired, her nerves began to fray and she became increasingly on edge. An Allied bombing raid on the nearby German ammunition dump at Michenon in early May left her shaken, and gradually her health began to deteriorate until she eventually collapsed. A hospital was a place that résistants and agents generally tried to avoid, as they were continually watched by the Nazis and any member of the staff could be a collaborator. It was especially dangerous for Muriel as she was delirious, and might blurt something out or speak in English which would give her away in an instant. But she needed medical attention and de Vomécourt stayed by her side in the ambulance and at the hospital.

SOE historian M.R.D. Foot maintained that the shock of the bombing raid on Michenon caused this breakdown in her health, but the attending doctor diagnosed meningitis and she was immediately hospitalised in Romorantin under a false name. An operation was undertaken to try to save Muriel's life, but it was too late. With D-Day only a matter of days away, de Vomécourt remained by her bedside, willing her to recover, but to no avail. She died in his arms on the evening of 23 May, aged 25. She was buried under a false name in a zinc coffin, placed temporarily in a vault so that it would be possible to transport her body to Britain after the war.[54]

Lise de Baissac also arrived in France in early April (9/10), for her second mission. Tony Brooks of PIMENTO had requested a female courier, 'someone first class', mature and plain in appearance. 'He wanted someone who had been trained at Beaulieu, could handle verbal or written messages, possessed prior operational experience and would hold no allegiance other than to himself.'[55]

Unable to parachute due to her prior injury, Lise came by Lysander to a STATIONER reception and, after waiting a day for a train, arrived in Montauban. Her first rendezvous did not go well: she was wearing Parisian fashion, which made her stand out, and then forgot the password. When she met Brooks later that day she commented that 'he seemed very surprised to see me and made me understand straight away that I was not the person that he wanted'. In spite of this the two agreed to start work as soon as possible.[56] Over dinner that night Brooks concluded that Lise was not what he wanted in a courier, especially with regard to her demeanour and appearance.

Lise, too, was unhappy with the situation in which she found herself, especially when Brooks informed her that her work would be limited to passing information between various groups once a week and collecting papers to be delivered to an agent called 'Julien'. Lise told Brooks that F Section had given her the impression that she would be taking over the Lyon branch of his circuit as its leader, rather than simply working as his courier; instead, she was to become nothing more than a 'mailman', which she 'found less than amusing', but she agreed nevertheless to do Brooks's work to the best of her ability, although it was not to her liking.[57] Also, Lise did not sympathise with the circuit's socialist leanings, making her feelings known when she enquired if SOE should really be arming them at all.[58] She later said she found the environment 'totally alien' to her.[59]

Over the course of the next week, Lise focused her energies on finding her brother Claude, who had also just returned to France for his second mission.[60] In her absence, Brooks ascertained that the dislike of Lise spread across the whole circuit. She had made it clear that the work was not 'sufficiently important' for her, she turned her nose up at 'eating with a worker or sleeping on the floor ... she wants to know and do everything' other than her actual job, and what she really wanted was to 'run an organization and give orders'. One member expressed his disdain by saying she would never be allowed to cross his threshold again.[61]

Brooks sent a message to London: 'I feel that Marguerite [Lise] is not exactly the kind of person we need'; she found the work was not 'sufficiently important' and would prefer something with 'responsibility', and 'to be able to do something worthwhile'. A second message reiterated this, as well as suggesting that 'she found the work strenuous and not in the least interesting due to my security measures'. He also reported that his group leaders resented her 'intrusion' into their matters. She wished simply to 'work with people' she understood.[62]

Lise made a second attempt to find her brother. On her return she was informed by Brooks that a decision had been made and she would no longer be working for him or his circuit. On 5 May, a message was received saying that Claude de Baissac was waiting for Lise in Paris and she should join him there. Leaving a circuit that she felt no affinity towards, Lise transferred via Paris to the SCIENTIST circuit in Normandy where she felt she would be better respected and valued. There, alongside her brother Claude, she assisted in the organisation of several resistance groups and gathered military intelligence that could be used against the Germans.[63]

Lise and Claude worked well together and, after the problems with PIMENTO, Lise was able to utilise her exceptional skill. Claude allowed her to deputise for him and handle delicate contacts that he did not want to deal with himself. She frequently cycled 60 to 70 km a day with compromising material on her person, on one occasion being arrested when carrying wireless schedules and crystals. With her 'calm and *sang froid* she hoodwinked her captors and escaped' to deliver the crystals, which enabled the circuit to 'maintain contact with the United Kingdom at a critical time'.[64] When it was clear her circuit was going to be overrun by the Allies, Lise asked for her uniform to be sent to France and greeted her liberators in full FANY finery.

On 29/30 April 1944, more help arrived in the form of Nancy Fiocca (née Wake). Born in Wellington, New Zealand, on 30 August 1912, she was the youngest in a family of six and grew up at Neutral Bay, Sydney, where the family had settled. In December 1932 she set out alone to explore Europe, via Vancouver and New York, and made her living as a freelance journalist. She left London for Paris, from where she sent reports to American press agencies. Then, after Hitler's rise to power, she travelled to Vienna and witnessed the Nazi brutality of which she had heard from German refugees. It was on seeing Jews being persecuted she 'resolved there and then that if I ever had the chance I would do anything to make things more difficult for their rotten party'.[65]

In the summer of 1936, Nancy met a 'charming, sexy and amusing' man called Henri Fiocca and, even though he had a reputation as a playboy, they married on 30 November 1939. Nancy was an ambulance driver during the Battle of France in 1940. Once France was overrun she and her husband went to Marseille, and there she had a chance meeting in a bar with Ian Garrow, who ran an escape line. Nancy's potential was recognised and he asked her to become his courier. She accepted, and Henri also offered to help fund the enterprise. The Gestapo soon became aware of Nancy's work, reputedly nick-naming her the 'White Mouse' because of her ability to elude capture. She managed to evade them for some time, but the net was closing in and she took the opportunity to escape to England. Henri promised he would follow, she kissed her husband one last time and fled.[66] In Toulouse, while she waited for her chance to get over the mountains into Spain, she was arrested in a random round-up and accused (falsely) of blowing up a cinema. She was released after four days and began the first of several attempts to get out of France. On the last of these, she had to leap from a train window before finding guides who hid her in the back of a coal truck. She eventually reached Gibraltar and joined a convoy that landed her in England in June 1943. She first tried to join the France Combattante (Fighting French), but was rejected, and was then approached by F Section, who gladly welcomed her experience. She was given an appointment in the FANY and began her SOE training.

Her work was to act as courier to the FREELANCE circuit alongside John Farmer. The pair parachuted in near Montluçon; although Farmer landed perfectly on the guide lights, Nancy dropped some 300 yards away from the field. She was eventually found by the search party, still in her parachute and dangling from a tree with her 'revolver in hand ready to shoot'. 'I hope,' said Henri Tardivat, the resistance fighter who greeted her, 'that all the trees in France bear such beautiful fruit this year.' The straight-talking Nancy replied, 'Cut out that bullshit and get me out of this tree.'[67] The two agents were taken to a safe house and from there were collected by Maurice Southgate of the STATIONER circuit, who was to show them around the area and introduce them to Émile Coulaudon, known as 'Gaspard', leader of the Auvergne Maquis with whom they were expected to work. First, Southgate decided to return to his house in Montluçon to check in on his new wireless operator, René Mathieu – and both he and his new operator were arrested there by the Gestapo. To avoid the same fate, Nancy and Farmer decided to steal a car and travel to Massiac. They did not dare risk staying in the town and spent the night in some woods before heading to a château where they hoped to meet 'Gaspard'. After a week's waiting, he arrived, and Farmer handed over the money and military targets that he had been given – at least that part of his mission was now complete.

They then moved their HQ to Chaudes-Aigues and Nancy began work, finding fields for drop zones or landing grounds, distributing arms, helping with the finances and assisting the local Maquis, who by the beginning of June already numbered 4,000 men. The region's forces were swelled still further by members of Coulaudon's Maquis who had survived a German airborne attack, launched in retaliation for their attacks on factories and communications in the Auvergne; Farmer reported that the enemy suffered great losses, but did not note how many Maquis were killed. The survivors made their way to FREELANCE and joined Nancy's resistance circuit. The number of Maquis whom she helped to manage now ran to approximately 7,500 men. During a sabotage raid on Air Liquide, a gas and oxygen plant at Massiac, Nancy 'behaved in a most outstanding manner' when she took charge of a section of ten men, whom she led to 'within face of the enemy, ordered fire and withdrew'. She was said to show 'exceptional courage and coolness in the face of enemy fire' and contributed to the safety of the men, who had not done the work before and were 'rather lost'.[68]

Nancy cycled huge distances to help maintain contacts across circuits. In the aftermath of the attack on Coulaudon's men, a member of FREELANCE panicked and destroyed his code books, fearing he would soon be captured. This left the circuit without any means of contacting F Section. Nancy cycled 200 km from Auvergne to Châteauroux, and then back again, a journey which took her seventy-two hours, in an attempt to re-establish contact using their wireless set. Initially, it looked as if the bike ride had been for nothing as she did not have a password and the first wireless operator she contacted refused to help her. Luckily, she found another resistance wireless operator who informed London of the situation. Nancy later recalled in an interview that 'when I got off that damned bike I felt as if I had a fire between my legs. I couldn't stand up. I couldn't sit down, I couldn't walk. I just cried.' With her thighs rubbed raw, it took her days to recover – and she never rode a bicycle again.[69]

Pearl Witherington, too, had become heavily involved with the Maquis. Since Southgate's arrest on 1 May 1944, London had approved a plan for Pearl and Maingard (the STATIONER circuit's main radio operator) to divide the network between them into two independent circuits. Maingard was to head SHIPWRIGHT and Pearl was to lead WRESTLER. It was a remarkable leap of faith for F Section – never before had a woman been given command of a circuit – but it was recognised that Pearl was known and trusted by many and would therefore make a good circuit leader. Pearl was not keen at first, maintaining that she was employed as a liaison officer between the French resistance and HQ in England, and not as a leader. But, before she knew it, 1,500 Maquis were seeking her help, and WRESTLER was born in its own right.[70] Pearl continued to send messages to F Section saying that she needed a military commander, but, when no one was sent, Pearl was forced to take command. And she did, with astounding fortitude and against all the odds. France was a patriarchal society, so for a woman (and an English one at that) to not only lead but gain the respect of so many men was truly remarkable.

Running a Maquis group was difficult. They needed food and money, and there was also a lot of 'in-fighting' and pettiness. In some ways this was unsurprising; the men were frustrated and keen to get the job done so that they could go home to their families. Pearl observed that they squabbled among themselves, stole food and weapons from one another, and constantly trod 'on each other's toes'. Her solution was to divide them into four groups, each one with a designated leader whom she chose herself, and then each section had to promise to keep themselves to themselves. When an officer arrived from a 'Jedburgh' team, he found Pearl's system to be very satisfactory and did not change a thing.[71]

During her time as leader of WRESTLER, Pearl was responsible for arming and training the Maquis. The training was difficult: 'you cannot make a guerrilla out of a soldier,' she said, 'because a soldier fights for his ground whereas a guerrilla just hits and runs, and to do that you have to know your territory. The territory was usually in woods because that was where you needed to hide, and we had no tents but had to sleep somewhere ...'[72] For about six weeks, Pearl slept rough in the woods alongside the Maquis, in a tent made from parachute silk hung from an oak tree and filled with hay to sleep on. It was comfortable, unless it rained, in which case they strung up two parachutes – though this did not make much difference. Pearl also had a puppy that Henri had brought for her from a nearby farm; 'he was completely mad', Pearl remembered, but he lived with them in the woods and entertained Pearl by chewing on her plaits as she tried to sleep.[73]

While Pearl was keen to be involved in most aspects of life in the Maquis, she refused to take part in any actual fighting as she believed that a woman is 'made to give life, not take it away'.[74] She did, however, organise sabotage missions, and her Maquis caused considerable damage to the Michelin works in Clermont-Ferrand during a sabotage attack. She also ensured that German columns were slowed down as far as possible by roadblocks and guerrilla attacks. Pearl attended supply drops, and was responsible for twenty-three successful parachute operations, the first of which consisted of three aircraft that delivered so much equipment it took her three days and nights to put it all into the woods.[75] Pearl remained in charge of her own circuit until well after D-Day and maintained command of some 3,700 men.[76]

D-Day was drawing closer and agents were arriving in ever greater numbers, while at the SOE's training schools agents' courses were being cut short. Marguerite 'Peggy' Knight received only three weeks' training. Born in Paris on 19 April 1920, the daughter of Alfred Rex Knight and his Polish wife, Charlotte Ditkowskito, Peggy was brought up in the French capital and in 1936 came to Britain to continue her education at Canterbury, where she qualified as a short-hand secretary. She joined the WAAF but was invalided out with pneumonia and, upon her recovery, gained secretarial work for ASEA Electric in Essex. It was at a company office party that she had a short conversation with the firm's owner in French, who invited her to contact him again – this conversation led to Peggy joining F Section in April 1944.

She was dropped with her colleague, Henri Bouchard, on 6/7 May, near Marcenay in the Côte-d'Or, where the agents landed off-course and Bouchard's parachute got tangled up in a tree. Things deteriorated when the reception committee made it clear that they were not expecting agents and then went on to talk loudly and smoke while keeping the new arrivals waiting. It seemed that they only wanted weapons and ammunition, not personnel – least of all a woman.[77]

The new arrivals were eventually taken to the nearest village, where they stayed in a safe house for two days. Ordinarily, newly dropped agents remained hidden away and as few people as possible would know of their existence – but on this occasion the whole village came out.[78] Horrified by this blatant lack of security and disregard for their safety, Peggy asked to be moved and they spent the next few days in an isolated shed on a farm. They were then collected in a car by Henri Frager, head of the DONKEYMAN circuit, and Alain de la Roussilhe, a local resistance leader. Bouchard left his wireless set behind and went to Paris with Frager, while Peggy remained with de la Roussilhe at Ailant-sur-Tholon. The DONKEYMAN circuit was preparing for the Allied invasion and was expecting to be busy once it came, so Peggy helped with parachute drops, made arms inventories, ran errands and cycled around delivering messages. But her group's lack of security made her increasingly nervous, especially as she was introduced to its members as 'the English parachutist'.

Eventually Frager made contact again, but he asked Peggy to stay with de la Roussilhe for the time being and then to head towards Paris where he would meet her. Bouchard had also returned. His wireless needed to be retrieved from Marscenay and de la Roussilhe insisted that they all travel together in a car (with no permit) to collect it, along with some arms. The trip was risky as only 2 km outside of Marsenay an attack on German forces had just taken place and in all likelihood the area would be inundated with Germans rooting out resisters and the enemy. They left at 6.30 the next morning to try to avoid the roadblocks that had been put in place, making it there and back –but 'were lucky to get through'.[79]

Peggy soon began to realise that de la Roussilhe did not want her to go to Paris; she thought that perhaps she had become too valuable to him. Frager had arranged a rendezvous with her but she missed her train and arrived six hours late for the meeting. Peggy went to the address of a safe house she had been given and waited for Frager there, but he never arrived. Later that evening two SOE agents, one of whom was Lilian Rolfe, came to tell her that she was in danger and must leave in the morning. Peggy went to another safe house and eventually began her work for Frager in earnest. She told him that she 'didn't think much' of de la Roussilhe and that 'some discipline and reorganisation was necessary'. Then a report was received that de la Roussilhe and a recently arrived additional agent for the circuit, Richard Lansdell, had 'accidentally' wounded someone in the knee. Frager agreed that something must be done and he requested that Peggy go back to collect some messages for him, and return by the next day. She waited hours for de la Roussilhe to turn up. When he arrived he was drunk and 'was very rude, refused to give me the wireless set, said Bouchard was miles away and he could not be bothered to fetch the messages'. He then told her he needed her help with a *parachutage* which overran and yet again she missed her train.[80]

Her frustration grew; de la Roussilhe seemed determined to make her life as difficult as possible. Peggy's unease was justified. The next day she was taken to a farmhouse with other members of the circuit, including Frager, but was told that she was not allowed outside where a meeting was taking place. Heated discussions followed and then she heard gunshots. Wondering what was happening she ran out of the house and saw de la Roussilhe 'running up the yard' pursued by the others. Frager saw her and told her to go inside because 'a very painful job had to be done'. More gunshots were fired and two bodies were brought out to be buried. It was Alain de la Roussilhe and Richard Lansdell – they had been executed as traitors.

As Peggy had worked with the executed men, there was suspicion that she might have been involved in the extortion and robbery schemes of which they had been accused. Luckily, enough evidence was gathered to prove that any suspicions were unfounded and she was able to continue her work, on one occasion walking 35 km to carry out an act of sabotage on a German troop train. She helped Frager make new contacts and, as the Allied invasion approached, plans were made to 'form a small Maquis and train men to use their arms, do sabotage etc'.[81] When there was no courier work to be done, Peggy spent her time peeling potatoes, cleaning arms and undertaking sentry work.

Madeleine Lavigne, a native Frenchwoman, had grown up in Lyon where she had been born in February 1912. At the age of 19 she married Marcel Lavigne and they had two children, Gui and Nöel, who lived with her parents in Lyon. Her husband had fought with the army at the Battle of France and had been taken as a POW. Meanwhile, Madeleine was recruited by Nicholas Boiteaux of the SPRUCE network and worked with him as his courier in the Lyon area for over a year. She forged papers to assist downed airmen and POWs who wished to leave on the local escape line, and lent Boiteaux money.

When the circuit was blown she began working for wireless operator Henri Borosh and hid his sets in her house. Borosh intended to set up a new network, and he and Madeleine visited various towns to scope the possibilities. In January 1944 they were warned that the French police were closing in on them and they requested help to get out of France. Madeleine later discovered that she left just before she was due to be arrested in Lyon and in her absence was tried for being a terrorist and sentenced to forced labour for life.

Madeleine's husband had been repatriated in November 1943, but the couple were not reunited before she left for Britain and were soon divorced. Madeleine arrived on 5 February 1944, the day before her thirty-second birthday, to begin her formal SOE training, which was shorter than usual owing to the fact that her mission was already planned and she spoke perfect French (indeed, she barely spoke any English).[82] She returned to France on 23 May 1944 to help lay the ground for D-Day. Reunited with Borosh, she accompanied him on his mission to Paris and Épernay to help set up the SILVERSMITH circuit in the Saône-et-Loire department in Burgundy. It was to have two sections, the first based in Reims in the north and the second in the lower Saône valley. Little is documented about Madeleine's work in the field, but she did undertake wireless training with Borosh and made friends with some restaurant proprietors (the Benazets) in Epernay in the hope of securing Borosh some safe houses. She inspired such confidence in them that they offered to rent her two of their houses, one in Epernay and one in Ay, which proved to be most useful.

On the eve of D-Day, Buckmaster described himself as like 'the producer of a play before the curtain rises on the first night'.[83] Everything was ready. BBC messages and codes had been prepared, and when these messages were broadcast the army of shadows would finally break cover and launch a series of coordinated sabotage raids on railways, roads, communications and power supplies throughout France. Their aim: to disrupt the occupying Germans just as the Allied troops were landing on the Normandy beaches and to ensure that D-Day was a success.

1. Violette Szabó was one of three SOE women to be awarded the George Cross. She was executed at Ravensbrück concentration camp in early 1945 alongside Denise Bloch and Lilian Rolfe. Her orphaned daughter Tania was touchingly presented with her mother's medals by the king and is pictured here with Sir Archibald Wavell.

2. During the Second World War, Wanborough Manor in Surrey was requisitioned by SOE and became known as Special Training School (STS) 5. It served as F Section's preliminary training school where potential agents were trained in the use of weapons and explosives as well as perfecting their French and Morse code.

3. In 1944, Violette Szabó suffered an accident during her parachute training in which she badly twisted her ankle. During her convalescence she met Harry Peulevé and struck up a close friendship with him. Her weak ankle continued to plague her, and slowed down her getaway during a German ambush, in which she was eventually arrested.

4. Krystyna Skarbek, also known as Christine Granville, was a Polish national who originally worked for Section D before undertaking exceptional courier work for the JOCKEY circuit of F Section alongside Francis Cammaerts. The two worked together on the Vercors plateau and narrowly avoided the final massacre by travelling over 100 km in just twenty-four hours.

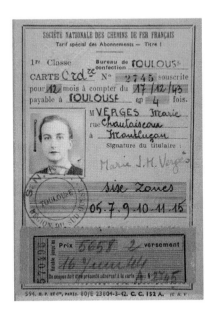

5. Rail travel was perhaps the most dangerous way to travel through occupied France, as spot checks on papers could leave an agent trapped with no means of escape. Agents had to be on their guard and never fall asleep so that sleep-talking didn't give them away.

6. The Fairbairn–Sykes fighting knife was named after its inventors, two former Shanghai policemen turned SOE instructors. It was issued to SOE, British Commandos, the airborne forces, the SAS and many other units throughout the war.

7. Julienne Aisner was living in France when it was invaded. In 1941 she was sent to Cherche Midi prison for slapping a German who had indecently propositioned her. There she was injected in the breast with an unknown substance. After her release she was courier to the FARRIER circuit and the supposed mistress of Henri Dericourt, a suspected double agent.

8. False ID papers were produced by SOE's camouflage section, using examples brought over by refugees or returning agents. The ink, stamps and paper had to be precise copies of those issued by the Germans in occupied France, which were frequently changed to catch out counterfeits. This is Yvonne Cormeau's false ID card.

9. Agents from Jedburgh team AUBREY prepare to be taken into occupied France post D-Day. Unlike undercover agents, they are in uniform. Their female escorting officer is also pictured.

10. Many agents who were parachuted into occupied France wore a 'striptease' suit over their civilian clothes, donned a cloche hat and carried a pistol. Some even had money belts strapped round their waist. The female agent pictured is believed to be Sonia d'Artois (née Butt), who arrived by parachute a few days before D-Day.

11. This image of a resistance fighter has met with many spurious assertions to its origins, including claims that it depicts Nancy Wake. However, this young man was a member of the Maquis of the Chartreuse mountains and Grésivaudan valley, to the north-west of Grenoble in the French Alps – which had no links to SOE. The image is one of a series and the men are all dressed in some semblance of 'uniform'.

12. Pearl Witherington (far right) with her fiancé and fellow résistant Henri Cornioley (third from left) in their uniforms. Also pictured are French resisters who worked with them after D-Day and the liberation. Pearl and Henri married after the war, and lived near where she had been dropped in the Loire valley.

13. Canisters full of weapons, equipment and supplies were dropped to the resistance and Maquis all over France; they had to be removed as quickly as possible to avoid the Germans finding them. Cars and lorries were too easily detected so horse- or mule-drawn vehicles were frequently used. Pictured is the collection of such containers on the plateau of Beuil-les-Launes on 12 August 1944.

14. Rail sabotage was considered to be a highly effective way of slowing down the German war effort and movement of troops. Blowing up a railway line could cause weeks of delays and disruption, especially in the run-up to D-Day when hundreds were damaged by resisters. Here a resistance fighter places explosives on a French railway line.

15. 84, avenue Foch, 16th arrondissement, Paris was an address that struck fear into every resistance and SOE member. If arrested, agents could be taken to this house where they were interrogated and possibly even tortured in an attempt to gain information about their associates and activities. It was from the top floor that Noor Inayat Khan attempted to escape across the rooftops.

16. Sturmbannführer Hans Josef Kieffer was head of the Sicherheitsdienst in Paris and was closely involved with Noor Inayat Khan's incarceration and 'Funkspiel'. After a failed escape attempt, Kieffer insisted that Noor sign a statement saying she would not try again. When she refused he had her transferred to Pforzheim prison where she was kept in chains.

17. Noor Inayat Khan was the first female wireless operator to be sent to France by SOE F Section, in spite of fears that she was unsuitable, as was deemed by her instructors and colleagues. After the fall of the PROSPER circuit Noor refused to return home and stayed at her post, providing vital wireless contact until her arrest. She is pictured here at the dunes near The Hague, Netherlands, in 1934.

18. The SS at Ravensbrück concentration camp exploited prisoner labour by forcing them to break rocks, dig and build in order to expand the camp. Prisoners also undertook work in armament factories or for manufacturers such as Siemens. Camp inmates were sometimes forced to do meaningless and demeaning work, such as shovelling sand from one pile to another, as punishment.

l'appel du bloc 5 étages (bloc 32)

19. While at Ravensbrück, resistance member Violette Lecoq produced thirty-six line drawings graphically detailing life and death in the camp. During *Appell* (roll call) a register was called and could take several hours; many prisoners collapsed or even died due to this forced period of exposure to the elements.

20. Medical experiments were carried out on prisoners at Ravensbrück, including purposely infecting wounded limbs with dirt, glass or debris to cause gangrene. Some were treated with sulphonamide drugs whilst others were left to die. Known as the Ravensbrück Rabbits, many of the victims were Polish. This is a clandestine photograph of one such Polish political prisoner.

21. Virginia McKenna (left) portraying Violette Szabó in the 1958 film *Carve Her Name with Pride*, on set with Odette Hallowes and Maurice Buckmaster. Both this film and *Odette* eight years earlier ensured that their heroines became, and remained, household names.

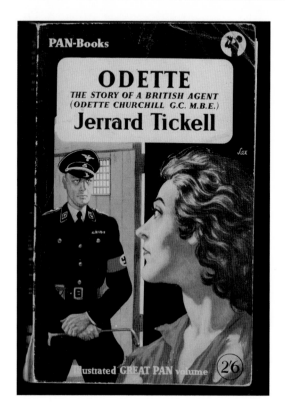

22. The front cover of the 1955 edition of *Odette* by Jerrard Tickell. Originally published in 1949, the book was an instant hit, selling over 500,000 copies with 4 impressions printed within a year. The book remains in print today.

5

D-DAY

She was the bravest woman I ever knew, the only woman who had a positive nostalgia for danger. She could do anything with dynamite, except eat it.

Sir Owen O'Malley, British Ambassador to Hungary,
regarding Kyrstyna Skarbek[1]

The groundwork for the invasion was now prepared. By June 1944 there were fifteen F Section women active in the field, ten in prison and one, Mary Herbert, still in France nursing her baby daughter but no longer active as an SOE agent.[2] The active agents knew exactly what was required of them and the resistance was armed and ready for the fight that lay ahead. However, not all those who had landed with the hope of participating were able to. For the imprisoned, D-Day was just something they would hear about on the grapevine, but it nevertheless brought them hope in their darkest hours.

The resistance learnt about the imminent approach of the Allied invasions through the wireless. It had been agreed that there would be a two-stage system of messages for SOE in preparation for D-Day: a 'stand-by' message and an 'action' message for each target. On 1 June 1944, the first of the stand-by messages came through and the agents knew that the invasion was at hand. The next few days were full of activity as weapons were prepared, reconnaissance on targets was updated and supplies were gathered.

On 5 June, the crucial message arrived from the BBC's Radio Londres – the attack was coming. That evening 306 'action' messages were heard by hundreds of agents, résistants and Maquis all across France. In those few hours before the first Allied troops landed on the Normandy beaches, over 960 sabotage strikes were made against railway lines across France. Many German soldiers, who were to be desperately needed to repel the Allied invasion, were turned to the task of hunting down and routing the resistance groups, and quickly, before they could hamper German movements further. These attacks on the transport network were crucial to the success of D-Day. With trains out of action and roads blocked, the Germans struggled to get reinforcements to the front. The work of the resistance helped cripple any potential for a significant counter-attack.[3] Buckmaster recognised that:

> the main achievement was the hindrance caused to the German panzer divisions, particularly the Hermann Göring from the Spanish border getting into the battle front in Normandy, and the same thing with the Das Reich division in the south-west, where in each case the resistance put up such an amount of ambush and barricades and stoppages on the route that the total strength of the panzer division crossing the Loire was minimal and they had no effect on the fighting at all ... [I]f they had been able to attack the British and American troops as they landed, God knows what might have happened, they may well have been back into the sea.[4]

The SOE-backed resistance also carried out their plans to attack German communications. Operation 'Violet' saw thirty-two telecommunications sites destroyed, meaning the Germans were forced to use radios which could readily be intercepted. Unknown to Nazi high command, thanks to the breaking of the Enigma cipher machine codes the Allies could read a vast array of high-level signals; consequently, the attacks on phone lines by the resistance helped the Allies get access to German plans.

At dawn on 6 June 1944, 160,000 Allied troops landed along the heavily fortified and staunchly defended 80-km stretch of Normandy coastline. They stormed five beaches codenamed 'Sword', 'Juno', 'Gold', 'Omaha' and 'Utah'. The sheer scale of the invasion was unprecedented, comprising more than 5,000 ships and 13,000 other vessels. After 1,739 days of war, the liberation was under way.

On 8 June, Ginette Jullian and Violette Szabó arrived in France by parachute. The view from their respective aircrafts that night must have been something to behold – the sea still full of ships, landing craft and the quiet hope of liberation.

Ginette joined F Section in 1943. She was born in 1917 in Montpellier and educated at the Couvent Sacré Coeur before marrying Paul Lucien Egg in December 1935. Their marriage lasted five years and, as soon as the divorce was settled, Ginette left for England, arriving in June 1940. She joined the Air Transport Auxiliary (ATA) and then transferred to the Bureau Central de Renseignements et d'Action (BCRA), the French intelligence service run by the Free French, from where she was sent to SOE to begin her training. Described by her F Section instructors as 'security minded' and someone who was 'interested and enthusiastic about her job', Ginette was sent into the field, landing alongside Gerard Dedieu in Saint-Viâtre, in the Loir-et-Cher department, south of Orléans, where they were met by a man called Antoine.[5] Her brief was to work as a wireless operator for Dedieu's PERMIT circuit and to train locally recruited helpers in the use of wireless sets, as they needed as many operators as possible to deal with the huge increase in wireless traffic after D-Day. Another aspect of the mission was to make contact with circuits in the Somme department.

Dedieu and Ginette made the long and painstakingly slow journey to Paris. Acting on advice given to her by Antoine, Ginette had left her wireless set behind, having been assured she would find several in Souppes, Oise or the Somme department, which meant she had no means of communication. In Paris they attempted to make contact with the list of people Antoine had given them, but all of their houses were empty and there were no forwarding addresses, indicating that they had either fled or been arrested. Dismayed, Ginette and Dedieu then went to Beauvais where the last contact on their list lived. They discovered that not only had she fled, but that the entire town had been completely abandoned by its residents and occupied by the Germans. Perturbed by such strange events, they withdrew into the Parisian suburb of Saunois (Côte Pontoise). Ginette made contact with Antoine and arranged to visit him so she could collect more information, but by the time she got there his underground hide-out had been attacked by Germans and he had fled. Ginette managed to borrow a wireless from a US section so that she could inform London of what was going on; F Section informed her that she was required to go to Eure-et-Loir, and it was there in late June that the 'actual work started'.[6] She set about sending wireless messages to Baker Street and arranged for 450 containers of arms and supplies to be air-dropped to the resistance fighters. She commented that 'from a technical point of view I was extremely satisfied – each contact is excellent, the failed skeds are caused by electricity current (jams), discharged storage batteries, or nearby danger. There's not much more to say.'[7]

During the Allied advance, Ginette was instructed by London to move forward with the Allied forces towards Dijon. An army officer, Major Hume Boggis-Rolfe, was keen to utilise her wireless skills and engaged her in a new mission which had two teams working alongside each other gathering information; Ginette and a US officer focused on air attack strikes and aerial objectives, which she then communicated directly to the army via radiophone.[8]

Ginette's work was curtailed by the rapid advance of the Allied forces that swept up from Normandy and from the south, taking Dijon on 11 September 1944. Ginette was overrun and her mission was over; she had only been in Dijon for three days. During this time Ginette sent sixty-seven messages and received fifty-two; a post-operation report stated 'these messages allowed PERMIT to arm his five underground hideouts which carried out ambushes on a magnificent scale, and took part in the liberation of several towns in Eure-et-Loir. The sabotages were also very significant on the railways and enemy convoys.'[9] It was also noted that 'Ginette did not want to return to England, she did not want to continue working with [Dedieu] ... there was evidently some friction in the group, but they did not tell me [the interviewer] the cause'. Regardless, Ginette's contribution, though short-lived, had an important impact.[10]

Violette Szabó was infiltrated for her second mission on the same night as Ginette. She parachuted into the Limousin region at around 4 a.m. alongside her team, Philippe Liewer, Bob Maloubier and Jean-Claude Guiet, and began her work establishing contacts and laying low. Two days after her arrival, however, disaster struck the Limoges area. On 10 June, the whole of Limousin was searched by the 4th SS Panzer Grenadier Regiment 'Der Führer' of the 2nd SS Panzer Division 'Das Reich'. They were trying to find SS Sturmbannführer Kämpfe, the head of the 3rd Battalion, who had been captured by the Maquis and bundled into a lorry the night before.[11] Later that day, information was received by the Germans that 'there was a Maquis headquarters in Oradour', which was possibly where Kämpfe had been taken, and that the village was full of weapons and explosives stashes. The 3rd Company 1st Battalion 'Der Führer' occupied the village of Oradour-sur-Glane.[12] The men were shot, the women and children were put into a church which was set alight, and the village was razed to the ground.[13] The massacre left 642 people dead; only 80 villagers survived. There remains no reliable information about Kämpfe's fate, but it seems certain that sometime after his disappearance he was killed by the Maquis.[14]

On that same day, just after 10 a.m., working under Liewer's instructions, Violette was on her way by car to make contact with members of the Maquis in the Corrèze and Dordogne, as well as Jacques Poirier, leader of the DIGGER circuit, in order to prepare a meeting between Liewer and him.[15] The mission was urgent: the Allies were trying to press home the advantage of D-Day and disrupt the German forces racing to Normandy. For speed, Jacques Dufour had offered to strap Violette's bicycle to the car and drive her halfway, to Pompadour, where he would introduce her to the Maquis leaders, and en route Dufour had picked up a friend, Jean Bariaud. None of them were expecting to run into a German checkpoint manned by 'Das Reich' soldiers. Up to that day the Maquis had been freely travelling by car and truck, and they 'had no knowledge of the presence of the "Das Reich" . . . their lack of intelligence was fatal'.[16]

Dufour stopped the car and, as the unarmed Bariaud ran off, he and Violette positioned themselves against the vehicle and opened fire on the

Germans.[17] Before they had set off Liewer had 'handed Szabó a Sten gun, loaded with two magazines for her, as she specifically insisted on carrying a weapon for the car journey'.[18] Now she put it to impressive use. Eyewitnesses recalled the gun fight, which lasted for 20–30 minutes, during which Violette kept the enemy at bay, killing at least one German, and provided covering fire for Dufour to retreat and successfully escape through the fields.[19] A recommendation for Violette's MBE praised her 'great coolness and gallantry … She only surrendered being completely exhausted and short of ammunition'.[20] Violette was arrested and taken to the Gestapo HQ at Limoges, where she was interrogated and refused to give any information about her mission or colleagues. She was then taken to Paris, to 84, avenue Foch.

At 8.30 a.m. the following day, it was the turn of Pearl Witherington to come under fire when her Maquis were attacked by 2,000 Germans at WRESTLER's headquarters at the château des Souches, a few miles east of Valençay. Taking shelter in a farmhouse, Pearl met up with Henri. She saw a German coming towards them and Henri took a potshot, hitting the enemy soldier in the head. Then the Germans opened fire. Pearl ran through the barn into a wheat field, hoping she could reach the nearby woods, but there was no way out; she was trapped in the field for almost twelve hours. From 11 a.m. until 10.30 p.m. there was constant stream of German lorries on the country roads. She later said, 'I thought I shall never see my life again, it is impossible, we were completely surrounded, it was bang bang bang all day'.[21] One of her Maquis and six communists were killed that day because they had stayed on the farm. Pearl managed to escape the field later that night, unscathed.

Pearl hoped that she might be able to rest a little and put her onerous tasks behind her, but on 4 August 'the "Jedburghs" arrived at WRESTLER with their own mission to undertake … and that is another story'.[22] They had parachuted behind enemy lines after D-Day wearing uniform, and worked alongside the resistance, SOE circuits and other Allied special forces (such as the Special Air Service). Pearl had been asking for help for months, but she had no idea that the 'Jedburghs' were on their way. She made sure they knew how cross she was:

'here you are parachuting into the middle of my ground and I didn't even know you were coming'. But she was soon grateful for their assistance as 'they did a great deal of damage to the Germans. The Germans seemed to come from everywhere, and that's really when my circuit started, after that ... and it grew and grew'.[23] By mid-September, WRESTLER had played a vital role in attacking German columns, as well as stopping them getting from west to east. The circuit had also assisted in forcing the surrender of the 18,000 German troops remaining in the region to the Americans, having caused approximately 1,000 German casualties over the previous four months.

Once the area was liberated, Pearl and Henri moved to Valençay, where they were visited by some locals. Henri was in uniform, and one of the locals noticed his pips and began to speak to him in English. Henri corrected him, saying that he was in fact French. The Frenchman retorted that he must therefore be considered a deserter of the French Army. For Pearl, 'I thought the sky was coming down on my head, having given everything we had, literally, because we were up to our necks and being considered a deserter of the French Army after everything that had been done, just because he was in a foreign uniform, I couldn't stomach it'. She cornered the man and set him straight: as far as she was concerned it did not matter whether you were British or French, 'we were both fighting to get the Germans out of the way'.[24]

Pearl was critical to WRESTLER's overwhelming success, but after the war she said, 'I'm only a tiny weeny dot in all this ... I helped them, but I didn't help the whole of France'.[25] She returned from France safely at the end of the war and remained in uniform until December 1945.

After the flurry of resistance activity that followed the Normandy landings, Robert Benoist, leader of the CLERGYMAN circuit, called his main members together for a meal at the Villa Cécile in Sermaise, which acted as their headquarters. Among the diners was his wireless operator, Denise Bloch. During the meal, Benoist received a message saying that his mother was on her deathbed and he must come quickly. He left immediately, saying that if he wasn't back by lunchtime the next day the rest of the network should disperse themselves. Although he was serious, the group considered it to be a throw-away comment. The success of the Normandy landings had, perhaps, made them less security conscious and more lax in their attitudes and actions.

The next day, 18 June 1944, Denise sent her wireless transmission as planned. It was a rainy day and she walked to the railway station with Garnier, another wireless operator, to see if there was any sign of Benoist. He was not there. They returned to the villa at about 8 p.m. No one had paid any heed to Benoist's warning, and preparations for dinner were well under way, with fresh eggs on the menu.

At about 8.20 p.m., the men, who were enjoying an aperitif on the porch, heard a convoy of cars coming along the road and realised they were about to be attacked. A warning was shouted out and everyone dispersed, scattering themselves across the grounds of the villa while the Germans opened up a volley of fire. Once inside the house an SD officer began to shout at the women, '*Line, Line, où est Line?*' This was the codename for Denise's wireless traffic; they clearly knew about her, and Denise stepped forward to be handcuffed. A wireless set and a stash of machine guns were uncovered, the villa was torched and the Germans and their prisoners drove away. Everyone in the villa that night was arrested except one man, a resistance fighter called Wimille (like Benoist, a champion racing driver), who hid in a nearby stream for two hours with only his face above water. He saw and heard everything.

On 25 June 1944, the biggest daylight drop of the war to date took place in the Jura department. Wireless operator Yvonne Baseden was 'on the ground for 48 hours and in constant touch with HQ. 32 Flying Fortresses delivered some 440 parachutes', which she helped distribute.[26] She recalled that it was an amazing and extraordinary sight 'seeing all these parachutes dropping and knowing that this was all equipment coming in successfully behind D-Day'.[27] Yvonne had been in the field for three months.

The first attempt to drop her was aborted as 'they weren't giving the right signals … That was very depressing because once we reached it [the drop zone] we had to come back to London, which was even more tricky because we felt we couldn't see anybody or talk about what we were doing, which lasted about a week and then we went off again to Tempsford'.[28] She finally dropped with field organiser and wireless operator Baron Marie Joseph Gonzague de Saint-Geniès on 18/19 March to a WHEELWRIGHT drop zone near Toulouse. Yvonne was met by circuit leader George Starr and some 'helpful farmers' before cycling to a farmhouse where she spent the night alone; Saint-Geniès went to a different farm and she did not see him again until she reached Jura. She then moved to a new farm where she stayed with Anne-Marie Walters, meeting several resisters including a young officer who had just blown up the Toulouse power station. Meanwhile, Starr had sent a contact to reconnoitre her journey to the east of France, where she was to be based in Dole. Word came back that she should travel accompanied by one of Starr's men and that she should also send her wireless set by a different route. Alphonse Guemneyer, described by Yvonne as 'one of our important French agents working in Saint-Étienne', arrived on 1 April to go with her. She travelled light, taking only her codes and papers, which, throughout her five-day journey, were never checked.[29]

Yvonne recalled that the most terrifying part of her journey was taking the train from Marseille to Dole, her first experience of public transport in Occupied France. She recalled that, while she knew her French was good, she worried that it was 'written all over me that I wasn't supposed to be here at all'.[30] She thought that everyone on the train would notice that she was different. She stayed awake so as not to sleep-talk and to keep guard of her possessions, and was careful to avoid police checks on the stations. She recalled her shock at seeing her first Nazi during the journey: 'it was in the train, there was one in the carriage where I was and it was quite a long journey … it was a question of getting used to the idea … also in Marseille in the railway station, it was dicey, as they were checking people who were sitting waiting for trains with papers'.[31] But she said she always found someone willing to help, be it with her luggage or getting the right connection.

In Dole, Yvonne had three wireless sets in different locations, one where she was staying and the other two at different addresses. Her work soon became routine: listening for messages, encoding and decoding them, and passing them on to Saint-Geniès telling him 'what they were all about' and 'hoping fervently that everything was "going to be alright"'.[32] According to Yvonne, the 'most busy time was just before D-Day when we spent practically all our time making up charges and choosing objectives for D-Day'.[33] After the daylight drop of arms three weeks after D-Day, the reception committee were exhausted and excited. They were supposed to go to a different safe house, but instead went to their usual headquarters at a cheese depot. It was here, fourteen hours later, that they were caught by the Germans.

Surprisingly, they were not arrested as a result of the parachute drop, but were unwittingly given away by a young man who was moving Yvonne's wireless. Yvonne recalled: 'we were supposed to go to one particular safe house and for some reason we unfortunately did not go there, but went to the centre where we were based. The young man ... was stopped and he gave away (thinking that we wouldn't be there) the address we actually were at. It's all very complicated and the poor chap didn't know and that is how we were all eventually found.' He was deported for carrying Yvonne's wireless.[34]

Yvonne thought 'it must have been roundabout lunch time that the Germans had arrested this chap and decided to find out what was there' at the address – just to take a look around, in other words, rather than conducting targeted search related to the *parachutage*.[35] The group had gathered for a meal when the German party arrived. Quickly, everyone dispersed and secreted themselves in various parts of the building. The soldiers couldn't find anyone. 'We all thought they don't seem to be getting anywhere, if only we can keep quiet and they go, eventually it'll get dark and we've got a chance to get over this.' The Germans 'left one chap in charge' as the rest of them drove off.[36] Hours went by in silence, but then one of the toilet cisterns made a noise. The German shouted, 'Is there someone around here?' and called for reinforcements. Yvonne recalled that 'they started moving all sorts of planks and things that we were hiding behind and eventually started finding one or two, of course that encouraged them to go on searching and that is how we were eventually found out and because they were getting fed up with searching they started shooting through partitions and the ceiling'.[37] It was then that the ceiling turned red: hiding on the floor above, Saint-Geniès had been mortally injured and, she said, had taken his cyanide pill to end his life. The rest of the group, seven in total, were arrested and taken away to the local jail by horse-drawn carts.[38]

The following day, George Wilkinson, leader of HISTORIAN, was caught with thousands of francs, a pistol, its silencer and a radio by the Gestapo at a house in Olivet.[39] His wireless operator, Lilian Rolfe, continued with her work, despite the fact that the area was still controlled by the enemy. For another month she regularly transmitted messages including ones arranging parachute drops, one of which comprised forty-seven containers and was considered by her colleague André Studler to be 'one of the best parachutings' he had ever seen.[40]

Lilian moved regularly to avoid the risk of detection. She transmitted from various locations, including the homes of resistance members, and her wireless was hidden in all kinds of places: a wine barrel, under a baby's mattress and in the roof of a dog's kennel. Lilian worked right up until her own arrest on 31 July. The Germans were looking for someone else when they raided the house in Nargis where she was staying, but they found her asleep on the bed with her wireless transmitter, codes and messages next to her; she was so exhausted that she had dropped off before concealing them. She was taken to the jail in Montargis. Pierre Charié, the resistance leader who had taken on Wilkinson's role, was desperate to try to rescue her. He found out that she was due to be moved to Orléans and tried to anticipate the route the convoy would take to stage an ambush, but in the event the Germans took a turning off their usual route. Studler never forgave himself for the failed rescue mission and kept a photograph of Lilian in his wallet for the remainder of his life.

Wireless operator Phyllis Latour, who had been in France since the beginning of May, was only permitted to undertake her true work after the

Normandy landings. The only child of Phillippe, a French doctor, and Louise, an Englishwoman living in South Africa, Phyllis was born in 1921 on a Belgian ship moored in Durban. Her father went to work in the Congo, but when there was civil unrest he sent her and her mother back to South Africa. He was killed in the troubles when Phyllis was just three months old, and three years later her mother remarried. She recalled that her 'stepfather was well-off, and a racing driver. The men would do circuits and they would often let their wives race against each other. When my mother drove the choke stuck and she couldn't control the car. She hit a barrier, the car burst into flames, and she died.'[41] Orphaned, Phyllis went to live with her father's family in the Congo.

At the age of 20 Phyllis moved to England and joined the WAAF as a flight mechanic for air frames. In November 1943 she was interviewed for F Section and was infiltrated in May 1944 to work alongside Claude de Baissac of the SCIENTIST circuit. She 'had 17 sets hidden around the countryside both indoors and in tin boxes outside'. Considered 'too valuable as a W/T operator to be allowed to participate in any operations', she was 'never allowed to participate in reception committees' or other work.[42] Ever security conscious, Phyllis worried about her appearance, commenting in her post-war interrogation that the clothes she had been supplied with looked too English and some 'still bore English markings'.[43] When she felt her safety was compromised on a trip to Lyon, she dyed her hair and bought coloured glasses to try to alter her appearance.

Following D-Day, Phyllis was 'soon in the thick of the battle area but continued her work, sending 135 messages . . . She had many narrow escapes and had to be on constant guard against D/Fings in this particularly difficult area. She was absolutely fearless and ready to run any risk.'[44] On one occasion, she was strafed on the road by the RAF as she travelled to her next transmission location. Another time, a German officer arrived at the farm from which Phyllis was transmitting; fortunately, it was dark, and he did not see her, and the quick-thinking farmer's daughter offered him a glass of cider to distract him and make sure he didn't go near the outbuilding where Phyllis was. On another occasion, two German soldiers who were looking for men to subject to forced labour stumbled across her as she was working; she told them that she was packing her suitcase to go away and convalesce since she had had scarlet fever, warning them that they should not come any closer. They soon left.[45] Phyllis's skeds were often disturbed by the military who were also using wireless sets in the area, and 'a continuous knocking noise ... prevented her from hearing when she was being D/F'd'. She had a near miss when the 'D/F auto was destroyed and the occupants killed by some unknown patriots'; at least she no longer had to worry about that particular van. Phyllis continued her duties until the circuit was overrun in August 1944.[46]

A cluster of circuits were overrun as the Allies broke through in the wake of D-Day, making their work no longer necessary. One of these was HEADMASTER, run by Sydney Hudson, with Sonia d'Artois (née Butt) as courier. Nineteen-year-old Sonia was the daughter of an RAF officer, but he left when she was young. She and her mother moved to the south of France, where Sonia was educated, returning to Britain at the outbreak of war. She had a 'definite devil may care streak in her veins' and had fallen in love with Canadian Army officer and fellow SOE trainee Guy d'Artois during her training.[47] The two shared a fascination with explosives and would go off together to blow things up. Sonia was not good at map reading but Guy was more than happy to teach her and soon their relationship became very obvious to all. The instructors were most concerned by what they saw:

[She is] very much in love with d'Artois and her entire life revolves around this fact, all other considerations being subordinated to it. If she works with him it is doubtful whether the arrangement would be good for either of them. If on the other hand she is separated from him she would not prove at all efficient. In these circumstances it is doubtful whether she be employed'.[48]

But the couple worked so well as a team that they managed to convince Buckmaster to put them on a mission together. They were to go to the

Saône-et-Loire department of eastern France where she would assume the role of explosives expert to DITCHER under the leadership of Guy. Everything was prepared for their mission and, on their last weekend's leave, the couple got married. After a 'lively' wedding reception at the RAF Club in Piccadilly, the couple were informed that now they were husband and wife, they could not work together; were it to be discovered by the Gestapo they might use that against them, and perhaps torture one of them in front of the other. Sonia was furious, saying if she couldn't go with Guy, she wouldn't go at all. But after Guy had departed she asked Buckmaster to send her on her own mission as soon as possible.

On 28 May 1944, just days ahead of the Allied invasion, Sonia parachuted into France near La Cropte, west of Le Mans, with Pierre-Raimond Glaesner and Francis Eugène Bec, to work as courier to HEADMASTER under its leader Sydney Hudson. She landed badly and wrenched her shoulder. Her suitcase, which was full of designer French clothes to assist with her cover of being a Louis Vuitton employee, landed on a nearby road and was picked up by a German convoy. Sonia only had the clothes she stood up in, but, more seriously, the Germans would know that a female parachutist had just arrived. She spent her first night in a safe house and then walked 18 km to a château near Le Mans where she could rest. After three days she began her liaison work between Hudson and the various groups. Assuming the Germans would expect her to lie low, Sonia made the brave decision to be seen out and about, eating in black market restaurants frequented by Germans and often sitting next to them. She engaged them in polite conversation and even flirted with the head of the Gestapo himself.

Glaesner took over the work in Le Mans, while Bec worked south of the town dealing with Hudson's contacts and moving explosives to the area ready for D-Day. While Sonia's work was as liaison for the entire area, she spent most of her time working alongside Hudson. The journey to Le Mans from the château was about an hour by bicycle and there was always the risk of encountering roadblocks and having their papers searched. To cut down on journey time and to increase security, Hudson rented a small house in the town to act as a base for them. But this was not the only reason for such a private and comfortable arrangement. Sonia and Hudson had met before in a club in London; she had been attracted to him, but he was already married, and she was about to marry Guy. So she pushed her feelings aside and got on with her training, but when she saw him again in the field she realised that she still had feelings for him, which became harder to supress as time went on and they got to know each other better. As the couple spent more and more time together – in order to maintain a decent cover for them both – they began an affair. Some years later Hudson admitted 'it was difficult not to fall in love' with her.[49]

Once D-Day arrived, the four agents helped to set up various Maquis groups in the forests of Le Mans, but the attitude of the locals made it so difficult to keep these going that, one after the other, they folded. Sonia and Bec stayed together for a short time, living with a Maquis group which she organised and did a little instructing for, allowing her to show off her skills with explosives and weapons. After a few days, she left the forest and, two days later, on 16 June, the band of Maquis was attacked by Germans and Milice. In the ensuing fight four resisters were killed, including Bec. Devastated, Sonia met up with the survivors and took them to another Maquis group that was being run by Glaesner, but the Germans were sweeping the forests looking for résistants, and so they moved on again.

From then on Sonia worked as liaison among all of the Maquis groups within HEADMASTER. Her work involved lengthy journeys by bicycle to the various groups, where she distributed food, messages and even explosives. After Le Mans was liberated on 8 August 1944, Sonia and Hudson undertook liaison work for the Americans. Posing as a married couple they carried out reconnaissance missions behind German lines. On one occasion, when they were returning from a three-day mission, they were shot at by SS while crossing a bridge over the Seine that they had been expecting Americans to be guarding. They left the car and ran, but were captured by a sentry further down the road and were held for four hours. During this time Sonia was raped by two German officers; Hudson was held overnight but released the next day. They were soon overrun by the Allies and their mission came to an end. They reunited with some other SOE agents in Paris, among them Guy d'Artois.[50]

A month after D-Day, one of SOE's most famous agents arrived to begin her work. Polish national Krystyna Skarbek, also known as Christine Granville, had already undertaken various roles for SOE (see Chapter 1). As she was fluent in French, Krystyna was deemed suitable to become an agent for the AMF Section of SOE, also known as 'Massingham', which infiltrated agents from Algiers into southern France. In the south-east of France, following the arrest of Cicely Lefort, Francis Cammaerts desperately needed a new courier in his JOCKEY circuit, which coordinated resistance groups across a vast region, including the Rhône valley, the Riviera and Grenoble. With her extensive experience in the field, and having already completed her wireless and parachute training at 'Massingham', Krystyna with her 'extraordinary qualities and experience' seemed to be just right.[51] She parachuted in near Vassieux, in the Vercors region of southern France, landing in the early hours of 7 July 1944. She had been blown 6 km off course and had landed so hard that her revolver was smashed and her coccyx was badly bruised, but within seconds she had got up and brushed herself down.

Described by Vera Atkins as a 'vital, healthy, beautiful animal with a great appetite for love and laughter',[52] Krystyna's original brief was to mobilise her Polish compatriots in France, of whom there were thousands who had either volunteered under duress or been pressed into work in German forced labour camps or units of the German Army. But first she and Cammaerts made a tour, during which she met with Cammaerts's contacts (of whom there were hundreds) before moving on to the Vercors plateau: a vast expanse of forests, ravines, foothills, wilderness and caves surrounded by rugged mountains and limestone cliffs. The area had already seen much activity and they arrived in the thick of things. The Vercors had long been a home for the Maquis – its forests and crags provided the ideal hiding place to set up and train a guerrilla army – and in early 1943 it had been decided that, when the time came, the area would also be a perfect landing base for Allied forces, who could use it to take Grenoble and Valence and cut off the retreating Germans. The plan was approved by the French authorities in exile and was named the 'Montagnards' (mountaineers) plan.

Cammaerts had visited the Vercors in August 1943 where he met with Eugène Chavant, who told him of a plan to use the Vercors as a redoubt and staging area for large-scale resistance activity. Cammaerts agreed that the Vercors could be used as drop zones for Allied paratroopers who could work with the local Maquis to defeat German military forces and assist the Allied forces after Operation 'Dragoon', the plan to invade southern France on the back of D-Day. The first SOE drop of arms to the Vercors Maquis was in November 1943, and in January the 'Union' mission, comprising three men, one each from the OSS, BCRA and SOE, arrived to assess the situation. Together with Cammaerts, they organised, trained and armed the Maquis to prepare them for an important role supporting the Allied invasion of southern France. (The 'Union' group departed France in May 1944.)

In the weeks leading up to D-Day, the Maquis received confusing and often contradictory guidance from the Allies. One consideration was whether the Maquis should rise in armed opposition to the Germans immediately after D-Day or wait until they could be of greatest assistance to the Allies. Eisenhower suggested caution be exercised, but a message from de Gaulle was interpreted as a call to arms. On D-Day, Cammaerts ordered the Maquis to remain hidden as 'it would be at least two months before they would be needed'. He was aware that similar uprisings had been crushed by the Germans. But the Maquis leader ordered his men to mobilise, assuring them that reinforcements would arrive soon in the form of paratroopers together with anti-tank guns and other heavy weapons.

Following D-Day, hundreds of volunteers converged on the Vercors anxious to participate with the Maquis in the upcoming fight. The Maquis were ready and requested that airborne troops be sent. They never came, and the Maquis became trapped by the Germans, who had occupied strategic points giving them direct access to the Vercors. Nevertheless, on 3 July, the Free Republic of Vercors was founded, the first independent territory in France since the beginning of the German occupation. It had its own flag comprising the French Republic tricolour with a Cross of Lorraine, the 'V' for Vercors and 'victory', and a coat of arms featuring a French alpine Chamois. Arms and weapons arrived by parachute over the course of the next few weeks, and, on 14 July, a daylight drop of over 800 containers rained down from 72 American B-17 Flying Fortresses, delivering weapons, anti-tank bazookas and much-needed supplies to the Maquis of Vercors. The Germans quickly launched air attacks to destroy the containers. The Maquis initially mistook the planes for Allied aircraft, but the black crosses on the wings' undersides were soon visible. The planes strafed the ground, destroying the equipment and killing and injuring those attempting to collect it. Krystyna recalled the strike: 'Having sprayed us lavishly with bombs, the enemy planes then inundated the plateau with dozens of grenades ... Vaissieux was on fire.'[53] Under attack, with her usual gusto, Krystyna got to work cutting away the parachutes and unpacking the dropped canisters, then stacking the various weapons, explosives and grenades neatly in piles to be distributed. In the village, makeshift hospitals were set up in schools in which to treat the wounded. The air attacks continued well into the night.

Mentally and physically exhausted, Krystyna and Cammaerts sought solace in one another's company and in a hotel in Saint-Agnan spent their first night together as lovers. As Cammaerts put it, they were 'absolutely certain that we were going to die the next day, it was all over, this was the end – the hotel was on fire, bombs were falling, the troops gathering on the side of the mountain ... we simply went into each other's arms.'[54] The next morning they were looking out of the window when they saw a fighter aircraft with a bomb strapped underneath it: 'we could see the pilot's face. I said if he releases it now we've had it – and on the word "now" he fired.' The bomb skidded across the roof of the hotel and landed in a mound of earth behind the building. It did not go off. Krystyna gripped Cammaerts's hand: 'They don't want us to die,' she said laughingly.[55]

On 21 July, the air raid ceased and was replaced by a large-scale ground attack. Not only did the Germans march onto the plateau in their thousands, they also arrived by air: 20 gliders brought 400 SS paratroopers carrying flame throwers, landing on the plateau's air strip which had been prepared for but rejected by the Allied air forces as too short – and now used with devastating effect by the Germans.[56] Vercors was under siege from all sides and the intense fighting went on for three days. Those who were caught by the Germans were brutalised and either shot or deported, whether they were Maquis or innocent bystanders; no one could get away and those who tried were routed and captured. Even the cave within which a Red Cross hospital was hidden was discovered; the patients, doctors and nurses were all murdered. It is estimated that 840 Frenchmen and women lost their lives in the fight for the Vercors plateau.

Krystyna and Cammaerts narrowly avoided the final massacre at the Vercors, leaving on 22 July. They travelled over 100 km in just twenty-four hours to Cammaerts's safe house in Seyne-les-Alpes, but not simply to escape. The following day, leaving Cammaerts behind, Krystyna crossed the mountains into Italy and made contact with a partisan group there. She recognised that their leader, 'Marcellini', had great potential and 'did all she could to help him' when he was attacked by over 500 Germans.[57] She put him, and what was left of his group, in touch with Major Hamilton, a 'Jedburgh' team leader in the area, whose job was to establish contact with partisans all along the frontier. 'Marcellini' proved himself 'to be the only leader capable of stopping Italian partisans from running immediately [when] they are attacked'.[58] These partisans helped prevent German advances by blowing up the roads and bridges around Briançon. Krystyna also managed to convince some 700 or so Poles, who had been pressed into working for the Germans as guards on the alpine frontier posts at the Col de Larche, to desert their posts and disable their guns.

Krystyna was accepted by her colleagues as an equal and a force to be reckoned with. She facilitated the escape from prison of Cammaerts and two British officers who had been arrested at a roadblock in Dignes on 11 August. At first she tried to enlist the help of the Maquis, but they were not able to assist in time; so she cycled around 40 km to the Gestapo HQ and walked straight in, knowing the risks she was about to take, as she demanded to speak to Albert Schenck, a French liaison officer working with the Germans. She declared herself to be not only a British agent but the niece of Field Marshal Montgomery. 'By a mixture of bluff and strength of character', including telling Schenk that an Allied invasion from the south was imminent and that he would be 'handed over to the mob' unless he cooperated with her, she managed to buy their freedom.[59] Krystyna offered 2 million francs, to be dropped by parachute the following day, and a guarantee of protection in return for the three prisoners' lives. Cammaerts and his puzzled companions were driven out of the prison literally hours ahead of their scheduled execution. Krystyna was waiting for them at a roadblock and the four made good their escape. A few weeks later the area where Krystyna was working was overrun. She filed her final report and returned to London.

In mid-August 1944, the second Allied invasion of France was launched: Operation 'Dragoon'. The aim was to speed up the liberation and to capture several large harbours in southern France. It was smaller in scope than the landings on the Normandy beaches some weeks before and the opposing German forces were weaker in both number and quality. It had originally been planned to launch this attack in conjunction with D-Day in June, but it became clear that the Allied war effort could not support two large-scale amphibious operations simultaneously and Operation 'Dragoon' was postponed. Churchill wished to cancel it completely. But the fighting in Normandy went on longer than anticipated, and the growing realisation that the northern ports could not cope with the offloading of all the necessary supplies led to the plan being revisited.

The 'Dragoon' landings took place on 15 August and, with the help of the resistance, the coastal defences were soon breached. The opposition forces crumbled quickly and the Americans progressed far more quickly than had been predicted, despite the Germans' fighting retreat in the Rhône valley which delayed the American advance. Meanwhile, French units liberated Marseille and Toulon, and captured two harbours which went on to play a substantial role in increasing Allied war supplies. In mid-September, Allied columns that had advanced from southern France met with the victorious units attacking from Normandy, forming the Western Front.[60]

Madeleine Lavigne's SILVERSMITH network in the area around Reims came into its own in helping to fend off the Germans and hold them back so that the Allies could advance. As the local towns were liberated one by one, Madeleine had little to do. She could not return home to Lyon in case her sentence for forced labour for life, handed down in absentia earlier in the year, still stood, so she went to Paris instead. Her final report calls her 'a most courageous and tactful woman, who rendered very great services to the cause. She was wise and brave ... she did her job unquestionably well and was of the greatest possible assistance to SILVERSMITH. A great-hearted lady for whom I have much respect and liking.'[61]

On the day of Operation 'Dragoon', news of the US breakthrough reached Peggy Knight. She had continued her work almost alone after the arrest of her leader Frager and his lieutenant, and had personally ensured that her network's D-Day work in the Yonne and Côte d'Or was carried out efficiently. Her Maquis hounded the Germans as they retreated, utilising their excellent guerrilla tactics to drive them out. Released from her duties on 12 September 1944, Peggy made her way to Paris to be collected by plane on 16 September. A British officer who had worked with her said that 'she took her place on the staff exactly as one of the men. She marched with them and took her turn at sentry with them, always a volunteer ... she was quite fearless and undertook work on the roads known to contain enemy barrages with a nonchalance which was the admiration of all ... but for her any derailments would not have taken place.'[62] The officer's words resonate with descriptions of most of the female agents who were involved with D-Day. Their devotion to duty, their willingness to continue their work in spite of increased dangers, and their ability to lead and organise played a great part in the success of the work of the resistance and SOE – which, in turn, made a significant contribution to the success of the Allied invasion and subsequent liberation of Western Europe.

In a letter to Colin Gubbins on 31 May 1945, General Eisenhower wrote that 'in no previous war ... no other theatre during this war have resistance forces been so closely harnessed to the main military effort ... I consider that the disruption of enemy rail communications, the harassing of German road moves . . . by the organised forces of the resistance played a very considerable part in our complete and final victory.'[63] This was in no small part due to the great skill with which the women of F Section took up their challenging and dangerous roles.

6

INCARCERATION

Oh! My beloved France, what has happened to you . . .
Inscription on the wall of Peter Churchill's cell at 84, avenue Foch[1]

While the 'active agents' engaged in the liberation of France, those who had
been captured could only wait for news of what was happening outside their
prison walls. For some of them it had been a very long wait. Odette Sansom
and Peter Churchill had been arrested over a year before D-Day, in April
1943. The couple had been separated from each other and handed over to
Italian troops. Odette claimed that she and Peter were married, and that he
was Winston Churchill's nephew, and managed to get a message to Peter to
corroborate the story.[2] She knew the name would resonate with her captors,
and, as the tide was turning against the Axis powers, it might get them
favourable treatment. It was a gamble, but she was willing to try.

The couple were detained in Annecy, and were initially treated fairly well;
'the friendly Italian soldiers gave Odette daily news of Raoul [Peter] and
Odette sent similar messages to Raoul. Raoul sent messages as a man would
to a woman he loved, and this appealed to the Italians.'[3] The NCO allowed
Odette to spend her days in his office as her cell had 'neither chair nor water'.[4]
Odette was not formally interrogated but was asked questions by the
inspector, which she refused to answer. Churchill tried to escape but was
discovered, and brutally beaten and bayoneted by the guard who caught
him, leaving him with a black eye, deep cuts and cracked ribs.[5]

After a week the couple were transported to Grenoble in a lorry, where
they were able to talk, agreeing that they would deny everything and try to

protect other members of their circuit who were still at large.[6] Odette was placed in a cell with two other women. From her cell window she could see that of Churchill, but it was only on her birthday later in the week that the Italians allowed her to see him in person, and then only for five minutes. After a week the pair were moved again, by train to Turin. Odette was taken to a convent, which was being used as a place for reforming prostitutes, and spent an interesting night there; the Mother Superior seemed very impressed by her surname, which appeared to prove Odette's theory correct. The next day they were taken by train to Nice, during which the Italians sang songs and gave them oranges, but the couple found it hard to converse and the enforced separation began to take its toll. In Nice they were collected by car and taken to a villa where they were held for nine or ten days; Odette was given an Italian guard who watched her every movement and even slept in her room. On 11 May 1943, Odette and Churchill were put in a truck and driven to Toulon. The Italians handed them over to the Germans, who drove them to Marseille, and from there they took a train for Paris.

Built in 1898, Fresnes prison was located just to the south of the city and by 1943 was the second largest prison in France. Since the occupation it had been used to house captured SOE agents, members of the French resistance and political activists, as well as common criminals.[7] Beneath the main prison was a dungeon where prisoners who had committed some sort of misdemeanour were kept in solitary confinement and total darkness, often denied a bed, blankets or a toilet, the walls streaming with damp and rats scampering across the floors.

Odette and Churchill arrived at Fresnes on 12 May. They were separated and could only glimpse each other at a distance, through the prison's dirty windows. Instead, Odette was greeted by the familiar, though far from welcome, face of Hugo Bleicher, the Abwehr sergeant who had arrested her some weeks before in Saint-Jorioz.

Odette was taken to the women's wing and locked in a small cell, number 108, which held just a bed, with a sheet and blanket, and a chair. There was a small frosted window behind bars which could not be opened, but through which Odette could just make out other prisoners exercising and sometimes catch a glimpse of a familiar face. Denied exercise, reading material or any privileges, Odette was for a time cut off from the rest of the prison and the rest of the world. Food was pushed through a hatch in her door and was meagre: acorn coffee, soup, bread or sometimes rancid meat. She could hear the moans and cries of other prisoners, footsteps outside, beatings, but no one came to see her for fifteen days. It was an experience she would have to endure numerous times over the coming months.

One evening, about three weeks into her time at Fresnes, some women in other cells were heard talking and being loud. The guards assumed Odette was one of the culprits: 'Two men and two SS women came to Source's [Odette's] room, pulled Source out of bed, and one of the women smacked Source's face twice'. The next day Odette demanded to see the captain in charge: 'the Captain was full of apologies and did not want Source to think ill of all Germans'. He sent her a parcel, told Churchill that she was well and instructed a German woman to look after Odette from now on.[8] But Odette's treatment varied greatly; she never knew what was going to happen, and that must have exacted a psychological toll.

Sometime in mid-June, Bleicher took Odette to see Churchill and they spent a couple of hours together. Peter was still bearing the scars of previous injuries and Odette was unsure as to whether he had been tortured. He told her that she looked pale, 'but she thought it was better to say nothing and talk of other things'. Odette hoped that, by behaving affectionately with Churchill, Bleicher would see that 'she would never give in to him'.[9]

During her time at Fresnes prison, Odette was taken for interrogation at one of the Gestapo's headquarters in Paris at 84, avenue Foch: a grand terraced house in the 16th arrondissement, and an address that struck fear into the heart of every resistance fighter and SOE agent in France. The reputation of the Paris Gestapo's HQs preceded them as places of brutal interrogations, mental and physical cruelty, torture and death. Many captured British agents were taken to 84, avenue Foch for interrogation. Some were accommodated in the cells of the house itself while others were brought in for questioning from Fresnes prison or makeshift cells at another of the SD's premises, 3 bis, place des États-Unis.

The house on avenue Foch was spread over six floors (including the ground floor). The first was used for interrogations of captured agents. The wireless section (IV) run by SD Lieutenant Dr Josef Goetz occupied part of that floor as well as the second floor. Here the 'Funkspiel' took place, in which wireless sets were played back to Britain as if still operated by their now captured wireless operators. This section had moved from 11, rue des Saussaies in January 1943. SD agent Ernst Ruehl worked on the third floor and said that 'one of my main jobs was connected with GRECO who had the back information service and transmissions from all over France'. The fourth floor was the office and living quarters of the commander of the Gestapo at no. 84, SS Sturmbannführer Hans Josef Kieffer, head of the Sicherheitsdienst, the SS intelligence service in Paris. Above his quarters on the fifth floor was a guardroom, interpreter's office and detention cells.[10]

Odette was taken by armed guard to 84, avenue Foch between twelve and fourteen times and was subjected to brutal torture there.[11] Torture was explicitly authorised at a number of Gestapo buildings such as 11, rue des Saussaies and 3 bis, place des États-Unis. At the latter, also known as the 'house prison', Josef Stork admitted using torture, including the *baignoire*. The method was to force the victim's head under the water until the point of drowning, when they would be dragged out and questioned, and the process would be repeated; the water might contain the bodily fluids of previous victims. At the avenue Foch, Hans Josef Kieffer employed Pierre Cartaud, known as 'Peter', who liked to use a riding crop on prisoners. According to a prisoner at no. 84, John 'Bob' Starr, 'Stork was one of the most brutal of the SS ... I have heard screams from the shed [where Stork interrogated people] and I have seen Stork come out. The victims had obviously been beaten up. I have seen people so treated in such a bad condition from the ill-treatment they had suffered that they could barely walk upstairs.'[12]

The torture at Odette's first interrogation was carried out by 'A Frenchman', who 'came into the room, and they made her sit on a chair and the tall thin interrogator held [her] hands behind her back. The Frenchman then burned [her] on the shoulder, with what she did not know ... They then left [her] alone for a while and the tall thin man said he would think of something else that might make her talk.'[13] At a later interrogation session her toenails were removed using a pair of pliers, and 'She was constantly threated with worse treatment'.[14] Throughout it all, Odette bravely refused to give away any information. Questions revolved around her work and the whereabouts of F Section wireless operator Adolphe Rabinovitch, who had escaped the arrests in Saint-Jorioz and who was still in the field – as was Francis Cammaerts. Odette was the only person who knew their whereabouts, as she had relocated them, and she was determined to protect them and the valuable work they could continue to do for SOE. Her interrogators also demanded information about Colonel Buckmaster, showed her photographs of men and women and asked her to identify them, and pressed her on the whereabouts of other agents – but Odette offered no information of value. She displayed considerable bravery, resilience and an unyielding stubbornness, as well as unswerving patriotism and devotion to the cause. Her George Cross citation recognised her contribution: 'The Gestapo tortured her most brutally to try to make her give away [certain] information ... Mrs. Sansom, however, continually refused to speak'.[15]

The Germans also employed rather different tactics in order to induce Odette to talk. On one occasion she was driven around the Arc de Triomphe by one of her interrogators; he believed that as a Frenchwoman she may like to see it. It would have been an all too rare excursion outside for Odette, but it did not have the intended effect – she still refused to reveal any information. Her blouse was even taken away for laundering by Bleicher, and at Fresnes she was offered books to read – she believed this 'kind treatment was because of her name'.[16] But Odette was wise to all Bleicher's ploys.

Still, her months of maltreatment at Fresnes took their toll. Simone Herail, who shared cell 337 with Odette from October 1943 to January 1944, later spoke of Odette's condition: 'for many months [she] been detained in solitary confinement ... her health was seriously impaired by this inhuman procedure so dear to the Nazis; her weakness was extreme; she could no longer even eat the small amount of filthy and repugnant food which was given to us. On some days she had not the strength to leave her paillasse, but at no moment did her courage or determination to survive falter.'[17]

Odette showed extraordinary tenacity during her harrowing time at Fresnes and would not be coerced into giving the Germans the answers they sought. Because of this, the Gestapo put her on trial in June 1943. She was in fact sentenced to death on two counts, once for being a member of the French resistance and one for being an English spy. She replied: 'then you shall have to make up your mind on which count I am to be executed, because I can only die once . . . I remember thinking, for which country shall I die? I will never know? It was quite ridiculous . . . There is an element of comedy in every tragedy. Comedy helps you survive.'[18] Odette spent her further months and years of captivity wondering if and when her sentence would be carried out.

Following her arrest in October 1943, Noor Inayat Khan was also taken to 84, avenue Foch for interrogation by Ernest Vogt (as Kieffer could not speak French). She refused to answer his questions. After several hours of trying (and failing), Vogt got tired and was about to send Noor to her room when she asked if she might have a bath first. This was a somewhat unusual request as most visitors to the avenue Foch would attempt to avoid baths at all cost, knowing of the *baignoire* method of torture sometimes used by Germans. Vogt agreed on the condition that the door was left ajar, as was the usual prac-tice. But Noor protested her modesty and they allowed the door to be closed. No sooner was it shut than Noor climbed out of the bathroom window and attempted to flee across the rooftops of Paris. Suspicious of Noor's motives, Vogt was in the next-door room and spotted her on the roof. Afraid she would fall if he shouted at her, he offered her his hand and, reluctantly, Noor came back inside.[19]

Noor was put in a room on the fifth floor of 84, avenue Foch where several other SOE agents, including 'Bob' Starr, Maurice Southgate and Gilbert

Norman, also had rooms. Despite the numerous stories of horrific privations associated with the address, these agents had a relatively comfortable existence. An agreement had been made by Starr 'to the effect that British agents would tell the truth, provided no innocent person suffered and the agents themselves were not shot'.[20] To this end, when Noor 'asked for writing materials, saying she was bored with having nothing to do', she was given pen and paper and began to write poems and stories for children. She also had access to a library and received adequate meals.[21] It wasn't just Noor who received this kind of treatment: Southgate was taken for day trips in a car, had accountancy books brought to him so he could study, and played chess with Starr in the evenings. On one occasion he was even invited to lunch with Kieffer.[22] Starr worked as a graphic artist; he drew maps and structure charts from information the Germans gave him and was once asked to check the English being used in the 'Funkspiel' to SOE HQ. The agents might be treated well, but only so long as they did what they were told.

Noor continued to be interrogated by the Gestapo and, according to Kieffer, showed 'great courage'. Although they 'got no information out of her [they had] found a good deal of material which helped in her interrogation.'[23] Noor's notebook had provided them with all they needed. This is confirmed by Robert Gieules, a resister who had been recruited to help F Section and who had been arrested in late September. He was told by his interrogator that, thanks to the 'code' seized on Rolande (Noor), the Germans had managed to decode many telegrams sent and received by her; they showed him the translations of the decoded messages.[24] Goetz, who ran the 'Funkspiel', confirmed that there was no need for him to interrogate Noor personally as he had all her messages to and from London and the codes.

Kieffer treated Noor relatively kindly because he needed her assistance in the 'Funkspiel' operation, playing her radio back to England. Noor's was codenamed 'Radio Diana' and F Section continued to receive messages on her frequency and from her wireless and believed that she was still operational in the field, despite the fact that doubts had been raised as early as December 1943 as to whether Noor was operating under duress. To try to clarify the situation, questions were included in messages sent to her to which she alone knew the answers. Vogt simply asked these of Noor, so he could answer them. She reputedly refused to tell him anything else about herself, but according to Rose Marie Holdwetz, a fellow prisoner, Noor confided in John Starr and 'told him the truth in confidence' – and Starr then passed on her replies to Kieffer. The Gestapo gleaned enough material to convince London that Noor was still at liberty and operating her own wireless.[25]

Over a four-month period in early 1944, SOE made several parachute drops to France as a result of the radio play to F Section. The first had been a request for twelve containers, and when only one was dropped the Gestapo wondered if London had 'twigged' and 'were not really deceived'. 'The second reception was the dropping of one container by a Mosquito. We [the Gestapo] asked for 500,000 francs and we also received this amount.'[26] The Gestapo received not only a great deal of material, but also a number of agents as the result of the 'Funkspiel' on Noor's wireless, all of whom perished in the camps. On 6/7 February, François Deniset (a Canadian arms instructor for Garry's circuit), Roland Alexandre (a wireless operator), Robert Byerly (an American who had served in the Canadian Army) and Jacques Ledoux (an Anglo-French captain in the Highland Light Infantry, his mission to set up a new network near Le Mans) parachuted into Poitiers: all four were arrested on landing. Then, three weeks later, on the night of 29 February 1944, the BRICKLAYER team of France Antelme, Lionel Lee and Madeleine Damerment suffered the same fate and were taken to the avenue Foch.[27]

Madeleine and her BRICKLAYER colleagues should have been heading to Britanny to see what had become of the blown PARSON circuit, whose agents were all in captivity, after which their mission was to set up a new circuit to prepare the ground ahead of D-Day. Madeleine had joined F Section in June 1942, having previously spent two years working on the PAT escape line, during which time she had helped save seventy-five British pilots. When the Gestapo began to make enquiries about her work, she and her sister escaped to Toulouse. In May 1941, with the Germans having lost interest in her, she had been escorted back across the demarcation line by her fiancé Roland Lepers, and she resumed her work until the line was denounced. She and Roland escaped across the Spanish border, arriving in

Barcelona in March 1942. Roland was sent to Britain, while Madeleine was arrested and held at Miranda de Ebro, a concentration camp for foreign prisoners and those who had crossed the border illegally. Eventually, with the help of the British consulate, she was released and sent to Britain by plane later that month, where she found her way to F Section. Now she was at 84, avenue Foch awaiting her fate.

Noor remained determined to escape from prison and, in the early hours of 25 November, Kieffer awoke to news that Noor, John Starr and Leon Faye, a fellow prisoner who was in the French resistance, had made an attempt to do so. This plan had been arranged by 'leaving written notes in a certain spot in the lavatory'. With a screwdriver that Starr had procured while fixing the cleaner's carpet sweeper, the three managed to remove the grilles from their windows and make it out onto the rooftops during an air raid. Then, 'by means of strips of blankets and sheets knotted together they let themselves down on to the balcony in the third storey of a neighbouring house and there smashed a window and entered the apartment'. Intrepid as they were, all three were soon recaptured.[28]

The disappointment at this setback was doubtless immense, not only for the prisoners but also for the Gestapo interrogators, who felt they had come to an understanding with their prisoners. The Germans drew up a document for the agents to sign, promising not to attempt escape again. Noor would not sign – she felt it was tantamount to suicide to give up her hopes of freedom. Faye also refused, but Starr shook Kieffer's hand and gave him his 'explicit word of honour in the presence of witnesses that he would not attempt to escape again'. Ruehl reported that Noor's refusal 'angered Kieffer very much and as in any case she had not helped us in any way, Kieffer arranged with Berlin to have her sent to Germany'.[29] Faye suffered the same fate.

Noor became a *Nacht und Nebel* prisoner at Pforzheim prison in Germany, meaning that she was to be cut off completely from the outside world, moved frequently and apparently at random, and no records would be kept either of her imprisonment or even her death, so anyone connected to her would remain uncertain as to her fate or whereabouts. As a political prisoner, she was to be kept 'on the lowest rations, in solitary confinement and moreover, she was to be chained hand and foot'. Wilhem Krauss, the prison governor, obeyed the orders at first, but soon 'felt sorry for the English girl' and removed the chains from her hands, enabling her to feed herself. A call from Gestapo HQ Karlsruhe reprimanded him for 'not observing the regulations about the chains': they were replaced, and not removed again.[30] While at Pforzheim, Noor was interrogated again by officials from Paris in relation to getting information for 'Radio Diana'. It is not known whether or not she helped them but, given her refusal to do so at avenue Foch, it seems unlikely that she told them anything. A fellow prisoner, Yolande Lagrave, confirmed that Noor's 'hands and feet were manacled' and that she was 'very unhappy, she was never taken out and I could hear that she was beaten up'. Noor and Yolande had been communicating by means of scratching words on a mess tin, and Lagrave recalled that 'the mess tin arrived with this message "I am going" written in a quick and nervous hand'.[31] Before leaving Pforzheim, Noor managed to let Yolande know 'her pseudonym ... by means of her mess tin' and her address back home.[32] After the war, Yolande sought to find out what had happened to her friend.

A few weeks after Noor's capture, on 18 November 1943, Diana Rowden was arrested alongside wireless operator John Young by a man whom she believed to be André Maugenet, also known as 'Benôit', one of five newly landed agents. Unbeknownst to Diana, the real Maugenet had been arrested in Paris the same day he landed, 16 November. He was interrogated by the Gestapo and during questioning gave them his name and the address of his safe house, and handed over letters and documents that he had brought from England. At around 7.30 a.m. on the morning of 18 November, Diana saw, from behind the curtain at the Juif house, someone arrive whom she assumed was Benôit – he knocked on the door of a neighbouring house, which was his designated first contact. Handing over a box of matches containing instructions, as well as a handwritten letter from Young's wife, the man established his credentials as Benôit and appeared to be legitimate. He said he needed to collect a suitcase that he had left behind in Lons-le-Saunier. Diana accompanied him. She must have been pleased to have news from home and someone new to talk to; he was a welcome addition. They had a drink at a café with a member of the Saint-Amour resistance before returning in the early evening to the house where Diana lived and where Madame Juif was preparing dinner.

Soon after they reached the Juif house, the door burst open and the room was overrun by armed German military police. Diana and Young were handcuffed as the German imposter 'Benôit' looked on, gun in hand. He had infiltrated the circuit, gained their trust and then facilitated the agents' arrest. Later he went back to the house and demanded that the Juif family hand over Young's wireless and crystals. The family refused and, after a thorough search, nothing was found; the crystals had been hidden under the baby's mattress. The two agents were first taken to a prison in Lons, and then Diana was taken to Paris, remaining at Gestapo headquarters for two weeks, where, after the war, an inscription was found on the wall of a cell giving her name, rank and the date.[33] She was then taken to Fresnes prison and brought back to 84, avenue Foch for questioning, where Bob Starr reported seeing her in March 1944.[34]

In January 1944, Yolande Beekman had begun to sense that the Germans were aware of her wireless signals and realised that they must be closing in on her. Born Yolande Elsa Maria Unternährer in Paris on 28 October 1911, her family background was Swiss but she grew up in France, moving to London in her teens where she lived near Hampstead Heath. She enjoyed doing children's illustrations and also worked alongside her mother as a *modiste* in Camden Town and Highgate. As Europe descended into war, she joined the WAAF and, as with the other agents, it was her language skills (French, German and some Italian) that attracted the attention of SOE. She was interviewed in November 1942.[35]

It was while training, in August 1943, that she met and fell in love with Jaap Beekman, who was training for the Dutch Section of SOE, and they married later that month.[36] The couple agreed to undertake their missions regardless of their new marriage and the possibility that Yolande was pregnant.[37] So, on 18/19 September 1943, Yolande was taken by Lysander to France where she would work as a wireless operator for the MUSICIAN network and its leader Gustave 'Guy' Biéler in Saint-Quentin. She landed near Tours and made the journey via Paris to Lille alone while carrying her incriminating wireless set. When she arrived she found Saint-Quentin to be a very difficult and dangerous place to work: enemy troops were thick on the ground and she had to be continually on her guard, no matter what she was doing, in case she came under suspicion or the D/F units picked up her wireless signal. In spite of this, she undertook numerous skeds during which she organised arms deliveries of much-needed weaponry for the resistance and sent news of sabotage actions to London. She also attended twenty parachute drops. This was extremely dangerous work as it involved being out after curfew and threatened the arrest of the all-important wireless operator.

In spite of her efforts, Yolande had made a fundamental error: her security was poor, and she had continually operated her wireless from the same attic room. When she saw a German D/F van passing her house in January 1944, she realised she was close to being discovered. She moved her wireless set to the house where she was living but, on 12 January, her host, Monsieur Boury, noticed a man walking down the street with his collar upturned: he thought that perhaps he was wearing earphones and listening out for illegal wireless traffic. Desperate to escape, Yolande moved again, this time to the Café Moulin Brûlé in Omissy, just outside Saint-Quentin, where Biéler (and his newly arrived assistant Paul Tessier) were now also staying.

Flustered and anxious, Yolande perhaps wished that she had had the foresight to move her wireless more often before the D/F units had begun to close in on her. But it was too late now; all she could do was try to hide herself and stay safe. On the morning of 14 January, Tessier had just left for Paris and Yolande and Biéler were in a café discussing the circuit's next move. The Gestapo arrived brandishing pistols – escape was impossible. The café had quickly been identified as the new source of Yolande's transmissions. She was taken to Gestapo HQ in Saint-Quentin for questioning. Some days later she was taken to the pharmacy, where Monsieur Boury worked, as the Gestapo wanted to collect some money that belonged to her which Boury was keeping safe. The owner of the pharmacy feigned ignorance and the Gestapo left empty-handed. It was reported that on this visit Yolande's face 'was swollen and she had clearly been beaten'.[38] Any plans for her escape were thwarted when she was moved to Paris and held in Fresnes prison, where she remained until May 1944.

Only days after Yolande's arrest, locally recruited courier Sonia Olschanesky was also arrested. Described as 'strong, discreet, intelligent and entirely without fear', Sonia was born in Paris on Christmas Day 1912 to Russian parents and grew up to become a dancer. This was not her first arrest – Sonia was Jewish, and in June 1942 she had been arrested as part of a round-up and sent to Drancy internment camp in a north-eastern suburb of Paris, where she and thousands of other Jews awaited deportation. When her mother heard the news, she contacted friends in Germany who managed to produce false papers stating that Sonia had 'economically valuable skills' that were needed for the war effort. Remarkably, she was freed.[39]

By November 1942 Sonia had become a courier for the JUGGLER circuit and, when the circuit leader had to escape, she assumed its leadership. She was never sent to Britain so received no SOE training. However, she had long experience of agents in the JUGGLER and PROSPER circuits and had managed to sit out the worst of the arrests in the latter, which had taken place during the autumn of 1943. That October, Sonia became aware of Noor's arrest; she tried to warn F Section that Noor's radio was probably in German hands and that the messages sent from it could not be relied upon. London considered Sonia's message to be from an unreliable source (she was unknown to them as she had never been to England) and they chose to ignore it. As a result, agents continued to be sent from England and arrests continued to be made across Paris, including her own.

On 21 January 1944, Sonia attended a rendezvous that had been arranged by wireless message: she was to meet with an agent who had been sent to replace Biéler at Soleil d'Or near the Galeries Lafayette. However, when her contact arrived in a black Citroën he was accompanied by three Gestapo agents who had caught him upon landing. Sonia had been caught up in a 'Funkspiel' carried out by means of Yolande Beekman's wireless set and had been convinced of its authenticity as it contained details of Biéler and Yolande (including something about the latter's lipstick). Sonia was imprisoned at Fresnes prison and questioned.

Meanwhile, a complex set of events was unfolding in Poitiers. Mary Herbert, who had severed all ties with the resistance when she gave birth to Claude de Baissac's daughter at the end of 1943, had moved to Poitiers after hearing that she and other resistance members were being hunted by the Gestapo in Bordeaux. She took up residence in the flat formerly belonging to Claude's sister Lise de Baisac, who had herself left Poitiers for her own safety – so it is rather odd that Mary chose to live in a place that may have already come to the Gestapo's attention. But Mary had written to the flat's owner, Madame Gateau, who had said she thought it was 'quite safe'.[40] On the morning of 18 February 1944, the Gestapo, looking for Lise, found Mary in bed feeding her baby. They asked her if she was 'Madame Brisse' – Lise's cover name – and other questions relating to Lise's whereabouts. She was taken to Gestapo HQ for interrogation, leaving her child behind with her maid.

Mary was interrogated by the Gestapo at their Poitiers HQ. She was questioned about her life, her history and her relationship with Lise, and was shown photographs and asked to identify people in them (she said she did not know them). She was also asked to account for her 'queer accent', which she said was down to living in Alexandria and speaking 'French, English, Spanish and Italian plus a smattering of Arabic which was enough to upset anyone's pronunciation'.[41] She repeatedly declared her innocence saying she knew nothing of the woman who had the flat before her: 'There was no reason for the Gestapo to suspect Mary of not being the young French woman she said she was. It hardly seemed likely that a woman who had just given birth could be a British agent.'[42]

Mary was not tortured, but her time in solitary confinement made her ill. She was cold and uncomfortable; a stone slab served as a bed, she was not given any blankets, and there was nowhere else to sit as no chair was provided.[43] Mary was released on 9 April 1944 and told that if she talked about what she had seen or the questions she had been asked, she would be rearrested.[44] She was given back her belongings except a ring that had been mislaid, which was returned to her by the interrogators the next day 'with apologies'.[45] She discovered that her baby had been taken to a convent where she had been very well looked after. After convincing the nuns that she had been wrongly arrested, her daughter was restored to her.[46] Mary sought anonymity and tried to disappear with her daughter to a farmhouse near Poitiers.[47]

During this time, the Gestapo were closing in on agents and resistance circuits all over France. Eliane Plewman was arrested in Marseille. She had been working as a courier to the MONK network, which had been blown around 23 March 1944 when the safe house at 8, rue Mérentié was raided. The agents inside had met to discuss the contents of a recent parachute drop near Meyrargues, which consisted of twenty-four containers of arms and ammunition, all of which had to be distributed according to agreements between local resisters. During the meeting there was a knock at the door: it was armed Gestapo agents, who were acting on a tip-off about black marketeers. (Eliane had told another SOE agent that she was operating successfully on the Marseille black market, so there could have been some truth to this.) An Italian hairdresser who lived nearby reporting hearing gunshots, but no one was harmed. MONK's circuit leader Charles Skepper and a résistant were taken to the local Gestapo HQ. Some Gestapo stayed in the house and set up a *souricière* (mouse-trap) in the hope that there would be yet more agents to ensnare.[48]

The next morning, when Skepper didn't show up for an agreed rendezvous, Eliane and Arthur Steele (who was reportedly carrying his wireless set with him) went to the house to find out if there was a problem. Outside they met Antoine Pierangeli, a member of the resistance, who had arrived for a rendezvous. He had noticed that the blinds were down so he could not tell if the curtains were open or closed – the agreed signal for if the house was safe (open) or unsafe (closed). He told them that he had also encountered a gas company employee at the bottom of the stairs:

> when he rang the bell of Skepper's apartment on the first floor, to ask to read the meter, a man's voice called out that there was no one there. He rang the bell again and eventually, the door was half-opened and, as the meter was just inside, he was allowed in. He was unable to see anything as the doors from the hall were closed, but he suspected the presence of several men due to the heavy pall of cigarette smoke that hung in the air.[49]

Eliane, who was considered to be somewhat impulsive by members of the circuit, told the two men, 'If you're afraid, I'm not. I'm going up.' She drew her pistol, went up the stairs to the apartment and rang the doorbell. She was met by two Germans who seized her by the arm and dragged her inside the apartment. Pierangeli grabbed the wireless set from Steele and made a bid to escape; he was at the end of the road before the Gestapo caught him. Eyewitnesses said that they heard gunshots ringing out, but whether Eliane fired her pistol no one knows.[50] Eliane was taken to Gestapo headquarters, a Belle Époque building situated at 425, rue Paradis. It was here that she was brought from her solitary cell at Baumettes prison and interrogated over the next three or four weeks, and may have been mistreated. She was eventually transferred to Fresnes.

There were now eight F Section women imprisoned at Fresnes: Odette Sansom, Andrée Borrel, Vera Leigh, Diana Rowden, Eliane Plewman, Yolande Beekman, Sonia Olschanesky and Madeleine Damerment. The women could do nothing but wait in their cells, each one unaware that other

SOE agents were confined in the prison. They led a lonely and terrible existence, their days punctuated by interrogations and violence, some with sentences hanging over their heads, with no idea of what the next day would bring or what the outcome of the war would be.

On 12 May 1944, the eight women who had been imprisoned at Fresnes were moved to Karlsruhe prison in Germany. Details as to how and why they were moved remain a mystery. Georg Kaenemund, a political prisoner who worked in the reception office at the prison, said that the women 'arrived by *Sondertransport* (special transport) and were accompanied by men in civilian clothes'. To his knowledge they were not members of either the Karlsruhe or Dijon Gestapo; he did not know who they were. One must surmise that they had travelled with the women from Paris and had either been Fresnes staff or Paris Gestapo.[51]

The prison at Karlsruhe had a men's and a women's block. The women's section was on the first floor and divided by locked doors from the men's prison. There was a maximum of three women per cell, and at its height the prison held between 150–160 women. The SOE agents were put into cell numbers 11, 14, 16, 17, 20, 22, 24 and 25 with one or two other women, in the main German political prisoners.[52] Among them were Hedwig Muller, Else Sauer and Nina Hagen, who 'struck up a very real friendship with our girls and … did everything possible to help them by sharing their food and having their laundry washed'. In cell 16 was Eliane Plewman, and cell 25 belonged to 'the girl known as Yvonne', which was Yolande Beekman's alias. Cell 17 was shared by Else Sauer, Frau Wipfler and Madeleine Damerment, whom they knew as Martine Dussatouy.[53]

During their stay at Karlsruhe, prisoners were regularly interrogated. Sometimes the Gestapo came to them (both Yolande and Madeleine were interrogated there) and at other times they were taken to Gestapo HQ. According to Nina Hagen, who shared a cell with Yolande, she was 'interrogated on arrival and once again by the Gestapo … she had been ill-treated in France and was very worried about her mother, her husband, her sister and her children'.[54] Prison warder Zina Zoeller also said that Yolande 'was not well, she suffered with her legs'.[55]

Madeleine's interrogation was overheard by Georg Kaenemund: 'the interrogation was conducted in German which Martini [*sic*] spoke very well … I cannot remember the questions that were asked, but I do remember that she defended herself most energetically. She said that she was a lieutenant in the British Army, demanded to be brought before a proper court martial, and said that as a member of the armed forces she should not be in a civil prison.'[56] It seems that Madeleine was determined to fight back. But as she was not a member of the armed forces and had been working undercover behind enemy lines she was not protected by the Geneva Convention and therefore had no rights.

Other than being removed for interrogation, the women remained held in their cells. The warders had been given 'strict instructions that the English women were not allowed to be in the court for exercise at the same time. For this reason, in the first few weeks they could only be exercised every 3 or 4 days. After some of them had gone they could be exercised more often.'[57] Prison warder Theresa Becker recalled that 'we were told that we would be required to keep them for a week, but as time went on no one came to collect them.'[58] The women remained at Karlsruhe with no idea of what would become of them.

Just a few days after D-Day, Violette Szabó was arrested and imprisoned at Fresnes, then taken to 84, avenue Foch for interrogation. Her George Cross citation states: 'She was [then] continuously and atrociously tortured but never by word or deed gave away any of her acquaintances or told the enemy anything of any value.'[59] Within her SOE file there is an early draft of her GC citation which refers more specifically to Violette being kept in solitary confinement at Fresnes and having 'had to endure … the torture of the cold douche and others'. But past this, the historical record on her experiences during this period is sadly lacking: the Gestapo files were mostly destroyed; Violette, of course, did not survive to give an affidavit; and the friends in whom she might have confided at the time perished with her.

Eyewitnesses who claimed to know her in prison did come forward later. In 1947, one Mme Meunier, who said she had shared cell 'No. 435, 4th floor, 3rd division, German section' with Violette at Fresnes, fleshed out the day-to-day reality of Violette's prison experience and painted a vivid picture of her extraordinary cellmate. Meunier recalled that Violette was distressed, believing that there was a traitor in London, and repeatedly saying 'I know who has denounced us. He is a member of French section, he is, at the moment in London, and he is the one who told the Germans about our real identity.'[60] This suspicion would have undoubtedly played on Violette's mind and perhaps made her imprisonment all the harder, spending her hours of confinement obsessively playing out scenarios of who had betrayed her without very much hope of redress. Yet it is also possible that her German interrogators deliberately mentioned names and details in order to make her think they knew more than they did, and to make her doubt the organisation for whom she worked.[61]

Fresnes and the avenue Foch were places designed to break a person down until they spoke using the various methods of intimidation and interrogation at the Gestapo's disposal. Huguette Desore, Violette's cellmate at Fresnes prison, remembered her returning after one interrogation and saying, 'Something unimaginable happened to me! He [the interrogator] was furious tonight, crazy and furious, unbelievably worked up.' While Violette did not specify what had happened to her, she was constantly threatened with rape, as were all female prisoners; as Tania Szabó writes, 'women are always vulnerable in certain areas – and these areas do not show the marks of abuse or torture'.[62] During her time in prison Violette was also forced to witness several atrocities. One such was being forcibly shown a 'badly tortured a young resistance fighter, [the Gestapo] showed her how they had smashed his face'; another was being made to watch five resisters being mown down by machine-gun fire.[63] The ill-treatment and torture of agents often occurred in the regional office or prison of the Gestapo, or at 11, rue des Saussaies in Paris.[64] In the face of all this violence and intimidation Violette demonstrated extreme fortitude and bravery throughout her captivity.

Denise Bloch was arrested a few days after Violette and arrived at 84, avenue Foch at 1 a.m. on 18 June. She was held separately from the others as it was already known that she was an English agent. Little is known of Denise's time at Gestapo HQ. It may be assumed that, because she was a wireless operator, she may have been asked about her codes and transmissions, but London never heard from her again so presumably her wireless was not played back. She was allowed to visit Robert Benoist 'in his cell and stay there on occasions'. Eventually she was taken to Fresnes prison.[65]

On 25 June, Yvonne Baseden and her colleagues who had also been arrested were taken to Dole prison where they stayed for 'a couple of nights'. Yvonne was kept with the caretaker's wife, and believed that the intention was to move everyone to Dijon prison where they could be dealt with more effectively; after five days she was taken there along with some black marketeers and the young boy with the wireless set who had inadvertently given her away. A plan was made by local resisters to rescue Yvonne during this journey, but the Germans 'let it be known that any rescue attempt would lead to the immediate execution of the rest of the party'. Once in Dijon, Yvonne was taken to Gestapo headquarters at 32, rue Talant, a control centre through which Berlin directed some of its Gestapo activities in occupied France. On arrival Yvonne's papers were checked and she was put into a cell without being interrogated.[66]

Yvonne said that during her first interrogation, which lasted for two or three hours, she stuck to the false story she had decided on, giving her name as Yvonne Gernier and reciting parts of her cover story, 'but', she recalled, 'unfortunately details of my previous work in Paris were difficult to follow up and on them asking me the name of my boss they saw I hesitated and decided I was not telling the truth'.[67] She refused to tell them the truth and was taken to the basement of the Gestapo HQ building, where she was put in a cell 'which had no light and one tiny window blacked out, and which only had two boards to act as beds one of which was completely covered with blood and with one blanket'. She was 'left in this cell for three days and three nights without any food, water or amenities'. She consoled herself with the knowledge that her arrest had been three weeks after D-Day, and her circuit had done all the work that was required of them for the Allied invasion.

During her incarceration, Yvonne was visited twice and asked if she was prepared to talk yet. She was pressed for details of her employer's name, her job and life in 1942, when, according to her cover story, she should have been working in Paris. The next day her interrogator spoke to her in English and referred to her as 'Odette', which was her code name, but she pretended not to recognise it.[68] On the morning of the fourth day she was taken back to the interrogation room and was 'there confronted with the full facts of what had actually happened before my arrest'. She recalled:

> it was clear to me from what I was told by the Germans that they knew who I was, what I was doing, how I had arrived in the country and in fact all about me and my part in the organisation of which I was a member. To all this I replied nothing but was then asked from what aerodrome in England I had set out and on my stating that I did not know (which was true) I was taken down to the cell wherein I had spent the previous four days by the German interrogator and his interpreter and again asked the same question. When I replied I did not know the German interrogator drew his revolver and fired one or two shots into the ground directly between my feet . . .[69]

The Gestapo knew that Yvonne was a British agent, that her field name was 'Odette', and that she had landed by parachute in the south of France. Yvonne had no idea how they knew so much about her nor where the information had come from, but she continued to feign ignorance, all the while terrified as to what else they might know. At least they were willing to accept the contention that as a wireless operator she was not likely to know much about the working of the circuit. She was also shown a large file containing photographs of Orchard Court personnel with a page left blank in readiness for a picture of Colonel Buckmaster. She said that she did not recognise anybody but was careful 'not to show undue interest in this particular page'.[70]

She was interrogated at regular intervals for about two months by a Gestapo officer with the assistance of a civilian interpreter, and, on occasion, by plainclothes interrogators. She maintained that she was not physically maltreated, except 'from time to time when they would tread on her feet'. She considered that she was 'extremely lucky in having a "reasonable" interrogator dealing with her'.[71] Yvonne's testimony of her arrest and time in prison gives a valuable insight into what life and conditions were like. It is unusual to have such an informative description. For many agents who were incarcerated no such accounts exist as they did not survive to leave any.

Eileen Nearne was among the fortunate few to be able to tell her experiences. She had been arrested on 25 July 1944 when, against her chief's orders, she had gone to her safe house to transmit an urgent message. After setting up her wireless and aerial she transmitted her encoded message as quickly she could. As she was finishing she heard banging from the house next door, a sound that all wireless operators dreaded hearing. Frantically packing away her set, hiding it in a little room and getting rid of her messages, the banging began on her door. She opened it to a man pointing a pistol at her face. He looked around the flat and then called for his colleagues next door to come. They searched the flat room by room and found her wireless, codes and gun. She was handcuffed and driven to Paris. Everything happened so fast and everything that the Gestapo found was so horribly incriminating that Eileen must have endured an agonising journey.

She was taken to 11, rue des Saussaies in the 8th arrondissement of Paris. Here, the Gestapo had one of their notorious offices, consisting of eight holding cells and two interrogation rooms. They occupied the building from June 1940 until August 1944 and in that time countless acts of torture, barbarity and cruelty were inflicted on 'enemies of the state' such as résistants, Jews, communists and criminals. In one of the rooms there was a *baignoire*; other methods of torture included electric shocks to sensitive areas of the body, teeth filing, nail removal, the cutting of the victim's feet before forcing them to walk on salt, burning, kicking, punching, rape and dousing in cold water. One interrogator interspersed his cruelty with breaks when he offered his victims tea, coffee or even brandy. Evidence uncovered on the walls of the prison after the liberation show what a cruel and terrrifying place it was. 'I am afraid,' wrote one prisoner awaiting interrogation. 'Never confess' and 'Don't talk' were etched into the plaster nearby. 'Believing in yourself gives one the power to resist despite the bathtub and all the rest,'[72] reads another, referring to the *baignoire*, with which Eileen would become all too familiar.

During interrogation Eileen was asked questions such as 'what nationality was she, whose was the gun they found in her house? She replied that she was French ... There was a gardener who used to work at the house, the gun had been left by him.'[73] She was also asked how long she had been a wireless operator and for whom she worked. She replied: 'three months and most of the codes were made up by my chief. They then asked me what organisation I worked for. I said that I had joined in France, and that I met my chief in a coffee shop and he engaged me there. They asked me if I had any other friends working with me. I made up some addresses of people. They put me in a cold bath [the *baignoire*] and tried to make me speak but I stuck to my story.' Asked by the Gestapo interrogators if she had 'had a nice bath', Eileen replied, 'yes, I'll complain to the town hall for what you've done.'[74]

Still wet from the immersion, she was taken to a railway station where she had claimed she was to have a rendezvous with her chief: 'we went to the Gare St Lazare at 7 o'clock and waited until 7.15pm. No one came but an air raid warning was sounded and I said he must have been delayed because of it. They then took me back to interrogate me again. The chief of the Gestapo said he would give me a last chance. I stuck to the same story. They then found out that the addresses I had given them were false.' Eileen goes on to report that 'they said they'd given me the benefit of the doubt but they were sending me to a concentration camp, it will not be like here, it'll be your punishment for working against us ...'[75]

Elizabeth Deveraux Rochester also spent time at the rue des Saussaies, where she was kept in solitary confinement for two months. Her second interrogation occurred halfway through this internment. She said that 'naturally I found it very sticky' but she was not treated badly 'except for one crack over the skull'. She stuck to her cover story. At her third interrogation, the Germans told Elizabeth who had denounced her. Elizabeth was tried for possessing a false identity card and was given three months in prison, after which she was sent to Vittel to be interned as a US citizen, managing to escape four days after her arrival, though she was swiftly rearrested. Terrified that she would be deported to Germany as a result of her escape attempt, she told the Germans that she had done it in a fit of homesickness. They left her alone and she remained in prison at Vittel until 18 September 1944, when the camp was liberated by the French and she was freed. She made contact with some local Maquis and asked that a message be sent to Buckmaster; she also asked someone to help her get to Paris so that she could arrange the arrest of the two women who had denounced her. Upon her return to England, Elizabeth once more showed her willingness and dedication to the cause, asking for two months' leave to visit her ailing mother before undertaking 'any further work that may be available'. However, her work for SOE was over.

Lilian Rolfe was arrested a week after Eileen's capture. Almost immediately she was transported to Fresnes, from where she was taken to 84, avenue Foch to undergo interrogation. But time was running out for the Germans: resistance and SOE networks had helped to clear the way for the Allied forces and the advance was well under way. In early August, just weeks before the liberation of Paris, the Gestapo realised they were beginning to lose their iron grip on the city and made one final gesture: they began to kill the prisoners at Fresnes. The women agents held there escaped that fate, but that was not the end of the story.

On 8 August 1944, just eleven days before the liberation of Paris, a train left France for Germany with thirty-seven SOE men and women, including Lilian Rolfe, Denise Bloch and Violette Szabó, and other prisoners on board. Prior to departure, the prisoners had been assembled in the main hall at Fresnes. Some of them recognised one another; some had not seen another person, let alone a familiar face, for months. It must have been a time of great relief, but also great worry: why were SOE agents being transported together, and where to? They were taken to the Gare de l'Est and boarded a train bound for Germany. The male agents were handcuffed in twos and put in a prison carriage while, under close guard, the women, also chained in pairs, sat in the third-class compartment. Among the male agents was

'Tommy' Yeo-Thomas, the most famous agent from SOE's RF Section; he had been brutally tortured and became the first agent to receive the George Cross. There was also F Section agent Harry Peulevé. On his first mission he had broken his leg on landing and, after a painful recovery, escaped across the Pyrenees. He had met Violette while recuperating and the two had become very close, but had not taken their relationship too seriously due to their imminent departure for the field.

The next afternoon at around 2 p.m. the train was attacked by Allied aircraft and one of its carriages was destroyed, bringing the train to a halt. The hand-cuffed SOE men could not move freely and, unsurprisingly, many of them began to panic. They were also parched with thirst as all the water from the Red Cross bottles had been consumed during the night. Yeo-Thomas said that 'we all felt deeply ashamed when we saw Violette Szabó, while the raid was still on, come crawling along the corridor towards us with a jug of water which she had filled in the lavatory. With her, crawling too, came the girl to whose ankle she was chained.'[76] It was an act of courage which demonstrated Violette's selfless-ness, staying to help her fellow SOE prisoners rather than attempting to escape.

The prisoners passed an uncomfortable night in some stables, where, though chained to others, Violette and Peulevé talked for hours through a chink in the wooden stalls about old times and their experiences in France. As Peulevé recalled:

Bit by bit everything was unfolded – her life in Fresnes, her interviews in Avenue Foch. But either through modesty or a sense of delicacy, since some of the tortures were too intimate in their application; or perhaps she did not wish to live again through the pain of it, she spoke hardly at all about the tortures she had been made to suffer. She was in a cheerful mood. Her spirits were high. She was confident of victory and was resolved on escaping no matter where they took her.[77]

It was the last time they would ever see one another. The next day the prisoners were taken in trucks via Metz to Saarbrücken, where the men and women were separated.

The Gestapo camp of Neue Bremm at Saarbrücken was on the French border, and many prisoner transports from collection camps in France were brought there; among the prisoners were political opponents, POWs, resistance fighters, 'asocials' and the work-shy, and numerous nationalities – French, Belgian, British and Italian. The camp was set up as an extended police prison due to overcrowding at the main prison in Saarbrücken, and so, unlike the concentration camps which were run by the Economic and Administrative Office of the SS, it was run by the local Gestapo. This meant the Gestapo had *carte blanche* to do whatever they liked without answering to any other authorities – and they did. Initially the camp staff were supposed to discipline the prisoners for a few weeks and then release them. However, many prisoners were incarcerated for longer: some would be sent to concentration camps, while some would never leave and were murdered at Neue Bremm.

The camp was divided into two wings, one for male and one for female inmates, in the middle of each of which was a pool of water to be used in the event of fire breaking out. These pools became a cruel device used by the Gestapo to torture or, in some cases, kill their victims. Those who were not sent on work details clearing debris from air raids were given exercise doing 'camp-sports'. A survivor testified that the ' "Pastime" of the whole day was so-called "Sport", i.e. between 8 am and 5:30 pm, with hourly break for dinner. Those "sporty" exercises on Commandos [POWs' working parties] "*hinlegen – rollen – auf! – marsch, marsch – hüpfen*, etc." led to daily casualties of an average of five persons.'[78] Sports included prisoners being forced to hop around the edge of the pool for hours in a crouched position with their hands clasped behind their necks. The guards threw those who collapsed or lost consciousness through exhaustion into the pool, and several prisoners drowned after guards forced their heads down with wooden clubs. Many prisoners were deliberately starved and died of malnutrition, others from the sadistic abuse they received from their guards. Those prisoners who needed medical attention were denied it, or, as some sources suggest, the Gestapo doctors simply killed them with a lethal injection. Conditions were so bad that some of the inmates who were taken on to various concentration camps later testified that Neue Bremm was worse than Buchenwald or Dachau.[79] However, the SOE women at Saarbrücken were joined by Yvonne Baseden, who later said that none of them seemed to have been 'ill-treated'.[80]

Yvonne Rudellat, who had been in prison since the summer of 1943, was taken to a different camp, the Fort de Romainville on the eastern outskirts of Paris. It has been described as a 'brutal stone giant ... a bloated, moated, impregnable monstrosity'.[81] It was a prison, transit camp and place of summary execution for civilian prisoners who did not toe the line of the Nazi regime. The inmates consisted of resistance fighters, political prisoners, communists and intellectuals. For them the privations at Romainville were harsh, the punishment cruel and death a constant threat, be it for their own crimes or someone else's.

Prisoners at Romainville were among the pool of 'criminals' from which the Nazis selected their victims to be executed in reprisal for acts of resistance. For example, 116 prisoners were shot in revenge for an attack on German soldiers at the Rex cinema in Paris. Another 16 were shot in retaliation for the assassination of a German officer in Nantes. On most occasions the condemned did not even know why they were being killed. The wave of terror that rolled through the camp was chilling: no one knew who was going to be next or why. Communist resistance fighter Danielle Casanova tried to draw strength from the atrocities. In a letter written in the camp she said: 'Be sure to tell everyone that the friends whose husbands were shot have borne this terrible ordeal with great courage and they are in every way worthy of those who are not ... know only that they died as heroes ... in them, in the love of our country and of our Party, we draw strength to withstand the hardships of imprisonment, and we are ready for anything.'[82]

Romainville was described as 'Death's waiting room' where 'Alles ist verboten' was painted on the door of each cell – 'Everything is forbidden'. According to Danielle Casanova, there was 'iron discipline, or rather bullying and inhuman treatment'. She was imprisoned for four days without food and spent a further eight 'lying on the floor, no blankets or coats'. She wrote: 'since we're here, we continue to suffer terribly from hunger, and we are reduced to eating cabbage stalks thrown away and potato peelings ... we do not have the right to receive parcels'.[83]

Despite being closely monitored, the prisoners could mingle in the large courtyard and, as a result, relationships and friendships were formed. Two British prisoners, Anthony Faramus and Eddie Chapman, began relationships with two female inmates. Likewise, acts of resistance and patriotism occurred within the camp, such as the small handwritten underground paper called 'Patriot Romainville fort', which contained the news from the war and tried to boost its readers' morale.[84]

It was here that Yvonne Rudellat waited to learn what was going to happen to her. There were no other SOE agents there to give her solace; she made friends but, partly due to the head wound she had sustained before being arrested, was never really sure of herself nor why she was there at all. But she did not have to wait too much longer for a reunion of sorts. On 21 August 1944, Yvonne, together with her fellow agents Violette Szabó, Lilian Rolfe and Denise Bloch, was transported to a women's concentration camp.

PART III
DEATH AND DELIVERANCE

7

NIGHT AND FOG

[E]fficient and enduring intimidation can only be achieved either by capital punishment or by measures by which the relatives of the criminals do not know the fate of the criminal ... The prisoners will vanish without a trace.

Nacht und Nebel Erlass (Night and Fog Decree), 7 December 1941[1]

The concentration camp of Natzweiler-Struthof was 50 km south-west of Strasbourg, in the annexed French region of Alsace-Lorraine. The camp opened in May 1941 and received 1,500 prisoners who had previously been kept in the Hotel Struthof (hence the camp's name). The prisoners worked in nearby granite quarries on construction projects, including at the camp itself. By the summer of 1943, many prisoners, including members of the French resistance, were detained at Natzweiler-Struthof in a marked attempt to subdue resistance activity across Western Europe. That summer, a gas chamber was also constructed at the camp in a building that formed part of the hotel compound. The bodies of eighty gassed Jewish prisoners were sent to the University of Strasbourg where the anatomist Dr August Hirt collected Jewish skeletons to establish Jewish 'racial inferiority'. Medical experiments were also carried out at Natzweiler, including tests to find treatments for typhus and yellow fever.

By 1944, there were about 50 sub-camps with 20,000 prisoners working, living and dying in them. The main camp had now swelled to approximately 7,000 prisoners, who were required to provide forced labour to help produce arms and construct underground armament manufacturing facilities. Over the course of four years, between 19,000 and 20,000 people died in the Natzweiler-Struthof camp system.

On 13 May 1944, on the orders of the RSHA (Reich Main Security Office), eight SOE women were transported from their respective Gestapo prisons and put into protective custody at Karlsruhe prison until further orders were received.[2] After the women had been in the prison some weeks, the chief warder Theresa Becker and her deputy Ida Hager had grown frustrated with the extra burden of housing these special prisoners, so they approached prison director Geisendoerfer and asked him what was to be done with them. Knowing he could only act on direct orders from above, he contacted RSHA in Berlin, who eventually issued a telexed reply instructing him to arrange for the execution of four of the eight women in a convenient, though unspecified, camp.[3] Natzweiler-Struthof was chosen by Gestapo officers Wassmer and Roesner because, being 165 km from Karlsruhe, it was one of the closest. The four women chosen were Sonia Olschanesky, Vera Leigh, Diana Rowden and Andrée Borrel.

These four women, as well as those deported in the subsequent transports from Karlsruhe, were part of the *Nacht und Nebel* policy. Hitler had issued the secret directive since called the *Nacht und Nebel Erlass* (Night and Fog Decree) on 7 December 1941. The same day, an executive ordinance was issued by Armed Forces High Command Feldmarschall Wilhelm Keitel, and on 4 February 1942 the directive and ordinance were published to the police and the SS. The decree targeted political activists and resisters and ordered for them to be 'disappeared', imprisoned or killed. It was the intention of the Nazis that *Nacht und Nebel* prisoners would be depersonalised and stripped of identity before vanishing without a trace. In the case of Sonia, Vera, Diana and Andrée, it was a success, as very little information identifying the women remains. Furthermore, in contrast to those who were sent to Ravensbrück, the women sent to Natzweiler did not meet other prisoners. Any recollections are snatched and very few corroborate one another as the testimonies come from prisoners and perpetrators alike – all of whom, by the end of the war, had very different motives for speaking out.

On receipt of the instructions to move the four women, Josef Gmeiner, chief of the Gestapo head office at Karlsruhe, instructed Roesner to make the necessary arrangements for their transportation from Karlsruhe to Natzweiler. The female agents he chose for the first executions were all captured in 1943, but they were never put on trial. Nor were they ever officially informed that they had been sentenced to death.

Between 4 and 6 a.m. on 6 July 1944, quite a substantial party assembled at Karlsruhe prison: Wassmer, Roesner, prison guard Frau Simon, an unnamed typist and an unnamed member of the Karlsruhe Gestapo. They fetched the women from their cells and took them by car to the station. The SOE agents must have wondered what was going on as so many people had been brought out to accompany them. They still had no idea where they were going, but wherever it was they were under a close guard.

In any other circumstance the journey by train would have been a pleasant one, passing through woodlands, countryside and green fields. Through the windows they would have seen day-to-day life continuing at farms, schools and villages – the like of which the women had not seen since their arrests. They carried their belongings in suitcases, folded their coats over their arms and, to other passengers, would have looked more or less like anyone else. But the women who boarded the 08.10 train to Strasbourg were under heavy guard. Once at Strasbourg, the German women who accompanied them were sent back to Karlsruhe. The party then caught a local train to 'a station not far from Natzweiler', probably Schirmeck, where they were picked up by a car driven by the camp commandant, SS Obersturmbannführer Fritz Hartjenstein. This procedure was rather unusual in itself and emphasised that they were indeed special prisoners.[4]

The journey brought them up a steep winding mountain pass lined with trees. Near the top of the mountain they passed a hotel, in the grounds of which, unbeknownst to them, was the camp's gas chamber. After a mile or so they reached the camp, arriving mid-afternoon, when they would have attracted maximum attention as work parties were returning and evening *Appell* (roll call) was approaching, so the camp was busy as inmates went about their business. As the car pulled into the camp it caused quite a stir. It was very unusual to see a car in the camp at all, but then, according to prisoner and escape line organiser Albert Guérisse (also known as 'Pat' O'Leary), 'Hartjenstein took the car on a curious lap of honour around the camp.' Guérisse had only been in the camp for a couple of weeks, but he was already alert to any suspicious behaviour that might be deemed of interest after the war.[5]

Witnesses were amazed still further to see four women get out. Natzweiler was a men's camp and the sight of these well-dressed young women was a novelty that few would ever forget. In a letter dated 8 June 1946, W.Ch.J.M. van Lanschot, a former camp inmate, recalled:

> I remember that I saw those four girls when they arrived at Natzweiler. In the morning I was working with potato peelers outside the kitchen when we saw four girls going down in the direction of the bunker ... It was the first time we saw women in Natzweiler and everybody was interested in the reason for which they were brought in. Anyhow the general opinion was that they were too good to start a 'puff' [a brothel] with.[6]

Rumours were rife in the camp. Some prisoners thought they were there to start an SS brothel; others believed that they were inspectors.[7] According to camp guard Conrad Schultz, 'Commandant Hartjenstein had informed the women that they would be employed in the SS kitchen or in the SS officer's Mess.'[8] As far as can be ascertained, no one ever told the women that they were there to be executed.

Guérisse saw them as they arrived, as did SOE F Section agent Brian Stonehouse. For him it was also 'the first time that I had seen women at this camp, the occurrence clearly stamped itself in my mind.'[9] Stonehouse made a mental note of what they were wearing and how they looked; he later painted a picture of the women as they arrived at the camp which now hangs in the lounge at the Special Forces Club. He recalled:

The four women were carrying various parcels and one was carrying, what I remember thinking at the time was that it was not a very good fur coat. There was one tall girl with very fair, heavy hair. I could see that it was not its natural colour as the roots of her hair were dark. She was wearing a black coat, French wooden-soled shoes and was carrying a fur coat on her arm. Another girl had very black oily hair, and wore stockings, aged about 20 to 25 years, was short and was wearing a tweed coat and skirt. A third girl was middle height, rather stocky, with shortish fair hair tied in a multi coloured ribbon, age about 28. She was wearing a grey flannel short 'finger-tip' length swagger coat with a grey skirt which I remember thinking looked very English. The fourth woman of the party [was wearing a brown tweed coat and skirt]. She was petite ... she had short brown hair. None of the women wore makeup and all looked pale and tired.[10]

Wassmer handed the agents to the camp staff and gave them the 'movement and execution order which had been sent from Amt IV, Berlin'. Hartjenstein gave him a receipt for them and said that the notice of execution would be forwarded. Wassmer and the Karlsruhe contingent then left. Their job was done and orders had been followed; as far as they were concerned what happened next had nothing to do with them.[11]

Vera, Andrée, Sonia and Diana had been left in the Politische Leitung, the office of the political department of the camp. There, the SS dentist remembered seeing 'three or four women who were busy unpacking their kit – one was brushing her hair'. He offered one of the women a cigarette.[12] Once the agents had been registered, they proceeded, under SS guard, down the Lagerstrasse, which was the main camp street. On either side loomed the camp barracks, buildings of concrete and wood in which hundreds of prisoners were crammed in appallingly squalid conditions. They walked down the steps of this strange landscape towards the Zellenbau (prison cells) at the far end of the camp. The women did not know where they were, why they were there, nor what their future held.

Stonehouse saw them go, saying they walked so near him he could 'observe them very closely. They went down the full length of the path and turned to the left towards the crematorium building where they disappeared from my view'.[13] Initially the women were put in a cell together, then in twos and finally alone. Vera, Diana, Sonia and Andrée had some friendly conversations with fellow prisoners during their last hours. A Dutch prisoner, George Boogaerts, 'tried at once to enter into contact with one of them and as the windows of the infirmary looked on to the Zellenbau I managed to enter into communication with two of them who shared a cell. They opened their window and [they] exchanged a few words . . . one of the women was dark and . . . called herself Denise, I was able to pass her some cigarettes and in gratitude for this she sent me, through Franz Berg, a small tobacco pouch'.[14] 'Denise' was Andrée Borrel's field name; after the war Boogaerts identified a photograph of her as the woman he had spoken to.

Boogaerts also saw to it that Guérisse managed to snatch some words with the women. He had worked on the PAT escape line with Andrée before she became an SOE agent. It was not until after the war that he realised to whom he had been speaking. He recalled that he went to the window, whistled and 'saw a woman appear at a window in her cell. I told her "I am a British officer." I asked her "who are you?" She said "I am British". She wished me the best of luck and I wanted to keep talking but unfortunately the SS appeared, a guard', and the conversation came to an abrupt halt.[15]

At 6 p.m., Franz Berg, a prisoner who worked in the crematorium, was ordered 'to have the crematorium oven heated to its maximum by 9.30pm and then to disappear'.[16] Since there were no dead bodies from the camp to burn that day, this could only mean one thing: an execution was due to take place. As evening drew on all the prisoners were told they must be in their huts by 8 p.m. with the blackout covers in place over the windows; no one was to look out or attempt to see anything of what was occurring. Those who did would never forget what they saw that night.[17]

The SS wanted to get their engagement with the SOE agents over with relatively swiftly that evening, as their colleague Dr Röhde was leaving Natzweiler and there was a farewell party for him that night. At 7 p.m. Conrad Schultz and Peter Strauss went to see the women in their cells in the Zellenbau. They looked in at them through trap doors and Strauss commented, 'beautiful things, what?' The women were taken to the crematorium, accompanied by 'SS men with torches'.[18]

At 9.30 p.m., Berg, who was still stoking the ovens, saw an SS party arrive at the crematorium. He identified them as Dr Röhde (who was in civilian clothes), his replacement, Dr Plaza, and Commandant Hartjenstein, as well as other officials: Oberstrumführer Johannes Otto, Shutzhaftlagerführer Wolfgang Zeuss and Arbeitdeinstführer Emil Bruttel. Dr Plaza then ordered Berg back to his room that he shared with two other prisoners within the crematorium building. A few minutes later the SS guards checked to see if the men were sleeping; many were pretending to. One of the cell's occupants, Georg Fuhrmann, had a top bunk and could see through a fanlight into the corridor; he was able to give a running commentary on what little he saw to Berg, who later relayed it at the Natzweiler trial. 'We heard low voices in the next room,' he said, 'and then the noise of a body being dragged along the floor . . . at the same time that this body was brought past we heard the noise of heavy breathing and low groaning combined.' Fuhrmann then saw another two bodies being dragged past, with the same noises and groans:

> the fourth woman, however, was different, she resisted, *'pourquoi'* and I heard a voice which I recognised as that of the doctor in civilian clothes say *'pour typhus'*. We then heard the noise of a struggle and the muffled cries of a woman. I assumed that someone held a hand over her mouth. I heard this woman being dragged away too. She was groaning louder that the others. From the noise of the crematorium oven doors which I heard, I can state definitely that in each case the groaning women were placed immediately in the crematorium oven.[19]

Each time the crematorium door was opened flames flew from the chimney. Those prisoners who were peering from behind curtains or round corners recognised the unmistakable sign that a body had been placed in the oven. Guérisse claimed to see the flames four times, one for each woman he had seen being led into the crematorium.[20]

It is at this point that the women lose any sense of individuality and their story now takes on a decidedly impersonal air. They are no longer Vera, Diana, Andrée and Sonia: they are simply 'the women' by all who talk about them. None of the eyewitnesses knew who they were, let alone who was who, and the German staff did not care; they simply had orders to obey. Most of the evidence concerning their deaths comes from affidavits given after the war to Vera Atkins or testimonies at the Natzweiler trial held in Wuppertal on 29 May 1946.

What exactly happened to Diana, Vera, Sonia and Andrée in that room within the crematorium building to make them insensible? Dr Werner Röhde gave his testimony at the Natzweiler trial, telling the court that each woman had received a lethal injection. When the first woman was brought in, he 'gave her an intravenous injection in the arm': 'I think that it was 20cc injection of Evipan or a similar preparation. Death was instantaneous. Peter Strauss then took the body away. I was so upset by this that I was unable to give the injection to the second woman who was brought in, and Plaza took over from me.' Each of the women was dispatched in this manner and taken away to be burnt by Peter Strauss, the camp executioner and man in charge of the crematorium.[21]

Röhde seemed unsure as to what substance he was actually injecting but he knew it to be lethal. Further evidence given at the trial suggests that the injection was in fact phenol (carbolic acid) rather than Evipan, which can be used as an anaesthetic. However, delivering lethal injections was not the usual method of execution at Natzweiler – it was shooting or hanging. So why were the women treated differently?

One reason for the use of injections was that, in the Nazis' eyes, it was more humane – the perpetrators' dissonant word – for the victim, as it ensured that the death was less public and less drawn out than hanging. Injections could also be given without the victims knowing that they were being executed. The doctors claimed that they were doing the best they could for the women since they could do nothing to 'alter or cancel their sentence.'[22] At the Natzweiler trial the doctors and their attorneys defended their actions. The attorney for the defence, Dr Groebel, stated that:

Until this time this camp received only men. These were the first females who had been executed there. I can imagine it must be something exceptional for a soldier whether he has to shoot a man or whether he has to shoot a woman, and I can imagine that he is even less capable of hanging a woman than he is a man. And I can also imagine that a further way out was found which one can say, if it had been properly carried out, would have been the most humane way.[23]

The idea to inject rather than hang was Dr Röhde's suggestion. At his trial he said it was 'more humane to kill [the women] with painless injections than to let Peter Strauss hang them',[24] and that his 'only solace is that [he] could save these women from being hanged'.[25] However, from the evidence available, the women were not humanely killed by the injections, but merely rendered temporarily unconscious; Berg suggested that the women were groaning in the corridor, while Dr Plaza claimed that death was immediate. At the trial, Dr Plaza described in detail how the injections worked, assuring all who listened that the women agents had died within seconds of having the injection and any noise was air being expelled from their lungs:

After the dose had been injected into the main vein of the left arm, in about 10 to 20 seconds sudden paralysis or cramp spread over the whole body. The breathing stopped, the pupils of the eyes rolled upwards, the muscles of the face were paralysed, and this condition remained for several seconds. This paralysis was then relieved by a complete muscular collapse. This collapse was quite apparent in the face which took on a waxen colour, the lips lost colour, the body became limp, the pupils of the eyes again returned to their normal state and the eyes were half closed so that only half of the pupils were visible. I think later that air escaped out of the lungs caused by the paralysis. The pulse could not be felt anymore, and breathing entirely stopped.[26]

There is more evidence to the contrary which suggests that not only were the women still alive, but that one woman actually regained consciousness as she was being put into the crematorium oven and attacked Strauss. At the trial, Strauss denied being involved in the executions, stating that he was on leave at the time. But eyewitness accounts put him at the scene of the crime and he himself admitted later that night what had happened to Conrad Schultz.[27]

After the executions, the members of the SS went to their party to bid farewell to Dr Röhde. Some men drank too much, including Strauss, who was apparently 'very drunk' when he started talking to Schultz: 'He said to me in the presence of Alex Wagner "I have been in Auschwitz for a long time, in my time four million people have gone up the chimney, but I have never experienced anything like this before. I am finished". I noticed that Strauss's face had been severely scratched.'[28] Strauss then described the events of that evening, saying that the four women were brought into the corridor in the crematorium which led from the dissecting room to the ovens. There they were told to sit on a bench and then asked to undress for a medical inspection. They refused to do so unless a female doctor was called, but there was not one at Natzweiler. Strauss also said that at this point the women were told they would be vaccinated against illness, and that their suspicions were raised by the fact that by now they were trapped with no means of escape. 'The first was taken by Strauss and injected in the upper arm by the doctor. Strauss told [Schultz] that he helped this first woman back to the bench, where she sat down next to the others who were still waiting. When Strauss arrived back with the second after she had been injected, he said he found the first was sitting stiff and in a stupefied condition.' All four were rendered unconscious. At no point did Strauss say that they were dead, 'he said they were finished. They were stiff, but the word dead was never mentioned.'[29]

They were then dragged along the corridor to the ovens, where they were placed alternately head or feet first. Strauss told Schultz that when the last woman 'was halfway in the oven (she had been put in feet first) she had come to, and had screamed and resisted. As there were sufficient men there, they were able to push her into the oven, but not before she resisted, scratched Strauss's face and shouted "*vive la France*".'[30] There is no way of knowing which agent this was. All four women went to their deaths in the same way and there is no means of identifying who was who. This was *Nacht und Nebel* as the Nazis intended it: the victims were faceless, nameless and went to their deaths in such a way that, without the war trials, it would have been impossible to find out what had happened to them.

The accounts vary on exactly how soon after being injected Andrée, Vera, Sonia and Diana died. The SS doctors maintained that they had died within seconds of the injections being administered and that it was impossible for any of them to have regained consciousness and therefore to have been burnt alive. Röhde even commented that 'in concentration camps the most impossible rumours about the most impossible things' occur, implying that the camp grapevine had twisted the story even further.[31] According to Tadeusz Paczuła, a Polish prisoner at Auschwitz, 'it was known that an intravenous dose of 10 millilitres [cc] of phenol caused death'.[32] An eye-witness at Natzweiler who was the camp's medical orderly, Bruttel, testified that 'in each case 10cc of liquid phenol were used. According to the doctors it was pure phenol.' He also recalled that he was the one who had collected it from the store (when it transpired there was not enough Evipan) and that he was ordered by Dr Plaza to bring along 'the phenol and a 10cc syringe as well as one or two strong needles'.[33]

It could be construed from the testimonies, unreliable as they are, that the first three women had been rendered insensible, or perhaps even been killed by the injections. For the fourth unfortunate woman, whoever she was, it may have been that the doctors did not have enough phenol to kill her or were unable to deliver a lethal dose. She lost consciousness but regained it when near the heat of the ovens where she screamed and fought for her life. We will never know the whole story.

In the immediate post-war period, Vera Atkins tried to ascertain what had happened to Vera, Sonia, Diana and Andrée. Belatedly receiving an honorary commission in the WAAF as a Flight Officer, later promoted to Squadron

Officer, Vera had stepped down from her role as the 'power behind the throne' of Buckmaster and now made it her business to find out what had happened to the missing agents of F Section: 118 in total, including 12 women. She travelled all over France and Germany tracing their footsteps, interviewing people who might have known them and interrogating German guards and perpetrators. She had a list of the missing, but one agent who was killed at Natzweiler was not on it.

Sonia Olschanesky was not officially on the SOE casualty list as she was recruited in the field and not through SOE HQ in London. Her description matched that of Noor Inayat Khan who, by the end of the war, was also missing. Through a series of interrogations and interviews which have been quoted above (and which were used in the war trials), Vera Atkins managed to ascertain what had happened to Diana Rowden, Vera Leigh and Andrée Borrel, and she believed that Noor had been the fourth victim at Natzweiler. A detailed letter was sent to each woman's family outlining their final hours, their death by lethal injection and the immediate cremation of their bodies. So, initially, Noor was listed as one of the Natzweiler dead, and Vera wrote to Noor's brother in June 1946: 'We regret to inform you that we have now received definite information that this officer who has been reported missing from operations with effect from October 1943, was killed at Natzweiler on approx. 25 July 1944.'[34] At the commencement of the war crime trials, another letter was sent to Noor's mother: 'In view of the distressing circumstances in which she was killed, we are most anxious to spare you any further pain which such publicity might entail, and should you desire, I should be only too willing to endeavour to arrange for the suppression of her name from any reports which may be published.'[35] But it proved impossible to do so, and Noor's name was printed alongside those of the other three women. The letter to Noor's mother was sent in May 1946. In the meantime, Vera had made a discovery.

While she was sure that the fourth woman executed at Natzweiler was Noor, she had had no documentary evidence to support it; she had relied on testimony and eyewitness accounts. The name in the Karlsruhe registers was Sonia Olschanesky. However, Vera still believed that this could have been an alias that Noor adopted (just as Madeleine Damerment used Martine Dussautoy). It was not until revisiting several files and examining those at Pforzheim that Vera discovered the truth. Noor had not been sent to Natzweiler in July 1944, she had been moved to Dachau in the autumn.

On the morning of 11 September 1944, Noor was taken from her cell at Pforzheim prison, where she had been chained and manacled for several months, to Karlsruhe where three other SOE agents were being held: Madeleine Damerment, Yolande Beekman and Eliane Plewman.[36] The orders received by teleprinter were to take the women to Dachau; according to Gestapo chief Josef Gmeiner, the message from RSHA in Berlin was that 'the last of the British women . . . were also to be transferred to a concentration camp'.[37] Gmeiner maintained that he had no choice in either obeying the orders or in choosing which camp the women went to.

In the very early hours of 12 September, Noor, Madeleine, Yolande and Eliane were prepared for their transfer. Dressed in civilian clothing, they greeted one another and 'were delighted and surprised by how well they looked'.[38] They had all been in solitary confinement for nine months; seeing other women and fellow agents must have brought intense relief and yet raised fears as to why they were being grouped together. Some of them knew one another from happier times in England – Yolande and Noor had trained together. The women were handcuffed 'two together in the usual manner'; the Gestapo Officer, Christian Ott, had been told to 'exercise every care' with the women.[39]

According to Ott, Allied bombing had disrupted train lines and so it was decided that the prisoners should be taken by car to Bruchsal and from there take the train to Stuttgart, where they would change. Another guard, Max Wassmer, met the prisoners at Bruchsal junction, where they arrived at 2.30 a.m. to begin their 200-mile journey. Ott expressed surprise that the women were being sent to Dachau, as it was a men's camp. Wassmer showed him the telex: 'the four prisoners will be transferred from Karlsruhe to KZ Dachau and will then be immediately executed'. It was signed by Ernst Kaltenbrunner, head of the RSHA. Ott also stated that he wished he hadn't come, as the women had made a 'good impression on me and I regretted their fate'.[40]

Instead of the cramped cattle trucks that one associates with transports to concentration camps, the women travelled in a train compartment. Although under guard, they experienced more freedom than they had in months; they could admire the passing scenery, which must have seemed a novelty after months in prison, and they talked to one another in English, catching up on the latest news since the Allied invasion.[41] They ate bread and sausage that they had brought with them for the journey and smoked English cigarettes. Once these had run out, they smoked German ones offered to them by their guards.[42] They changed trains at Stuttgart, where they waited for an hour or so. The women stood apart from their guards, continuing to chat and enjoying one another's company.[43] They then boarded a train to Munich when they also talked to Ott, who later recalled:

I did not tell them of the fate in store for them, on the contrary I tried to keep them in a happy mood. They wanted to know where they were being taken. Wassmer told them they were going to a camp where farming was done. They were not told that they were going to Dachau. The Englishwoman [possibly Yolande, assuming that Ott and the woman were speaking in German, as she was the only one of the four able to do so fluently] told me that all four were officers in the women's auxiliary forces. She said she had the rank of major and one of her companions was captain and two were lieutenants. On closer questioning she told me that she had been dropped by parachute into France and had worked in the secret service.[44]

At Munich the women changed trains again, this time for a local service that would get them within 2 km of Dachau. The time of arrival varies according to various sources, but it was late, sometime between 10 p.m. and midnight. As the women walked through the chilly night air towards the camp, the search-lights swept over them, lighting up the camp and revealing the endless rows of barracks, the *Appellplatz* (roll call square), the barbed wire and the gallows.

The camp had been built eleven years previously, in 1933, as a prison for political prisoners, but soon housed Jehovah's Witnesses, homosexuals,

Roma, Sinti, political prisoners from occupied territories and Jews. Such was the reputation of Dachau that it became a model concentration camp and included an SS training school where guards could hone their skills in brutality and violence.

The women were taken through the gate bearing the words '*Arbeit macht frei*', 'Work sets you free', but they would neither work at this camp nor would they ever be free again. They were handed over as prisoners to the camp guards and their possessions were seized. Ott recalled the guards making comments about the 'pretty watches and jewellery, rings with sapphire stones and gold bangles', all of which were taken from them. Whether or not they were put into camp uniform is not mentioned, but, as the intention was to kill them almost immediately, it seems unlikely. Ott then left the women and never saw them again.[45] In stark contrast to the relatively comfortable journey and the brief solace they had found in being together, the four women were led to their cells and were incarcerated separately for the remainder of the night.

There are two versions of what happened next. When Vera Atkins interviewed Ott he told her what Wassmer had told him: 'the four prisoners had come from the barracks in the camp, where they had spent the night, into the yard where the shooting was to be done. Here Wassmer announced the death sentence to them. Only the Lagerkommandant and two SS men had been present. The German speaking English woman had told her companions of the death sentence ... all four had grown very pale and wept.' The women asked if they could appeal, and were told they could not. They also asked for a priest, which was declined on the grounds there was not one at the camp:[46]

The four prisoners now had to kneel with their heads towards a small mound of earth and were killed by the two SS, one after another by a shot through the back of the neck. During the shooting the two Englishwomen held hands and the two French women likewise. For three of the prisoners the first shot caused death, but for the German speaking Englishwoman a second shot had to be fired as she still showed signs of life after the first shot.[47]

Vera Atkins wrote in July 1946 to the women's relatives that 'the only consolation I feel able to offer is that, until the end, they were cheerful and of good faith, and that whilst perhaps suffering equal hardship, they were spared the horrors of the concentration camp'.[48]

But, within a few years, evidence came to light which suggested such consolation was misplaced. In 1958, a letter was sent to Jean Overton Fuller, later the biographer of Noor Inayat Khan, which stated that an eyewitness had seen what happened to the women before they were shot.

The letter came from Lieutenant Colonel H.J. Wickey, who was an officer in Canadian Military Intelligence. After the war he became military governor of Wuppertal-Eberfeld in the British zone of occupation, where he met a German officer who had spent time in Dachau and who claimed to have witnessed the deaths of the four agents. Wickey stated that the story was very different from Ott's version and that the women had not all been shot together. Eliane Plewman, Yolande Beekman and Madeleine Damerment were 'handled very roughly' before their execution: 'one of them had her face slapped several times; they were all kicked several times'. They were partially undressed and in rags when death came from a gunshot to the back of the neck, after which they were immediately cremated.[49]

Noor had been separated because she was still considered to be 'very dangerous'. At Dachau, a special kind of torment had been reserved for her and she was to be given the 'full treatment'. As Wickey did not know who he was identifying, he referred to Noor as the 'Creole', due to the darker colour of her skin in comparison to the others.

> The Creole was kept outside, chained and almost naked. She was subjected to ridicule, was slapped and kicked several times, apparently by this same man who was very fond of this type of sport. She was left all night lying on the floor in a cell and the next day, rather than drag her to the crematorium, they gave her some more rough handling. Finally in a cell they shot her with a small pistol and dead or half dead she was dragged by some other inmates and thrown in to the furnace.[50]

Further evidence stated that a guard named Yoop said that she had been 'stripped, kicked, and abused all night by an officer called Ruppert. When Ruppert got tired and the girl was a "bloody mess", he told her that he would shoot her. He ordered her to kneel and put his pistol against her head. The only word she said before dying was "*liberté*".'[51]

The deaths of Sonia Olschanesky, Vera Leigh, Diana Rowden and Andrée Borrel in July at Natzweiler-Struthof, and Eliane Plewman, Yolande Beekman, Madeleine Damerment and Noor Inayat Khan in September at Dachau, would not be known of at home for months. At F Section, the women were put onto the casualty list; their whereabouts and fates were unknown and there was nothing that could be done to find out while the war was still being fought. Nobody at home knew if they were alive or dead, and it would be a long time before they were able to find out.

The only ones who knew what had happened were the perpetrators, those who had transported the women from Karlsruhe to the camps and those who had carried out their murders in cold blood. The killings were done unquestioningly and without any thought of saving the women, or keeping them alive as prisoners, as a direct result of orders from Berlin. For the women arriving at the two respective camps there was to be only one outcome – their deaths.

8
RAVENSBRÜCK

As we walked or rather staggered, bone weary between the dark camp barracks day in and day out, across the black cinders of the ground beneath our feet, I was struck with the absolute certainty that there was indeed a worse fate than death: the destruction of our souls, which was the purpose and goal of the concentration camp universe.

Geneviève de Gaulle on entering Ravensbrück[1]

Ravensbrück concentration camp was established in May 1939 near the town of Fürstenburg, 95 km north of Berlin. It was continually expanded throughout the war and by 1942 was the biggest women's concentration camp with over 40 satellite camps. Approximately 120,000 women from 30 countries passed through Ravensbrück's gates. They had been arrested for being Jewish, Jehovah's Witnesses, 'asocials' (including Roma or Sinti), 'work shy', prostitutes, criminals, involved in resistance activities or having anti-Nazi political affiliations. Among their number were 800 children and babies (some of whom were born within the camp confines), and from April 1941 there were also 20,000 men, who lived and worked in a separate camp.

Alongside the beatings, brutality and malnutrition, a strict regime was upheld in the camp. The camp siren woke prisoners early, sometimes at 3.30 a.m. In the hour before roll call they had to attempt to wash, dress, tidy their barracks, make their beds (in a very specific way, which was punishable if it was not correct) and try to snatch a cup of ersatz coffee. Then, in lines of five they filed outside to *Appell* where, regardless of the weather, they would be kept standing until all prisoners were accounted for. Sometimes this took hours. The work details were then assigned and the slave labour began. Most of this work was heavy manual labour, such as digging or carrying huge weights. There was a short midday break and work continued until evening *Appell*, the average workday lasting between eight and twelve hours. Free time was permitted on Sundays, but once the prisoners had tidied their blocks there was little time left.[2]

Accommodation was in wooden barracks, which were originally designed for 100 people, but sometimes housed up to 500 or more. Prisoners slept in three-tier bunks and each barrack had one washroom and toilet. There was also a sick bay, warehouse, prison and penal bock. The camp soon became overcrowded: in 1940 there had been 3,000 prisoners, but by the end of the war there were approximately 30,000, resulting in widespread disease including epidemics of typhus and dysentery.

To help deal with the overcrowding, a tent – which had no side walls, only a pitched roof and straw on the ground, and with no washing or toilet facilities – was erected in August 1944. At times 4,000 people were housed here, and it soon became infested with fleas and vermin. A survivor described the tent as:

> dirty, lice-infested straw – [still] with no water. Days under the burning-hot canvas and in the crowded quarters were terribly stuffy – the nights on the other hand, were cool. During bad weather, rain would come through the open sides, and the wind toppled the tent poles and even the main posts in the middle, which meant that the whole tent was in danger of collapsing.[3]

It is estimated that approximately 1,000 prisoners a month died as a result of living in such squalid conditions. The camp staff removed the tent in late February–early March 1945.

The most common causes of death in Ravensbrück were starvation, exhaustion and disease, but there were also many executions. In 1941, 500 women were executed at the camp. In 1942, the SS selected 1,600 women and 300 men to be killed in the '14f13' campaign: these people, deemed unfit to work due to the fact they had asthma, tuberculosis (TB) or other diseases, were taken to Bernberg and Hartheim 'euthanasia' facilities and gassed. Mass shootings became commonplace and, from early 1945, selected women were taken behind the crematorium and shot in groups of fifty, or were killed by poison gas in a temporary gas chamber at the camp.

Those who were to be gassed were usually first taken to an adjoining camp known as Uckermark, the former *Jugendlager*, or juvenile protective custody camp. Many of the prisoners had been tricked into agreeing to go, believing the conditions to be less harsh than in the main camp. In reality, they were left to starve to death or were killed, either by lethal injection or a poisonous 'white powder'. Some were taken in lorryloads of 150 to the gas chamber. It is estimated that between 5,000 and 6,000 women were murdered in the frenzied period of killing in early 1945; approximately 2,300 of these were killed in the gas chamber.[4]

Murder was routine but medical experiments were commonplace too: forced sterilisation was carried out on numerous women, most of whom wore a black triangle denoting them as 'asocials'. The medical staff also infected women's limbs with gas gangrene, in particular Polish victims, who became known as 'rabbits', and many of whom died. The total death toll at Ravensbrück is estimated to be 25,000 out of a total of 120,000 prisoners. Approximately 20 prisoners were British, 7 of whom were members of SOE.[5]

The first SOE agent to be sent to Ravensbrück was Cicely Lefort. Arrested in September 1943, she had spent several months at Toulouse military prison along with Yvonne Rudellat and Odette Sansom. On 1 February 1944, Cicely was taken to a railway station on the outskirts of Paris. Among her travelling companions were a number of prostitutes, a group of women who had been caught while working on the 'Comet' escape line, some French Red Cross nurses, an opera singer and Geneviève de Gaulle, niece of the leader of the Free French.[6] Some of them wore wool or fur coats and carried inside their suitcases lingerie, makeup and perfume. Several of the women hoped that they were travelling to a work camp in Silesia, from where they believed they would be liberated after the forthcoming Allied invasion.[7]

When the women arrived at the station, they found that the train had cattle wagons in place of carriages. Sixty women were shoved into each cattle wagon, designed to take forty men and eight horses. As the train pulled away, some of the women frantically pushed letters through the gaps in the sides of the wagon and onto the tracks, in the hope that that the rail workers might pick them up and post them on their behalf. Cicely wrote one for her husband which simply read 'Leaving for Germany. C'. Inside the train there was little ventilation, nowhere to sit down, no water to drink and only a single bucket in which the wagon's occupants could relieve themselves. The train stopped occasionally to empty the slop buckets and only once, as it crossed the border into Germany, was food – soup – offered to the women. In spite of the conditions, the passengers remained optimistic, and even as the train pulled into Ravensbrück two days later at 2 a.m. the women had little realisation of what lay ahead.[8]

There is no record of what Cicely thought as she entered the camp, but accounts of other women on her transport show that reactions were varied. Some women were shocked at what they saw. Denise Dufournier, a young Frenchwoman betrayed while working on an escape line in Paris, said 'the reality was so brutal and so hard we could hardly grasp it', while others remember the 'healthy smell' of the woods and water.[9]

After delousing and showering, the newly arrived women were taken to a temporary block for the rest of the night, terrified of the skeletal figures they saw around them. The next day they were brought some beet soup, which they refused to believe was for them. One woman suggested they eat the food they had brought with them instead, and so they picnicked on bread and cheese; the guards were so surprised at their tenacity they did not stop them.[10] The women were quarantined and then assimilated into the life and routine of the camp.

Some months later, Odette Sansom arrived, via several prisons, at Ravensbrück. On 18 July 1944, she was taken from Karlsruhe, where she had spent two months in a cell with three German criminals, to Frankfurt on a train packed with German male prisoners. After a week there she went to Halle prison, which was so overcrowded that she and thirty-seven women (who were mostly Ukrainian) were confined in the loft. There was one basin with a 'little water and they had to sleep on the floor; whenever anybody moved the dust flew up and choked them'. Odette also said that she was beaten by a policeman who asked her if she was English and then 'struck her twice'.[11] She stayed there just one night, leaving on 26 July. On that journey, Odette said:

> one of the SS men took the opportunity to express his dislike for me and to say that he would be only too pleased if we would have an accident because he could kill me. He added it would not really matter, for we were [being] taken to a place, where, after working for them, we would all be killed. In my case, in order to impress me, he showed me a piece of paper written in German, the text being underlined in red, telling me that this was my death sentence.[12]

She arrived in Fürstenberg the next day and walked the last 5 km to Ravensbrück. Odette recalled that the camp was in chaos and noted 'the sheer misery of it all'. She was overcome by the size of the place as well as 'the appalling number of women there who were no longer looking like human beings, more like wounded animals'. She spent the first night on the concrete floor of the shower room believing that 'they were not organised enough' to receive her, before being transferred not to the barracks but to an underground bunker where she spent three of a total of nine months in solitary confinement.[13] The reason, she was told, was that she had at one stage held plans of the naval base at Marseille and, thanks to her tenacity to not break under torture, a successful invasion had just taken place in the south of France.[14] Another reason offered was her supposed relation to the British prime minister, though she was no longer to be known by her assumed name of Churchill, and was registered under the name Frau Suhrer.[15]

Odette's cell was through a barred gate, along an artificially lit corridor and down a staircase; it was 'about ten feet by six, very dark, and in it . . . a wooden bunk with some straw, two rugs, the usual table against the wall and a wooden stool'.[16] The cell was underground 'with the window completely blocked, bricked off with just holes so I could get some air but not see through.'[17] She was left there for weeks, her days only interrupted by the delivery of her meagre rations, which were sometimes simply pushed through the hatch in her door. Her punishment 'consisted of leaving [her] entirely in the dark, there was no light and no artificial light and never seeing anybody come into my cell ... once a month he [camp commandant Fritz Suhren] would come to my door. "Have you anything to say" and I would say "No". I couldn't see him. "No", the door would close again and that was it.'[18] For more than three months she lay in darkness, not knowing night from day and, to add to the torment, her cell was right next to the punishment cell.

Beatings and floggings were a regular part of life at Ravensbrück. Sometimes victims were chosen at random, sometimes it was a punishment for such indiscretions as stealing food or talking back to a guard. Victims were strapped face-down over a wooden horse or *bock* and received twenty-five lashes from an oxhide whip on the buttocks. Some were so weak and frail that they died in the process. Odette recalled that from her cell 'you could hear everything, you could hear everybody screaming ... and every evening it was like another punishment ... every evening there used to be women being beaten, I could count every stroke, I could hear everyone, I could hear the screams.'[19] Keeping her in the vicinity of such barbarity was another way for the guards to punish her.

Odette's treatment varied between being given food and water one week to being forced to starve in complete darkness with the heating turned up full the next – the latter a punishment for the part she played in the successful Allied invasion of southern France, and which left her delirious and ill.[20] Odette had chronic problems with her glands and the prolonged periods in a darkened cell did nothing to improve her health. By early October she was very unwell. Fritz Suhren came to her cell and had her X-rayed. Odette was informed that she had TB, but, rather than receiving immediate treatment, she was put back into her bunker. The camp doctor reputedly said that if she continued to be held in such horrendous conditions she would be dead within two months. She recalled reading a book before the war that said if you had TB you should starve yourself to help cleanse your body. Owing to

213

the fact she was already being starved and kept immobile she thought that this might actually aid her recovery.[21]

Fortunately for Odette, Suhren believed, as the Gestapo interrogators had before him, that she was in some way related to Winston Churchill. While this meant she deserved 'special punishment' in terms of being kept in solitary confinement, it also meant that she was a prisoner worth keeping alive, for the time being at least. As a result, she was given infra-red treatment and vitamins and was treated for scurvy. This was in early October; from the snippets of news whispered to her by the camp nurse, she knew it would not be long until all of Europe was liberated.[22]

While Odette lay incarcerated in solitary confinement, Cicely sent a letter to her husband, Dr Alix Lefort. She gave her address as 'Konzlager, Ravensbrück, Fürstenberg, Mecklenburg'. He informed Vera Atkins that he had received news of Cicely and gave her the details. Vera had heard of Ravensbrück and decided to investigate it a little further. She asked the War Office for details; they told her, 'Ravensbrück camp as such is comparatively unknown to us and we have no record of any British internees being in Brandenburg now.'[23]

Alix took the opportunity to keep lines of communication open with his wife, but he had no idea of the conditions under which she was being kept. If he had, perhaps he might not have chosen this time to write to her telling her that he wanted a divorce. He felt that Cicely had endangered him by undertaking resistance work; later evidence reveals that he had also met another woman. Devastated, Cicely found the means to rewrite her will in the camp, cutting him out, and even finding a camp doctor to witness the document.

The summer of 1944 also saw the arrival of several more female SOE agents at Ravensbrück: Eileen Nearne on 15 August, and Denise Bloch, Lilian Rolfe, Violette Szabó and Yvonne Rudellat on the 21st. The women spent two weeks in the camp before they began work, during which time Eileen had bumped into 'Violette Szabó and another girl, Denise Bloch. "Oh," she said, "you too?" '[24] Eileen told Violette that she was passing herself off as French and also informed her about the *baignoire*. Violette was horrified and tried to convince Eileen to change her story and admit to being English; she felt sure this would mean Eileen would receive better treatment. Eileen was adamant that she would stick to her story. She maintained her cover name of Jacqueline du Tertre and was always nervous around the other women agents for fear they would give her away. In the end, Eileen was right to maintain her cover.

On 3 September, Violette, Denise, Lilian, Eileen and Yvonne Rudellat were sent on work detail to one of Ravensbrück's satellite camps. Torgau was a three-day train journey from the main camp. On the march from the railway station the women passed a POW camp, where the men looked healthy and talked cheerfully about 'the end' being near.[25] Lilian was already quite weak and relied on the help of a friend she had made to support her as she walked. At Torgau conditions were surprisingly good; the barracks had a mattress on each bed, heating and running water. The prisoners were even addressed politely at *Appell* and told they would soon have everything they needed; their evening was topped off with a meal of fresh bread, sauerkraut and sausage. Noticing how cold they were, the officer said that they could attend *Appell* in their blankets from then on, and a weary, poorly Lilian was admitted to the well-equipped *Revier* (camp hospital). The work included farming vegetables, digging roads and working in machine factories.[26] The SOE women worked in the factory where the labour was hard, but the conditions were much better than at Ravensbrück.

At Torgau, Violette, who was described by a fellow prisoner as being 'in good spirits', began to plan her escape.[27] The camp was less closely guarded than Ravensbrück, and 'behind the washroom was a hut inside a barricade, beyond the barricade there was a wall with a door in it, beyond the wall was an open field'.[28] She got a key cut with the help of a fellow prisoner in the camp and told Eileen Nearne of her plan. Eileen wanted to escape immediately but Violette said it would be better if it was properly planned. However, before they had a chance to use the key Violette was denounced to the authorities.

There was unrest on a large scale at Torgau, which was, among other things, a munitions factory. The women were unaware at this stage that, not only were they making munitions, they were making parts for the V-2 rocket. One of the communist prisoners advised the other women to stop working on munitions that will 'kill our brothers'.[29] Another woman, Jeannie Rousseau, went up to a German guard and said that, while she was prepared to work, she could not and would not work on munitions. The officer said that 'if you refuse to work in the factory you can go back to Ravensbrück'.[30] Jeannie was imprisoned and the other women continued working, but the unrest continued.

No one knew what to do; they were told that 'they would be wise to stay where they were and work in the munitions factory where conditions were far superior to Ravensbrück'.[31] Nonetheless the Torgau camp authorities were unable to deal with the situation and Fritz Suhren, commandant of Ravensbrück, came to the camp to impose order. He decided to send 250 women to work in Leipzig and another 250 to Königsberg, a harsh work camp in east Prussia. Among the women sent to the latter camp were Denise, Violette and Lilian. Frail and ill, Lilian was out of the hospital but frustrating her colleagues by refusing to eat her meagre rations 'because she didn't like' the food.[32] Even so she was sent to Königsberg to undertake even tougher work.

Another agent whose health was failing was Yvonne Rudellat. Aged 46, with white hair, she had been sent with the others to Torgau but did not stay long; unfit and ill she was probably considered unsuitable for the work and was sent back to Ravensbrück. Marguerite Flamencourt, one of Yvonne's friends, knew that her chances of survival were greater if she could get in a work party. Marguerite herself worked in a factory making upholstery strips for cars and aircraft. Although the work was repetitive and laborious, it was easier than most other jobs at the camp and the punishments were relatively light by comparison to other places. Marguerite tried to help Yvonne by attempting to pass her off as fit to work by positioning her within the ranks of workers: 'At *Appell* she [Yvonne] was placed next to me and we went off in a column but the guard realised that there was one too many and made [Yvonne] come out of our ranks. So she had to re-join those who didn't work.'[33] After this Yvonne was told to go and clean her block and do some knitting; she would still have to attend *Appell* which could go on for hours in the heat of the sun, the rain or the freezing sleet or snow. Yvonne received a pink card which showed that she was not fit for hard labour; it also noted that she was a *Nacht und Nebel* prisoner. This meant she could not send or receive letters or parcels; no one knew where she was and, if she died, she would be virtually untraceable.[34]

Yvonne was housed in Block 17 with other *Nacht und Nebel* prisoners; one was a French prostitute, another a communist who would lash out, unprovoked, at other prisoners. Yvonne had a top bunk near a window which was broken, so she always had fresh air, in a manner of speaking. Block 17 also had two working sinks and five usable toilets, which was luxury in comparison with some of the others. However, it did not mean that the block was in any way sanitary. The washrooms were where the corpses of those who had died overnight were kept, and this could be as many as ten a night. The bodies were covered with a curtain until the cart came to take them away to be burnt. It was in this block that Yvonne remained for the duration of her stay at Ravensbrück.[35]

While the other agents had been labouring at Torgau, another small transport of fifty or so women had arrived at Ravensbrück in early September 1944. Among their number was Yvonne Baseden, who recalled that, on her arrival, 'we were marched to the camp by SS German women guards and the following day our particulars were recorded and having been ordered to parade in the shower baths for a shower all our personal possessions were taken from us and we were issued with a form of uniform which consisted of a civilian dress with a large cross on the front and back made by insertion of different coloured material'.[36] Yvonne was given the number 62947 and had a variety of jobs, including 'uprooting trees and on another occasion unloading trains which arrived at the station usually from Warsaw laden to capacity with loot of all kinds, linen, silver, crockery, and all kinds of household effects'.[37] The railway siding was only a mile or so from the main camp, and it was here that Yvonne had a near miss with an irate guard:

I nearly got badly injured on one occasion because I was unloading pillows of all things and the guards were throwing them for us to pick up and put somewhere else and one of the cushions burst open as I was

getting it and went all over this chap, he was furious and he had something in his hand which was something like a revolver . . . he was furious
and tried to hit me with this thing, I just missed it, I was lucky because he
could have used that revolver . . . I didn't get injured on that occasion. But
they were liable to do anything.[38]

After the working day, Yvonne returned to the main camp, recalling that
'you got back and tried to wash, which you couldn't do really, you didn't have
any soap or anything and then to bed to try and sleep'. The next morning the
whole thing would begin again:

every day we had a parade, in other words we all trooped out and had to
stand in rows . . . we just stood around every morning for a couple of
hours. I suppose then they checked numbers to see that we were all there
and on occasion we were sent out to work either in other parts of the
camp or outside the camp. It was on a marsh really and they were making
another camp, they knew the war was over but they had to find something for us to do.[39]

That autumn, Cicely Lefort, complaining of swollen legs and stomach
pains, was diagnosed with stomach ulcers (possibly cancer) by one of the
camp's senior medical staff, Obersturmführer Percival 'Percy' Treite, a
pre-war gynaecologist who was now conducting medical experiments on
the ovaries of female inmates. He operated on her, presumably to remove a
tumour, after which she was allowed to recuperate in the *Revier* before going
back into the main camp.[40]

Having received treatment for her various conditions, including
swollen glands, scurvy and chest pains, Odette was moved to a new cell.
Here she had light from a window and was allowed to exercise, albeit only
for a few minutes a day, and which was sometimes overlooked completely.
She was no longer in darkness, but she was still in solitary confinement,
and the reality of her new situation began to sink in. Her new cell was next
to Crematorium II and consequently it was 'full of dust and hair'. She

reported hearing screaming women being taken into the crematorium and believed that they were being burnt alive: 'The guards had opened a small gap in my cell window to let in some air. The ashes of the dead seeped into the cell every day. My cell was covered with pieces of hair and cinders of the crematorium. I did not see victims but I heard them, I heard everything.'[41]

It was around the same time that Odette was moved from her underground cell that Eileen Nearne, who had returned from Torgau, was sent to Abteroda, a sub-camp of Buchenwald. Here, women were required to work at the BMW plant, where their smaller hands and fingers were considered useful when it came to assembling the delicate parts of Messerschmitt aircraft. The women worked twelve-hour shifts, and Eileen found the work painstaking and tiring. Asking herself why she should contribute to making aircraft that would be used against her own people and the Allied cause, she decided to stage her own rebellion, and stopped working. The guards shaved off her hair as punishment and forced her to work at gunpoint, with just one ration of clear soup a day. But she continued to work as slowly as she dared and damage pieces here and there when no one was looking.

Her behaviour aroused the suspicions of the supervisor, who pulled her aside for questioning. She said that she had heard Eileen speak English and questioned her nationality. Eileen replied in English, saying that she had never said she was English, just that she spoke it. She returned to her work, but her health was failing and she was exhausted, so much so that during an Allied air raid she actually fell asleep, and woke up believing that she was back in England.[42] During her time at Abteroda, Eileen mentioned that 'the SS commandant from Torgau came looking for two English girls who had escaped from Torgau and there were rumours that it was Violet [sic] and Lynne [Denise]. They were always with a girl called Lilian.'[43] News of her fellow SOE agents cheered her, especially when she thought they might have escaped as she was so desperate to do so herself. But it was not to be, not yet. Confused, weary and unwell, Eileen was transported from Abteroda to Markkleeberg, near Leipzig.[44]

At Markkleeberg, which was administered by Buchenwald concentration camp, Eileen worked twelve hours a day, wearing dark grey overalls with a red triangle on the left sleeve to mark her out as a political prisoner. The main work at this camp was at the Junkers aircraft factory; other jobs included paving roads, digging ditches, felling trees and loading bricks. Like Ravensbrück, the camp was situated in remote countryside. As was the case with the other camps, the women were treated harshly, sometimes being worked to death. Dysentery was rife and food was scarce. Eileen struggled to cope, but said that 'the will to live. Will power. That's the most important. You should not let yourself go. It seemed that the end would never come but I always believed in destiny and I had hope. If you are a person who is drowning, you put all your efforts into trying to swim.' Markkleeberg was the last camp Eileen would work in.[45]

Meanwhile, Violette, Lilian and Denise were working at another sub-camp. They had briefly returned to Ravensbrück from Torgau in October 1944, where they were seen by Yvonne Baseden, who recognised them from their shared time at Saarbrücken:

> I next saw Danielle [Denise] and Violette about two months later on their return to the camp [from Torgau] and was told that Lilian was with them although I did not see her ... I understand they refused to work in the factory and were given work in the kitchens. On their return to the camp they were very keen on leaving it again. Having been lucky in this transport they thought they might be again.[46]

This was not the case. On 19 October, the three women left Ravensbrück and were sent to Little Königsberg, on the River Oder, where the work was much harsher than at Torgau and the conditions were exacerbated by the severe weather. The women worked on a frozen airfield, then had to dig a trench for a narrow-gauge railway, after which they laid the track. Inadequately dressed – Violette was described as wearing a 'blue silk frock, a fringe from hem to her knees and short sleeved', and ill-fitting clogs[47] – they worked in sub-zero conditions, with frostbitten hands and feet.

Sunday was a rest day, and the women huddled in their blocks. Violette befriended a woman called Christiane Le Scornet, who described her companion as having 'a rare loyalty, a rare courage'. She also helped create a picture of how the SOE women were faring, describing Lilian as thin and shockingly pale, Denise as suffering with sores (the result of malnutrition) and Violette as 'the cheeriest of them all', talking about her daughter and singing songs at Christmas.[48] Another camp inmate and friend, Marie Lacomte, described how, as time wore on, Violette became depressed. In a letter sent to Violette's parents after the war, Marie recalled an incident when Violette arrived back at her hut out of her mind, chilled, disconsolate, exhausted and crying, repeating 'I am so cold, so cold.'[49]

The winters were harsh at Königsberg and January especially so. The dreaded *Appell* now became a way of finishing off the weak. Forced to stand for hours in the Prussian winter, those who fell were left to die on the frozen ground, unless their friends were able to pick them up and get them to the *Revier* – which had no medicine, no heating and no blankets. One of the victims of *Appell* on such a bitter winter morning was Lilian Rolfe, who collapsed in a fit of coughing. Another woman helped her to the *Revier* where she then stayed. Denise and Violette went on working parties in the forest, digging up tree stumps from the frozen soil. The work involved long treks through deep snow and Denise's foot turned gangrenous. Unable to undertake the walk or work, she remained behind in the block. Violette was the only one of the three fit enough to work, and apparently still talked of escape. Her hopes were raised on 20 January, when the three women were told to get ready to leave Königsberg.

At around the same time, Cicely Lefort left the main camp at Ravensbrück and was taken to Uckermark, the *Jungendlager*, the neighbouring sub-camp originally set up as the juvenile camp and now the waiting room for the gas chambers. Cicely and her friend Mary O'Shaughnessy volunteered to go to the camp, impelled by the rumours of extra blankets, individual mattresses, no work and no *Appell*. Sometime between 13 and 20 January, Cicely, Mary and hundreds of other inmates were lined up in ranks of five and taken through gates at the back of the main camp compound. The walk was little more than half a mile, but it took them over an hour and a half to get there, so weak were some of the women. Amputees, the disabled and those too exhausted to walk were brought along in carts at the back. The women trudged through the snow, passing the men's camp and eventually arriving at the youth camp which, with only five barracks, seemed disconcertingly small.

Cicely was put into a small block with seventy other women; there was no room to sit or lie down. The prisoners were told that this was a temporary arrangement and that their new accommodation was still being prepared. The women remained crammed inside that hut for three days, with no food, water or sanitation, and soon there was urine and excrement all over the floor. Then, after a meal of soup and bread, Cicely was moved to a larger block which housed hundreds of prisoners. There were planks fixed to the walls as beds, on top of which were straw mattresses which were home to thousands of lice and were literally crawling.[50]

After a few days, having told prisoners there would be no *Appell*, the guards woke them at 3.30 a.m. and forced them to stand outside for six hours, during which time some of them collapsed and died. At the next *Appell* the guards took any blankets and coats from the prisoners and when they returned to their barracks they found that the windows were jammed open. The women quickly began to sicken and freeze. At the next *Appell* the women stood outside in thin summer clothing and realised they had been harshly tricked; they had been brought here to die slow, lingering deaths. Those who did not die quickly enough were sent back to the main camp, where the gas chambers were now fully operational.

Accounts from survivors of Ravensbrück and the *Jugendlager* differ, but the most credible accounts suggest that, after about two or three weeks, Cicely was selected for the transport back to Ravensbrück. She fulfilled the criteria to return to the main camp: she was not disabled or particularly ill, nor did she have a pink card. It also does not seem that her life as an SOE agent had caught up with her; those SOE agents who had been executed to date had been killed with other SOE women, not taken in a mass round-up. But there was nothing that could be done to save her and, sometime in early February, Cicely was put into a truck and taken back to the main camp. The truck stopped some 50 metres from the crematorium. Cicely and the other women were unloaded and taken into an anteroom where they were told they were going to be treated for lice and ordered to strip. In groups of about 150, they were taken into the gas chamber and there they were murdered. Cicely Lefort was 45 years old.[51]

Freezing and exhausted at Königsberg, Violette Szabó, Denise Bloch and Lilian Rolfe received word at 10 p.m. on 20 January 1945 to prepare themselves for a journey back to Ravensbrück; they would be leaving at 5 a.m. There was speculation as to why, and the women firmly hoped that they were about to be repatriated via Sweden or Switzerland or even a British camp.[52] They were given clean clothes, soap and a comb; Violette even got a coat and shoes, and she washed her hair, asking her friend Marie to help her remove the lice. She was on the way to feeling human again. Denise and Lilian remained weak and frail, but, buoyed by the news of Allied advances and the prospect of being freed, the three cheerfully made their way back to Ravensbrück.

But orders to free the women never came. On the contrary, directives had been sent to all the camps with the names of British prisoners who were to be made to disappear under Hitler's *Nacht und Nebel* policy. The women were taken first to the punishment block, and from there to the bunker. Sometime between 25 January and 5 February 1945, all three were led along a passage behind the crematorium. Lilian was so weak she had to be carried on a stretcher, and Denise had to be supported to walk to the place of execution. They were killed by a 'single shot to the neck', Violette being the last to die.[53] In his post-war affidavit, Obersturmführer Johann Schwarzhuber said that 'Suhren read out the execution order, they were shot by Corporal Schult [SS] with a small-calibre gun in the back of the neck. Present were Dr. Trommer and Dr. Hellinger, the dentist.' He also said that 'all three were very brave and I was deeply moved', and that Suhren was 'impressed by the bearing of these women'.[54] Suhren was reputedly furious that the Gestapo had not carried out the execution themselves.

After the murders, rumours abounded about what had happened to the three women. A nurse at Ravensbrück said they had been hanged, believing that 'she had seen [Violette's] clothes in the disinfection room and [that] there was blood on them'. The clothes, she said, 'were identified by Marie Lacomte as being Violette's'.[55] Others said that their clothes were cremated with them. However, not everyone believed they were dead. Another prisoner even thought they had been repatriated and had heard rumours that Denise and Lilian had been seen in Switzerland and France.

Yvonne Baseden was as confused as everyone else: 'no one knew, it was extraordinary, they had been brought back, we heard through the grapevine that they had come back to the punishment block and eventually we heard that their clothes had been burnt, we thought they had been executed ... I never knew anything, except that they had been executed.'[56] For Yvonne, life at the camp had deteriorated further; she had contracted tuberculosis and was in the *Revier*, and as the sick and frail were being liquidated her prospects of survival seemed low. But then, in March and April 1945, the Swedish Red Cross were, remarkably, given access to some of the prisoners and allowed to remove them from the camp – although only after being held up outside Ravensbrück for a few days while a frenzied spate of killing by means of a gas van took place. The Red Cross buses saved the lives of hundreds of women, among them Yvonne Baseden, who was on the last vehicle out of Ravensbrück. Her friend Mary Lindell, who had helped keep her alive while in the hospital, had ensured that she was given a place on the bus and planned to join her. But, at the last minute, Mary was called back by Suhren who told her she had to stay behind. Yvonne did not want to leave without her friend, but Mary insisted. Yvonne recalled:

our departure from the camp was a rather rushed affair, as I believe most of the German authorities in charge did not know of the move until it had been accomplished. Some of the German officers for some reason helped us to leave on the Swedish transport and within an hour of our being told we were going, we were out of the camp under Red Cross protection. We had been told the previous day that we would leave the camp as orders had been received from Berlin that we should be considered as hostages. I had practically given up hope then and when we were told to dash off felt rather suspicious as to where we were going to. As it was, we were at once presented to the Swedish Red Cross commander of the convoy who made quite sure all the British were out of the camp.[57]

The date was 29 April 1945. Yvonne was taken to Malmö in Sweden where she was quarantined in the Natural History Museum and slept under a dinosaur's skeleton. Racked with TB she spent two weeks there before returning to Britain, where she spent a year recovering in a sanitorium.

However, not all remaining SOE women had shared her good fortune. Yvonne Rudellat survived in Ravensbrück until the end of February 1945 when she and approximately 2,500 women, most of whom were elderly, infirm or ill, were told that they were being taken away to a 'convalescent camp'. This was the notorious Bergen-Belsen. Typhus, dysentery and TB were rife among the 60,000 starving inmates. Brutality and privation were the norm and the inmates had nothing left – no clothes, no food and no dignity. Yvonne arrived on 2 March 1945, still suffering from exhaustion and weakness, and she struggled to survive. She maintained her cover story, remaining 'Jacqueline Gautier', and did not disclose to anyone that she was British or that she was with SOE.

The camp was liberated on 15 April 1945 by British soldiers, but even after liberation the death rate was vast, with some 20,000 inmates dying in the first few weeks. Among them was Yvonne. The last time her name appeared on any list was 19 April; a fellow inmate thought she saw her alive on 22 April, but after that there was nothing. She is believed to have died between 19 and 27 April. Her fragile remains were buried in an unmarked mass grave alongside the nameless thousands who were murdered at Bergen-Belsen.

As the Allies began to liberate the concentration camps of Europe, the Nazis started to clear them, getting rid of their prisoners and destroying any evidence. A series of death marches began, during which emaciated, maltreated and weary prisoners were forced to walk in all weather conditions; those who could not keep up were shot en route and corpses littered the roadsides that led away from the camps. Eileen Nearne was put on one such march when she was forced to leave Markkleeberg in April 1945. She recalled:

> Two French girls and I decided to escape and while we were passing a forest I spotted a tree and hid there and then joined the French girls in the forest. One of the girls was named Yvette Landais ... we stayed in a bombed house for two nights and the next morning walked through Markelberg [sic] and slept in the woods. We were arrested by the SS who asked us for papers. We told them a story and they let us go. We arrived at Leipzig and at a church a priest helped us and kept us there for 3 nights and the next morning we saw white flags and the first Americans arriving and when I said that I was English they put us in a camp.[58]

Eileen relayed her story to the men she thought were her saviours, but they didn't believe her and treated her badly. They said that she was 'unbalanced' and acted as if she was 'impersonating someone else'.[59] They also thought that her story was 'invented' and suggested she be handed over to the British for 'further investigation'. It was far from the hero's welcome that one might have hoped for. Months of hiding her true identity in order to survive evidently took its toll on Eileen; the mental scars of torture endured by the Gestapo and the physical scars of forced labour in several camps had made her frail and a shadow of her former self. She was on the verge of collapse.[60]

It was 1 May when liberation finally began for Odette. Just days after her thirty-third birthday and Hitler's suicide, she left her solitary cell for the first time in over six months, having spent nine months in solitary confinement. She was initially blinded by the sunlight and then overwhelmed by what she saw. Ravensbrück was in disarray: records were being destroyed, prisoners moved around freely, and the camp personnel were in state of panic that they would be overrun by the Allies and their grotesque secrets discovered. Fritz Suhren had decided that Odette would be a very useful pawn in his bid for freedom and exoneration of his crimes. He knew he could not survive against the advancing Russians and had decided to take his chance with the Americans. Stuffing piles of papers in his car, he personally drove Odette in the direction of the American lines. Odette recalled passing through two other camps but could not remember their names. All the while she believed that Suhren would stop the car near some woods and kill her, but he did not.[61] 'At about ten o clock we were stopped by the Americans,' Odette recalled; 'he said "this is Frau Churchill she has been my prisoner." And I said "This is the commandant of Ravensbrück you make him your prisoner", they broke his gun and gave it to me.' They offered to find her a room for the night, but Odette insisted on sleeping in the car under the stars. Having spent so long under lock and key and in horrendous conditions, this must have been a welcome experience – but it was also an extremely clever move in the name of duty: the car boot was rammed full of incriminating documents which Odette ensured got back to England.[62]

Suhren didn't remain a prisoner for long; handed over to the British, he managed to escape from Neuengamme camp before his trial, but was rearrested under an assumed name by the US authorities in 1949 and handed over to the French, who were then conducting another Ravensbrück trial in Rastatt. Suhren received the death sentence and was shot in June 1950. Odette was repatriated and treated at the expense of SOE for her various medical conditions that arose from her maltreatment in Germany, including an abscess in her teeth. As the dentist was digging around in her mouth he commented, 'I hear you were a prisoner of the Germans ... how very tiresome for a woman.' Odette said she knew then that she 'was back in England – the land of the stiff upper lip. But nothing has ever done me so much good. The war didn't matter anymore. To this day I love that dentist for it.'[63] Odette was awarded the George Cross, as was Violette Szabó, who was murdered within feet of Odette's cell.

Ravensbrück was liberated on 30 April 1945 by Soviet forces. They found 2,000 women who had been too ill to go on the death marches. A total of 120,000 women were incarcerated at the camp during its six-year existence, among them 8,000 French women, one-fifth of whom did not survive their internment. It is estimated that a total of 25,000 women and 2,500 men lost their lives at the concentration camp.

9

AFTERMATH

'Missing presumed dead' was a terrible verdict . . .

Vera Atkins, speaking of the SOE women who did not return[1]

Just days after the liberation of Ravensbrück concentration camp, the guns fell silent in Germany's capital and the battle for Berlin was over. The last few days of fighting had seen the suicides of many high-ranking Nazi officials and the Reich's capital lay in smoking ruins. As the dust settled over the rubble of once great buildings, the citizens of Berlin, who had been hiding in cellars and basements, came blinking into the sunlight and were faced with the stark realisation that it was over. The thousand-year Reich was gone, Hitler was dead, Germany had lost: 8 May 1945 was declared Victory in Europe Day by Britain and the United States, and their respective leaders announced that the war in Europe was officially over.

In 1945, the agents who were still in the field or liberated from the camps slowly began to make their way home. They now had the difficult task of adjusting to their new lives as civilians in peacetime. Just as the transition to becoming skilled SOE agents had taken time and patience, so did the reverse process. Some agents had difficulty reacclimatising to life back in England. Pearl Witherington recalled that:

I was asked one day, were you stressed, we didn't know the word until after the war and I said I don't know . . . when I think it over, in 1953 I was going down from the Palais de Compiègne with my daughter, who was five years old . . . in a few steps I came up face to face with three Germans

228

in uniform. I nearly passed out, I wasn't expecting it and six years of war came down on me like that. It was stress . . . just like the black Citroën that was always used by the Germans – as soon as one stopped anywhere near me for at least five years I just [*mimes shock*], I couldn't help it. I thought this is ridiculous, there are a lot of us who are terribly marked by a lot of things.[2]

Those who had survived the camps had an arduous rehabilitation task ahead as they sought to overcome the mental and physical damage. When asked about the attitude of the returning agents, Vera Atkins recalled a sense of 'huge relief . . . of course they came back in varying degrees of ill health but it was a very wonderful thing to be able to take them back to their families or wherever. They were seen by medical people, they were all passed through medical examination with our own medical staff but some had to go into hospital.'[3]

Eileen Nearne was very ill when she was brought back to England in 1945; for months she lived in a state of physical and emotional collapse and was nursed by her sister Jacqueline. While her physical strength returned, her mental health did not and she never fully recovered from her experiences at the hands of the Gestapo in Paris and the SS staff at Ravensbrück, saying 'these things live with you'. She turned to painting to help express the mental images and thoughts that still held her captive. Her pictures were violent and graphic in content, which expressed the horror of her captivity and the deprivation of the camps in which she was held.[4]

It was not just her capture, interrogation and imprisonment that haunted her: her life as a secret agent did too. On a TV interview for *Timewatch* in 1997, Eileen donned a wig, dark glasses and a head scarf; she spoke French and gave her name as 'Rose', which had been her codename, as if still trying to keep her identity a secret. She said of her life as an agent that 'it was a life in the shadows, but I think maybe I fitted it. I could be a bit hard and secret. I could be lonely. I could be independent. I was not bored – I liked the work. After the war I missed it. I even tried to find a job doing radio operating but it wasn't the same.' The psychological damage Eileen suffered never truly went away and she remained a recluse until her death in 2010.[5]

Odette Sansom, by contrast, spoke of her experiences when she got back to England after the liberation of Ravensbrück. She remained affected by what she had endured, however, suffering an acute attack of rheumatism, a weakened heart muscle and anaemia, among other illnesses. The doctor employed by F Section to comment on agents' suitability to return to service noted some 'troublesome symptoms which, I feel are in the most part psychological and are undoubtedly a direct result of her two years in solitary confinement'.[6] The doctor, who treated both Odette and Eileen, also reported that in his opinion both women were 'suffering from psychological symptoms which undoubtedly have been brought on by their service in the field. These symptoms interfere to a considerable extent with their efficiency for future employment and it is likely that they may continue to do so for some time to come.' 'These agents', he want on to say, 'come under a class of their own', and he recommended that SOE 'see its way to giving these two gallant women the appropriate compensation'.[7]

Odette and Peter Churchill married soon after the war, but found themselves at odds in how they wanted to move on with their lives. Odette wished to forget about the war and rebuild a normal existence with her daughters and with her husband. Churchill on the other hand 'wanted to go on with it, writing about it and lecturing about it. He didn't want to leave it behind', Odette said.[8] Though neither of them pushed for the limelight, they quickly became celebrities. Reluctant as she was to be in the public eye, Odette realised she could use her fame to highlight the work of her fallen SOE comrades.

Yvonne Baseden also had a long recovery ahead of her. She had told the officials at Malmö her name, rank and organisation, and Vera Atkins was contacted and verified Yvonne's identity, passing on the happy news to Yvonne's father that, despite their fears for the worst, his daughter had survived the war. But Yvonne was far from well: the tuberculosis she had contracted in the camp still racked her lungs, and she needed treatment. She was flown to Leuchars, and from there to London, where she had an emotional reunion with her father. She was then taken to the King Edward VII sanatorium near Midhurst, Surrey, where she was treated at the expense of the WAAF. There she had 'a lung operation', endured excruciating pain and was 'tormented by fearful dreams' during her nine-month stay.[9] In 1946, she married Major Desmond Bailey and moved to Rhodesia. She was remarried in 1966 to Anthony Burney; they lived in Zambia and Lesotho until retiring to Portugal in 1972. She did not speak of her wartime experiences again until her return to England in 1999.

For most female agents, the end of the war also marked the official end of their service. They were debriefed when they came home from their missions. They were usually demobbed through the FANY or the WAAF and given some assistance to return to civilian life. Help was often given in finding new work through references and contacts, and financial aid was also offered to those who needed it. The transition from active agent to living a 'normal life' could be tough and the women had to get used to no longer being in an occupied country, where the threat of arrest or denunciation was a constant worry.

Three women agents, however, were able to return to liberated France between September 1944 and March 1945, as part of a mission to thank the French community who helped SOE, and also to help bring closure to those involved in the organisation. Lise de Baissac, Yvonne Cormeau and Jacqueline Nearne joined the Judex Mission, which involved a team of SOE personnel, led by Colonel Maurice Buckmaster and accompanied by Vera Atkins, visiting the former F Section and resistance networks in France and meeting those who had assisted the agents throughout the war. Lunches were held and speeches given in which the members of Judex thanked the locals for offering SOE agents food, support and comfort when they were at their loneliest and most vulnerable. They also provided updates and brought news of agents' whereabouts, and, where necessary, gave remuneration for expenses incurred or for money that had been lent. That said, the mission report stated that 'money was, generally speaking, the last thing that these gallant people would ask for and it was comparatively rare that the matter be raised by them'.[10]

Judex was not just about expressing gratitude; it had several aims and purposes. For each circuit it needed to investigate 'any friction or victimisation of people who had worked with British officers; meeting and shaking hands with all colleagues of the British organiser; checking lists of citations for decorations; settlements of any outstanding financial problems including the handing over of cases of pensions to the French and collection of W/T sets, S-phones, Eurekas' – the latter two being radio equipment for communication between incoming aircraft and agents on the ground, and which would be used in the Far East. The mission was surprisingly successful regarding the latter and they were pleased to discover that great care had been taken to maintain and clean these instruments, so that they were still in good working order.[11]

The Judex reports (there were two missions, one in 1944 and one in 1945) are vitally important in that they give an on-the-ground impression of the state of France after liberation, in much the same way that Virginia Hall's reports did early in the war. That said, the purpose of Judex was not to provide a complete report on post-war France. The resultant written analysis also served to provide a justification for what was essentially a junket enjoyed by SOE officials at public expense. By celebrating France's resistance activities and subsequent liberation it also served to counteract the more sinister undertone of the punishment of women for *collaboration horizontale*, or sleeping with the enemy, in which some 20,000 French women had their heads shaved, as well as the *épuration*, during which thousands of Frenchmen and women were 'purged' in local executions.

Nonetheless, the Judex reports offer an interesting, if limited, view into life after the liberation. The state of France was reported to be in far better condition than had seemed possible given the dangers and difficulties it had suffered and was trying to rid itself of. Indeed, German prisoners had been put to use mending bridges with 'pretty good results', although the workers were 'arrogant and sulky'.[12] The Judex officers witnessed a 'patriotic fervour' that had been unleashed and increased steadily ever since D-Day, and they were impressed by the fact that the country seemed to have a 'fresh impetus' and was directing its energy towards the reconstruction of its 'domestic needs and national economy'. This was, they believed, due to the fact the resistance was made up of people from a complete cross-section of French national life, that they came from 'every walk of life and there was no *shibboleth* other than a true desire to serve the country'. Marquis and *cheminot* [railway worker], farm labourer and industrialist were united in the passionate desire to rid France of the hated enemy and the extermination of the Germans...'[13]

The people of France, it was observed, were united in the 'admiration and esteem in which they held Great Britain since we stood alone in 1940', and wherever officers went they witnessed 'great admiration and affection for England'. Some of the French even asked if they could continue to serve under British command or come to Britain themselves. Vera Atkins recalled displays of national pride and unity, and was present at a review of troops in 'Lyon on 11 November 1944 ... which lasted about two hours – they were people filing past who had worked in the resistance and the FFI [Forces Françaises de l'Intérieur] and so forth and we took the salute' from the steps of the local mayor's office.[14]

It was noted that some of the French had a 'great yearning for British marks of favour' and the F Section heads made recommendations for decorations, including the King's Medal for Service and the King's Medal for Courage in the Cause of Freedom. A letter from Field Marshal Montgomery or the newly promoted Colonel Buckmaster might also be sent to reward the French for their part in the country's liberation. This patriotic fervour and support for the British SOE seems at odds with de Gaulle's insistence within a few hours of the country's liberation that any British SOE agent should remove themselves from France. For instance, SOE agent Peter Lake met de Gaulle on 18 September 1944. When de Gaulle asked Lake what he was doing there, he replied that he was 'training certain troops for special operations'. De Gaulle replied: 'Our troops don't need training. You have no business here ... we don't need you here. It only remains for you to leave ... You too must go home. Return, return quickly. *Au revoir*.' F Section agents George Starr and Roger Landes, who served for far longer and contributed more than Peter Lake, also got the same treatment, and there were several similar cases.[15]

The Judex Missions also observed sites that had been the targets of sabotage attacks and used these visits as a tool to assess how successful SOE training had been and what might have been done to improve it should the war have continued. A more substantial report on the effect of sabotage operations was established and a detailed survey undertaken by F Section circuit leader, Tony Brooks, and a BCRA saboteur, Pierre Henneguier. The Judex reports evaluated the differences in conditions in which sabotage was carried out (daytime, night-time, number of guards, methods of transportation), provisions of supplies (such as plastic explosive and time pencils) and methods of storage. It was concluded that the training had 'been along the right lines' but that more time should have been devoted to the subject of sabotage. It was suggested that images as well as diagrams should have been added to the handbook, which was dropped with most explosives, so even those with no training could use them. The reports are full of detailed descriptions and evaluations of various acts of sabotage, such as those carried out on the Dunlop works in Montluçon, the Peugeot factory in Clermont Ferrand, and the Ratier works and Carmaux Mines power station, both in Figeac.[16] Further evaluation of training noted that the 'physical fitness acquired in Scotland has more than a few times been the saviour of our men in a tight spot . . .' It was also noted that wireless training was excellent, but that it was a pity that more wireless operators had not been recruited in the field.[17]

The Judex reports also show the more enjoyable side of the mission and are scattered with references to champagne, black market lunches, tea (which had been saved since 1940 for when a British officer passed by), cigars, 'colossal' dinners, good food, good wine and reminiscences on an epic scale, resulting in late nights and sore heads. A more sombre part of the mission was visiting the graves of SOE agents, résistants and locals who had been killed in action; widows were consoled and funerals held for those who had not had one before. Members of the Judex team visited people who had been directly involved with SOE agents or Allied personnel and brought them news of their fates or successful return home. During these visits, the families would often reminisce about what they had done to help agents out.[18]

On one such visit to Madame Coutelle, who had housed two locally recruited members of the SCIENTIST network, an elderly gentleman who believed he was 'too old for active forms of participation' regaled the officers with tales of how he had stood guard while a wireless operator worked from their home. The same family was also said to be tearful at the thought of losing Lise de Baissac, who was returning to England as her mission was over. She 'had become a philosopher and friend for all the local inhabitants' and was also one of the organisers for this part of the Judex Mission – a role that she had handled so efficiently that the mission reported 'there was comparatively little left to do'.[19]

Another role of the mission seemed to be to tie up loose ends while everyone was still in the same place. Many post-mission interrogations were carried out: for instance, Pearl Witherington and Sonia d'Artois were interviewed on 2 October 1944. Later that day, Buckmaster visited the British embassy in Paris and conducted more interviews, in addition to submitting the names of selected male agents (Cammaerts, Millar and Cowburn) for work at the Foreign Office. Filling a day with this type of activity seemed typical while on the tour.

The Judex Missions ran for several months, and the reports show that they helped Buckmaster draw conclusions from SOE's activities in France. One such conclusion was that 'the British officers sent to the field during the years 1941 to 1944 did a very great deal, by their courage, and their devotion to duty, to counteract German propaganda put out through the Vichy media that the British always get other people to fight their wars'. The British had indeed helped 'set Europe ablaze' and yet Judex also acknowledged one fundamental flaw in the system: 'One of the greatest problems that confronts a country section is to know whether a W/T operator is genuine or operating under duress or being impersonated. There appears to be no fool-proof method of establishing this fact.'[20] The acknowledgement that this was still a problem, even as late as 1944, was an admission that F Section knew its wireless traffic had never been secure and that therefore they could not have had confidence that those they were sending were landing in the right hands. Regardless, F Section had continued to infiltrate agents and, as a result of the 'Funkspiel', several landed in the enemy's lap, as in the case of Madeleine Damerment.

SOE's successes and failures were detailed in a further, far more comprehensive report by Major Bourne-Paterson, published on 30 June 1946 and entitled 'The British Circuits in France'. The initial task of SOE to 'set Europe ablaze' is clearly set out:

> the purpose behind the work of these circuits was the encouragement of sabotage in Occupied Europe ... there were two types of activity which quite definitely formed no part of what it was intended that an F section network should perform, and into which, equally, they were pitch forked by the logic of events in the later stages. Firstly they were not 'Intelligence' circuits. They were for action, and intelligence was a waste of time and – more valuable still – of vital wireless space ... secondly the F section circuits were sabotage circuits and not designed for guerrilla warfare and still less for open warfare ... .[21]

Historians' views on the resistance and the SOE are, at best, varied. It has been argued that 'as an individual act resistance was liberating, satisfying and necessary; on a co-ordinated level it seems to have been seldom effective, sometimes stultifying, frequently dangerous and almost always too costly'.[22] Others maintain that SOE's contribution in France was significant. After the war General Eisenhower wrote, 'Throughout France the resistance had been of inestimable value in the campaign. Without their great assistance the liberation of France would have consumed a much longer time and meant greater losses to ourselves.' Eisenhower estimated that the efforts of the resistance in preventing German troops from attacking the Allied invasion forces were the equivalent of fifteen Allied divisions. Eisenhower also commented that it was not just the practical assistance that the SOE and the resistance provided that was vital to the liberation: 'they had, by their ceaseless harassing activities, surrounded the Germans with a terrible atmosphere of danger and hatred which ate into the confidence of leaders and the courage of soldiers'.[23]

Regardless of its many successes and failures, in December 1945 F Section began to wind down and agents received correspondence from HQ stating that this 'branch, which has been operational, is now closing'. In order to give former members of SOE somewhere to gather and a 'home from home' in London, the Special Forces Club was founded in 1945 largely under the auspices of Major General Sir Colin Gubbins, the last head of SOE. In a leafy corner of Knightsbridge and a stone's throw from Harrods department store, the club was to be a meeting place solely for those who had served in SOE and their compatriots, such as members of the Special Duties Squadrons, OSS and resistance movements. The club was somewhere agents could reminisce and talk with others who had shared similar experiences.[24]

However, the way in which SOE's closure was dealt with was – and is – very controversial. Vera Atkins was surprised at the speed with which it all happened:

> we left many loose ends and I think it is, in many ways, most regrettable that a decision was made ... to close SOE and before any real assessment could be made of its work or an ordered handover of what remained of historical interest or indeed any conclusions drawn from this work, and I think we wasted a good deal of goodwill created by SOE in various Occupied territories ranging from Norway right round the coast of Europe to Greece, where post war, the people heading the government were people who had cooperated with SOE in wartime.[25]

The cases of missing agents and outstanding queries were entrusted to other government offices such as the War Office, the Foreign Office and SIS. Most critically, other files began to disappear.

As early as mid-August 1944, a special instruction had been issued to all directors, regional heads, section heads and heads of country establishments to conduct a survey of documents as to what should be permanently retained, what could be given a more 'limited life', and what could be immediately destroyed. Even as SOE country sections were in the winding-up stage, preparations were being made for the compilation of handbooks and official histories which would draw on existing SOE files.[26] Records were chosen for destruction by the remaining staff, and instructions were given for all files to be 'weeded of ephemeral material'. It was feared that 'some officers took advantage of the instructions to dispose of material which they thought would be unduly sensitive should their contents ever be disclosed'.[27]

Mrs Pawley, who worked in the SOE offices as they were closing down, revealed how files were chosen for destruction: 'it was called weeding', she said, 'and you were given a master plan of how to put things. Missions, directives, this and that, you know, and anything that was trivial you chucked out. And you put things into the master plan, kept the things that were necessary ... and there were piles on the floor and I just went through one after the other ...'.[28] In his memoirs, Sir Douglas Dodds-Parker of SOE's 'Massingham' mission in North Africa wrote that 'a FANY said to me that as she saw the last paper curl up in the flames she realised that with it went the only record of two years of great interest and effort'.[29]

By April 1946, the sum total of SOE's documented history comprised 66,000 files contained in 214 steel filing cabinets, 81 steel cupboards and 7 wall safes. By the end of May 1947, this had been further reduced to 169 filing cabinets (7 of which pertained to France), 9 cupboards and 4 cupboards of card indexes. It was estimated that by the end of 1949, 'something like 100 tons of material had been destroyed'.[30]

In addition to the deliberate destruction of files by personnel, a fire at Baker Street in 1946 damaged an unknown quantity of records. Norman Mott, formerly of SOE's directorate and appointed to handle outstanding SOE matters while the office was closing down, recalled that the fire had broken out in a stationery store between his office and the rooms dedicated to the FANY administration section. 'The whole floor was gutted and a large proportion of the FANY records destroyed altogether,' he said, some of which 'related to the activities in the Field of the SOE FANYS agents'.[31] The files that survived, which included a number of papers pertaining to the Belgian section, included singed papers with charred edges.

But how important were any of these documents? Dodds-Parker said that 'from 1940 it has been said "the less paper, the more action"', and with relation to F Section Buckmaster maintained that full records were not kept during the war anyway, as he had work to do: 'it was unwise to take notes then, owing to the danger of such information getting into the wrong hands.[32] Buckmaster maintained that he was not in the business of making records for future generations of historians to study.[33] His opinion was reiterated by Vera Atkins, who stated that 'we were not keeping records for history but for our own reference on day to day work and no regard for posterity', and 'the idea one would be asked to give information subsequently never entered anyone's head'.[34]

During the 1950s, the weeding continued, but access to the files was increasingly requested by former agents and authors. Dame Irene Ward MP pressed parliament for the release of the SOE records for her own book *F.A.N.Y. Invicta* as well as the *Official History of SOE in France, Death Be Not Proud* and *Madeleine*. Eventually, in the 1970s, the final phase of filing was lodged in the Public Record Office (now The National Archives).[35] The archivist responsible described that 'of the surviving files ... we have documentary evidence that at least 87% were destroyed in London between 1945 and 1950' and that those files were in a 'confused state' having been dealt with by 'inexperienced archival staff' without the knowledge or time to complete the task. Today the archive comprises 15,000 files.[36]

As F Section's missions were fulfilled and its remit became redundant, its staff began to leave the organisation to find other work. Vera Atkins remained to undertake the huge task of finding out what had happened to the agents still missing. Vera was efficient and clever. She had seen as many agents off on their missions as possible, years later recalling that 'the burden of stress was probably on the person who was seeing them off, [in] the realisation that they were going out on a very dangerous mission, and this was probably the last glimpse they would have of the lovely countryside through which you were travelling with them, while you remained quite safely at the end'. Aware of the considerable strain she put herself under, she considered that she must have been 'extraordinarily tough'.[37]

During the war, Vera was one of the staff officers who kept in touch with agents' next of kin, a job that must have been especially trying when the agents were arrested or, worse, disappeared. Vera found solace in the information from returning agents which helped her piece things together. The 'returning agents and the information they brought was more than interesting and more than harrowing ... seeing people back when you had given up hope of them was very exciting'.[38] But there were those who did not come back, and the longer she waited the more she wanted to find out what had happened to them – thirteen of whom were women, one-third of the total who were infiltrated.

One of the female agents' deaths was already accounted for: that of Muriel Byck, who had died of meningitis. For those whose fates remained unknown, Vera believed it was of vital importance to investigate so that their families could be told; she thought ' "missing presumed dead" was a terrible verdict'.[39] Finding she 'could not just abandon their memory', Vera felt strongly that she should be the one who went to find out what had happened to the missing agents: whoever went would have 'to know every detail of the agents, names, code names, every hair on their heads, to spot their tracks'.[40] SOE agreed that she was well qualified for the job 'in view of her intimate knowledge of the set-up of various circuits comprising the "Réseau Buckmaster" and, during her time working with the organisation, she had secured much valuable information'.[41] She was also fluent in German and had good French.

Vera's first request to go to Germany was denied by her superiors but, according to Vera's biographer Sarah Helm, a number of factors began to make them realise that these cases needed solving. Charles Bushell, Violette Szabó's father, was angry that he had had no information about his daughter's whereabouts and, having been shuttled from the Red Cross to the War Office and back again, had involved his local MP. In doing so he threatened the secrecy that surrounded the work of the SOE and its use of women, which in turn could have caused a national controversy. Another factor was that news had been received that instead of simply coming home, as Buckmaster had hoped, some SOE agents had been killed at Mauthausen, Flossenbürg, Sachsenhausen and Dachau concentration camps, among them Jack Agazarian and Gilbert Norman. This meant that others may too have perished: they deserved to be found and their families informed. Also, as

Vera herself later highlighted, those who had been in camps which now sat within the newly created Russian zone of occupation might find themselves stranded, particularly in light of the fact that relations between Britain and the Soviet Union were deteriorating.

Eventually, Vera was given permission to go. Her first trip, in December 1945, lasted for four days, during which she had to prove that she was the right person for the job and could get the results that she needed. Initially, the mission was led by SOE but, with its impending dissolution in January 1946, arrangements needed to be made if the investigations were to continue. For 'a time it looked likely that all further attempts to secure detailed information regarding the fairly considerable number of agents still unaccounted for would have to be abandoned at a time when it appeared that a few more months of work would see the task completed.'[42] Fortunately, Vera was given permission to become attached to the staff of the Judge Advocate General's (JAG) Office, War Crimes Section, and the newly promoted Squadron Officer Atkins arrived in Bad Oeynhausen, the headquarters of the British Army of the Rhine, on 10 January 1946. Vera reported that 'from that date the investigations [were] handled with quite outstanding success.'[43] Vera was very clear in her aims: 'I was only interested in tracing the people who had gone to concentration camps, and who had not returned and find out how and where they were killed.'[44]

As she began her work in earnest it became clear that her task was gargantuan. She was to travel to 'numerous camps and prisons' and undertake 'interviews with the German officers responsible for the British prisoners'. She would not rest until she found out how and where the missing 118 SOE agents had been killed, and if any had survived that she did not already know of.[45]

During her work Vera traced and interrogated dozens of people, from civilian internees to the prison guards at Karlsruhe, the head of Gestapo HQ at avenue Foch and eyewitnesses in the concentration camps who saw some of the women being led to their deaths. She interviewed Hugo Bleicher, who had caused havoc for many members of the resistance and F Section, notably Odette Sansom and Peter Churchill. Bleicher recalled that Vera:

turned out to have more aplomb than all the other officers put together ...
she boxed me in with astonishing ease and consummate tactics. Luckily my
memory is good or she might well have put me in an awkward position. She
seemed also quite tireless in her questioning and if the conducting officer
had not felt hungry at lunchtime and urged her to break off the interrogation, she would have kept me on tenterhooks for a good deal longer.[46]

Through her interviews Vera managed to get details of imprisonment
conditions, interrogation and torture methods that had been used, deportation details and dates. Eventually, through painstaking research into files
and registers, and piecing together the various interview notes, she traced
the fates of the 118 missing F Section agents, 117 of whom had been killed,
among them 12 of 'her girls'.[47]

Vera said that 'each case was different' and that it was very difficult to
'trace people who were moved from camps in the Russian zone and where
the trials took place within the Russian zone'.[48] The one unresolved case was
an agent who had been sent to Marseille with 3 million francs in his pocket.
It was thought that, unable to resist the temptation, he went to Monte Carlo
and gambled the money. It was never discovered whether he had won and
was living off his winnings in secret or whether he had lost and committed
suicide or simply disappeared.

Vera attended the war trials relating to the deaths of the female agents at
Natzweiler-Struthof, Dachau and Ravensbrück, where Odette testified wearing
her FANY uniform, having been personally selected by the prosecution's chief
counsel for her 'ability to give a clear and unbiased account without embellish-
ments'.[49] Vera also attended the trial relating to Sachsenhausen, the camp near
Berlin where several male agents had been murdered. She also attended the
Hamburg trial, which, although not related to her own work, concerned
the men who fabricated the gas 'which was used throughout Germany for the
killing of humans', and attended the Nuremburg trials as a spectator. When
asked if she was satisfied with the outcome, she simply answered 'yes'. She
attempted to keep the names of the victims from the press, but was not
successful, and stories of the executions made it into the public arena: 'British

Women Burned Alive' was a headline in the *Daily Telegraph* on 30 May 1946 and, on 22 May 1948, an article entitled 'Women who died for their country' appeared, featuring the portraits of eleven women who had been executed. Their stories have continued to be retold in newspapers ever since.

The grim fascination with the fates of the women who died for SOE gripped the public, and an organisation which was supposed to remain top secret for years suddenly burst onto the public stage. Described as 'the least secret of the British secret services', as early as 1945 its story was being told far and wide.[50]

The intense public interest in SOE seems to have been born with a statement in the House of Commons but then took on a life of its own. Writing in the 1960s, M.R.D. Foot stated:

> at the end of the war Sir Archibald Sinclair revealed in parliament that some young women had been parachuted into France to assist resistance operations. This precipitated a flurry of excited newspaper comment, and since then official revelations have been few indeed. History and journalism, like nature, abhor a vacuum, and into the vacuum of official silence ghastly imputations about what happened to these girls has been freely inserted by sensation mongers.[51]

One of the early galvanising factors was the awarding of several decorations to agents – including the George Cross to three female agents, posthumously to two of them – and the resultant media coverage. The public desired ever more exciting stories about the SOE and accordingly the national press published the lives of particular SOE members, making some of them into what we would now call celebrities.[52] Awards made in respect of F Section women agents by the British, French and US authorities included the George Cross, George Medal, OBE, MBE, Mentioned in Despatches, King's Commendation for Brave Conduct, Croix de Guerre, Légion d'honneur, Médaille de la Résistance Française, Presidential US Medal of Freedom and Distinguished Service Cross. Pearl Witherington was awarded the MBE (civil division). She recalled:

> I was called up to the office in Paris. 'Read this,' so I read it, it was all more or less what I had done and at the end it said I had been awarded the MBE civil commission. I said, 'What is all this about?' and he said, 'It is a press release,' so I said, 'What!' I said, 'I am sorry but I am not going to accept an MBE civil thank you,' and he said 'I quite agree with you'! And there and then I said they could keep it; if they can't do the job, don't do it at all. I didn't do this for decoration. But why give this to someone who hadn't even done this type of job before? I said, 'Why give us the same decoration as someone who has been sitting behind a desk for the whole war?' I said, 'No thank you, unless they changed it to military' . . . Yvonne Cormeau (who had a whole year as a radio operator with George Starr) and I were both put in for military medals, and the reply came: 'not awarded to women.'[53]

Some months later in September 1946 Pearl was awarded the MBE (military division) along with four other female agents. This was upgraded to a CBE in 2004. She said, 'I never thought of anyone as being an amazing hero, we were just doing our work.'[54]

Yvonne Cormeau was dismayed at the decoration she received: 'at the end of the war we all got MBEs, except for Odette[55] and Noor Inayat Khan who got the George Cross. Pearl and I were put up for it too, for working in the field for a long time, but no as "we hadn't been caught". It's a funny condition – as Hilaire [George Starr] said, you have to fail before you get it.'[56] Sydney Hudson agreed, also saying it was 'disgraceful' that the women agents should be recommended for civil and not military decorations.[57] A memo in the FANY archives dated 22 October 1945 read: 'a number of these young women have given service in the field which, had they been male officers, would have earned between them gallantry awards or other recognition of every grade from DSO and CBE (Mil) downwards. They are however debarred from receiving such awards.'[58] Buckmaster commented that:

though many of SOE's officers earned decorations, we and certainly they did not necessarily think more highly of them than those that fought and received no reward, or of those who died in agony to protect a trivial secret or conceal information already known to the enemy. In no other department of war did so much courage pass unnoticed. In no other department of war were men and women called upon to die alone, to withstand agony of mind and of body in utter solitude, to face death, often ignominious and pain-racked, uncertain whether they might not have saved themselves by the revelation of petty secrets. In no other department of war were civilians asked to risk everything in order to conceal a man whom they had never seen before and might never see again.[59]

The most prominent decorations were the three awards of the George Cross (GC). On 20 August 1946, Odette Sansom became the first woman to ever receive this prestigious medal. An account of the ceremony on 19 November 1946 when King George VI conferred the GC upon her appeared in many British newspapers: ' "You are the first and only woman to be awarded the G.C. . . . Did you know that?" "Yes, your majesty" replied Mrs Sansom "I know I am the first woman G.C. The price I paid was very small for such an honour and such a reward." "No" said the King, "it was not." '[60] Odette's self-effacing attitude made her very popular with the public; she said that what she was receiving, she was receiving for those women who did not return from the camps.

The two other awards to women agents were made posthumously: on 17 December Violette Szabó's medal was touchingly collected by her orphaned daughter, Tania, and then Noor Inayat Khan was gazetted for her GC on 5 April 1949.[61] However, even these decorations were not without their drama. Dame Irene Ward MP in particular made her very strong opinions known, lobbying the prime minister to have Violette awarded the Victoria Cross. The implication was that, in Ward's view, one award, the VC, was superior to the other.

The George Cross was a relatively new award, created by King George VI at the height of the Blitz and bestowed, as he said, 'for acts of the greatest heroism or of the most conspicuous courage in circumstances of extreme danger ... [It is] a new mark of honour for men and women, in all walks of civilian life.' Ward's campaign went to the very top. She began a personal correspondence with Prime Minister Harold Macmillan, in August 1963 telling him that: 'there had always been a tremendous feeling that Violette Szabó was not awarded the Victoria Cross ... She certainly was the bravest of them all and satisfied the two essential conditions.'[62] The two conditions are, first, conspicuous bravery and, second, some daring or pre-eminent act of valour, self-sacrifice or extreme devotion to duty in the presence of the enemy. In November 1963, Ward claimed that 'Violette's particular contribution was that she sacrificed herself to allow her leader to get away and did not seek to escape with him.'[63] Ward's insistence that one decoration was superior to the other reached its apogee when she said the GC was merely a 'civilian' award. Her derogatory comments were not well received in the press, and by spring 1964 the Victoria Cross and George Cross Society began to show their irritation. In a letter dated 8 April, the chairman wrote that he rather hoped that Ward would have 'piped down' by now, but on the contrary she was making 'every effort behind the scenes' to get the decorations exchanged, pursuing this matter 'hotly', and he feared she would petition the Queen herself if she did not get her way.[64] It was explained to Ward in no uncertain terms that the awards were equal, that there was no virtue in one over the other, nor was either reserved exclusively as a 'military' or 'civilian' award, and that it would be derogatory to exchange one for the other unless a gross error had been made in the initial award. It was decided that the change would have 'far reaching and undesirable effects and there is no case for it', and Ward's claim was rejected.[65]

The first book about SOE, and the first personal account of SOE's work, was *Maquis*, written in 1945 by SOE agent George Millar.[66] It was an instant success. Despite paper shortages, 70,000 hardback volumes were printed by Heinemann to much public and critical acclaim.[67] General de Gaulle was impressed by its candid nature, saying 'this is the truth about the Maquis', predicting correctly that 'the Maquis is something that will be untruer, year-by-year, for decades ahead'.[68] SOE HQ had been less enthusiastic, telling Millar that it would have to pass its censors before it was put into print. Vera Atkins asked Millar, 'must you write a damned book, it seems rather a cheap idea, as though you did what you did to make money out of it and I know you did not'.[69] Regardless, *Maquis* is an exciting and realistic account of life in the French resistance as well as a frank personal account.

In 1946, *Moondrop to Gascony* by Anne-Marie Walters was published just two years after the author's infiltration into France. This work contributed significantly to the SOE records and was the first autobiography by a female agent.[70] Walters, who was courier to the WHEELWRIGHT circuit, did not attempt to make her work seem glamorous, nor did she oversell her achievements as an agent. Nevertheless, *Moondrop to Gascony* has all the elements of a great war story – near misses, gunfights, torture and betrayal – and is told with sincerity and clarity. It was awarded the John Llewellyn Rhys Prize in 1947.

That same year a semi-documentary film, *School for Danger* (also known as *Now It Can Be Told*), was made by the RAF as an informational film for its pilots, but it was also released to the public. It 'stars' two former SOE agents, Captain Harry Rée and Lieutenant Jacqueline Nearne, who 'as agents Felix and Cat . . . recreate for the camera some of their adventures in France'.[71] The film depicts agents' training and life in the field, and the narration, albeit scripted, gives a clear impression of how the agents felt about it all: while on the 'death slide', Rée comments, 'they took a delight in making us climb up things then jump down or slide down'; while Nearne says, as she shoots a gun, 'we were taught all about firearms, British and foreign', and about parachuting, 'the first jumps were pretty nasty . . . the balloon jump was the worst, the awful silence as the earth receded and the gathering noise of the wind as we went higher'. Colonel Buckmaster makes a brief appearance, as do former agents Blanche Charlet, Brian Stonehouse and Marcel Rousset. Despite not being a true documentary (in that it was scripted and agents took on roles that were not theirs in real life) *School for Danger* is the closest depiction to reality that F Section have ever received on the big screen.

The increasing interest in SOE was fuelled by the newspaper accounts of the Natzweiler trials. To counteract the horrors recounted in the press, SOE wanted to share a more positive story of success and triumph. It was through the medium of the press in the late 1940s that the majority of the general public discovered that women had actually been used behind enemy lines as secret agents. The thirst for knowledge and a desire to feed the public's imagination was born.

Jerrard Tickell, who worked as the War Office publicist, conducted a series of interviews with both Odette and Peter, the result of which was his book *Odette*, an account of their time in France. Odette and Buckmaster also assisted with the writing of it. Due to his role as publicist Tickell enjoyed access to War Office files and wireless messages, and training notes and other similar information are dotted throughout the book. Tickell even refers to members of the SS who helped fill in the 'many sinister gaps in the story'. Published in 1949 it was an instant bestseller, with over 500,000 copies sold and four impressions printed within a year.[72] The book received rave reviews and was made into a successful film in 1950, turning Odette Churchill into a household name. Then, in 1956, Violette Szabó received similar treatment in R.J. Minney's *Carve Her Name with Pride*, the film version of which was released two years later.

The way in which these two books are written, and how the women are characterised, typifies the attitudes of the post-war years. They are very much books of their time. Tickell and Minney intended their works to tug at the heartstrings of their readers and bring to life the sensational stories of Odette and Violette that had filled the newspapers. Some liberties were therefore taken, and the books are sometimes overindulgent and romantic. And although Odette's and Violette's courage is rightly at the forefront, sadly they come across as somewhat two-dimensional – a shadow of their real selves.

The influence of *Odette* and *Carve Her Name with Pride* is huge, yet it is not widely recognised that the films inspired by the books made subtle adjustments to the events they depict. The films had SOE personnel as advisers, and SOE was therefore in a position to mould an image of F Section that suited its post-war needs. As such the films emphasised themes of self-lessness, bravery and patriotism, which informed the public perception of SOE and embedded the received wisdom regarding F Section for genera-tions to come.

Another three books, also written in the 1950s, changed the course of SOE studies and led to a demand to make the official files more accessible, high-lighting the need for an official history. *Madeleine* by Jean Overton Fuller was published in 1952. Jean was a personal friend of Noor Inayat Khan and wanted to discover the full details of her friend's recruitment and work with F Section, as well as the circumstances of her arrest, imprisonment and execution. In her preface Fuller states: 'The War Office were able to give hardly any information about the people [Noor] met, worked and lived with.'[73] But Fuller became friends with two other authors who were undertaking their own research into F Section, Dame Irene Ward and Elizabeth Nicholas. The women shared information with one another and followed up leads together.

Madeleine makes extensive use of letters and personal recollections. While this does not necessarily guarantee accuracy, it does give a sense of energy and clarity that makes the book very readable; M.R.D. Foot said the 'many trivial inaccuracies hardly impair the dramatic force of the story'[74] and, on its publication as a paperback in 1957, that it not only contained 'fresh material' but 'fresh mistakes'.[75] That said, Fuller did not have access to official archives, and so had to rely on sources such as eyewitnesses and friends to build up her construction of Noor's life. Even though Fuller was a close friend of Noor's, she does not hesitate to include material such as Noor's security lapses or her fragile state of mind. The work is on the whole unbiased and, though 'dramatic' in its tone, *Madeleine* provides the historian with an interesting and predominantly accurate account of Noor's life.[76]

After writing her book *F.A.N.Y. Invicta*, Dame Irene Ward put to the House of Commons many 'probing' – and many unsubstantiated – questions about SOE in France. Her work, which is predominantly about the FANY, explores the relationship between FANY and SOE, the circumstances in which women became involved with SOE as agents, and the details of several F Section women, including Odette Sansom, Noor Inayat Khan, Pearl Witherington and Yvonne Baseden.

Ward also assisted Elizabeth Nicholas, whose investigation into Rowden's execution, *Death Be Not Proud*, was published in 1958. Nicholas was a journalist and travel writer for the *Sunday Times* and had been at school with Diana Rowden, where the two had shared a room. Through her research into her friend's work and death, Nicholas travelled throughout France and visited places where Diana, and the other F Section women killed at Natzweiler and Dachau, had been. She met and spoke with those who had known the agents in the field and became close to several of their families. It was in this way that she came to uncover details about the women's missions and arrests, and it is this that gives Nicholas's book an intimacy and immediacy which makes it an emotive read. She also became convinced that there had been some conspiracy, and that the collapse of PROSPER led directly to ten out of the twelve female F Section deaths. She implies that that they were used as a decoy, sacrificed in some sort of game to mislead the Nazis with regard to British awareness of the collapse of the network. Its publication was said to leave the 'press and public wondering just how good British intelligence really was'.[77]

The research done by Fuller, Ward and Nicholas inspired others to follow in their footsteps and uncover more SOE stories. Eventually there was a slight relaxation regarding access to F Section files for researchers and authors. These works, as mentioned, highlighted the need for an official history of SOE in France, but the Foreign Office seemed to have concerns about the repercussions that such a book would have, as demonstrated in this letter which was drafted from the foreign secretary to Dame Irene Ward in May 1960:

> I know it would please some individuals, particularly those who feel that
> the books hitherto published have given a distorted picture of what really

happened, and that unless there is an authoritative account of the part played by this country, our contribution to European resistance is likely to be misrepresented. But I have to think of the national interest; and I have to think of it in terms of the present and future rather than of the past ... Some of our activities, moreover, although justifiable in war, could cause us a lot of embarrassment if publicly admitted now. Then I have to consider the effect on our relations with our wartime allies, and whether the inevitable revival of old controversies and re-opening of old wounds would not do more harm than good.[78]

Nonetheless the history of SOE in France was sanctioned in 1960 and a year later the Foreign Office commissioned Oxford graduate and British intelligence officer M.R.D. Foot to undertake the task.

In the preface to the book Foot gave a brief outline of its origins: 'The project derives from the continuing concern expressed, both in parliament and outside it, that there should be an accurate and dispassionate account of SOE's activities in the war of 1939–1945.'[79] The research and writing of such a book was unprecedented, as it constituted 'the first officially sponsored account of a British secret service made available to the general public'.[80] It was 'officially considered a "companion volume to the official histories"' of the Second World War, and was described later by Foot as a 'quasi-official' history.[81] The result of years of research, *SOE in France* was published in 1966, and was heavily criticised for aspects of its coverage; Foot subsequently retracted statements and issued an apology, with an amended edition published in 1968.

The book deals with all aspects of SOE's work in France, explaining its origins, modus operandi and the activities of F Section agents – detailing their sabotages, successes with the resistance and notable individual stories. Foot was somewhat critical of the way in which agents' stories had already been portrayed by the press. What is striking about the book is that it entered public discussion at precisely the point where historical record and public contention converge. This led to controversies at the time. For instance, Foot had been granted access to closed files but only limited access to veteran SOE personnel – and no contact with F Section agents themselves. The fact that he had not interviewed several agents irritated Vera Atkins for one. 'I think it is a great pity that *SOE in France* was published before the author was able to see who he would have wished to see, which included head office staff like Colonel Buckmaster and myself, a number of others and a much wider cross-section of agents, it is very discernible as a book and I can pick out those he had seen as against those he had not seen and it does leave an imbalance.'[82] Atkins's interviewer was under the impression that Foot was restricted by Whitehall as to whom he could interview. Certainly, although the book was vetted by a number of people before publication, it was not seen by any of the agents themselves. Thus, despite its monumentality in the story of SOE, it is a source that is debated as much today as it was when it was written over fifty years ago.

After the war, many of the other F Section agents slipped back into civilian life and left their war work behind them.

Madeleine Lavigne saw the liberation of Paris, but then, on 24 February 1945, she died quite suddenly of a blood clot. Captain Fraser Campbell, an SOE FANY staff officer, attended her funeral and laid a wreath of behalf of her SOE colleagues. Her final report says 'at all times she conducted herself with the greatest gallantry and devotion to duty, and it was mainly due to her energy and tact that one of the two main groups was established on a firm basis.'[83]

In recognition of all she had done, SOE kept Krystyna Skarbek on full pay until the end of 1945, when they began to close up shop, and she became a British citizen in 1946. In May 1951, Krystyna was working as a steward on the maiden voyage of New Zealand cruise liner MV *Ruahine* from Southampton to Wellington. It was a requirement that all staff should wear their war medal ribbons and she became a subject of great interest and some envy among crew and passengers alike. One person who took particular note of her was 43-year-old steward Dennis Muldowney, but it was not reciprocated: Krystyna was still very much commited to her long-term lover

Andrzej Kowerski. Muldowney became obsessed with her. In April 1952, while Krystyna was staying at the Shelbourne Hotel in Kensington, Muldowney took a job as a porter at the Reform Club. On 15 June, a day before Krystyna was due to fly to Belgium to meet Kowerski, Muldowney followed her back to her room. After a brief argument, he took out a dagger and stabbed her in the chest: she was dead within minutes. Muldowney was hanged at Pentonville prison on 30 September 1952.

In 1946, Julienne Aisner was reunited with her son, but her health was in rapid decline and, though she begged to receive treatment at the Curie Institute in Paris, nothing could be done to save her. Her son believed that her cancer was caused by the injections she received at Cherche Midi prison. She died, aged 47, in February 1947.

After the war, Ginette Jullian married her fiancé Phillipe and moved to Tahiti. She died in a scuba diving accident in 1962. Yvonne Cormeau worked in the British Coal Control Commission in the Ruhr and in Brussels. She was also a guest on *This Is Your Life* and historical adviser on the first series of *Wish Me Luck*, a dramatised, fictitious account of F Section made by London Weekend Television in the 1980s. Sonia d'Artois went to live in Canada with her husband Guy, where they had six children. Francine Agazarian made a visit to Flossenbürg in 1967, where her husband Jack had been murdered; seeing his cell and walking in his footsteps to the yard where he was shot, she admitted she had never been able to free herself 'entirely from grief'.[84] Jacqueline Nearne served in the protocol department of the United Nations, and her portrait, painted by Brian Stonehouse, hangs proudly and prominently on a wall in the bar of the Special Forces Club.

Virginia Hall married OSS Lieutenant Paul Guillot, with whom she had fallen in love during the war. When the OSS became the CIA in 1947 she was one of the first women to be taken on, and remained with them in both office and field work for many years.

Mary Herbert and Claude de Baissac were married in November 1944 but never lived together. Mary gave French lessons while raising her daughter, Claudine. Pearl Witherington and Henri Cornioley married in November

1944 and had a daughter, and Pearl worked for the World Bank. In 1991, Pearl and Henri helped to establish the Valençay Memorial, commemorating 104 SOE agents, in the Loire valley. On retirement they moved close by.

In spite of only knowing each other for three days in perilous conditions on the Spanish mountains, Odette Wilen married Santiago Strugay, her escape line guide, and they remained together until his death in 1997. Peggy Knight returned home and became a housewife, with three children, as did 'Paddy' O'Sullivan, who married a former SOE instructor and had two sons. Anne-Marie Walters moved to France and married in 1946. She travelled throughout the rest of her life, living in New York, Barcelona and France, working as an editor and translator for various publishers. Lise de Baissac married interior designer Gustave Villameur, and the couple lived in Marseille. Yvonne Fontaine married a Frenchman called Dumont. Because she was recruited in the field, Vera Atkins did not count her as an official F Section agent and, as such, the proposal for her Croix de Guerre and OBE were never approved.

After the war Phyllis Latour married an engineer and the couple went to live in Australia, where they had four children, and then moved to Fiji. Phyllis decided to move back to Australia with the children and brought them up alone in the Auckland region. She had no wish to speak of her wartime exploits and it was not until 2000 that her own children found out what she had done and insisted she send off for her medals. Similarly, Blanche Charlet and Marie-Thérèse le Chêne kept themselves to themselves after they came home from the war and never spoke publicly. Likewise, Elizabeth Deveraux Rochester was released from prison after the liberation and returned to a quiet life, out of the public eye, in France.

What unites these women, other than their service to France during the war, is their silence after it. For some women this silence was a matter of choice – they had fulfilled their job and wanted a return to normal life. Despite originally wanting this for herself, Odette was pushed into the lime-light. She divorced Peter Churchill in 1956 and married former SOE agent Geoffrey Hallowes. She spent much of her life involved with various veterans charities as well as Amnesty International.[85] Odette also vigorously supported and donated to a campaign for a plaque to be placed at Ravensbrück dedi-cated to the F Section women who were murdered there. In 1995, alongside former agents, family members and historians, Odette unveiled the plaque, affixed to the Wall of Nations at the camp memorial.

Nancy Wake also enjoyed publicity with her first biography, written by Russell Braddon and published in 1958, making the 'White Mouse' a house-hold name. After the war Nancy worked in the intelligence department at the British Air Ministry. In 1949 she unsuccessfully ran for the Australian parliament, returning to England in 1951 to work as an intelligence officer at the Air Ministry in Whitehall. In December 1957 she married RAF officer John Forward and they went back to Australia in the early 1960s.

As is evident from these women's later lives, there is a disproportionate amount of publicity around the different agents. Some chose to speak out, some went to ground never to be heard of again, while others came out in later life to discuss their wartime experiences. The press's 'ghastly imputations about what happened to these girls ... freely inserted by sensation mongers' meant that their stories were dominated by betrayal, interrogation, torture, prisons, concentration camps and executions, which, as we have seen, were not always experienced by the female agents, some of whom enjoyed a high degree of success while in the field and the majority of whom returned home safely. Whether or not agents chose to speak after the war should not detract from the incredible work they undertook and the sheer peril in which they placed themselves. But was it all worth it?

EPILOGUE

Her grandeur of character bore a classic hall-mark: she was not conscious of being remarkable.[1]

SOE member Patrick Howarth, about Madame Rossi,

a female résistant

The contribution made to F Section by its female agents was unique. In a society where sexual equality was virtually unheard of, and where a woman's perceived duty was to raise the family or work in non-combatant areas of war work such as munitions or driving, the recruiting, training and employing of women to bear arms and to be infiltrated to work behind the lines as secret agents was groundbreaking in every sense.

SOE demonstrated a hitherto unprecedented degree of broad-mindedness by actively seeking out suitable women for work in the field. In accordance with the body's usual principle, to 'go straight for the objective, across any social or military conventions that may get in the way', F Section ignored all precepts and prejudices by recruiting and deploying women.[2] Although the use of women was questioned in the aftermath of war, during the war years it demonstrated that SOE was a relatively progressive organisation with a policy of equality whereby women did exactly the same training as the men. Their roles in the field, certainly as wireless operators, were the same as their male counterparts, and in some extraordinary cases women even stepped into leadership roles after the arrest of their circuit head or were actively involved in sabotage.[3]

Thirty-nine F Section women were active in the field during the Second World War. Some women got through the war without a hitch, others had near misses; sixteen were caught, imprisoned and eventually deported to concentration camps; and thirteen did not return. Up until now there has been a vast amount of literature, press interest and films about the women who served with SOE and yet some stories are untold, while others are simply not true. M.R.D. Foot himself recognised that 'A few highly accomplished and gallant [women] were agents operating in France ... on these few, there is a large amount of popular literature, almost all of it is worthless and much of it about the wrong people.'[4]

This book has attempted to tell the true story of all the women agents, those who have become household names and national heroines as well as those who have remained in the shadows. I have re-examined well-worn, oft-told narratives and revealed some hitherto little known or uncelebrated stories of heroism and bravery, as well as frustration, failure and betrayal. Looking at agents' true personalities and contributions has been enlightening in different ways. Instead of viewing these women as two-dimensional icons or names glancingly referred to in the files, I have aimed to find the real women within – normal women, women to whom we can relate and with whom we can empathise.

All the women who were infiltrated into France by F Section were extraordinary. Only consider Yvonne Baseden, the skilled wireless operator who received one of the biggest daylight drops of supplies of the war and who was betrayed to the Gestapo the very next day. Or Lilian Rolfe, who travelled from Brazil to join the Allied war effort and who sent sixty-seven faultless wireless messages over three months, even engaging with the enemy before being arrested and sent to her death. Or Denise Bloch (so often simply mentioned in passing as one of the agents who died alongside Violette Szabó), the Jewish girl who had fought with the French resistance before escaping to England and who was arrested two weeks after D-Day. Or the achievements of pioneering agents such as Pearl Witherington, who took command of some 1,500 men and was responsible for arming and training them;[5] of Eliane Plewman, whose 'untiring devotion to duty and willingness to undergo any risk largely contributed to the successful estab-lishment of her network' and sabotage on a huge scale;[6] of Yvonne Cormeau, who over the course of a year sent 400 wireless messages from the field. All too often these women have been overlooked by authors and journalists hunting for stories of derring-do or the high drama of interrogations, torture and imprisonment, or because the spotlight didn't shine on them in the post-war years.

This book has tried to ensure that their stories have been told and that they have been given the recognition they deserve. It has been my aim to redress the balance by approaching the work of all the agents with suitable gravitas: to tell all of their stories and to set them within the framework of SOE F Section as a whole. I have investigated how the various agents' lives interconnected with the resistance networks across France, and have charted the deployment of these women in the context of wider SOE tactics in the field and the progress of the war and beyond. I have shown how their relationships with one another, with fellow agents and even with Germans affected them and their missions. I have charted the work of all thirty-nine women and investigated their roles, contributions, foibles, successes and failures. It is clear that these women did not work alone, that they had a network of people behind them, and that the role of male agents was just as important and dangerous as theirs; and also that the female agents worked incredibly efficiently given the dangers that they faced, not only the obvious ones in wartime but also the threats of exhaustion, illness and childbirth.

The sacrifice and bravery of those who were captured, facing imprison-ment, interrogation and the concentration camps, is exemplary and inspiring. The three women who survived the camps suffered greatly, both mentally and physically, during and after their incarcerations. But all those who came back had undertaken immensely dangerous missions in enemy-occupied territory. Between them they had cycled thousands of kilometres, sent hundreds of wireless messages, faced identity checks, dealt with the daily fear of the Gestapo and collaborators, and endured privations that it is almost impossible to imagine. They worked tirelessly and risked everything for the cause in which they wholeheartedly believed. The contribution of these women to the work of F Section played a pivotal role in the liberation of France from Nazi occupation, and in bringing an end to the Second World War by helping to secure an Allied victory.

AGENTS WHO SURVIVED

Agazarian, Francine
Aisner, Julienne
Baseden, Yvonne
Butt, Sonia
Charlet, Blanche
Cormeau, Yvonne
de Baissac, Lise
Deveraux Rochester,
    Elizabeth
Fontaine, Yvonne
Granville, Christine
Hall, Virginia
Herbert, Mary
Jullian, Ginette
Knight, Marguerite
Latour, Phyllis
Lavigne, Madeleine
le Chêne, Marie-Thérèse
Nearne, Eileen
Nearne, Jacqueline
O'Sullivan, Patricia
Sansom, Odette
Wake, Nancy
Walters, Anne-Marie
Wilen, Odette
Witherington, Pearl

AGENTS WHO DIED IN THE FIELD

Beekman, Yolande
Bloch, Denise
Borrel, Andrée
Byck, Muriel
Damerment, Madeleine
Khan, Noor Inayat
Lefort, Cicely
Leigh, Vera
Olschanesky, Sonia
Plewman, Eliane
Rolfe, Lilian
Rowden, Diana
Rudellat, Yvonne
Szabó, Violette

APPENDIX
GEORGE CROSS CITATIONS

Numb. 38578

1703

SUPPLEMENT TO

The London Gazette

OF FRIDAY, 1st APRIL, 1949

Published by Authority

Registered as a newspaper

TUESDAY, 5 APRIL, 1949

CENTRAL CHANCERY OF THE ORDERS
OF KNIGHTHOOD.

*St. James's Palace, S.W.*1.

5th April, 1949.

The KING has been graciously pleased to approve the posthumous award of the GEORGE CROSS to:—

Assistant Section Officer Nora INAYAT-KHAN (9901), Women's Auxiliary Air Force.

Assistant Section Officer Nora INAYAT-KHAN was the first woman operator to be infiltrated into enemy occupied France, and was landed by Lysander aircraft on 16th June, 1943. During the weeks immediately following her arrival, the Gestapo made mass arrests in the Paris Resistance groups to which she had been detailed. She refused however to abandon what had become the principal and most dangerous post in France, although given the opportunity to return to England, because she did not wish to leave her French comrades without communications and she hoped also to rebuild her group. She remained at her post therefore and did the excellent work which earned her a posthumous Mention in Despatches.

The Gestapo had a full description of her, but knew only her code name "Madeleine". They deployed considerable forces in their effort to catch her and so break the last remaining link with London. After 3½ months she was betrayed to the Gestapo and taken to their H.Q. in the Avenue Foch. The Gestapo had found her codes and messages and were now in a position to work back to London. They asked her to co-operate, but she refused and gave them no information of any kind. She was imprisoned in one of the cells on the 5th floor of the Gestapo H.Q. and remained there for several weeks during which time she made two unsuccessful attempts at escape. She was asked to sign a declaration that she would make no further attempts but she refused and the Chief of the Gestapo obtained permission from Berlin to send her to Germany for "safe custody". She was the first agent to be sent to Germany.

Assistant Section Officer INAYAT-KHAN was sent to Karlsruhe in November; 1943, and then to Pforsheim where her cell was apart from the main prison. She was considered to be a particularly dangerous and unco-operative prisoner. The Director of the prison has also been interrogated and has confirmed that Assistant Section Officer INAYAT-KHAN, when interrogated by the Karlsruhe Gestapo, refused to give any information whatsoever, either as to her work or her colleagues.

She was taken with three others to Dachau Camp on the 12th September, 1944. On arrival, she was taken to the crematorium and shot.

Assistant Section Officer INAYAT-KHAN displayed the most conspicuous courage, both moral and physical over a period of more than 12 months.

Air Ministry, 5th April, 1949.

Air Commandant F. H. HANBURY, M.B.E., Women's Royal Air Force, is appointed Honorary Air Aide-de-Camp to the KING. 28th Mar. 1949.

Matron-in-Chief H. W. CARGILL, R.R.C., Princess Mary's Royal Air Force Nursing Service, is appointed Honorary Nursing Sister to the KING. 28th Mar. 1949.

ROYAL AIR FORCE.

GENERAL DUTIES BRANCH.

Appointment to commission.

As Wing Commander (permanent):—
Donald Arthur GARNER, D.S.O. (40528). 20th Sept. 1948.

As Squadron Leaders (permanent):—
Edward Leslie WEST (42926). 22nd June 1948.
Thomas Walter Clayton FAZAN (37093). 16th Aug. 1948.
Anthony David LAMBERT, D.F.C. (80832). 10th Sept. 1948.

15th Sept. 1948.
George Edward GOODE, D.F.C. (81675).
Guy MARSLAND (41940).

Henry Gilbert FLETCHER, D.F.C. (40173). 4th Oct. 1948.
Peter Evan LEWIS, D.F.C. (40400). 7th Oct. 1948.
Edward Quentin MOODY (40006). 29th Oct. 1948.

10th Nov. 1948.
Gerald Frederick Reader ALFORD, A.F.C. (108852).
Edmund DONOVAN, D.F.C. (117677).

Colin Norman BIRCH, A.F.C. (41519). 16th Nov. 1948.
James Donald Wakefield WILLIS, A.F.C. (44972). 23rd Nov. 1948.
Kenneth Victor GILLING, A.F.C. (41171). 2nd Dec. 1948.

Numb. 37693

4175

THIRD SUPPLEMENT
TO
The London Gazette

Of FRIDAY, the 16th of AUGUST, 1946

Published by Authority

Registered as a newspaper

TUESDAY, 20 AUGUST, 1946

CENTRAL CHANCERY OF THE ORDERS OF KNIGHTHOOD,

St. James's Palace, S.W.1.
20th August, 1946.

The KING has been graciously pleased to award the GEORGE CROSS to:—

Odette Marie Celina, Mrs. SANSOM, M.B.E., Women's Transport Service (First Aid Nursing Yeomanry).

Mrs. Sansom was infiltrated into enemy-occupied France and worked with great courage and distinction until April, 1943, when she was arrested with her Commanding Officer. Between Marseilles and Paris on the way to the prison at Fresnes, she succeeded in speaking to her Commanding Officer and for mutual protection they agreed to maintain that they were married. She adhered to this story and even succeeded in convincing her captors in spite of considerable contrary evidence and through at least fourteen interrogations. She also drew Gestapo attention from her . Commanding Officer on to herself saying that he had only come to France on her insistence. She took full responsibility and agreed that it should be herself and not her Commanding Officer who should be shot. By this action she caused the Gestapo to cease paying attention to her Commanding Officer after only two interrogations. In addition the Gestapo were most determined to discover the whereabouts of a wireless operator and of another British officer whose lives were of the greatest value to the Resistance Organisation. Mrs. Sansom was the only person who knew of their whereabouts. The Gestapo tortured her most brutally to try to make her give away this information. They seared her back with a red hot iron and, when that failed, they pulled out all her toe-nails. Mrs. Sansom, however, continually refused to speak and by her bravery and determination, she not only saved the lives of the two officers but also enabled them to carry on their most valuable work.

During the period of over two years in which she was in enemy hands, she displayed courage, endurance and self-sacrifice of the highest possible order.

———

CENTRAL CHANCERY OF THE ORDERS OF KNIGHTHOOD,

St. James's Palace, S.W.1.
20th August, 1946.

The KING has been graciously pleased to give orders for the undermentioned appointments to the Most Excellent Order of the British Empire, for the following awards of the British Empire Medal, and for the publication in the London Gazette of the names of those specially shown below as having received an expression of Commendation for their brave conduct.

To be an Additional Officer of the Civil Division of the Most Excellent Order of the British Empire:—

Captain James Alexander TAYLOR, Master, m.v. "Empire Patrol." (Prince Line Ltd.).

To be Additional Members of the Civil Division of the Most Excellent Order of the British Empire:—

Paul Francis Johns HUNTER, Chief Officer, m.v. "Empire Patrol" (Prince Line Ltd.).

John Douglas HUGHES, Senior Second Engineer Officer, m.v. "Empire Patrol" (Prince Line Ltd.).

The "Empire Patrol" was carrying Greek refugees, mainly women and children, from East Africa to Greece, when a fire broke out on board.

Rumb. 37820

6127

FOURTH SUPPLEMENT

TO

The London Gazette

Of FRIDAY, the 13th of DECEMBER, 1946

Published by Authority

Registered as a newspaper

TUESDAY, 17 DECEMBER, 1946

CENTRAL CHANCERY OF THE ORDERS
OF KNIGHTHOOD.

St. James's Palace, S.W.1.
17th December, 1946.

The KING has been graciously pleased to
award the GEORGE CROSS to:—

Violette, Madame SZABO (deceased), Women's
Transport Service (First Aid Nursing Yeomanry).

Madame Szabo volunteered to undertake
a particularly dangerous mission in France.
She was parachuted into France in
April, 1944, and undertook the task
with enthusiasm. In her execution of the
delicate researches entailed she showed
great presence of mind and astuteness. She
was twice arrested by the German security
authorities but each time managed to get
away. Eventually, however, with other
members of her group, she was surrounded
by the Gestapo in a house in the south west
of France. Resistance appeared hopeless but
Madame Szabo, seizing a Sten-gun and as
much ammunition as she could carry, barri-
caded herself in part of the house and, ex-
changing shot for shot with the enemy,
killed or wounded several of them. By constant movement, she avoided being cornered
and fought until she dropped exhausted. She
was arrested and had to undergo solitary
confinement. She was then continuously and
atrociously tortured but never by word or
deed gave away any of her acquaintances
or told the enemy anything of any value.
She was ultimately executed. Madame Szabo
gave a magnificent example of courage and
steadfastness.

———

CENTRAL CHANCERY OF THE ORDERS
OF KNIGHTHOOD.

St. James's Palace, S.W.1.
17th December, 1946.

The KING has been graciously pleased to
give orders for the undermentioned appointment to the Most Excellent Order of the British

Empire, and for the publication in the London
Gazette of the names of those specially shown
below as having received an expression of Commendation for their brave conduct.

*To be an Additional Member of the Civil
Division of the Most Excellent Order of the
British Empire:—*

Gerald James WRIGHT, Burma Civil Supplies
Board, Lashio, Burma.

In April, 1942, Wright and his family who
were prevented by the Japanese from leaving
Namkhan, took refuge at Myanchoung in
the Kachin Hills. In May, several British
officers and a platoon of Indian troops entered Myanchoung, after an engagement with
the Japanese. Wright at once rendered first
aid to several wounded in the party although
he knew that the Japanese would shortly
enter the village. On three other occasions
Wright sheltered British troops at great risk
to himself. He concealed one party for 18
months, cared for the sick and wounded and
organised their escape. He was arrested by
the Japanese and kept in captivity for six
months. During this time he was tortured
but did not reveal the whereabouts of any
of the troops he had befriended. Wright
showed courage without regard for self.

———

KING'S COMMENDATIONS FOR BRAVE
CONDUCT.

Patricia, Mrs. Friend, British resident in Monte
Carlo.

For special services during the enemy occupation of France.

———

William Reynolds (deceased), Hotel Manager,
Brussels.

For special services during the enemy occupation of Belgium.

———

The appointment of Miss Lalita Hensman
announced in Gazette No. 37771 of 29th
October, 1946, page 5307 is now dated 18th
May, 1946.

NOTES

PROLOGUE

1. William Mackenzie, *The Secret History of SOE*, St Ermin's Press, London, 2000, p. 65. The attendees at this meeting were Lord Lloyd (secretary of state for the colonies and chairman of the British Council), Lord Hankey, Dr Dalton (minister of economic warfare), Sir Alexander Cadogan, Colonel Menzies, Mr Desmond Moron (representing the prime minister) and Mr Gladwyn Jebb.
2. Ibid.
3. Hugh Dalton, *The Fateful Years*, Frederick Muller Ltd, London, 1957, p. 366.
4. M.R.D. Foot, *SOE in France*, HMSO, London, 1966, pp. 21–2.
5. Liane Jones, *A Quiet Courage*, Corgi, London, 1990, p. 26.
6. Foot, *SOE in France*, p. 47.
7. Ibid., p. 46.
8. Irene Ward, *F.A.N.Y. Invicta*, Hutchinson, London, 1955. Irene Ward was elected to parliament in 1931. After the war she published this account of the Women's Transport Service and lobbied for an official history of the SOE. She became Britain's longest serving woman MP until she stood down in February 1974. *Oxford Dictionary of National Biography*, accessed online, 9 January 2011.
9. Imperial War Museum (IWM), Sound Archive, 9331, Selwyn Jepson, 3 July 1986.
10. Ibid.
11. Information provided by Tania Szabó.
12. Marcus Binney, *The Women Who Lived for Danger*, Coronet, St Ives, 2002, p. 1.
13. Through films such as *Carve Her Name with Pride*, dir. Lewis Gilbert (Network, 1958), *Charlotte Gray*, dir. Gillian Armstrong (4dvd, 2001), *Female Agents*, dir. Jean-Paul Salomé (Revolver Entertainment, 2008) and *Odette*, dir. Herbert Wilcox (Wilcox–Neagle, 1950).
14. Russell Miller, *Behind the Lines*, Pimlico, London, 2002, p. 267.
15. Second World War Experience Centre, Mrs Pawley, reel 2996 (14 September 2005).
16. Duncan Stuart, '"Of Historical Interest Only": The Origins and Vicissitudes of the SOE Archive', in Mark Seaman (ed.), *Special Operations Executive*, Routledge, Abingdon, 2005, p. 228.
17. Maurice Buckmaster, *Specially Employed*, Batchworth Press, London, 1952, p. 7.
18. Wilcox, *Odette* (film).

1 SETTING EUROPE ABLAZE

1. W.E. Fairbairn, *All-in Fighting*, Faber & Faber, London, 1942.
2. SIS records, quoted in Clare Mulley, *The Spy Who Loved*, Macmillan, London, 2012, p. 33.
3. Ibid., pp. 47–8.

4. Sonia Purnell, *A Woman of No Importance: The Untold Story of Virginia Hall – WW2's Most Dangerous Spy*, Virago, London, 2019, p. 30.
5. Interview by author with Yvonne Burney (née Baseden), Napier Gardens, London, 23 May 2003 and August 2003.
6. Cynthia Sadler, *War Journey*, Artemis Publications, Croydon, 2003, p. 17.
7. TNA, HS9/77/2, Mary Herbert, Personnel File.
8. Hugh Popham, *FANY*, Leo Cooper, London, 1984, p. xii.
9. IWM, Sound Archive, 9331, Selwyn Jepson, 3 July 1986.
10. In the RAF documentary-drama *School for Danger* (later known as *Now It Can Be Told*), Jacqueline Nearne (who plays a wireless operator, despite actually having been a courier in the field) is handed a lipstick and told 'Your tablets are in the lipstick,' while Nancy Wake famously always had her Chanel lipstick in the pocket of her silk pyjamas.
11. Mackenzie, *The Secret History of SOE*, p. 719.
12. Interview by Juliette Pattinson with Gervase Cowell, 3 June 1999, 'Behind Enemy Lines' (PhD thesis, University of Lancaster, October 2007).
13. TNA, HS7/121, Use of women in F Section.
14. TNA, HS9/114/2, Yolande Beekman, Personnel File.
15. Interview by *Army News* editor Judith Martin with Phyllis Latour, 2009. See https://www.stuff.co.nz/national/63516307/pippas-astonishing-story-recognised
16. IWM, Sound Archive, 9478, Odette Sansom, 31 October 1986.
17. IWM, Sound Archive, 9331, Selwyn Jepson, 3 July 1986.
18. Anne-Marie Walters, *Moondrop to Gascony*, Macmillan and Co., London, 1946, p. 3.
19. IWM, Sound Archive, 9331, Selwyn Jepson, 3 July 1986.
20. IWM, Sound Archive, 9478, Odette Sansom, 31 October 1986.
21. IWM, Sound Archive, 9331, Selwyn Jepson, 3 July 1986.
22. The phrase derives from a comment made by Claude Dansey of SIS. See Geoffrey Elliott, *I Spy: The Secret Life of a British Agent*, Little, Brown, London, 1997, p. 68.
23. *SOE Syllabus*, intro. Denis Rigden, PRO, London, 2001, p. 2.
24. Walters, *Moondrop to Gascony*, p. 4.
25. Peter Fitzsimmons, *Nancy Wake*, HarperCollins, London, 2001, p. 114.
26. Ibid., p. 115.
27. Each agent was assigned an operational code name before leaving for France. F Section's were taken, for the most part, first from trees, such as REDWOOD, and later from trades and professions, such as PLUMBER. It was the norm that each circuit organiser gave their name to the circuit, for example Guy Biéler was MUSICIAN and his circuit was MUSICIAN. One important divergence was in the case of Francis Suttill, who was PHYSICIAN, but his circuit became more commonly known by his field name, PROSPER. In France, agents had a field name, normally a French Christian name or nickname such as 'Annette' or 'Ambroise', for daily use in the circuit, while code names were more generally used by SOE HQ. Lastly, there was also the French name which appeared in an agent's false identity papers.
28. TNA, HS9/653/1, Joyce Hanafy, Personnel File.
29. *SOE Syllabus*, p. 2.
30. Susan Ottaway, *Violette Szabo: The Life That I Have*, Leo Cooper, Barnsley, 2002, p. 54.
31. Eric Sykes, *SOE Close Combat Syllabus*, 1943, PRO, London, 2001.
32. Fitzsimmons, *Nancy Wake*, p. 177.
33. Judith Pearson, *The Wolves at the Door*, Lyons Press, Guilford, CT, 2005, p. 70.
34. TNA, HS9/1289/7, Yvonne Rudellat, Personnel File.
35. Fitzsimmons, *Nancy Wake*, p. 178.
36. M.R.D. Foot, *SOE: An Outline History*, Greenwood Press/BBC, London, 1984, p. 61.
37. Russell Braddon, *Nancy Wake*, Book Club, London, 1956, p. 122.
38. Stella King, *Jacqueline*, Arms and Armour, London, 1989, p. 91.
39. TNA, HS9/836/5, Noor Inayat Khan, Personnel File.
40. *SOE Syllabus*, p. 141.

41. Braddon, *Nancy Wake*, p. 123.
42. Ibid.
43. King, *Jacqueline*, p. 96.
44. Sharabani Basu, *Spy Princess*, Sutton, Stroud, 2006, p. 68.
45. Interview by author with Yvonne Burney (née Baseden), Napier Gardens, London, 23 May 2003 and August 2003.
46. Ibid.
47. Brandon, *Nancy Wake*, p. 125.
48. Walters, *Moondrop to Gascony*, p. 4.
49. TNA, HS9/836/5, Noor Inayat Khan, Personnel File.
50. Leo Marks, *Between Silk and Cyanide*, HarperCollins, London, 2000, p. 311.
51. TNA, HS9/836/5, Noor Inayat Khan, Personnel File.
52. Foot, *SOE in France*, p. 57.
53. Rigden, *SOE Syllabus*, p. 85.
54. TNA, HS9/836/5, Noor Inayat Khan, Personnel File.
55. TNA, HS9/1435, Violette Szabó, Personnel File.
56. Ibid.
57. Jones, *A Quiet Courage*, p. 179.
58. TNA, HS9/1654, Madeline Damerment, Personnel File.
59. TNA, HS9/114/2, Yolande Beekman, Personnel File.
60. IWM, Sound Archive, BXC 8680 1 and 2, Maurice Buckmaster.
61. TNA, HS9/648/4, Odette Sansom, Personnel File.
62. TNA, HS9/1089/4, Jacqueline Nearne, Personnel File.
63. Ibid.
64. Popham, *FANY*, p. 99.

2 TRAILBLAZERS

1. HS9/1091/1, Henry Newton PF.
2. *New York Post*, 4 September 1941.
3. Ibid.
4. Ibid.
5. Anne Sebba, *Les Parisiennes*, Orion, London, 2016, pp. 31–2.
6. *New York Post*, 4 September 1941.
7. Purnell, *A Woman of No Importance*, p. 68.
8. TNA, HS9/647/4, Virginia Hall, Personnel File.
9. Ibid.
10. TNA, HS9/1651, Benjamin Cowburn, Personnel File.
11. The twelve were Michael Trotobas, Georges Bégué, Marc Jumeau, Jean Pierre Bloch, Jean Bougennec, François Garel, Jack Hayes, Jean Philippe le Harivel, George Langelaan, Philippe Liewer, Robert Lyon and Raymond Roche, alongside their guard José Sevilla.
12. These included Hayes, Liewer, Lyon and Trotobas. Foot, *SOE in France*, pp. 203–4.
13. *New York Post*, 14 November 1941.
14. Foot, *SOE in France*, p. 161.
15. Ibid.
16. TNA, HS9/647/4, Virginia Hall, Personnel File.
17. All biographical information provided by Julie Clamp, Yvonne's granddaughter.
18. King, *Jacqueline*, p. 65
19. Ian Ousby, *Occupation*, St Martin's Press, New York, 1998, p. 66.
20. Drop zones had to be clear of trees or electricity pylons, and, as technological innovations were introduced, pilots could be guided to the correct area using specialised equipment (Eurekas or S-phones) to allow them to locate and communicate with agents on the ground. The prescribed pattern of lights for a reception committee varied during the war,

from a straight line of three lights (bonfires were sometimes used instead of torches) to an isosceles triangle, both versions accompanied by a flashing signal light sending a prearranged letter in Morse code so the pilot knew he was in the correct place. If no lights were seen, or the incorrect code letter flashed, the pilot was expected to turn back for home without dispatching his cargo.

21. Foot, *SOE in France*, p. 196.
22. King, *Jacqueline*, p. 211.
23. TNA, HS9/165/8, Denise Bloch, Personnel File.
24. TNA, HS9/298/6, Blanche Charlet, Personnel File.
25. King, *Jacqueline*, p. 69.
26. TNA, HS9/298/6, Blanche Charlet, Personnel File.
27. Foot, *SOE in France*, p. 170.
28. TNA, HS9/165/8, Denise Bloch, Personnel File.
29. The STO was an extension of *Relève*, the Vichy policy implemented in early 1942, whereby specialised voluntary workers would be sent to Germany in exchange for the return of prisoners of war (three workers for one prisoner). 'Originally the STO specified a two-year stint in Germany, for which men between the age of 20 and 22 were required to register. Miners and farmworkers, as well as the unfit, were exempt and students were granted deferrals . . . Yet by 1944 successive changes to the regulations had enlarged the scope of the STO at every point. Farmworkers, for example, had lost their exemption and the age range of those eligible spanned men from 18 to 60 and childless women from 18 to 45. Not all of them had to work in Germany. Men over 45 and all the women could remain in France under the authority of Albert Speer's Organisation Todt, whose main achievement was to build the Atlantic Wall in anitication of the Allied landings.' Ousby, *Occupation*, p. 251.
30. Jean-Luc E. Cartron, *So Close to Freedom: A World War II Story of Peril and Betrayal in the Pyrenees*, Potomac Books, Nebraska, 2019, p. 24.
31. A D/F van was a German vehicle capable of tracking down an illegal wireless signal.
32. Miller, *Behind the Lines*, p. 79.
33. TNA, HS9/1096/8, Alfred Newton, Personnel File.
34. TNA, HS9/647/4, Virginia Hall, Personnel File.
35. Ibid.
36. She was awarded an MBE in July 1943, the news reaching her while she was serving in Madrid.
37. TNA, HS9/647/4, Virginia Hall, Personnel File.
38. TNA, HS9/648/4, Odette Sansom, Personnel File.
39. Beryl Escott, *The Heroines of SOE*, The History Press, Cheltenham, 2010, p. 69.
40. TNA, HS9/304/1, Henri and Marie-Thérèse le Chêne, Personnel File.
41. Ibid. The SOE interviewer was not impressed and surmised that 'she is a silly old woman who is telling lies and must be treated as such'. He went on to say that 'her work in the field was not outstanding' and that he 'was not averse to giving her a more serious punishment' than the warning she had received.
42. IWM, Sound Archive, 9478, Odette Sansom, 31 October 1986.
43. Jones, *A Quiet Courage*, pp. 87–8.
44. Hugo Bleicher, *Colonel Henri's Story*, Kimber, London, 1954. Bleicher also posed as 'Colonel Henri' and claimed to be anti-Nazi with a desire to defect to the Allies, while actually intent on arresting members of the resistance and SOE. After the war he was arrested by the Dutch and put on trial and subsequently imprisoned by the Allies.
45. IWM, Sound Archive, 11238, Francis Cammaerts.
46. M.R.D. Foot, *SOE: An Outline History*, Greenwood Press/BBC, London, 1999, p. 10.
47. Ray Jenkins, *A Pacifist at War*, Arrow, London, 2010, p. 70.
48. The *Messages Personnels*, which were broadcast after the news, were a vital way of communicating with resistance groups throughout the war. A pre-arranged message in French would be broadcast if a mission was due to take place, with agents and resisters listening attentively for messages such as 'Aunt Maud has flu' or 'the donkey wears

pyjamas'. If these messages related to their code message they knew to set off to receive a parachute drop, or undertake whatever mission that the message related to.

49. TNA, HS9/315, Peter Churchill, Personnel File.
50. Jenkins, *A Pacifist at War*, p. 69.
51. TNA, HS9/648/4, Odette Sansom, Personnel File.
52. Ibid.
53. King, *Jacqueline*, p. 281.
54. TNA, HS9/165/8, Denise Bloch, Personnel File.
55. TNA, HS9/647/4, Virginia Hall, Personnel File.
56. Albert would follow her to France in October 1943, where he headed the DITCHER network, located in the region of Cluny (Saône-et-Loire). On 14 July 1944 he organised the largest daylight weapons drop during which the US Air Force used tricolour parachutes.
57. TNA, HS9/1195/1, Eliane Plewman, Personnel File.
58. Quoted in *8, rue Mérentie* by Jean Contrucci, with the collaboration of Jacques Virbel, a pamphlet published by Alliance Française. Private correspondence with a member of the Plewman family; also 'Journal d'une Longue Nuit' by Pierre et Marthe Massenet – recollections of local resistance leader and his wife; also private correspondence between Garcin and the Steele family. See https://www.alliancefrancaise.london/8-rue-Merentie-ENG-AFL.pdf
59. Bob Maloubier, *Agent secret de Churchill*, Tallandier, Paris, 2011 (translated).
60. TNA, HS9/1195/1, Eliane Plewman, Personnel File.
61. Jones, *A Quiet Courage*, p. 200.
62. IWM, Sound Archive, 7369, Reel 1, Yvonne Cormeau.
63. Jones, *A Quiet Courage*, pp. 178–80.
64. IWM, Air Ministry document to Vera Atkins, 27 July 1946.
65. TNA, HS8/999, Use of women in F Section and IWM, Air Ministry document to Vera Atkins, 27 July 1946.
66. IWM, Air Ministry document to Vera Atkins, 27 July 1946.
67. Ibid.
68. Elizabeth Deveraux Rochester, *Full Moon to France*, HarperCollins, London, 1977, pp. 1–5.
69. TNA, HS9/1250/1, Elizabeth Deveraux Rochester Reynolds, Personnel File.
70. Ibid.
71. Ibid.
72. Ibid.
73. Richard Heslop, *Xavier: A British Secret Agent with the French Resistance*, Biteback Publishing, London, 2014, p. 246.
74. Ibid.
75. Ibid.
76. TNA, HS9/1250/1, Elizabeth Deveraux Rochester Reynolds, Personnel File.
77. TNA, HS9 647/4, Virginia Hall, Personnel File.

3 THE FALL OF PROSPER

1. TNA, HS9/836/5, Noor Inayat Khan, Personnel File.
2. TNA, HS9/183, Andrée Borrel, Personnel File.
3. *Sunday Times*, 'The Dirty War on Our Doorstep', 15 March 2009.
4. Ibid.
5. Rita Kramer, *Flames in the Field*, Penguin, London, 1996, p. 91.
6. They were arrested on 22 April 1943 and killed at Ravensbrück in March 1945.
7. Kramer, *Flames in the Field*, p. 93.
8. TNA, HS9/183, Andrée Borrel, Personnel File.
9. Francis Suttill, *Shadows in the Fog*, The History Press, Stroud, 2014, p. 37.
10. In a conversation between Francis Suttill (son of PROSPER's Suttill) and Gilbert Norman's school friend Nicolas Laurent in 2002, Laurent told Suttill that Andrée and Gilbert

Norman were lovers and that is why she was staying with him on the night of their arrest. This cannot be verified as both Norman and Borrel were executed. Information disclosed in an email between Suttill and the author, 12 June 2019.

11. Interview by author with Yvonne Burney (née Baseden), Napier Gardens, London, 23 May 2003, and with Pearl Cornioley (née Witherington), Grand Hôtel Saint Aignan, 3 June 2003.

12. IWM, Sound Archive, 8680, Maurice Buckmaster.

13. TNA, HS9/183, Andrée Borrel, Personnel File. The 'moon period' refers to the nights preceding, during and after the full moon – usually the fifteen or so nights between first and last quarter. This is when the moon reflects enough light to be useful for an aircraft crew to navigate across country, flying low enough to pick out individual features on the landscape below. The Special Duties squadrons, and everyone involved with them – planning staff, ground crews and agents – knew these periods of bright moonlight as 'moon periods'. See https://beforetempsford.org.uk/moon-periods/

14. Ibid.

15. A chapter in M.R.D. Foot's book *SOE in France* is dedicated to 'Déricourt's loyalties' and Jean Overton Fuller devoted an entire book, *Double Webs*, Putman, London, 1958, to the theory that Déricourt was not a traitor or double agent. At his trial after the war Déricourt was acquitted based on Bodington's reply to the question if he would again trust his life to an operation by Déricourt: 'Certainly, without hesitation.' Foot, *SOE in France*, p. 305.

16. TNA, HS9/77/1, Lise de Baissac, Personnel File.

17. Ibid.

18. Ibid.

19. Ibid.

20. Ibid.

21. TNA, HS6/567, Mary Herbert, Personnel File.

22. Jones, *A Quiet Courage*, p. 208.

23. Binney, *The Women Who Lived for Danger*, p. 146. Binney conducted a personal interview with Lise de Baissac.

24. TNA, HS6/567, Mary Herbert, Personnel File.

25. *Memoirs of Julienne Besnard*, January 1946, translated by Aileen Lauler and provided by Louis Lauler.

26. Ibid., p. 6.

27. Ibid., p. 7.

28. TNA, HS9/10/2, Francine Agazarian, Personnel File.

29. Ibid.

30. Jones, *A Quiet Courage*, p. 63.

31. Ibid.

32. TNA, HS9 11/1, Jack Agazarian, Personnel File.

33. TNA, HS9/10/2, Francine Agazarian, Personnel File.

34. TNA, HS9 11/1, Jack Agazarian, Personnel File.

35. *Memoirs of Julienne Besnard*, p. 9.

36. TNA, HS9/910/3, Vera Leigh, Personnel File.

37. *Memoirs of Julienne Besnard*, p. 10.

38. TNA, HS9/140/7, Julienne Besnard, Personnel File.

39. Elizabeth Nicholas, *Death Be Not Proud*, Cresset Press, London, 1958, p. 83.

40. TNA, HS9/1287/6, Diana Rowden, Personnel File.

41. Ibid.

42. 'Juif' is French for 'Jewish', perhaps an unwise choice of safe house given the anti-Semitic activities of both Vichy France and the Nazis.

43. Ibid., p. 82.

44. Interestingly, her service records (both WAAF and SOE) list her as having been born in Ireland in 1900 with the maiden name McKenzie, whereas her actual date of birth was a

year earlier. This surname has led many historians and writers to assume that she was of Irish origin. Perhaps the scandal surrounding her birth and childhood still haunted her and she wished to move on. There are also several misspellings of her name Cicely, such as Cicily or Cecily, which has also resulted in some confusion. Paul McCue, 'Lefort', Secret Learning Network Lecture, 2016.

45. TNA, HS9/908/1, Cicely Lefort, Personnel File.
46. Ibid.
47. Ibid.
48. Ibid.
49. Jenkins, *A Pacifist at War*, pp. 94–5.
50. Ibid.
51. TNA, HS9/258/, Francis Cammaerts, Personnel File.
52. TNA, HS9/908/1, Cicely Lefort, Personnel File.
53. Information from Carol Ann Sokoloff, family friend to Hidayat Khan and his daughter Inayat Bergum. Also author of *A Light Unbroken* (a long poem on the life of Noor Inayat Khan), Ekstasis Editions, Toronto, 1986. Private correspondence, 2020.
54. Ibid.
55. TNA, HS9/836/5, Noor Inayat Khan, Finishing report, 21 May 1943.
56. Ibid.
57. Marks, *Between Silk and Cyanide*, p. 308.
58. Ibid., p. 315.
59. Jean Overton Fuller, *Madeleine*, EW Publications, The Hague, 1988, p. 133.
60. Ibid., p. 133.
61. Sarah Helm, *A Life in Secrets*, Little, Brown, London, 2005, p. 15.
62. Ibid., p. 17.
63. TNA, HS9/836/5, Noor Inayat Khan, Personnel File.
64. Foot, *SOE in France*, p. 317.
65. He was executed, alongside twelve other Allied officers, at Flossenbürg on 29 March 1945.
66. Suttill, *Shadows in the Fog*, p. 241.
67. Foot, *SOE in France*, p. 146.
68. Ibid.
69. Overton Fuller, *Madeleine*, p. 168.
70. Ibid., p. 179.
71. TNA, HS9/836/5, Noor Inayat Khan, Personnel File.
72. Jean Overton Fuller, *Noor-un-nisa Inayat Khan: Madeleine*, East West Publications, The Hague, 1988, p. 191.
73. Ibid.
74. Mark Seaman, *Saboteur*, John Blake Publishing, London, 2018, p. 228.
75. Basu, *Spy Princess*, p.181.
76. Ibid., p. 135.
77. These were Bodington, Antelme, Benoist and Lise and Claude de Baissac.
78. In fact there were other wireless operators in Paris as of 24 June 1943: André Dubois, a 'freelance' W/T (wireless telegraphist) originally based in the Tours region but relocated to a Paris suburb, who had acted as W/T for many people via couriers until his arrest in November 1943; Marcel Clech, also based in Paris and not arrested until November 1943; and Marcel Rousset, operating not far from Paris, who was arrested in the city on 7 September 1944. In addition, the remnants of JUGGLER, Weil and Olschanesky, sent and received messages through Weil's contacts in Bern, Switzerland.
79. Basu, *Spy Princess*, p. 153.
80. Ibid.
81. After the war, Renée was tried, but escaped conviction by one vote. She was recompensed 25,000 francs by SOE for her services.
82. TNA, HS9/836/5, Noor Inayat Khan, Personnel File.

4 THE ARMY OF SHADOWS

1. TNA, HS9/356, Pearl Witherington, Personnel File.
2. Interview by the author with Pearl Cornioley (née Witherington), Grand Hôtel Saint Aignan, May 2003.
3. Ibid.
4. TNA, HS9/1089/4, Jacqueline Nearne, Personnel File.
5. Ibid.
6. Ibid.
7. Ibid.
8. Ibid.
9. Ibid.
10. Interview by the author with Pearl Cornioley (née Witherington), Grand Hôtel Saint Aignan, May 2003
11. Ibid.
12. TNA, HS9/1424/7, Odette Strugo Garay Wilen née Sar, Personnel File.
13. Ibid.
14. David Hewson, 'Introduction', in Anne-Marie Walters, *Moondrop to Gascony*, Moho Books, Chippenham, 2009.
15. Ibid.
16. HS6/574, Anne-Marie Walters, post-tour report.
17. Ibid.
18. Walters, *Moondrop to Gascony*, p. 15.
19. TNA, HS9/1407/1, George Starr, Personnel File.
20. Ibid.
21. Hewson, 'Postscript', in Walters, *Moondrop to Gascony*, 2009, p. 232.
22. Ibid., p. 231.
23. Foot, *SOE in France*, p. 436.
24. *Memoirs of Julienne Besnard*, p. 15.
25. Ibid.
26. Ibid., p. 16.
27. Julienne was aware of Déricourt's treachery and the accusations that he been a double agent and had betrayed many British agents who were sent to France and met their deaths as a result of his actions. She said that she believed he would 'pay for his crimes with his life. He should lose it a hundred times over for the punishment to fit the crime.' However, he was tried in June 1948 and was acquitted.
28. Susan Ottaway, *Sisters, Secrets and Sacrifice*, Harper Element, London, 2013, p. 32.
29. Ibid., p. 67.
30. Ibid., p. 32.
31. TNA, HS6/437, Eileen Nearne, Personnel File.
32. Ibid.
33. Foot, *SOE in France*, p. 370.
34. TNA, HS9/1427/1, Paddy O'Sullivan, Personnel File.
35. Ibid.
36. Ibid.
37. Ibid.
38. TNA, HS9/1427/1, Paddy O'Sullivan, Recommendation for MBE, Personnel File.
39. TNA, HS9/1427/1, Paddy O'Sullivan, Personnel File.
40. Ibid.
41. Ibid.
42. Ibid.
43. Thomas Childers, *In the Shadows of War*, Henry Holt and Co., New York, 2004, p. 130.
44. TNA, HS9/457/6, Yvonne Fontaine, Personnel File.
45. Paul McCue, The Secret WW2 Learning Network, via correspondence.

46. Ibid.
47. It would appear that accounts suggesting that Violette's infiltration on 5/6 April 1944 was by parachute are incorrect. It was first documented in M.R.D. Foot's *SOE in France* in 1966, and has appeared numerous times since (e.g. Ottaway, *Violette Szabo*, p. 84). Violette's personnel file states 'she was landed by air'; while this is unusually unspecific (other files are far more explicit about the mode of entry, e.g. Lise de Baissac's personnel file clearly states that her first infiltration was by Lysander and her second by parachute), it does indicate Lysander. Further, flight logs indicate that there were no B-24 flights that night. Records do however show that there were Lysander flights, and Liewer flew on the same dates, 5/6 April, which would indicate that they went together. Hugh Verity's *We Landed by Moonlight: Secret RAF Landings in France, 1940–1944* (Ian Allan, Manchester, 1979) does not list them, but this source is not always complete or fully accurate, compiled as it was after the war with the available information Verity could piece together. André Studler who also flew that night alongside Lilian Rolfe mentioned two agents who set off 15 minutes before them from RAF Tempsford and said they 'were on their way to Paris' (TNA, HS9/1425/6, André Studler, Personnel File). This would also indicate that Violette and Liewer were infiltrated by Lysander.
48. Freddie Clark, *Agents by Moonlight*, Tempus Publishing, Stroud, 1999, pp. 232–3.
49. TNA, HS9/1435, Violette Szabó – 109957, undated.
50. Malraux and Newman were taken via Compiègne to Germany; they were executed at Mauthausen concentration camp on 6 September 1944. Mayer survived the war and was awarded the Military Cross.
51. Interview by the author with Bob Large, Hythe, Kent, 22 May 2003.
52. IWM, Air Ministry document to Vera Atkins, 27 July 1946.
53. TNA, HS9/250/2, Muriel Byck, Personnel File.
54. Ibid. Muriel's body remained in France and for many years her grave was tended by local people. A commemoration was held on the anniversary of her death and she was heralded as a heroine of the resistance. Her remains were later moved to the Pornic War Cemetery.
55. Seaman, *Saboteur*, p. 226.
56. TNA, HS9/77/1, Report, April to May 1944.
57. Seaman, *Saboteur*, pp. 233–5.
58. Ibid.
59. Ibid., p. 235.
60. TNA, HS9/77/1, Lise de Baissac, Personnel File.
61. Seaman, *Saboteur*, pp. 232–3.
62. Ibid., pp. 233–5.
63. Ibid.
64. TNA, HS9/77/1, Lise de Baissac, Personnel File.
65. Nancy Wake, *The Autobiography of the Woman the Gestapo Called the White Mouse*, Sun Books, Melbourne, 1985, p. 4.
66. Henri Fiocca was arrested, tortured and murdered by the Gestapo. When Nancy returned to France after the war she discovered his fate. Her much-loved dogs had survived.
67. Fitzsimmons, *Nancy Wake*, p. 195.
68. TNA, HS9/1545, Nancy Wake, Personnel File.
69. Fitzsimmons, *Nancy Wake*, p. 243.
70. IWM, Sound Archive, Pearl Witherington, 8689 (1983).
71. Interview by the author with Pearl Cornioley (née Witherington), Grand Hôtel Saint Aignan, May 2003.
72. Ibid.
73. Ibid.
74. IWM, Sound Archive, Pearl Witherington, 8689 C 1 and 2 (1983).
75. Interview by the author with Pearl Cornioley (née Witherington), Grand Hôtel Saint Aignan, May 2003.
76. Ibid.

77. Buckmaster, *Specially Employed*, p. 131.
78. Ibid.
79. TNA, HS9/849/7, Marguerite Knight, Personnel File.
80. Ibid.
81. Ibid.
82. TNA, HS9/895/6, Madeleine Lavinge, Personnel File.
83. Buckmaster, *Specially Employed*, p. 191.

5 D-DAY

1. Sir Owen O'Malley, *Phantom Caravan*, 1954. p. 208.
2. The active agents were Yvonne Cormeau, Pearl Witherington, Anne-Marie Walters, Denise Bloch, Eileen Nearne, Yvonne Baseden, Paddy O'Sullivan, Yvonne Fontaine, Eileen Rolfe, Lise de Baissac, Nancy Wake, Phyllis Latour, Marguerite Knight, Madeleine Lavigne and Sonia d'Artois. Those in prison were Yvonne Rudellat, Andrée Borrel, Odette Sansom, Vera Leigh, Noor Inayat Khan, Cicely Lefort, Diana Rowden, Eliane Plewman, Elizabeth Deveraux Rochester and Madeleine Damerment.
3. Jones, *A Quiet Courage*, pp. 313–14.
4. IWM, Sound Archive, 8680, Colonel Maurice Buckmaster, Reel 2.
5. TNA, HS9/815/3, Ginette Jullian, Personnel File, translated by Caroline Ridler. No surname for 'Antoine' is given.
6. Ibid.
7. Ibid.
8. Ibid.
9. Ibid.
10. Ibid.
11. Jones, *A Quiet Courage*, p. 173.
12. Ibid., p. 183.
13. See Sarah Farmer, *The Martyred Village*, University of California Press, Los Angeles, 1999, pp. 13–29, and Max Hastings, *Das Reich*, Henry Holt & Co., London, 1982, pp. 181–202. These books provide a corrective to the sometimes-heard assertion that the Germans were mistaken in the Oradour they moved against – that they should have attacked Oradour sur Vayres some 20 miles to the south-west where the Maquisards they sought were to be found. As Hastings states, there is no evidence to support this view.
14. Hastings, *Das Reich*, pp. 181–202.
15. TNA, HS9/1435, Violette Szabó, Personnel File. Information provided by Tania Szabó suggests that Violette was to pass on urgent instructions from Liewer and London to cause as much disruption as possible to the movements of the SS Panzer Division 'Das Reich'.
16. Hastings, *Das Reich*, p. 176.
17. *Sunday Times*, 27 April 2003, and TNA, HS9/1435, Violette Szabó, Personnel File – 109957. Unfortunately it was impossible to reinterview Dufour to ascertain further information as he was killed in Indo-China in 1946.
18. TNA, HS9/923/4, Mark Staunton, Personnel File.
19. Information from Tania Szabó, which also mentions that Violette was wounded in the shoulder by gunfire and retreated behind an apple tree to provide covering fire for Dufour after twisting her ankle in the wheat field while retreating – her ankle had been weakened when she landed awkwardly during her parachute training.
20. TNA, HS9/1435, Violette Szabó, Personnel File – 109957, 30 December 1944.
21. Interview by author with Pearl Cornioley (née Witherington), Grand Hôtel Saint Aignan, May 2003.
22. Ibid.
23. Ibid.

24. Ibid.
25. Ibid.
26. IWM, Air Ministry document to Vera Atkins, 27 July 1946.
27. Interview by author with Yvonne Burney (née Baseden), Napier Gardens, London, 23 May 2003.
28. Ibid.
29. TNA, HS6/437, Yvonne Baseden affidavit.
30. Interview by author with Yvonne Burney (née Baseden), Napier Gardens, London, 23 May 2003.
31. Ibid.
32. Ibid.
33. Ibid.
34. Ibid.
35. Ibid.
36. Ibid.
37. Ibid.
38. Ibid.
39. Wilkinson was taken to the prison in Orléans where he was tortured in the *baignoire*. He was then taken to Paris, where he was seen in Fresnes prison, from where he would most likely have been taken to avenue Foch for further interrogation. It was later discovered that he had been betrayed by a double agent called Annick Boucher.
40. Lilian Rolfe, citation for Croix de Guerre, 16 January 1946, English translation.
41. Interview by *Army News* editor Judith Martin with Phyllis Latour, 2009.
42. TNA, Phyllis Latour, HS9/888/9, Personnel File.
43. IWM, Air Ministry document to Vera Atkins, 27 July 1946.
44. Ibid.
45. Ibid.
46. Ibid.
47. TNA, HS6/56/7, Sonia and Guy d'Artois, Personnel File.
48. Ibid.
49. Sydney Hudson, *Undercover Operator*, Pen and Sword, Barnsley, 2003, p. 68. After the war Sonia 'did not leave Guy under any illusion about what her relationship with me had become and yet she was totally determined to make her future life with him'. Ibid., p. 108.
50. David Stafford, *Ten Days to D-Day*, Little, Brown, London, 2004, p. 208. After the war Sonia returned to Le Mans with Guy to pay back some money that had been borrowed from the local Abbé: 'we got the money from London ... and the briefcase was full of French notes'.
51. TNA, HS9/612, Christine Granville, Personnel File.
52. Madeleine Masson, *Christine*, Hamish Hamilton, London, 1975, p. xxvii.
53. Ibid., pp. 192–3.
54. Jenkins, *A Pacifist at War*, p. 174.
55. Ibid., p. 172.
56. Paul McCue, The Secret WW2 Learning Network, via correspondence.
57. TNA, HS9/612, Francis Cammaerts's report of Christine Granville.
58. TNA, HS9/612, Christine Granville, Personnel File.
59. Ibid.
60. Four weeks of fighting cost the Allies about 25,000 casualties; the German army lost about 150,000 men, mostly taken as prisoners.
61. TNA, HS9/895/6, Madeleine Lavigne, Personnel File.
62. TNA, HS9/849/7, Marguerite Knight, Personnel File.
63. General Dwight Eisenhower, letter to the executive director of SOE and to the director of OSS, London, 31 May 1945, quoted in Foot, *SOE in France*, pp. 441–2.

6 INCARCERATION

1. Peter Churchill, *The Spirit in the Cage*, Hodder & Stoughton, London, 1954, p. 32.
2. Penny Starns, *Odette: World War Two's Darling Spy*, The History Press, Stroud, 2009, p. 83.
3. TNA, HS9/648/4, Odette Sansom, Personnel File.
4. Churchill, *The Spirit in the Cage*, pp. 13–15.
5. TNA, HS9/648/4, Odette Sansom, Personnel File.
6. Mitchell Roth, *Prisons and Prison Systems: A Global Encyclopaedia*, Greenwood, Westport, CT, 2005.
7. TNA, HS9/648/4, Odette Sansom, Personnel File.
8. Ibid.
9. TNA, WO 208/4679, interrogation of Ernst Ruehl by Squadron Officer Vera Atkins, 24 October 1946.
10. TNA, HS9/648/4, Odette Sansom, Personnel File contains evidence from Dr T. Markowicz that 'the nails on her toes were missing and there was a rounded scar on her back'. Odette's George Cross citation and her Disability Pension Claim state that she was burnt on her back and that her toenails removed. A letter from Peter Churchill provides testimony to her toenails being pulled out, and suggests that Major Ireland, 'who saw Mrs Sansom on several occasions' immediately upon her return, be consulted for a second medical certificate. Testimony from fellow Fresnes prisoner Simone Herail, although not specifically referring to the nature of the torture, provides further evidence of Odette's treatment during captivity.
11. TNA, WO 208/4679, interrogation of Ernst Ruehl by Squadron Officer Vera Atkins, 24 October 1946. Josef Stork was officially Kieffer's chauffeur, but was also his 'eyes and ears' as well as his 'enforcer' in terms of interrogation and torture.
12. TNA, HS9/648/4, Odette Sansom, Personnel File, 12 May 1945, p. 13.
13. TNA, HS9/648/4, Odette Sansom, Personnel File.
14. George Cross citation, *London Gazette*, 20 August 1946.
15. TNA, HS9/648/4, Odette Sansom, Personnel File.
16 Ibid.
17. IWM, Sound Archive, 9478, Odette Sansom, 31 October 1986.
18. Ibid.
19. Overton Fuller, *Madeleine*, p. 208.
20. IWM, Vera Atkins papers, File 8/1/11-13.
21. Overton Fuller, *Madeleine*, p. 227.
22. IWM, Vera Atkins papers, File 8/1/11-13.
23. Ibid.
24. TNA, HS 9/581/4, Robert Gieules, Personnel File.
25. Hodlwetz also claims that 'Noor gave nothing away under torture'.
26. TNA, HS9/836/5, Noor Inayat Khan, Personnel File.
27. Ibid.
28. TNA, HS9/836/5, report on Captain Starr by Kieffer.
29. TNA, WO 208/4679, Interrogation of Josef Goetz by Squadron Officer Vera Atkins, 3 September 1946.
30. TNA, HS9/836/5, Noor Inayat Khan, Personnel File, Deposition Wilhelm Krauss, 6 November 1946.
31. Helm, *A Life in Secrets*, p. 323.
32. TNA, HS9/836/5, Noor Inayat Khan, Personnel File, letter from Yolande Lagrave, 16 August 1946.
33. TNA, HS9/1287/6, Diana Rowden, Personnel File.
34. TNA, WO 208/4679.
35. TNA, HS9/1089/2.
36. Jaap was highly decorated and survived the war, dying in 2010.

37. In mid-1944 Yolande's mother, Mrs Unternährer, contacted SOE requesting an interview at which she stated that 'when her daughter parachuted into France last September her mother knew she was pregnant, and consequently expected by now to have some news of a new arrival'. SOE answered saying that 'we stated, as is the truth, that we had received no report on Mrs Beekman's health that confirmed that she was pregnant when she left, as Mrs Unternährer claimed she was'. Yolande's pregnancy is not mentioned anywhere else in her records, no eyewitnesses mention it, and so it seems implausible that she was pregnant, but the question remains unanswered to this day. TNA HS9/114/2, Yolande Beekman, Personnel File.
38. IWM, Vera Atkins papers, File 8/1/11-13.
39. *Oxford Dictionary of National Biography*, Sonia Olschanesky.
40. TNA, HS6/567, Mary Herbert, Personnel File.
41. Ibid.
42. Jones, *A Quiet Courage*, p. 209.
43. Ibid.
44. Easter Sunday was 9 April 1944, making her captivity approximately two months in duration.
45. TNA, HS6/567, Mary Herbert, Personnel File.
46. She was so successful in this that Claude had no idea where she and Claudine were. After Bordeaux was liberated in September 1944 the de Baissac siblings set out in a borrowed car to find them. Within days, Claude met his daughter for the first time, and then he sent them both to England, where in November 1944 Claude and Mary were married. Beryl Escott, *Mission Improbable*, Patrick Stephens, Somerset, 1991, pp. 57–9.
47. Ibid.
48. Contrucci, *8, rue Méréntie*. Also private correspondence with a member of the Plewman family; 'Journal d'une Longue Nuit', by Pierre et Marthe Massenet – recollections of local resistance leader and his wife; private correspondence between Garcin and the Steele family. See https://www.alliancefrancaise.london/8-rue-Merentie-ENG-AFL.pdf
49. Paul McCue, Secret Learning Network, via correspondence. Also Contrucci, *8, rue Méréntie*.
50. Ibid.
51. IWM, Vera Atkins papers, File 8/1/1-4, Deposition of Georg Kaenemund.
52. IWM, Vera Atkins papers, File 8/1/1-4, Deposition of Fraulein Hager.
53. Ibid.
54. IWM, Vera Atkins papers, File 8/1/1-4, Deposition of Nina Hagen.
55. IWM, Vera Atkins papers, File 8/1/1-4, Deposition of Zina Zoeller.
56. IWM, Vera Atkins papers, File 8/1/1-4, Deposition of Georg Kaenemund.
57. IWM, Vera Atkins papers, File 8/1/1-4, Deposition of Frau Habich.
58. IWM, Vera Atkins papers, File 8/1/1-4, Deposition of Frau Theresa Becker.
59. TNA, T350-3, Violette Szabó, George Cross citation.
60. Ottaway, *The Life That I Have*, p. 119.
61. Ibid., p. 120.
62. Tania Szabó, *Young, Brave and Beautiful: The Missions of Special Operations Executive Agent Lieutenant Violette Szabó, George Cross, Croix de Guerre avec Étoile de Bronze*, The History Press, Stroud, 2014, p. 410.
63. Ibid.
64. Robert Gellately, *The Gestapo and German Society*, Oxford University Press, Oxford, 1990, p. 130.
65. TNA, HS9/165/8, Denise Bloch, Personnel File.
66. TNA, HS9/240/2, Yvonne Baseden, Personnel File.

67. TNA, HS6/437, Affidavit by Yvonne Baseden. In the matter of war crimes and in the matter of ill-treatment of British nationals at Dijon, France and Ravensbrück, Germany, June 1944 and April 1945.
68. TNA, HS9/240/2, Yvonne Baseden, Personnel File.
69. TNA, HS6/437, Affidavit by Yvonne Baseden.
70. Ibid.
71. Ibid.
72. *Taipei Times*, 'France opens doors of Gestapo's Paris headquarters to public for first time', 19 September 2005.
73. Jones, *A Quiet Courage*, p. 278.
74. Interview on *Timewatch*, 'Secret memories', BBC2, 11 March 1997.
75. TNA, HS9/1089/2, Eileen Nearne, Personnel File.
76. TNA, HS9/1458, 'Tommy' F.F.E. Yeo-Thomas, Personnel File.
77. Minney, *Carve Her Name with Pride*, p. 169.
78. Lund, 27 November 1945. See www3.ub.lu.se/ravensbruck/interview5.pdf
79. Daniel Brewer and Patricia Lorcin (eds), *France and Its Spaces of War: Experience, Memory, Image*, Palgrave Macmillan, New York, 2009.
80. TNA, HS9/240/2, Yvonne Baseden, Personnel File.
81. Ben Macintyre, *Agent Zigzag*, Bloomsbury, London, 2007, p. 31.
82. See http://www.curagiu.com/la_sante_et_romainville.htm
83. Ibid.
84. For example, on 11 November 1942, prisoners turned to face Paris and sang the *Marseillaise* in defiance of the Nazis and their systematic brutality.

7 NIGHT AND FOG

1. Keitel expanded on this principle in a February 1942 letter stating that any prisoners not executed within eight days were 'to be transported to Germany secretly, and further treatment of the offenders will take place here; these measures will have a deterrent effect because – A. The prisoners will vanish without a trace. B. No information may be given as to their whereabouts or their fate.' Nürnberger Dokumente, PS-1733, NOKW-2579, NG-226. Cited in K.D. Bracher, *The German Dictatorship: The Origins, Structure and Effects of National Socialism*, Praeger, New York, 1970, p. 418.
2. Odette Sansom, Yolande Beekman, Eliane Plewman, Madeleine Damerment, Vera Leigh, Diana Rowden, Sonia Olschanesky and Andrée Borrel.
3. IWM, Vera Atkins papers, 8/1/1–11, Karlsruhe orders – 7 August 1946.
4. TNA, WO 309/282, Karlsruhe Gestapo, Germany: Killing and ill-treatment of British FANY and WAAF officers of French section.
5. IWM, Vera Atkins papers, 8/1/1–11, Interview with Albert Guérisse, 9 November 1945.
6. IWM, Vera Atkins papers 8/1/1–11, Eyewitness letter about Natzweiler girls, W.Ch.J.M. van Lanschot, Holland, 8 June 1946.
7. IWM., Vera Atkins papers, 8/1/1–11, Eyewitness letter about Natzweiler girls, W.Ch.J.M. van Lanschot, Holland, 8 June 1946.
8. IWM, Vera Atkins papers, 8/1/1–11, Statement of Conrad Walter Schultz, Gaggenenau, Germany, 26 April 1946.
9. IWM, Vera Atkins papers, 8/1/1–11, Interview with Albert Guérisse, 9 November 1945.
10. IWM, Vera Atkins papers, 8/1/1–11, Stonehouse, at Bad Oeyhnhausen, 5 April 1946. Stonehouse was a fashion artist hence his attention to their clothes.
11. IWM, Vera Atkins papers, 8/1/1–11, Deposition of Kriminal Sekretaer Max Wassmer, born 6 March 1890 in Bruchsal at present in camp 74.
12. This was possibly Diana, as he refers to her having 'blonde hair' and Diana had dyed hers in Clairvaux. Kramer, *Flames in the Field*, p. 109.
13. IWM, Vera Atkins papers, 8/1/1–11, Stonehouse, at Bad Oeyhnhausen, 5 April 1946.

14. IWM, Vera Atkins papers, 8/1/1–11, Affidavit of George Boogaerts.
15. IWM, Vera Atkins papers, 8/1/1–11, Interview with Albert Guérisse, 9 November 1945.
16. IWM, Vera Atkins papers, 8/1/1–11, Franz Berg, 27 December 1945.
17. Ibid.
18. Anthony M. Webb (ed.), *The Natzweiler Trial*, William Hodge and Co., London, 1949, p. 75.
19. Ibid., pp. 80–1.
20. IWM, Vera Atkins papers, 8/1/1–11, Interview with Albert Guérisse, 9 November 1945.
21. IWM, Vera Atkins papers, 8/1/1–11, Dr Werder Röhde, 14 April 1946.
22. Ibid.
23. Webb, *The Natzweiler Trial*, p. 100.
24. IWM, Vera Atkins papers, 8/1/1–11, Dr Werner Röhde, 14 April 1946.
25. Webb, *The Natzweiler Trial*, p. 151.
26. Ibid., p. 153.
27. IWM, Vera Atkins papers, 8/1/1–11, Statement of Conrad Walter Schultz, Gaggenenau, Germany, 26 April 1946.
28. Ibid.
29. Kramer, *Flames in the Field*, p. 119.
30. IWM, Vera Atkins papers, 8/1/8/1/10, Statement of Conrad Walter Schultz, Gaggenenau, Germany, 26 April 1946.
31. IWM, Vera Atkins papers, 8/1/1–11, Dr Werner Röhde, 14 April 1946.
32. Anna Dobrawolska, *The Auschwitz Photographer*, REKONTRPLAN GFR, Grupa Filmowa, 2015.
33. Kramer, *Flames in the Field*, pp. 120–1.
34. IWM, Vera Atkins papers, 8/1/1–11, 11 April 1946. From Junior Commander Di Gorrum. No. 9901 A/SO N. Inayat Khan. WAAF.
35. TNA, HS9/836/5, Noor Inayat Khan, Personnel File.
36. TNA, WO 309/282, Karlsruhe Gestapo, Germany. Killing and ill-treatment of British FANY and WAAF officers of French section.
37. TNA, HS9/59/2, Vera Atkins, Personnel File.
38. TNA, WO 309/282, Karlsruhe Gestapo, Germany, Killing and ill-treatment of British FANY and WAAF officers of French section. Ernst Ott.
39. Ibid.
40. Ibid.
41. Ibid.
42. Ibid
43. Ibid
44. Ibid.
45. Ibid.
46. Yolande Beekman is the only one of the four listed in her Personnel File as speaking German, TNA, HS9/114/2.
47. Ibid.
48. TNA, HS9/1195/1, Eliane Plewman, Personnel File.
49. Letter to Jean Overton Fuller from Colonel H.J. Wickey, 9 May 1975.
50. Ibid.
51. Basu, *Spy Princess*, p. 179.

8 RAVENSBRÜCK

1. Geneviève de Gaulle, *The Dawn of Hope*, Arcade Publishing, New York, 1999, p. 16.
2. Alyn Beßmann, *The Ravensbrück Women's Concentration Camp*, Metropol, Berlin, 2013, p. 114.
3. *Voices from Ravensbrück*, Polish Documentary Institute, 31 December 1945. Testimony written personally by witness no. 434.

4. See https://www.jewishvirtuallibrary.org/history-and-overview-of-ravensbr-uuml-ck
5. Beβmann, *The Ravensbrück Women's Concentration Camp*, p. 239.
6. Sarah Helm, *If This Is a Woman*, Little, Brown, London, 2015, p. 347.
7. Sebba, *Les Parisiennes*, p. 198.
8. Ibid.
9. Ibid., p. 349.
10. Helm, *If This Is a Woman*, p. 350.
11. TNA, HS9/648/4, Odette Sansom, Personnel File.
12. TNA, HS9/648/4, sworn affidavit of Odette Sansom, 14 December 1946.
13. IWM, Sound Archive, 9478/3/2, Odette Sansom, 31 October 1986.
14. TNA, HS9/648/4, Odette Sansom, Personnel File.
15. IWM, Sound Archive, 9478/3/2, Odette Sansom, 31 October 1986.
16. TNA, WO 235/305, Ravensbrück-Prozess in Hamburg, 16 December 1946.
17. IWM, Sound Archive, 9478/3/2, Odette Sansom, 31 October 1986.
18. Ibid.
19. Ibid.
20. Jerrard Tickell, *Odette*, Chapman and Hall, London, 1956, p. 170; Starns, *Odette*, p. 103.
21. IWM, Sound Archive, 9478/3/2, Odette Sansom, 31 October 1986.
22. Tickell, *Odette*, p. 272.
23. TNA, HS9/908/1, Cicely Lefort, Personnel File.
24. Jones, *A Quiet Courage*, p. 313.
25. Helm, *If This Is a Woman*, p. 424.
26. Jones, *A Quiet Courage*, p. 314.
27. TNA, HS9/1435, Violette Szabó, Personnel File – 109957.
28. Ibid.
29. Ottaway, *Violette Szabo*, p. 143.
30. Helm, *If This Is a Woman*, p. 425.
31. Ottaway, *Violette Szabo*, p. 143.
32. Helm, *If This Is a Woman*, p. 427.
33. King, *Jacqueline*, p. 366.
34. Ibid.
35. Ibid.
36. IWM. Affidavit by Yvonne Baseden. In the matter of war crimes and in the matter of ill-treatment of British nationals at Dijon, France, and Ravensbrück, Germany, June 1944 and April 1945.
37. Ibid.
38. Interview by author with Yvonne Burney (née Baseden), Napier Gardens, London, 23 May 2003.
39. Ibid.
40. Helm, *If This Is a Woman*, p. 489.
41. IWM, Sound Archive, 9478 A, Odette Sansom, 31 October 1986.
42. TNA, HS6/437. Security files: repatriated prisoners-of-war; interrogations; war crimes; missing personnel; concentration camp lists.
43. Ibid.
44. Jones, *A Quiet Courage*, p. 316.
45. Ibid.
46. Interview by author with Yvonne Burney (née Baseden), Napier Gardens, London, 23 May 2003.
47. Ottaway, *Violette Szabo*, p. 146.
48. Helm, *If This Is a Woman*, p. 522.
49. Ottaway, *Violette Szabo*, p. 144.
50. Helm, *If This Is a Woman*, p. 498.
51. Mary Lindell de Monchy reported a slightly different version – that Cicely never returned to the main camp and that she was killed by lethal injection while still in the *Jugendlager*.

Following her death, by whatever means, Cicely's body would almost certainly have been disposed of in the Ravensbrück crematorium.

52. Helm, *If This Is a Woman*, p. 498
53. Gritt Philipp, *Kalendarium der Eriegnisse im Frauen-KZ Ravensbrück 1939–44*, Metropol, Berlin, 1999.
54. TNA, WO 235/309 Bl.11, Judge Advocate General's Office, War Crimes Case Files, Second World War, Ravensbrück case, exhibits 1–8, March 1946.
55. Ottaway, *Violette Szabo*, p. 151.
56. Interview by author with Yvonne Burney (née Baseden), Napier Gardens, London, 23 May 2003.
57. TNA, HS6/437. Security files: repatriated prisoners-of-war; interrogations; war crimes; missing personnel; concentration camp lists. Yvonne Baseden.
58. TNA HS6/437. Security files: repatriated prisoners-of-war; interrogations; war crimes; missing personnel; concentration camp lists. Eileen Nearne.
59. Ibid.
60. Ibid.
61. IWM, Sound Archive, 9478 A, Odette Sansom, 31 October 1986.
62. Ibid.
63. Ibid.

9 AFTERMATH

1. IWM, Sound Archive, 9551/3, Vera Atkins, 6 January 1987.
2. Interview by author with Pearl Cornioley (née Witherington), Grand Hôtel Saint Aignan, May 2003.
3. IWM, Sound Archive, 9551/3, Vera Atkins, 6 January 1987.
4. Jones, *A Quiet Courage*, p. 334.
5. Ibid.
6. TNA, HS9/648/4, Odette Sansom, Personnel File.
7. Ibid.
8. Ibid.
9. Jones, *A Quiet Courage*, p. 334.
10. *Sunday Express*, 9 March 1952.
11. TNA, HS7/134, Report on Judex Mission.
12. Ibid.
13. Ibid.
14. TNA, HS7/134, Report on Judex Mission.
15. IWM, Sound Archive, 9551/3, Vera Atkins, 6 January 1987.
16. TNA, HS9/877/5, Peter Lake, Personnel File.
17. TNA, HS7/134, Report on Judex Mission.
18. Ibid.
19. Ibid.
20. Ibid.
21. Ibid.
22. TNA, HS7/122, Major R.A. Bourne-Paterson, 'The British Circuits in France', London, 30 June 1946.
23. Milward, Alan, 'The Economic and strategic effectiveness of Resistance', in *Resistance in Europe: 1939–1945*, edited by Hawes and White, 1975, pp. 188–9.
24. Dwight D. Eisenhower, *Crusade in Europe*, Garden City, NY, Doubleday, 1948, p. 296. But with such success again came reprisals and these were 'even more savage than before'. In March 1944 an entire Maquis band numbering more than 1,000 resistance members were wiped out in the Haute-Savoie region. In July 1944 another Maquis force of similar size was destroyed at Vercors.

25. Today the club has many members, including members of FANY and Special Forces units. On the staircase walls there are many photographs of members of F Section and short biographies. The frames of the images of those who did not come back are black. In the lounge is Brian Stonehouse's picture of the four women at Natzweiler, and his portrait of Jacqueline Nearne hangs in the bar on the first floor.
26. IWM, Sound Archive, 9551/3, Vera Atkins, 6 January 1987.
27. Stuart, '"Of Historical Interest Only"', pp. 220–1.
28. Ibid., p. 222.
29. Second World War Experience Centre, Leeds, tape 2996, Mrs Pawley, 14 September 2005.
30. Douglas Dodds-Parker, *Setting Europe Ablaze*, Springwood Books Ltd, Windlesham, 1984, pp. 163–4.
31. Stuart, '"Of Historical Interest Only"', pp. 223–5.
32. Ibid., p. 225.
33. Buckmaster, *Specially Employed*, p. 7.
34. Buckmaster also clarified this point in a letter to Cynthia Sadler, author of *War Journey*.
35. IWM, Sound Archive, 9551/3, Vera Atkins, 6 January 1987.
36. Stuart, '"Of Historical Interest Only"', p. 227.
37. Ibid., p. 228. C.B. Townshend's report of 17 December 1974 held by Duncan Stuart.
38. IWM, Sound Archive, 9551/3, Vera Atkins, 6 January 1987.
39. Ibid.
40. IWM, Sound Archive 9551/3, Vera Atkins, 6 January 1987.
41. Ibid.
42. TNA, HS9/59/2, Vera Atkins, Personnel File.
43. Ibid.
44. Ibid.
45. IWM, Sound Archive, 9551/3, Vera Atkins, 6 January 1987.
46. Jones, *A Quiet Courage*, p. 327. Vera Atkins's work on finding out about the thirteen missing women is retold in some detail in Sarah Helm's *A Life in Secrets*.
47. Helm, *A Life in Secrets*, p. 107.
48. Vera was present when the JAG team questioned Rudolf Höss, commandant of Auschwitz. When he was asked if he was responsible for the murder of 1.5 million Jews, Höss corrected his interrogator, saying the correct figure was 2,345,000. The evidence was used to convict him at the Nuremberg Trials in 1947.
49. Information provided by Penny Starns.
50. IWM, Sound Archive, 9551/3, Vera Atkins, 6 January 1987.
51. Mark Seaman, 'A glass half full – some thoughts on the evolution of the study of the Special Operations Executive', *Intelligence and National Security* 20:1 (2005), 27–43.
52. Foot, *SOE in France*, p. 48.
53. IWM, Vera Atkins papers 8/1/1–11, Various newspaper clippings (GB62/IWM) including *Daily Herald*, 24 April 1950, and *News Chronicle* article, undated.
54. Interview by author with Pearl Cornioley (née Witherington), Grand Hôtel Saint Aignan, May 2003.
55. Ibid.
56. Odette Sansom was awarded an MBE as well as the George Cross.
57. Jones, *A Quiet Courage*, p. 339.
58. Interview with Sydney Hudson for *Behind Enemy Lines*, Channel 4, 2002.
59. 'Some examples of discrepancies in civil/military awards', 22 October 1945. Box labelled 'SOE' at FANY HQ. Cited in Juliette Pattinson, *Behind Enemy Lines: Gender, Passing and the Special Operations Executive in World War Two*, Manchester Unversity Press, Manchester, 2007, p. 198.
60. Maurice Buckmaster, *They Fought Alone*, Popular Book Club, London, 1958, p. 205.
61. *Yorkshire Evening Post*, 19 November 1946.
62. For citations see Appendix II.
63. TNA, WO 32/20708, Violette Szabó: proposal (by Dame Irene Ward MP) that her GC be converted to a VC.

64. Ibid.
65. Ibid.
66. Ibid.
67. George Millar, *Maquis*, Pan, London, 1945.
68. Mark Seaman, 'Good Thrillers, but Bad History: A Review of Published Works on the Special Operation Executive's Work in France during the Second World War', in *War, Resistance and Intelligence: Essays in Honour of M.R.D. Foot*, ed. K.G. Robertson, Routledge, Abingdon, 2006, p. 120.
69. George Millar, *The Road to Resistance*, Pan, London, 1945.
70. Seaman, 'Good Thrillers, but Bad History', p. 120.
71. Walters, *Moondrop to Gascony*.
72. Description of the film from the VHS sleeve, *Now It Can Be Told*, distributed by IWM, 2001.
73. Jerrard Tickell, *Odette*, Chapman and Hall, London, 1956, p. 9.
74. Starns, *Odette*, p. 125.
75. Jean Overton Fuller, *Madeleine*, Gollancz, London, 1952, Preface.
76. Foot, *SOE in France*, p. 461.
77. Ibid.
78. Ibid.
79. *Time*, 15 December 1958.
80. TNA, PREM 11/5084, draft letter to Dame Irene Ward, DBE, MP, from the secretary of state, foreign office, undated.
81. Foot, *SOE in France*, pp. ix–x.
82. Christopher Murphy, 'The origins of SOE in France', *Historical Journal*, 4 (2003), pp. 935–52.
83. In a memo prepared for Harold Wilson, the civil servant Burke Trend noted that the book was not considered an official history 'in the full sense of the term' due to the fact that 'it has not been written by a team of historians, as are the ordinary official histories of the war, or subjected to the full process of departmental scrutiny which the official histories undergo'. Rather, it was classed as 'a companion volume to the official histories', prefaced 'with a statement that the author had had full access to all relevant material and was alone responsible for the opinions which he expressed'. Ibid., p. 936.
84. IWM, Sound Archive, 9551/3, Vera Atkins, 6 January 1987.
85. After the war Odette involved herself with a host of charitable endeavours, including the Poliomyelitis Trust, the VC and GC Association and the St Dunstan's Ex-Prisoners of War Association. She also served as President of the East Ham RAF 282 Squadron Air Cadets Training Corps, was Vice President of the FANY and was a co-founder of the Woman of the Year luncheon, celebrating extraordinary British women from all walks of life in the UK.

EPILOGUE

1. Howarth, *Special Operations*, p. 154.
2. Foot, *SOE in France*, p. 47.
3. Popham, *FANY*, p. 68.
4. M.R.D. Foot, 'Was SOE any good?', *Journal of Contemporary History* 16:1 (1981), p. 174.
5. In 2004 Carole Seymour-Jones wrote a biography of Pearl entitled *She Landed by Moonlight*, Hodder & Stoughton, London, 2014. Pearl's own memoir, *Codename Pauline*, was published after her death in 2015 by Chicago Review Press.
6. TNA, HS9/1195/1, Eliane Plewman. Personnel File.

BIBLIOGRAPHY

AUTOBIOGRAPHIES

Aubrac, L., *Outwitting the Gestapo*, trans. K. Bieber, University of Nebraska Press, Nebraska, 1993.

Beevor, R.G., *SOE: Recollections and Reflections*, Bodley Head, London, 1981.

Besnard, Julienne, *Memoirs of Julienne Besnard*, trans. Aileen Lauler, 1946.

Bleicher, Hugo, *Colonel Henri's Story*, Kimber, London, 1954.

Buckmaster, M., *Specially Employed: The Story of British Aid to French Patriots of the Resistance*, Batchworth Press, London, 1952.

——, *They Fought Alone: The Story of British Agents in France*, Popular Book Club, London, 1958.

Churchill, P., *Duel of Wits*, Hodder & Stoughton, London, 1953.

——, *Of Their Own Choice*, Hodder & Stoughton, London, 1952.

——, *The Spirit in the Cage*, Hodder & Stoughton, London, 1954.

Dalton, H., *The Fateful Years: Memoirs, 1931–1945*, Frederick Muller, London, 1957.

Davidson, B., *Special Operations Europe: Scenes from the Anti-Nazi War*, HarperCollins, London, 1987.

de Gaulle-Anthonioz, G., *The Dawn of Hope: A Memoir of Ravensbrück*, Arcade Publishing, New York, 1999.

——, *God Remained Outside: An Echo of Ravensbrück*, Souvenir Press, Paris, 1999.

Deveraux Rochester, E., *Full Moon to France*, Harper Collins, London, 1977.

Dormer, H., *Hugh Dormer's Diaries*, Jonathan Cape, London, 1947.

Fairbairn, W.E., *All-in Fighting*, Faber & Faber, London, 1942.

Fairbairn, W.E. and Sykes, E.A., *Shooting to Live*, Paladin Books, Boulder, CO, 1987.

Fourcade, M., *Noah's Ark: The Secret Underground*, Dutton, Toronto, 1974.

Friang, B., *Parachutes and Petticoats*, Jarrolds, London, 1958.

Heslop, Richard, *Xavier: A British Secret Agent with the French Resistance*, Biteback Publishing, London, 2014.

Hudson, S., *Undercover Operator: An SOE Agent's Experiences in France and the Far East*, Pen and Sword, Barnsley, 2003.

Hue, A. and Southby-Tailyour, E., *The Next Moon: The Extraordinary Story of a British Agent behind Enemy Lines*, Viking, London, 2004.

Katona, E. and Macnaghten, P., *Codename Marianne: An Autobiography*, HarperCollins, London, 1976.

Khan, N.I., *Twenty Jataka Tales*, George G. Harrap & Co., London, 1939.

Maloubier, Bob, *Agent secret de Churchill*, Tallandier, Paris, 2011.

Maloubier, R., *SOE Hero: Bob Maloubier and the French Resistance*, The History Press, Cheltenham, 2019.

Masterman, J.C., *The Double-Cross System: The Classic Account of World War Two Spy-Masters*, Yale University Press, London, 1972.

BIBLIOGRAPHY

Marks, L., *Between Silk and Cyanide: A Code Maker's War, 1941–45*, Free Press, London, 1999.
Millar, G., *The Horned Pigeon*, Pan, London, 1973.
——, *Maquis*, Pan, London, 1957.
——, *The Road to Resistance*, Pan, London, 1945.
Neave, A., *Little Cyclone: The Girl Who Started the Comet Line*, Hodder & Stoughton, London, 1954.
Sweet-Escott, B., *Baker Street Irregular*, Methuen, London, 1965.
Sykes, E., *SOE Close Combat Syllabus*, 1943, PRO, London, 2001.
Ten Boom, C., *The Hiding Place*. Hodder & Stoughton, London, 2004.
Verity, H., *We Landed by Moonlight*, Ian Allan, Manchester, 1979.
Wake, N., *The Autobiography of the Woman the Gestapo Called the White Mouse*, Sun Books, Melbourne, 1985.
Walters, A.M., *Moondrop to Gascony*, Macmillan, London, 1946, reprinted, Moho Books, Chippenham, 2009
Witherington, P. and Atwood, K., *Code Name Pauline: Memoirs of a World War II Special Agent*, Chicago Review Press, Chicago, 2013.

BIOGRAPHIES

Basu, S., *Spy Princess: The Life of Noor Inayat Khan*, Omega Publications, Stroud, 2007.
Bles, M., *Child at War: The True Story of a Young Belgian Resistance Fighter*, Sphere, London, 1990.
Braddon, R., *Nancy Wake: World War Two's Most Rebellious Spy*, The Book Club, London, 1956.
Fitzsimmons, P., *Nancy Wake: The Inspiring Story of One of the War's Greatest Heroines*, HarperCollins, London, 2002.
Foot, M.R.D., *Resistance: An Analysis of European Resistance to Nazism, 1940–45*, Methuen, London, 1976.
——, *Six Faces of Courage* (revised edn), Pen and Sword, Barnsley, 2003.
——, *SOE: An Outline History of the Special Operations Executive 1940–1946*, Greenwood Press/BBC, London, 1984.
——, *SOE in France: An Account of the Work of the British Special Operations Executive in France 1940–1944*, HMSO, London, 1966.
Helm, S., *A Life in Secrets: Vera Atkins and the Lost Agents of SOE*, Little, Brown, London, 2005.
Jenkins, R., *A Pacifist at War: The Silence of Francis Cammaerts*, Arrow, London, 2010.
King, S., *Jacqueline: Pioneer Heroine of the Resistance*, Arms and Armour, London, 1989.
le Chêne, E., *Watch for Me by Moonlight: British Agent with the French Resistance*, Methuen, London, 1973.
Loftis, L., *Code Name Lise: The True Story of Odette Sansom*, Mirror Books, London, 2019.
McDonald-Rothwell, G., *Her Finest Hour: The Heroic Life of Diana Rowden*, Amberley Publishing, Stroud, 2017.
Macintyre, B., *Agent Zigzag: The True Wartime Story of Eddie Chapman: Lover, Traitor, Hero, Spy*, Bloomsbury, London, 2007.
Marshall, B., *The White Rabbit: Wing Commander F.F.E. Yeo-Thomas*, Cassell Military Paperbacks, London, 2002.
Masson, M., *Christine: A Search for Christine Granville, G.M., O.B.E, Croix de Guerre*, Hamish Hamilton, London, 1975.
Minney, R.J., *Carve Her Name with Pride*, George Newnes, London, 1958.
Mulley, C., *The Spy Who Loved: The Secrets and Lives of One of Britain's Bravest Wartime Heroines*, Macmillan, London, 2012.
Ottaway, S., *Sisters, Secrets and Sacrifice: The True Story of WWII Special Agents Eileen and Jacqueline Nearne*, Charnwood, London, 2014.
——, *Violette Szabo: The Life That I Have*, Leo Cooper, Barnsley, 2002.

Overton Fuller, J., *Noor-un-nisa Inayat Khan: Madeleine*, East West Publications, The Hague, 1988.

Pearson, J., *Wolves at the Door*, Lyons Press, Guilford, CT, 2005.

Perrin, N., *Spirit of Resistance: The Life of SOE Agent Harry Peulevé*, Pen and Sword, Barnsley, 2008.

Purnell, S., *A Woman of No Importance: The Untold Story of Virginia Hall – WW2's Most Dangerous Spy*, Virago, London, 2019.

Sadler, C., *War Journey: Echo of Times Remembered*, Artemis, Croydon, 2003.

Seaman, M., *Bravest of the Brave: The True Story of Wing Commander 'Tommy' Yeo-Thomas – SOE Secret Agent – Codename 'The White Rabbit'*, Michael O'Mara Books, London, 1997.

——, *Saboteur: The Untold Story of SOE's Youngest Agent at the Heart of the French Resistance*, John Blake Publishing, London, 2018.

Seymour Jones, C., *She Landed by Moonlight: The Story of Secret Agent Pearl Witherington: The Real 'Charlotte Gray'*, Hodder & Stoughton, London, 2013.

Starns, P., *Odette: World War Two's Darling Spy*, The History Press, Stroud, 2009.

Stroud, R., *A Lonely Courage: The True Story of the SOE Heroines Who Fought to Free Nazi-Occupied France*, Simon & Schuster, London, 2017.

Suttill, F., *PROSPER: Major Suttill's French Resistance Network*, The History Press, Stroud, 2018.

——, *Shadows in the Fog*, The History Press, Stroud, 2014.

Szabó, T., *Young, Brave and Beautiful: The Missions of SOE Agent Lieutentant Violette Szabó*, The History Press, Stroud, 2014.

Tickell, J., *Odette*, Chapman and Hall, London, 1956 [1949].

GENERAL

Beßmann, A., *The Ravensbrück Women's Concentration Camp*, Metropol, Berlin, 2013.

Binney, M., *The Women who Lived for Danger: The Women Agents of SOE in the Second World War*, Hodder & Stoughton, London, 2002.

Bracher, K.D., *The German Dictatorship: The Origins, Structure and Effects of National Socialism*, Praeger, New York, 1970.

Brewer, Daniel, and Lorcin, Patricia (eds), *France and Its Spaces of War: Experience, Memory, Image*, Palgrave Macmillan, New York, 2009.

Cartron, Jean-Luc E., *So Close to Freedom: A World War II Story of Peril and Betrayal in the Pyrenees*, Potomac Books, Nebraska, 2019.

Childers, Thomas, *In the Shadows of War*, Henry Holt and Co., New York, 2004

Clark, F., *Agents by Moonlight*, Tempus, Stroud, 1999.

Cobb, M., *The Resistance: The French Fight against the Nazis*, Simon & Schuster, London, 2009.

Collins-Weitz, M., *The Sisters of the Resistance: How Women Fought to Free France 1940–45*, Wiley, New York, 1995.

Contrucci, Jean and Virbel, Jacques, *8, rue Mérèntie*, Alliance Française, undated.

Cookridge, E.H., *Inside SOE: The First Full Story of SOE in Western Euope 1940–45*, Arthur Barker, Liverpool, 1966.

Cunningham, C., *Beaulieu, Finishing School for Secret Agents*, Pen and Sword, Barnsley, 1998.

Dear, I., *Sabotage and Subversion: Stories from the Files of the SOE and OSS*, Cassell Military Paperbacks, London, 1996.

Delbo, C., *Convoy to Auschwitz: Women of the French Resistance*, Northeastern University Press, Boston, 1997.

Dobrawolska, Anna, *The Auschwitz Photographer*, REKONTRPLAN GFR, Grupa Filmowa, 2015.

Dodds-Parker, Douglas, *Setting Europe Ablaze*, Springwood Books Ltd, Windlesham, 1984.

Doneux, J., *They Arrived by Moonlight*, St Ermin's Press, London, 2001.

Dupuy, T.N., *European Resistance Movements*, Franklin Watts, New York, 1965, 1970.

Elliott, Geoffrey, *I Spy: The Secret Life of a British Agent*, Little Brown, London, 1997.

Escott, B., *The Heroines of SOE: F Section, Britain's Secret Women in France*, The History Press, Stroud, 2010.

——, *Mission Improbable: A Salute to the Royal Air Force Women of Special Operations Executive in Wartime*, Patrick Stephens, Somerset, 1991.

Farmer, S., *The Martyred Village: Commemorating the 1944 Massacre at Oradour-sur-Glane*, University of California Press, Los Angeles, 1999.

Foot, M.R.D., 'Was SOE any good?', *Journal of Contemporary History* 16:1 (1981), pp. 167–81.

Gellately, Robert, *The Gestapo and German Society*, Oxford University Press, Oxford, 1990.

Gildea, R., *Marianne in Chains: Daily Life in the Heart of France during the German Occupation*, Macmillan, London, 2002.

Gleeson, J., *They Feared No Evil: The Woman Agents of Britain's Secret Armies, 1939–45*, Pan, London, 1978.

Hastings, M., *Das Reich: The March of the 2nd SS Panzer Division through France, June 1944*, Henry Holt & Co., London, 1982.

Hawes, Stephen and White, Ralph (eds), *Resistance in Europe*, Allen Lane, London, 1973.

Helm, S., *If This Is a Woman – Inside Ravensbrück: Hitler's Concentration Camp for Women*, Little, Brown, London, 2015.

Jackson, J., *France: The Dark Years 1940–44*, Oxford University Press, Oxford, 2001.

Jones, L., *A Quiet Courage*, Bantam Press, London, 1990.

Kramer, R., *Flames in the Field: The Story of Four SOE Agents in Occupied France*, Penguin, London, 1995.

Mackenzie, W., *The Secret History of SOE: Special Operations Executive 1940–1945*, St Ermin's Press, London, 2000.

Marnham, P., *Resistance and Betrayal: The Death and Life of Jean Moulin*, Random House, London, 2002.

Mears, R., *The Real Heroes of Telemark: The True Sory of the Mission to Stop Hitler's Atomic Bomb*, Hodder & Stoughton, London, 2003.

Miller, R., *Behind the Lines: The Oral History of Special Operations in World War II*, Pimlico, London, 2002.

Nicholas, E., *Death Be Not Proud*, Cresset Press, London, 1958.

Noakes, L., *Women in the British Army: War and the Gentle Sex 1907–1948*, Routledge, London, 2006.

Nossiter, A., *The Algeria Hotel: France, Memory and the Second World War*, Methuen, London, 2001.

——, *France and the Nazis: Memories, Lies and the Second World War*, Methuen, London, 2003.

Ottaway, Susan, *Sisters, Secrets and Sacrifice*, Harper Element, London, 2013.

Ousby, I., *Occupation: The Ordeal of France 1940–1944*, St Martin's Press, New York, 1998.

Overton Fuller, J., *Conversations with a Captor*, Fuller D'Arch Smith, London, 1973.

——, *The German Penetration of SOE*, George Man Books, Bristol, 1996.

Overton Fuller, Jean, *Double Webs*, Putman, London, 1958.

Overton Fuller, Jean, *Madeleine*, Gollancz, London, 1952,

Pattinson, J., *Behind Enemy Lines: Gender, Passing and the Special Operations Executive in the Second World War*, Manchester University Press, Manchester, 2011.

Philipp, Gritt, *Kalendarium der Eriegnisse im Frauen-KZ Ravensbrück 1939–44*, Metropol, Berlin, 1999.

Popham, H., *FANY: The Story of the Women's Transport Service 1907–1984*, Leo Cooper, Barnsley, 1985.

Rees, L., *The Nazis: A Warning from History*, BBC Books, London, 1997.

——, *Their Darkest Hour: People Tested to the Extreme in WWII*, Ebury Press, London, 2007.

Robertson, K.G. (ed.), *War, Resistance and Intelligence: Essays in Memory of M.R.D. Foot*, Pen and Sword, Barnsley, 1999.

Rose, S., *D-Day Girls: The Spies Who Armed the Resistance, Sabotaged the Nazis, and Helped

Win World War II, Sphere, London, 2019.

Roth, Mitchell, *Prisons and Prison Systems: A Global Encyclopaedia*, Greenwood, Westport, CT, 2005.

Ruby, M., *F Section SOE: The Story of the Buckmaster Network*, Pen and Sword, Barnsley, 1988.

Seaman, M. (ed.), *Special Operations Executive: A New Instrument of War*, Routledge, Abingdon, 2005.

Seaman, Mark, 'A glass half full: some thoughts on the evolution of the study of the Special Operations Executive', *Intelligence and National Security* 20:1 (2005), 27–43.

Sebba, A., *Les Parisiennes: How Women of Paris Lived, Loved and Died in the 1940s*, Orion, London, 2017.

SOE Syllabus: Lessons in Ungentlemanly Warfare, World War II, intro. D. Rigden, PRO, Richmond, 2001.

Stafford, D., *Secret Agent: The True Story of SOE*, BBC Books, London, 2000.

——, *Ten Days to D Day: Countdown to the Liberation of Europe*, Little, Brown, London, 2003.

Tickell, J., *Moon Squadron*, Hodder & Stoughton, London, 1956.

Voices from Ravensbrück, Polish Documentary Institute, 31 December 1945. Testimony written personally by witness no. 434.

Ward, Dame I., *F.A.N.Y. Invicta*, Hutchinson, London, 1955.

Webb, A.M. (ed.), *The Natzweiler Trial: Trial of Wolfgang Zeuss and Others*, William Hodge & Co., London, 1949.

West, N., *Counterfeit Spies*, Little, Brown, London, 1998.

——, *Secret War: The Story of SOE, Britain's Wartime Sabotage Organisation*, Hodder & Stoughton, London, 1992.

INTERVIEWS CONDUCTED BY THE AUTHOR

Brenda Biehal (SOE employee), Leeds, West Yorkshire, 21 May 2004.

Tim Buckmaster (son of Maurice Buckmaster), Special Forces Club, London, 17 November 2005.

Yvonne Burney (née Baseden), Napier Gardens, London, 23 May and August 2003.

Pearl Cornioley (née Witherington) MBE, Grand Hôtel Saint Aignan, France, 2 and 3 June 2003.

Professor M.R.D. Foot, Saville Club, London, 14 January 2003.

Dee Gallie (SOE employee), Tamworth-in-Arden, Warwickshire, 28 April 2004.

Bob Large, Hythe, Kent, 22 May 2003.

Bob Lyndall (SOE instructor), Matlock, Derbyshire, 27 April 2004.

Bob Maloubier (SOE agent), Paris, France, 27 July 2006.

Yvette Pitt (daughter of Yvonne Cormeau), Surrey, 7 August 2006.

ARCHIVAL SOURCES

IMPERIAL WAR MUSEUM, LONDON

PRINTED RECORDS

Private papers of Squadron Officer V.M. Atkins CBE. Document 12636. Papers 8/1/1–8/1/11. Contents include:

Papers relating to war crimes investigations – 14 files: papers relating to Atkins's war crimes investigations including reports on individual female agents, Ravensbrück concentration camp and the diary of an SS doctor.

Correspondence relating to SOE agents and war crimes – 1 file.

Photographs and illustrations.

Publications, letters and obituaries written by Atkins – 1 file.

Papers and correspondence relation to Atkins' involvement with the Special Forces Club and French Resistance veterans' organisations – 2 files.

Published and unpublished pamphlets, memoirs, reviews and poems by others – 1 file.
Newspaper cuttings – 1 file.
Television and film scripts – 2 files.
Maps – 1 file.
Three-dimensional objects and ephemera – 1 file.

SOUND ARCHIVES

8680, Colonel Maurice Buckmaster (Reels 1, 2).
7369, Yvonne Cormeau (Reels 2, 4, 5).
9478, Odette Sansom (Reels 1, 2).
8689, Cecile Pearl Witherington (Reels 1, 2).
11238, Francis Cammaerts (Reels 2, 3).
10444, Robert Maloubier (Reels 1–5).
31587, Selwyn Jepson (Reels 1–3).

THE NATIONAL ARCHIVES, KEW, UNITED KINGDOM

HS6/437, Security files: repatriated prisoners of war; interrogations; war crimes; missing personnel; concentration camp lists.
HS6/437, Security files: repatriated prisoners of war; interrogations; war crimes; missing personnel; concentration camp lists. Yvonne Baseden.
HS6/437, Security files: repatriated prisoners of war; interrogations; war crimes; missing personnel; concentration camp lists. Eileen Nearne.
HS6/437, Baseden, Yvonne, affidavit.
HS7/134, Report on JUDEX Mission.
HS9/10/2, Agazarian, Francine, Personnel File.
HS9/11/1, Agazarian, Jack, Personnel File.
HS9/59/2, Atkins, Vera, Personnel File.
HS9/240/2, Baseden, Yvonne, Personnel File.
HS9/114/2, Beekman, Yolande, Personnel File.
HS9/140/7, Besnard, Julienne, Personnel File.
HS9/165/8, Bloch, Denise, Personnel File.
HS9/183, Borrel, Andrée, Personnel File.
HS9/250/2, Byck, Muriel, Personnel File.
HS9/258/, Cammaerts, Francis, Personnel File.
HS9/298/6, Charlet, Blanche, Personnel File.
HS9/315, Churchill, Peter, Personnel File.
HS9/1651, Cowburn, Benjamin, Personnel File.
HS9/56/7, d'Artois, Sonia and Guy, Personnel File.
HS9/1654, Damerment, Madeleine, Personnel File.
HS9/77/1, de Baissac, Lise, Personnel File.
HS9/1250/1, Deveraux Rochester Reynolds, Elizabeth, Personnel File.
HS9/457/6, Fontaine, Yvonne, Personnel File.
HS9/581/4, Gieules, Robert, Personnel File.
HS9/612, Granville, Christine, Personnel File.
HS9/647/4, Hall, Virginia, Personnel File.
HS9/653/1, Hanafy, Joyce, Personnel File.
HS9/77/2, Herbert, Mary, Personnel File.
HS9/836/5, Inayat Khan, Noor, Personnel File.
HS9/815/3, Jullian, Ginette, Personnel File.
HS9/849/7, Knight, Marguerite, Personnel File.
HS9/877/5, Lake, Peter, Personnel File.
HS9/888/9, Latour, Phyllis, Personnel File. Release date: January 2022.

HS9/895/6, Lavigne, Madeleine, Personnel File.
HS9/304/1, Le Chêne, Henri, Personnel File.
HS9/304/1, Le Chêne, Marie, Personnel File.
HS9/908/1, Lefort, Cicely, Personnel File.
HS9/910/3, Leigh, Vera, Personnel File.
HS9/1089/2, Nearne, Eileen, Personnel File.
HS9/1089/4, Nearne, Jacqueline, Personnel File.
HS9/1096/8, Newton, Alfred, Personnel File.
HS9/1427/1, O'Sullivan, Paddy, Personnel File.
Olschanesky, Sonia, no Personnel File as not official SOE employee.
HS9/1195/1, Plewman, Eliane, Personnel File.
Rolfe, Lilian, no Personnel File.
HS9/1287/6, Rowden, Diana, Personnel File.
HS9/1289/7, Rudellat, Yvonne, Personnel File.
HS9/648/4, Sansom, Odette, Personnel File.
HS9/1407/1, Starr, George, Personnel File.
HS9/923/4, Staunton, Mark, Personnel File.
HS9/1435, Szabó, Violette, Personnel File.
HS9/1458, Thomas, 'Tommy' Yeo, Personnel File.
HS9/1545, Wake, Nancy, Personnel File.
HS6/574, Walters, Anne-Marie, Personnel File.
HS9/1424/7, Wilen, Odette Strugo Garay née Sar, Personnel File.
HS9/356, Witherington, Pearl, Personnel File.
HS9/77/1, Report, April to May 1944.
HS9/836/5, A report on Captain Starr by Kieffer.

GENERAL SOE INFORMATION

HS7/1, A brief history of SOE.
HS6/585, Ambushes.
HS6/601/602, Appreciations of French Resistance.
HS7/122, Bourne-Paterson, Major R.A., 'The British Circuits in France', London, 30 June 1946.
HS6/576, Circuit and mission reports and interrogations, Nearne to Noyer.
HS6/576, Drop Zones.
HS6/587, Electric power for radios.
HS8/422, Evaluations of SOE activities in France.
HS7/244, F Section Jul–Sep 1942.
HS7/245, F Section Oct–Dec 1942.
HS8/998, F Section personnel, circuits and locations, Network agents in the field.
HS7/7, FANY.
HS8/241, France and F Section.
HS6/598/599, France.
HS8/999 and HS7/121, France; F Section, Also Employment after F Section, Use of women in F Section.
HS6/596, General situation in France.
HS6/575, Lack of training.
HS6/597, Maquis.
HS6/571, Milice.
HS6/566-84, Mission reports and interrogations.
HS6/579, Circuits and mission reports, St-Quentin to Sybille.
HS6/376, Numbers of French Resistance.
HS6/611, OSS war diary.
HS7/121, Personnel dropped by F Section.
HS6/657, German armistice terms.

HS6/576, Railway sabotage.
HS6/579, Reception by Octaine.
HS6/595, Resistance groups and freedom fighters.
HS6/579, Security rules for WHEELWRIGHT.
HS8/435, SOE Syllabus.
HS6/593, The situation in France.
HS6/609/610, Use of BBC.
HS8/881, War Crimes.
HS1/237, Weapons instruction.
HS6/568, Work of the W/T.

IMPRISONMENT AND CONCENTRATION CAMP RECORDS

HS6/629, Execution of F Section personnel.
HS6/438, Karlsruhe, ref. to Odette Sansom.
HS8/893, Missing agents index: Concentration camps.
HS6/438, Personnel in Ravensbrück.

WAR OFFICE PAPERS

WO 235/309, Bl.11, Judge Advocate General's Office, War Crimes Case Files, Second World War, Karlsruhe Gestapo, Germany: Killing and ill-treatment of British FANY and WAAF officers of French section. Ravensbrück case, exhibits 1–8, March 1946.
WO 309/282, Execution of F Section personnel.
WO 208/4679, Interrogations by Squadron Officer Vera Atkins.
WO 235/305, Ravensbrück-Prozess in Hamburg, 16 December 1946.
WO/235/1-594, Ravensbrück, Dachau.
WO 32/20708, Szabó, Violette: proposal (by Dame Irene Ward MP) that her GC be converted to a VC.

ACKNOWLEDGEMENTS

Among the many people to whom I am indebted for help in the preparation of this book I would like to thank Heather McCallum, Marika Lysandrou and Rachael Lonsdale of Yale University Press for their patience, time and guidance.

My thanks go to Mark Seaman for sharing his love of SOE with me and inspiring me to further my studies by undertaking the writing of this book; and to Richard Aldrich for keeping me going with enthusiasm and restorative normality. Thanks also to Paul McCue of the Secret WW2 Learning Network for his invaluable help and assistance.

I am indebted to Dr Mike Maddison who instilled in me a love of history in the schoolroom (even though it took me a while to realise it), and to Dr Peter Caddick-Adams for the lessons in wider Second World War history. My appreciation goes to Steven Kippax for sharing with me his copies of official files and documents, enabling me to undertake research swiftly and effectively; and also to Julie Clamp for telling me about her grandmother and Tania Szabó and Yvette Pitt for taking the time to talk to me about their mothers' work.

I would like to acknowledge those who have helped me by reading and rereading this text to ensure its accuracy and tone, and for offering me words of encouragement and motivation: Matt Broom, Keith Errington, Lesley Holmes, Daisy Vincent, Lynette Nusbacher, Kaitlyn Kernek, Alison Gagg, Nigel Mercer and Phil Lowes. And others too numerous to name.

Thank you to Claire Peacey for the quiet and solitude of her Derbyshire getaway where I began work, and where I wrote some of the most difficult and dark chapters of this book.

ACKNOWLEDGEMENTS

My gratitude goes to my peer reviewers for their comments and encouragement to keep going and to continue improving.

And most especially to my parents, Gus and Susan Vigurs, who have stood by me every step of the way.

INDEX

ACROBAT 93
Agazarian, Francine xii, 21, 87, 92
  background 87
  in the field 88–9
  post-war 253, 262
Agazarian, Jack 79, 82, 87–9, 92, 101, 240, 255
Aisner, Julienne xii, 86–7, 89, 101
  background 86
  work with Dericourt 87
  sent to England 89
  infiltration 90
  in the field 91–2, 117–18
  post-war 253, 262
Antelme, France 82, 103, 106, 168
Arisaig 28–30, 33
Aron, Jean 53–4
Atkins, Vera 5–6, 41, 98, 115, 117, 119, 154, 198, 201–2, 205–6, 214, 228–31, 233, 237, 248, 252, 254
  finding the missing 239
  war crimes 241
  war trials (Natzweiler Struthof, Dachau, Ravensbrück, Sachsenhausen, Nuremburg, Hamburg) 242
AUTOGIRO 78
avenue Foch (no. 84) 97, 101, 144, 161, 163–6, 168–71, 178–9, 184, 241

Baker Street 4, 11, 38, 51, 59, 62, 95, 98, 104–5, 122, 142, 238
Bariaud, Jean 143–4
Baseden, Yvonne xii–xiii, 8, 10, 21, 220, 250, 257, 262
  recruitment 21
  training 33–4
  daylight drop 146
  infiltration 147

in the field 147–8
  arrest 148–9
  prison 180–2, 187
  Ravensbrück 217–18, 220, 224
  Red Cross buses 224–5
  post-war 230
BBC 50, 60, 62, 87, 108, 116, 138–9
  Messages Personnels 62, 87, 118
Beaulieu 27, 36–8, 48, 98, 119, 129
Becker, Theresa 178, 192
Beekman, Yolande xiii, 21, 82, 173–4, 176–7, 262
  motive 24
  report 39
  training 64
  background 171–2
  infiltration 172
  in the field 172
  arrest 172
  deportation 203–5
  execution 205–7
Bégué, Georges 6, 46
Benoist, Robert 103, 145–6, 180
Berg, Franz 196–7, 199
Bergen-Belsen 25
Besnard, Jean 92, 117–18
Biéler, Gustav 'Guy' 172–3
Biggs, Earnest 54
Bleicher, Hugo 61–3, 78, 92, 162–3, 166, 241–2
Bloch, Denise xiii, 188, 220, 257, 262
  background 51–2
  in the field 53–6
  near miss 56
  crossing the Pyrenees 65
  interview 65
  training 66
  arrest 145–6

prison 179–80
train journey 184–5
Ravensbrück 214
Torgau 215–16
Little Königsberg 220–1, 223
execution 223–4
Bodington, Nicholas 5, 19, 92, 101, 103
Bordeaux 52, 58, 69, 84, 86, 97, 104, 174
Borosh, Henri 137–8
Borrel, Andrée xiii, 2, 8, 20, 78–80, 99, 176,
    207, 262
  infiltration 1, 80
  training 27, 48
  in the field 81–2, 89
  arrest 101
  deportation 192–3
  Natzweiler 194–7
  execution 197–201
  Atkins enquiry 201–2
Bourne-Patterson, Robert 5, 235–6
BRICKLAYER xiv, 82, 106, 168
Brittany 95, 123, 168
Brooks, Tony 129–31, 234
brothel 45, 60, 194
Browne-Bartroli, Albert 67, 69
Bucharest 5
Buchenwald 114, 187, 219–20
Buckmaster, Maurice 4, 5, 10–12, 39–40, 58,
    66, 73, 77, 81, 92–3, 98–9, 101, 104–5,
    110, 114, 119, 138, 140, 152, 181, 184,
    202, 231, 233, 235, 238–40, 244–5,
    247, 248, 253
Budapest 71
Bushell, Charles 240
Butt, Sonia see d'Artois, Sonia
Byck, Muriel xiv, 21, 240, 262
  background 127
  in the field 127–8
  illness and death 128

Cairo 18, 22
Cammaerts, Francis 61–3, 92, 95–7, 154–8,
    165, 235
Carré, Mathilde 78
CARTE 61, 80
Carve Her Name with Pride
  film 248
  book 249
Chaillan, Roger 63
Charlet, Blanche xiv, 247, 262
  training 27, 48,
  background 53–4
  arrest 55–6
  post-war 254

CHESTNUT 103
Churchill, Peter 60–3, 161–3, 230, 241,
    254
Churchill, Winston 3, 7, 9, 16, 158, 212,
    214
Clech, Marcel 90
CLERGYMAN xiii, 103, 145
code 6, 17–18, 21, 27, 29, 34, 36, 39, 41,
    61, 70, 83, 88–9, 95, 98, 100–3,
    114, 118–19, 123, 127–8, 133, 138,
    140, 146–7, 149, 167, 180–3, 229,
    240
collaboration horizontale 232
Colonel Henri see Bleicher, Hugo
Cormeau, Yvonne xiv, 10, 21, 116, 258,
    262
  report 39
  training 64
  background 69–70
  in the field 70–1
  Judex 231
  MBE 244
  post-war 253
courier xii–xxi, 7, 27, 36, 40, 51, 53, 55–6,
    58–60, 68, 72, 78–9, 81–2, 85, 91,
    93–4, 97, 100, 110, 113–14, 116,
    123–5, 128–9, 131, 137, 151–2, 154,
    173, 175, 247–8
Cowburn, Ben 45–6, 123–4
Culioli, Pierre 64, 99–100

D/F xi, 55, 105, 120, 128, 150–1, 172
Dachau 187, 203–7, 240, 242, 251, 292
  history 203–4
  arrival of women 205
  execution of women 205–7
Dalton, Hugh 3
Damerment, Madeleine xiv, 20, 106, 176–8,
    235, 262
  report 39
  background 168
  infiltration 169
  arrest 168
  deportation 203–5
  execution 205–7
d'Artois, Guy 151–3
d'Artois, Sonia xiii, 20–1, 235, 262
  background 151
  marriage 152
  infiltration 152
  in the field 152–3
  post-war 253
'Das Reich' 140, 143–4
Daujat, Raymond 96

D-Day 4, 107–9, 114–16, 120–1, 123, 127–8,
134–5, 138–9, 161, 168, 178, 180, 232
stand-by 139
action 140
plan 'Tortue' 108
plan 'Violet' 108, 140
plan 'Vert' 108
Normandy landings 140–1
de Baissac, Claude 58, 82–6, 101, 104,
129–30, 150, 174, 253
de Baissac, Lise xv, 2, 8, 21, 80–2, 104, 174,
262
infiltration 1
training 27, 48
background 82
in the field 83–5, 104
second mission 129–30
Judex 231, 235
post-war 254
de Gaulle, Charles 4, 56, 58, 155, 233, 246–7
de Gaulle, Geneviève 208, 210
de Guélis, Jacques 5, 41, 44, 49, 53–4
de la Roussilhe, Alain 35–7
de Vomécourt, Philippe 53, 56, 127–8
decorations 243–7
Dedieu, Gerard 141–2
Déricourt, Henri 82, 86–7, 89–90, 92–3,
103–6
Desore, Huguette 179
Deveraux Rochester, Elizabeth xv, 256
background 71
report 72
infiltration 72
in the field 72–3
arrest 73
prison 183–4
release 184
post-war 254
DIGGER 143
DITCHER 69, 152
DONKEYMAN xvii, 91, 135
Drancy 52–3, 173
Dufour, Jacques 143–4
Dufour, Maurice 79

Eisenhower, General Dwight 155, 159, 236
Electra House 2
épuration 232
explosion 64, 69
explosive 18, 32–3, 51, 69, 72, 82, 89, 94, 116,
143, 151–3, 156, 234

Fairbairn, Ewart x, 15, 30–1
felucca xiii, 28, 49, 54, 55, 58, 60

Fiocca, Henri 131
firearms 31–2, 248
First Aid Nursing Yeomanry (FANY) xi, 8,
11, 22–3, 35, 48, 83, 91, 111, 113–14,
119, 126, 130–1, 231, 238, 242, 251,
254
Flossenbürg 240, 253
Fontaine, Yvonne xv, 118
background 123–4
in the field 124
post-war 254
Foot, M.R.D. 10, 128, 243, 249, 251,
257
SOE in France 239, 251–2
Foreign Office 2–3, 235, 237, 252
Fort de Romainville 187–8
Frager, Henri 61, 91–2, 135–7, 159
FREELANCE 131
Fresnes prison 61, 102, 120, 162–5, 171,
173–4, 176–7, 179–80, 184
FS knife 30–1
'Funkspiel' 164, 167–8, 174, 235
FUSAG 108

Garbo, agent 107
Garry, Émile 99, 103, 106, 168
Garry, Renée 106
Geneva Convention 6–7, 178
Gestapo 8, 17, 38, 42, 52, 57, 59, 65–6, 69, 73,
78, 83–4, 87–8, 94, 96–7, 101–2,
105–6, 113–17, 120, 124, 126–7,
131–2, 149, 152, 158, 163, 186,
192–3, 203, 214, 223, 226, 229, 241,
247, 259, 262
Gibraltar 20, 54, 83, 111, 114, 131
Girard, Andre 61
Glières 109
Gmeiner, Josef 193, 203
Goetz, Josef 106, 164, 167
Granville, Christine see Skarbek, Krystyna
Gubbins, Major General Colin 6, 98,
159–60, 237
Guérisse, Albert (Pat O'Leary) 194, 196–7
Guiet, Jean-Claude 143

Hall, Virginia xvi, 6, 40–2, 50, 54, 57, 66, 73,
83, 114, 232, 262
background 18
'Cuthbert' 19, 57
US embassy 19
training 31, 34
infiltration 42
New York Post 43, 44, 47
prison break 46

escape from France 57
transfer to DF 57
return to F Section 66
OSS 73–4
post-war 253
Hanafy, Joyce 29
hand grenades 32, 82, 88, 109, 118, 156
Hartjenstein, Commandant Fritz 193–5, 197
HEADMASTER xiv, 151–3
HECKLER xvi, 45
Herail, Simone 165–6
Herbert, Mary xvi, 21, 139, 262
    background 22
    training 27, 48,
    infiltration 55–6
    in the field 58
    pregnancy 85–6
    arrest 174
    prison 175
    release 175
    post-war 253
Heslop, Richard 72–3
HISTORIAN xix, 127, 149
Hudson (aircraft) 28, 59, 86
Hudson, Sydney 151–5, 244
Hungary 17–18, 139

Inayat Khan, Noor xvi, 21, 77, 82, 92, 99,
        104, 173, 179, 244, 249, 250, 262
    training 35–6, 38, 64,
    report 32–6, 38, 39–40
    background 97–8
    WAAF training 98
    SOE training 98
    letter 98–9
    in the field 101–6
    Pierre Viennot 102–3
    France Antelme 103
    Poste Madeleine 105
    arrest 106
    prison 166–70
    'Radio Diana' 167–8, 170
    escape attempt 169
    mistaken identity 202–3
    deportation 203–5
    execution 205–7
    George Cross 45–6
INTERALLIÉ 78
INVENTOR xviii, 91

Jedburghs 4, 74, 117, 134, 144–5, 157
Jepson, Selwyn 5, 7, 23–6, 41, 65, 111, 119,
        125
JOCKEY xiv, xvii, 61, 96, 154

Jones, Sidney 90–1
Judex Missions 231–5
JUGGLER xix, 82, 173
Jullian, Ginette xvi, 262
    background 141
    in the field 141–3
    post-war 253

Kämpfe, Major 143
Karlsruhe prison 170, 177–8, 192–3, 195,
        202–3, 207, 211, 241
Kieffer, Hans 164, 166–9
Knight, Marguerite 'Peggy' xvii, 20–1, 262
    background 135
    infiltration 135
    in the field 135–7, 159
    post-war 254
Königsberg 216, 220–1, 223
Kowerski, Andrzej 17–18, 34, 253

LABOURER xxi, 114
Lansdell, Richard 136–7
Large, Bob 10, 126
Latour, Phyllis xvii, 11, 21, 262
    motive 24
    background 149–50
    infiltration 150
    in the field 150–1
    post-war 254
Lavigne, Madeleine xvii, 137, 262
    background 137
    infiltration 138
    in the field 138, 159
    post-war 252
le Chêne, Marie-Thérèse xvii, 20, 56, 262
    training 27, 48
    infiltration 55
    background 58
    in the field 58–9
    breach of Official Secrets Act 59
    friends with Andrée Borrel 80
    post-war 254
Lefort, Cicely xviii, 21, 92, 97, 99, 154, 262
    training 64
    background 94–5
    in the field 95–6
    arrest 96–7
    transportation 10–11
    Ravensbrück 211, 214, 218
    Jugendlager 221–2
    execution 223
Leigh, Vera xviii, 20, 82, 176, 207, 262
    infiltration 90
    background 90–1

in the field 91–2
deportation 192
Natzweiler 194–7
execution 197–201
Atkins enquiry 201–2
Liewer, Philippe 118, 125–6, 143–4
Loire river 1, 2, 90, 140
Luftwaffe 16, 19, 96
Lysander xii–xxi, 28, 62, 86–7, 89–90, 92, 97, 99, 106, 118–19, 125–6, 129, 172

Macalister, John 99
Maloubier, Bob 10, 67, 143
Maquis 55, 66, 72, 107, 109, 110, 114, 117, 127, 132–4, 137, 140, 143, 144, 153, 154–9, 184, 247, 248
Maquisards 66, 72, 109
Markkleeberg 220, 226
Marks, Leo 6, 36, 98, 101
MARKSMAN xvii, 72
Marsac, André 61–2
Marseille 46, 50, 53, 60, 63, 67–8, 94, 110, 131, 147, 158, 162, 175, 212, 242, 256
Mauthausen 240
Meunier, Mme 179
MI R 3
MI5 24, 72, 79, 88
MI6 16
Milice 37, 64, 72, 153
Millar, George 72, 235
  Maquis 246–7
Ministry of Information 67
Ministry of Labour 67
MONK xix, 68–9, 175
MONKEYPUZZLE 51
Montauban 129
Montbéliard 94
Monte Cassino 107
Montélimar 95–6
Montluçon 115, 131–2, 234
Montparnasse 101
Montpellier 141
Montrichard 64
Morel, Gerrard 5
motor gunboat xvii, xvi, 28, 123
MUSICIAN 172

Nacht und Nebel xi, 169, 191–3, 201, 217, 223
National Archive 10–11, 239, 290
  weeding of files 11
Natzweiler-Struthof 191–7
  Lagerstrasse 195
  Zellenbau 195, 196

crematorium 197
execution of the women 197, 201
Nearne, Eileen 'Didi' xviii, 111, 118, 184, 262
  background 118–19
  training 119
  infiltration 119
  in the field 120–1
  arrest 182
  prison 182–3
  Ravensbrück 214
  Torgau 215
  Abteroda 219
  Markkleeberg 220
  death march 225–6
  escape 226
  post-war 229–30
Nearne, Jacqueline xviii, 118–19, 229, 247, 262
  training 27, 48
  report 40
  background 110–11
  in the field 111–13
  Judex 231
  post-war 253
Neue Bremm (Saarbrücken) 186–7, 220
Nicholas, Elizabeth
  Death Be Not Proud 239, 250
Nobel 808 33
Norman, Gilbert 78, 81–2, 89, 100–1, 166–7, 240
Normandy 108–9, 130, 138, 140, 142, 146, 150, 158–9
Norway 3, 237
Now It Can Be Told (School for Danger) 247

O'Sullivan, Paddy xix, 21, 118, 262
  background 121
  infiltration 121
  in the field 121–3
  post-war 254
occupied France
  fall of France 15
  Armistice with Germany 16
  shortages 43 44, 49
  Rafle du Vél D'Hiv 52–3
  collaboration 47
  abolishment of demarcation line 56
Odette
  film 12, 248
  book 248
Office of Strategic Services xvi, 74, 127, 155, 255

Olschanesky, Sonia xix, 12, 176, 207, 262
  background 173
  in the field 173
  arrest 173–4
  deportation 192
  Natzweiler 194–7
  execution 197–201
  Atkins enquiry 201–2
Operation 'Bagration' 107
Operation 'Barbarossa' 17, 41
Operation 'Dragoon' 155, 158–9
Operation 'Fortitude South' 108
Oradour-sur-Glane 143
Ott, Christian 203–5
Overton-Fuller, Jean 206, 249
  Madeleine 239, 240, 249

Paris 2, 4, 5, 8, 15, 18, 22, 24, 42, 48, 51–4,
  61–2, 71, 73, 78, 80–4, 86, 88, 90–5,
  97, 99, 101–3, 105–6, 109, 111, 116,
  118–20, 124–6, 130–1, 135–6, 138,
  141, 144, 154, 159, 162–4, 166,
  170–3, 177, 179–82, 184, 187,
  210–11, 229, 235, 244
Pas-de-Calais 108, 111
PAT escape line 79, 168, 196
Périgueux prison 46
PERMIT xvi, 141–3
Pétain, Marshal Philippe 4, 16, 42–3, 50, 56
Peulevé, Harry 185
Pforzheim 169–70, 203
PHONO xvi, 98–9
PHYSICIAN xx, 78
Pickersgill, Frank 99
PIMENTO 129, 130
Pithiviers 53
place des États-Unis, 3 bis 163, 164
PLANE xvii, 58
plastic explosive 32–3, 82, 234
Plaza, Dr 197–201
Plewman, Eliane xix, 21, 82, 176, 177, 203,
  257–8, 262
  background 67
  infiltration 67–8
  in the field 68–9
  arrest 175–6
  deportation 203–5
  execution 205–7
Poirier, Jacques 143
Poitiers 81–3, 85, 87, 104, 111, 168, 174–5
Poland 16–18, 22
PROSPER 77, 78, 80, 81–2, 86, 87–8,
  89–91, 99–105, 173, 251
Pyrenees 57–9, 65, 72, 86, 111, 114, 116, 185

Rabinovitch, Adolphe 62, 165
radio 17, 27, 36, 41, 50, 66, 74, 100, 108, 111,
  120, 126, 133, 139, 140, 142, 149,
  167–8, 170, 173, 229, 232, 244
RAF xi, 1, 2, 21, 23, 33, 35, 70, 79, 98, 113,
  120–1, 126, 151–2, 248, 257
railway 16, 42, 56, 60, 64, 69, 89–90, 96, 108,
  109, 138, 140, 142, 146, 148, 183, 210,
  215, 217, 220, 233
Ravensbrück 192, 208–27, 255
  history 208–10
  Torgau 215–17
  Königsberg 216
  Jugendlager 221–2
  liberation 227, 228
Red Cross 93, 100, 127, 157, 185, 210, 224–5,
  240
resistance 1, 2, 7, 17, 20, 22, 24–5, 28, 41–2,
  44–5, 47, 50–1, 55, 57, 61–2, 64, 66,
  72, 74, 78–9, 83, 85–6, 91, 96, 100,
  102, 104, 108–9, 112, 117, 123,
  126–7, 130, 132–3, 135, 139–40, 142,
  145–6, 149, 154–5, 158–62, 163, 169,
  171–2, 174–6, 179, 184–5, 187, 191,
  208, 214, 231–3, 236–7, 241, 243,
  247–8, 258
Roesner 192–3
Röhde, Dr Werner 196–201
Rolfe, Lilian xix, 8, 21, 118, 136, 188, 220,
  257, 262
  personnel file 11
  background 22
  training 34
  in the field 126–7
  arrest 149, 184
  prison 184
  train journey 184–5
  Ravensbrück 214–24
  Torgau 221
  Little Königsberg 220–1, 223
  execution 223–4
Rowden, Diana xx, 21, 82, 92, 97, 99, 176,
  207, 250, 262
  background 93
  infiltration 93
  in the field 93–4
  arrest 170–1
  deportation 192
  Natzweiler 194–7
  execution 197–201
  Atkins enquiry 201–2
Royal Victoria Patriotic School 72,
  79, 82
RSHA xi, 192, 203

Rudellat, Yvonne xx, 10, 20, 53, 82, 210
  training 27, 32–3, 48
  background 48 49
  infiltration 49
  sabotage 64
  in the field 51
  arrest 99–100
  prison 187–8
  Ravensbrück 214–16, 225
  Torgau 215
  Bergen-Belsen 225
rue des Saussaies 73, 164, 182–3
Ruehl, Ernst 164, 169

sabotage 1–3, 9, 32, 36, 45, 59, 64, 69,
    78, 88–9, 96, 124, 128, 132, 134,
    137–8, 140, 142, 172, 234, 236, 247,
    258, 262
Sachsenhausen 240, 242
SALESMAN xx, 125–6
Sansom, Odette xx, 8–9, 27, 56, 58, 176,
    179, 210–11, 241, 244–5, 248, 250,
    262
  motive 25
  interview 25–6
  report 40
  training 34, 48
  background 59–60
  infiltration 55
  in the field 60–3
  arrest 63
  prison 161–3
  torture 164–6
  transportation 211–12
  Ravensbrück 212–14, 218–19, 226
  leaves Ravensbrück 226–7
  George Cross 227, 245
  post-war 230, 242
  later years 254–5
Savy, William 120
Schultz, Conrad 194, 196, 200
SCIENTIST xv, xvi, xvii, 58, 82, 84–6, 104,
    130, 150, 234
Secret Intelligence Service (SIS) 3
Section D 3–4, 16–18, 54
Service du travail obligatoire (STO) xi,
    7, 92
SFHQ 74
SHIPWRIGHT 13
SILVERSMITH xvii, 138, 159, 254
Skarbek, Krystyna xv, 6, 8, 262
  background 16
  Section D 17–18
  Cairo 18

  training 18
  infiltration 154
  in the field 154–8
  Vercors 154–7
  Italy 157–8
  post-war 252
  murder 253
Skepper, Charles 68, 92, 175–6
Southgate, Maurice 110–12, 114–15, 132–3,
    166–7
Special Forces Club 194, 237, 255
Special Operations Executive (SOE) 2
  'Massingham' (AMF) 4, 117, 154
  RF 4
  EU/P 4
  F 2, 4–6, 8, 9, 11, 12, 20–2, 24, 25, 28, 36,
    39–41, 44–8, 51, 54, 56–8, 61, 63,
    65–7, 69, 70, 72, 74, 78, 80, 84, 85, 88,
    89, 92, 95, 98, 99, 101, 104, 113, 114,
    116, 121, 127, 129, 131, 133, 135, 139,
    141, 142, 150, 160, 163, 167–9, 173,
    176, 185, 194, 202, 207, 230, 231,
    233–7, 239, 241–3, 247, 249–61, 268,
    271, 283, 288–92
  DF 4, 57, 95
  recruitment 20
  decision to use women 48
  discussion on SOE 236
  closure of SOE 237–9
  weeding of files 237–9
SPINDLE xx, 60–3
SPIRITUALIST 120
SPRUCE 137
Stalingrad 77
Starr, George 56, 64, 116–17, 147, 233, 244
Starr, John 'Bob' 93–4, 164–9, 171
STATIONER xviii, xxi, 110–11, 113, 129,
    132–3
Stonehouse, Brian 53–6, 194–5, 247, 253
Stork, Josef 164
Strauss, Peter 196, 198–200
Studler, André 118, 149
subversion 1, 3, 78
Suhren, Fritz 213–14, 216, 223–4, 226–7
Suttill, Francis 78, 80–2, 87–90, 92, 99, 101,
    103
Sykes, Eric 30–1
Szabó, Étienne 26, 124
Szabó, Violette xx, 8–10, 20, 118, 188, 220,
    262
  interview 26, 125
  training 31–2, 34, 66, 125
  report 38–9
  background 124–5

infiltration 125
in the field 125–7
second mission 141–3
arrest 143–4
prison 178–9
train journey 184–5
Ravensbrück 214–15
Torgau 215
Little Königsberg 220–1, 223
execution 223–4
George Cross 227, 245
father 240
Irene Ward campaign for VC 246

Tambour sisters 80–1
training programme 26
    preliminary 27–9
        Wanborough Manor 28
        Winterfold 28
    paramilitary 27, 29–33
        Silent Killing 30–1
        close combat 30
    parachute 27, 33 34
    Finishing School 27, 36 38
        Beaulieu 36
        mock interrogation 38
    wireless 27, 34–6
        Thame Park 34
        Morse code 34
    Students' Assessment Board 27, 29
    'Cooler' 29
    reports 38

VENTRILOQUIST xiv, 53–4, 127–8
Vercors plateau 154–7, 235
Vichy 16, 18, 37, 41, 42–4, 46–7, 50, 56, 235
Vogt, Ernst 106, 166, 168

Wake, Nancy xxi, 20, 262
    motive 24
    training 28–9, 30–4
    background 130–1
    infiltration 131
    in the field 132–3
    post-war 255
Walters, Anne-Marie xxi, 21, 147, 262
    interview 25
    training 28, 34, 66
    background 115
    infiltration 115
    in the field 116–17

Starr Affair 117
Moondrop to Gascony 247
post-war 254
Ward, Dame Irene 6, 245–6, 250–1
    F.A.N.Y. Invicta 239, 249–50
Wassmer, Max 192–3, 195, 203–5
Watt, André 117–18
WHEELWRIGHT xiv, xxi, 56, 65, 70, 116,
    147
Wickey, CH 206
Wilen, Odette xxi, 33, 39, 262
    training 33
    background 113
    infiltration 114
    in the field 114
    post-war 254
wireless 18, 21, 26–7, 35–6, 55, 59, 70–2, 78,
    84–5, 88, 90, 98–9, 101, 104, 106, 113,
    119–23, 127, 130, 135–6, 138–9,
    141–2, 146, 148, 151, 154, 164,
    167–8, 171–2, 174–6, 182, 234–6
wireless messages 9, 70, 84, 102, 105, 120,
    142, 173, 249, 259, 262
wireless operator xiii–xxi, 8, 23, 27, 34–6,
    39–40, 46–7, 53, 55–6, 59, 66, 69–71,
    78–9, 81, 89–92, 94, 97–9, 103, 105,
    113–23, 126–7, 132, 135, 137, 141,
    146–7, 149–50, 163–4, 168, 170, 172,
    180–3, 234–5, 258–9
Witherington, Pearl xxi, 10, 82, 107, 113–14,
    235, 244, 250, 257, 262
    motive 24
    training 30, 33
    background 109–10
    infiltration 110
    in the field 113
    command of Maquis 133–4
    near miss 144
    'Jedburghs' 144–5
    liberation 145
    post-war 228, 253–4
    MBE 243–4
    post-war 256
WIZARD xix, 119–20
Women Who Lived for Danger, The 9
Women's Auxiliary Air Force (WAAF) 21–3,
    25–6, 70, 93, 95, 98, 115, 121, 127,
    135, 150, 171, 201, 230
WRESTLER xxi, 109, 133–4, 144–5

Yeo-Thomas, Tommy 185
Young, John 94, 170